JUSTICE
AND THE MĀORI

For John Pocock,
with the warmest regards
of the author,

Andrew Sharp

1.3.98.

JUSTICE
AND THE MĀORI

The Philosophy and Practice
of Māori Claims
in New Zealand since the 1970s

SECOND EDITION

ANDREW SHARP

Auckland
OXFORD UNIVERSITY PRESS
Oxford Melbourne New York

OXFORD UNIVERSITY PRESS
NEW ZEALAND

Oxford   New York
Athens   Auckland   Bangkok   Bombay
Calcutta   Cape Town   Dar es Salaam   Delhi
Florence   Hong Kong   Istanbul   Karachi
Kuala Lumpur   Madras   Madrid   Melbourne
Mexico City   Nairobi   Paris   Port Moresby
Singapore   Taipei   Tokyo   Toronto

and associated companies in
Berlin   Ibadan

First published 1990
New chapter added 1997
© Andrew Sharp 1990, 1997

ISBN 0 19 558382 5

Cover designed by Anitra Blackford
Typeset by Desktop Concepts P/L, Melbourne
Printed through OUP China
Published by Oxford University Press
540 Great South Road, Greenlane,
PO Box 11–149, Auckland, New Zealand

Contents

Preface to Second Edition

In a final, sixteenth, chapter of this second edition of *Justice and the Māori*, I have written an essay on developments in political argument in New Zealand/Aotearoa from mid-1989 up until 1996. This has been difficult in view of the nature of the first fifteen chapters of the book, which I have left unchanged. My main intention in writing those earlier chapters (although I did not quite say it then) was to contribute to an emerging international philosophical debate on the nature of justice and to insist on the importance of the concrete and particular in time and place when that debate was being conducted. But I also felt obliged to record for New Zealanders something of their recent intellectual and political history that I thought had not, until then, been related in coherent form. So the original chapters took their time – mixing history, politics and political philosophy in a series of discrete sections. In the added chapter, long as it is, the history, politics, and the philosophy are treated much more briskly and are much less separated one from the other. Space, of course, was a problem but I also no longer feel the obligation to record so much; plenty has been written since, and Māori-Pākehā political interaction is now generally much better understood. Philosophers immediately saw what I was saying in the earlier chapters, and I hope they will not need the message of the last spelled out as fully as they might, in justice, expect.

Hampton Court, Auckland
22 November 1996.

Acknowledgments

My thanks still go, as I acknowledged in the first edition, to Bob Chapman, Conal Condren, Jim Evans, Dick Flathman, Richard Mulgan, the late David Palmer, Bill Pearson, Jane Sharp, John and Felicity Pocock, and to the editors of Oxford University Press then: Anne French and Jill Rawnsley. They helped me to build the book.

Since then I have continued to profit from conversations and correspondence with, in particular, Stephen Davies, Justin Fepulea'i, Barry Hindess, Paul McHugh, Manuka Henare, Jane Kelsey, Preston King, Mike Korenblat, Peter Laslett, Bridget McPhail, Michael Peters, John Pocock, Keith Sorrenson, Nicholas Thomas, Jim Tully, Andrew Vincent, Martin Wilkinson, Iris Young and Anna Yeatman. There have been many others, not least the participants at a conference in 1992 in Cambridge (UK) organized by Peter Laslett and Jim Fishkin, and also the participants at two conferences in the USA in 1996: one in New Orleans organized by John Pocock, the other in Cambridge organized by Michael Brown. My special thanks are due to Jane Kelsey, Paul McHugh, Bridget McPhail, Ann Sullivan and Ranginui Walker, who were kind enough – with little notice and less time – to comment on my final chapter.

No book can be written without an editor. I would like to thank Linda Cassells of Oxford University Press for inviting me to produce a second edition and then seeing it through the press so efficiently and kindly. I am again indebted to the University of Auckland and in particular my colleagues in the Department of Political Studies for their support. Mike Crawshaw (our Print Media Research Assistant) and Julienne Molineaux (our Research Assistant in the Robert and Noeline Chapman Audio-Visual Archive) deserve my special thanks for their years of help.

Part One
The Social and Conceptual Conditions for Claims to Justice

Chapter 1
The Māori Demand Justice, 1966–1988

This book is a history and analysis of recent demands for justice made against the Pākehā people and Government of New Zealand by and on behalf of the descendants of the country's aboriginal inhabitants, the Māori. It is also a history and an analysis of responses to those demands. Its recurring theme is that as a matter of fact Māori and Pākehā have separate and often contradictory conceptions of what justice demands. To take two common definitions: if justice demands giving 'to each their rights' or 'to each what is due to them', then Māori and Pākehā did not agree on what rights people actually had (or ought to have), or on what was due to them. The condition was one of passionate and sincere disagreement in which competing conceptions of justice were backed by argument and not merely asserted as self-evident. Not only did settlement of their differences prove difficult, but no plausible conception of a justice that could be adopted by both peoples emerged in the 1980s.

In the face of that failure to create a new conception of justice the inevitable occurred: appeals were made to sovereignty. Naturally enough *legal* sovereignty continued to be routinely asserted by the institutions of the state in their normal procedures of adjudication and legislation. Legal sovereignty included the right to authoritatively define the content of legal justice, and as a result, to override all conceptions other than the sovereign's as to who had legal rights to things. This is normal modern states-theory, and it was applied to the Māori demands. But another kind of sovereignty was asserted by those Māori and Pākehā who cared passionately about justice and yet who did not agree on what in fact justice required: *moral* sovereignty. Their conception of the morality that ought to obtain between the two peoples . was a legalistic one, and one largely derived from contemplating the form of the modern state. And it came to this: that each contender proposed to visit their own conception of justice on the other and thus still more systematically than before to render injustice to them. If the justice of the New Zealand state was to be Pākehā justice, then New Zealand was a Pākehā land; if justice in Aotearoa was to be that conceived by the tribes, then Aotearoa was a Māori land. The argument was about moral superiority and the moral right to say what was just. In brief, it was about moral sovereignty, and its tendency was to convert moral into legal superiority.[1]

That is one logic of the story of the contentions about justice as they unfolded. But there was another logic too. This was discoverable among those who decided to argue less about the strict demands of justice and more

---

[1] I take the distinction between moral and legal sovereignty from Rees, 'The Theory of Sovereignty Restated'. (A Finding List at the back of the book gives full references to what appears in the footnotes.)

about how to live together in conditions of severe disagreement about what those demands were. Their arguments were obviously less juristic in tone. They were less concerned, that is, with rights and duties (and with who should have authority) than as to what it might be a good idea to do; and they were considerably less heroic in their clarity of definition and imperativeness of demand. They spoke of deals and settlements that could be lived with rather than speaking the language of justice. They spoke more of politics than of the state. Unwilling to say that one or other conception of justice must predominate, they sought political settlements, impermanent no doubt, but which would enable the peoples to continue to live together in tolerable harmony. They argued that New Zealand was not exclusively a Pākehā land, nor Aotearoa exclusively Māori. They were happy to fudge questions of rights and of sovereignty.

In fact, and despite their obvious contradictoriness, the two logics were often fused in practice. The same people adopted both and argued each with equal conviction; the demands of justice and the desirability of imperfect settlement were asserted together in single documents or single tracts of speech. And in all this there were no great signs of strain. If this was perversity, it was a perversity deeply natural to the New Zealander.

Much of what is to be said on these matters lies in the detail of the following chapters as they traverse the events of the 1970s and 1980s, and focus especially on Māori claims to justice made in the 1980s. However, first the social conditions in which there were claims to justice by the one people against the other need to be understood – and most obviously the condition in which there was 'Māori' and 'Pākehā'. For without the two separate peoples there could have been no claims; and without an explanation of this condition, readers who are not New Zealanders will find it difficult to appreciate where the arguments were coming from.[2]

Since, too, the concept of justice informs the greater part of the history, some account of that concept and the various species of conceptions in which it can manifest itself needs to be given. So this and the following two chapters of the first part of the book attempt to provide an account of the political, mental and social conditions at issue: firstly of the emergence of the demand for justice; secondly as to what justice is (and what injustice is too); thirdly of the ways New Zealanders conceive themselves to be both separate from one another, at times embattled as Māori and Pākehā, and yet sharing a common interest. Overall, these are the conditions that made the demands for justice both possible and comprehensible; and they constituted too the real world in which the claims had to be answered.

---

[2] It will be a longer explanation than most of my New Zealand readers will think necessary. They will doubtlessly recognize it as drawn largely from arguments and from explanations of things which they have often heard and which are in fact part of the very issues of justice at stake; but I hope it will not be too obtrusive.

I

The Emergence of Māori Protest and Demands for Justice

The Polynesian ancestors of the Māori migrated to New Zealand across the
Pacific Ocean from the north east somewhat more than a thousand years
ago. Those who the Māori were to call the Pākehā were Europeans,
predominantly from the British and Irish archipelago, who began to settle
in the late eighteenth century. The map of New Zealand reflects the
intermingling of the races. The two main islands are unimaginatively called
the North and the South Islands; smaller ones are (to the south) Stewart
Island and (off to the east of the South Island) the Chathams. Most of the
main towns and cities also have English and Scots names. From the north
of the North Island they are Auckland, Hamilton, New Plymouth, Napier,
Hastings, Palmerston North, Masterton, Upper Hutt, Lower Hutt and
Wellington (the capital). In the South Island there are Nelson, Blenheim,
Greymouth, Christchurch, Dunedin and Invercargill. But there *are* Māori
names among the larger settlements. In the North Island there are Whangarei,
Tauranga, Rotorua, Taupo, and Wanganui. In the South Island (colder and
less populated by Māori when the Europeans arrived) are only Motueka,
Kaikoura, Hokitika, Rangiora, Timaru and Oamaru. But while the South
Island provincial areas have (now going northward) predominantly non-Māori
names: Southland, Otago (from the Māori, Otakau), Westland, Canterbury,
Marlborough and Nelson, in the North Island the balance hangs more even
and the names are constructed from both languages: Wellington, Manawatu,
Wairarapa, Horowhenua, Wanganui, Taranaki, King Country, Hawke's Bay,
East Coast, Poverty Bay, Bay of Plenty, Waikato, Thames-Coromandel,
Auckland and North Auckland. Smaller settlements, and natural features such
as rivers, lakes, bays and mountains similarly show a mixture of names –
names more densely Māori in the areas around and to the north and east
of Lake Taupo in the heart of the North Island where the bulk of the Māori
lived and still live.

Many different stories can be and have been told of the interactions between
the two races. Until the 1960s the most common sort was a story of mutual
respect, co-operation and integration, inevitably interrupted by mercifully
brief periods of antagonism, most notably in the first phase of the 'Māori
Wars', from 1860 to 1864. But another story emerged into the public arena,
especially from the mid-1970s. It was one of continued strife and of the
oppression of the Māori by the Pākehā. Tony Simpson told it in 1979 in
his book *Te Riri Pakeha: the White Man's Anger*; in 1984, Jane Kelsey told it
in an article, 'Legal Imperialism and the Colonization of Aotearoa';[3] Angela
Ballara told it in 1987 in *Proud to be White?* Other professional historians
told it with less obvious fire. But none denied its overall truth, in writing,
for instance, of Pākehā trickery and aggression in early colonization, in their

---

[3] 1988. See Kelsey in the Finding List.

precipitating the wars in 1860, in invading Parihaka in 1881 and Maungapohatu in 1916, and in writing, too, of the general tendency of Pākehā law and policy to ride, booted and spurred, over the Māori people. By the 1980s what was once a new and revisionist history was the established orthodoxy.[4]

For the Māori though, the general story was not a new one. In the 1960s, 1970s and 1980s they simply continued to tell the story in a long-established form though its precise content continued to vary from locality to locality; and it was a story that was to be retold officially in the findings of the Waitangi Tribunal, a quasi-judicial body which was instituted in 1975 and began to operate in 1977. In fact one of the most notable features of the Tribunal's work was the art and sophistication with which it listened to and relayed a Māori version of history to a wider audience. Professor Keith Sorrenson, himself an important revisionist historian, and since 1986 a member of the Tribunal, wrote in 1986 of the beginnings of a 'radical reinterpretation' of New Zealand history undertaken by the Tribunal. He was in a sense correct, though his judgement included the usual historian's tendency to search for a professional, historiographical point to hang his story on. But the real point of the reinterpretation is not so much to be found in the historiographical and academic as in the contemporary moral and political sphere. The new history was no less than a history of injustice; and it was largely the republication of an older Māori history, the point of which was largely to condemn past and continuing injustice, and to lay claim to a different and better future.[5]

Each of the forty-odd tribes (iwi) and many of the subtribes (hapū), had their own history. But now there was a pan-tribal story told. The story was that the Māori had been almost unrelievedly subject to wrongs and injustices at the hands of the new colonizers. The 'Māori Wars' were now to be seen as a justifiable reaction to Pākehā fraud and aggression. And they should be renamed. In 1982 the Chairwoman of the Church and Society Commission of the National Council of Churches explained why: 'These wars are now more properly referred to as the "land wars" as the term "Maori wars" suggests that the struggles over possession of the land were somehow the fault of the Maori people. The truth is that the Pakeha settlers, determined to force the Maoris to give up their land, provoked them into taking up arms in defence of what was rightfully theirs and then proclaimed

---

[4] The most notable works are: (at the origins of modern revisionism) Dick Scott, *The Parihaka Story* (1954), and the revised edition, *Ask that Mountain* (1975); Keith Sinclair, *The Origins of the Maori Wars* (1957) and M. P. K. Sorrenson: 'Land purchase methods and their effect on the Maori population 1865–1901' (1956). See also Sorrenson, 'The Politics of Land' (1965); 'Maori and Pakeha' (1981); and 'Towards a Radical Reinterpretation of New Zealand History' (1986 and 1989); Ian Wards, *The Shadow of the Land* (1968); Alan Ward, *A Show of Justice* (1973); Judith Binney *et al., Mihaia* (1979); Judith Binney and Gillian Chaplin, *Ngā Mōrehu* (1986); Alex Frame, 'Colonising Attitudes Towards Maori Custom' (1981); James Belich, *The New Zealand Wars* (1986); Claudia Orange, *The Treaty of Waitangi* (1987); F. M. Brookfield, 'The New Zealand Constitution' (1985 and 1989); Michael Litchfield, 'Confiscation of Maori Land' (1985).

[5] Sorrenson, 'Towards a Radical Reinterpretation'.

them to be in rebellion against the Crown'.[6]

Unjust wars were followed by unjust confiscations of land especially in the Waikato and in Taranaki – confiscations doubly unjust in the case of the lands of non-belligerents around Tauranga and elsewhere in the Bay of Plenty. Continued fraud and the unfair workings of an individualistic land law applied from then on to a collectivist people. Thus they lost most of their communally-held land; their own profitable and culturally-satisfying management of their remaining lands was denied them by a paternalistic state; their culture was seldom honoured and respected but was more often ignored, even despised and attacked; the use of their language was discouraged and hence it is on the point of death.

The story was told in varying accents of outrage; and it is one that will be told more fully when in a later chapter[7] the historiography and the jurisprudence of the Waitangi Tribunal are examined in their relationship to the demands it faced.

Nor do present times, according to those who have demanded justice, provide a happy ending to the story. To past wrongs must be added current inequalities. The Māori are now 75 per cent or more an urban people and outnumbered by something in the order of ten to one in a population of three million. Although, as shall be seen, precise figures of the Māori population are unreliable, a good idea of them can still be given. In 1971, the census showed 290, 501 persons of Māori descent in a total population of 2,862,631; the 1986 census showed 403, 185 persons of Māori descent in a total population of 3,261,783.[8] It will be noticed that there was substantial growth in the Māori population, which would tend to indicate the existence of congenial living conditions. But their urbanization since the 1950s and the increasingly strained economy of the country since the mid 1970s have left the Māori considerably worse off than the Pākehā on most uncontroversial counts of social well-being. They have suffered from what the sociologists call relative deprivation.

Indeed, figures demonstrating their deprivation compared with the Pākehā became something of a commonplace – a recurrent rhetorical figure in political argument. This was especially so after the publication of the *Hunn Report* on Māori affairs in 1961. After that, officials and commissions through to and beyond *The April Report* of the 1988 Royal Commission on Social Policy imitated the report, and elaborated, updated and refined its measures. The general shape of the facts of deprivation was always clear, as was their moral implication. And in 1988, Hon. Mike Moore, Minister of Overseas Trade and one of the more eloquent of his generation of MPs, was able to repeat in common speech and with punch what everyone knew and had been saying (with numerical variations) since the 1960s:

---

[6] H6:6/12/82. 'H' stands for the daily newspaper, *The New Zealand Herald*. All such abbreviated references can be found in the Finding List at the end of the book.

[7] Chapter 7, Section II.

[8] *The April Report*, i, p. 103.

How can any of us be proud of two nations? Half the Maori population . . . own their own homes while 70 percent of pakeha people own their own homes. Fifteen percent of Maori are unemployed as opposed to 6 percent of pakehas. The average Maori household takes home 20 percent less money than the average pakeha household. The average Maori lives 7 years less than the average pakeha. Sixty-two percent of Maori leave school without qualifications opposed to 28 percent of pakehas. For Maori New Zealanders under 20 years of age, the imprisonment rate is nearly 5 times that of non-Maori. Fifty-one percent of the prison population is Maori – although only 12 percent of the population . . .[9]

The Māori are victims of relative deprivation in a country of (in world terms) relative though declining prosperity.

This has been the undenied public perception of things; and since the late 1960s the Māori have been increasingly, and vocally, both remembering past wrongs and complaining of current inequalities. They have been demanding 'justice' from the Pākehā. Past wrongs and current inequalities were to be the themes of the accusations of injustice and the demand for justice.

The protests seemed to Pākehā New Zealand to spring to life fully armed in 1970 with the emergence of the protest group, Nga Tamatoa (the Young Warriors). This was not actually true. In fact the Māori had had a long history of sometimes locally-based, sometimes pan-tribal disaffection with their role in a Pākehā-dominated New Zealand. All the same, the 1950s and early 1960s were quiet years so far as the general public was concerned. There were indeed powerful objections to the assimilationist policies suggested in the *Hunn Report*. But these did not hit the streets, and they were delivered in academic and church papers not readily available to a Pākehā audience. Even those Pākehā sympathetic to the Māori cause and friends with many Māori did not predict an upsurge in protest. The novelist and academic, Dr Bill Pearson, reporting in 1962 on a series of Māori Leadership Conferences held since 1959, noted that the leaders had adopted a policy of slow and 'cordial adjustment' to the European occupation of New Zealand. They were seeking justice indeed, and preparing for the closer contact with the Pākehā that seemed inevitable as the Māori population became steadily more urban. But Pearson sensed at the meetings no suspicion that the government and the people of New Zealand could not be trusted to help them. He also reported hearing that Paul Robeson, the black singer and political activist, had 'failed to strike a chord' when speaking in the late 1950s to a Māori audience at the Auckland Maori Community Centre, 'pointing to the inequalities of economic status', and 'urging militancy'. 'Militancy,' he reported, 'does not attract Maoris, because they have an ideal of racial harmony.' Commenting too, on the 'pressure to integrate' that was being put on them he remarked on their quiet, polite, and determined resistance to that pressure. He judged there to be 'no fear of nationalism' – by which he meant exclusivist separatism – though he thought that there was plenty of room for Pākehā to take more seriously the Māori desire to preserve

[9] Hon. Mike Moore in NZPD1:42 (15 June 1988), p. 4391.

their way of life against those aspects of Pākehā living they disliked.[10] There is no evidence to suggest that Pearson was wrong in his reports, or that his judgement was wrong as to Māori attitudes to the Pākehā and the Pākehā state was astray. Things were just to change utterly.

The rumblings of disturbance were first widely heard when, in 1964, Māori political activists joined protests against sending an All Black (New Zealand representative) rugby team to play in South Africa without Māori players – who were objected to by the South African government as non-white. More significantly for the future articulation of Māori protest was the public release in February 1966 of the Prichard-Waetford Report on the Maori Land Courts and the adoption by the government of its crucial recommendations in the Maori Affairs Amendment Act of 1967. Whatever the intent of the legislators, the tendency of the legislation was evidently to make more easy the loss of 'Māori' land. Land owned by fewer than five persons was now to become subject to the laws and practices which governed 'General' (previously 'European' land); 'uneconomic' individual shares of blocks of land owned in severalty were to pass to the Crown, in the person of the Maori Trustee, for disposal. The loss would be both material and mental; and the loss would be added to those already sustained.

The report and the legislation united not indeed all, but many Māori of varied temperaments and political persuasions. Urbanized and Pākehā-educated leaders co-operated with the traditional leadership of the countryside. Hui (meetings) throughout the country discussed the complicated ramifications of the reforms and united to make submissions against them to Parliament.[11] The Young Maori Leadership Conferences, previously mediatory, became angry and aggressive, demanding that the Pākehā respect not only Māori land but also their language and their way of life. New Māori activist groups appeared: for instance the Maori Organization of Human Rights (MOOHR) which produced the occasional pamphlet, *Te Hikioi*. MOOHR was allied with the Pākehā left and the Trade Unions, and thus far from shared the ruling National Party and conservative Pākehā connections which the New Zealand Maori Council then mainly had. Yet MOOHR shared a clear Māori consciousness in common with the Council – not for nothing was *Te Hokioi* named after an anti-government Māori newspaper published in the Waikato before and during the New Zealand internal wars of the 1860s. And then in 1970 Nga Tamatoa began its career of confrontationist politics in the service of the land, the language and the mana of the Māori people. What Nga Tamatoa and other Māori had begun to call the 'Maori renaissance' – even though at this point their language included much imported Black Power rhetoric from the USA – had become public. The production of the history

[10] Pearson, 'Under Pressure to Integrate'. Further interpreted to me in conversation as he remembered the period and what he had been thinking of.

[11] Kawharu, *Maori Land Tenure*, Chapter 6 and Apps. 6–9.

of injustice and disaffection, once largely confined to marae (meeting centres)[12] papakāinga (villages) and to the seclusion of the universities, was one of the constituents of that renaissance.

In the mid-1970s came the first contact of Māori agitators with the 'indigenous' peoples of North America. The 'Trail of Broken Treaties', the remarkable Indian march on Washington D.C. in election week 1972,[13] soon found its parallel in New Zealand. In 1975 there was the Great Land March from Te Hapua at the extreme north of the North Island to Wellington at its extreme south. It was led by Te Matakite O Aotearoa ('The seers of Aotearoa/New Zealand'), and somewhere between 20,000 and 30,000 marchers joined Te Matikite to complain of the loss of Māori land and vowed that 'not one acre more' should be lost. They spoke of once owning the whole of Aotearoa, and of how from owning 60,000,000 acres they now owned only 3,000,000. They spoke now of the importance of valuing and practising te taha Māori (the particular traits and ways of being Māori; the Māori dimension or side of things). They spoke of being, like the American Indian, 'indigenous' to the land; and in this usage, to be 'indigenous' meant not just born and bred in a place but to be a member of a people who were in the place before all other peoples. It meant to be an aboriginal people – a people there from the beginning. In te reo Māori (the Māori tongue) they called themselves tangata whenua, 'people of the land': born of it, their generations buried in it, attached to it by indissoluble spiritual ties in a way that the Pākehā who regarded land simply as a commodity never could be. This made the loss of Māori land a more than merely material one. It went to the roots of their culture.

Two years later, in 1977, 500-odd protesters set up a tent town on land lying between the two headlands of Takaparawha and Bastion Point. They claimed the restoration of the land to those hapū of Ngati Whatua from whom it had been wrongly taken. This land was, as the media then said and were still to say in 1988 when a settlement of claims was (perhaps) reached, 'prime real estate' overlooking the Waitemata Harbour in New Zealand's largest city, Auckland. The tent people lived in a camp there for 506 days until they were ejected with the aid of police in May 1978.

In 1978 the protesters demanded the return of land in a rhetoric which still echoed that of Black Power, which continued to adopt the rhetoric of native Americans, which aligned itself closely with Pākehā conservationist groups, and which called on the distinctiveness, too, of being Māori.[14] It was a heady mix. At a photograph exhibition mounted by the protesters,

---

[12] Typically, but far from always, consisting of an open space for assembly, with attendant buildings (whare) including a meeting house and perhaps a house in which to eat.

[13] See De Loria, *The Nations Within: The Past and Future of Indian Sovereignty*, pp. 237–9 for a useful summary of events and Indian policy.

[14] On the growth of Māori ethnic ideology and organization, see Greenland, 'Ethnicity as Ideology'; and Greenland, 'The Politics of Maori Cultural Revival', Chapters 3–5. More concisely but less informatively, Ranginui Walker, 'The Maori People: Their Political Development'.

the image of Joe Hawke, a leader of the protest, was to be seen flickering on a TV screen as he made some of the first submission ever to the Waitangi Tribunal. He talked 'of the multiple wrongs' done the Māori in breach of the terms of the Treaty of Waitangi (1840). On the wall were the words of Tecumseh of the Shawnees: 'Will we let ourselves be destroyed in our turn without a struggle, give up our homes, our country bequeathed to us by the great spirit, the graves of our dead and everything that is dear and sacred to us?' Another message on the wall was: 'We (the Māori) have worked with nature not against it. We are the people of the land'; and further along the wall were the words of the then Governor-General, Sir Arthur Porritt, quoted from his speech at the Waitangi Day celebrations of 1977: 'in all honesty, it is apparent that the early settlers, the government and even the missionaries . . . used methods of land acquisition which could be described as contentious'.[15]

Events in the public drama then accelerated to a degree that defies brief description. In 1978 the nine-year-long, ultimately successful attempt by Tainui Awhiro, a sub-tribe of the Tainui, to regain their lands at Raglan began its public career. And many other claims to the restoration of lands, waters and other 'things treasured' ('taonga') in Māori culture emerged to the public eye.[16] In 1980, newspapers reported Tauranga Māori refusing a government offer of $250,000 compensation for unjust confiscation following the internal wars of the 1860s; in 1982 Ngati Awa claims to land in the Tarawera Forest surfaced. After 1983, land claims began to surface still more notably in the proceedings of the Waitangi Tribunal, which after a quiet start became prominent in public life. It is those claims to the Tribunal which this book will concentrate on most. But it was not only via the proceedings of the Tribunal that the public heard of them; and it was not only in the Tribunal that they were heard. The names of the places to which 'grievances' attached not only continued to recur in the literature and in the talk of radical critics of the status quo, they were by the early 1980s to begin to feature quite markedly in the newspapers and on the two TV channels. The general public began to hear of the places and the claims: of the Awhitu lands; the Coromandel mines; the confiscated lands in Taranaki and in the Waikato; the lands of the Muriwhenua people of the Far North around Te Hapua, their Ninety-Mile Beach and their fishing grounds. Then, reported best of all by the Christchurch *Press*, there were the claims by the predominant Māori tribe of the South Island, Ngai Tahu, to the restoration of huge tracts of land, and (by 1988) to 70 per cent of the sea fishing resources of the nation. Most of them destined for the Waitangi Tribunal, the claims and grievances nevertheless took on a public life of their own outside the ambit of the state's judicial processes: in pubs and in offices, common rooms and clubs, on TV, and radio.

That was not all. Sporadically from the early 1970s, then regularly each

---

[15] Sharp, 'Tangata Whenua at Snaps Gallery', p. 38.

[16] 'Taonga' were guaranteed the Māori in the Treaty of Waitangi. See Section II of this Chapter, and Chapter 7, Section II of this book.

year from 1979 onwards, there were very public demonstrations against the 'celebration' (later officially amended to 'commemoration') of the anniversary of the signing of the Treaty of Waitangi on 6 February 1840.[17] Yet this was the very Treaty that was widely supposed to provide the moral basis for the Pākehā presence in New Zealand, the basis of governmental legitimacy, and the basis for Māori-Pākehā co-operation in the activities of social life. There was more. In 1979 there was the widely-publicized 'Haka Party Incident', in Auckland, the city said in New Zealand to have the largest (racially) Polynesian population in the world. As a consequence of the incident a group of Māori and Polynesians were tried and most were convicted for assaulting a group of white students. An enquiry and 1982 report by the Race Relations Conciliator followed, stressing, in the words of its title, *Race Against Time*, that race relations in New Zealand were in a potentially dangerous state and ought to be rapidly attended to. In 1979, Hon. Matiu Rata, who had been Minister of Maori Affairs in the Labour Government of 1972–1975, defected from the party – since the 1930s the party of the four MPs representing the Māori electorates. He formed a separatist Māori party, Mana Motuhake, the name of which in that context meant something like 'The separate distinction [of being Māori]', something like the meaning of Sinn Fein, 'Ourselves Alone, (over-and-against you)'. Then in 1981 there was the Springbok Rugby Tour of the country. As the South Africans toured they were accompanied by huge and theatrical protest demonstrations captured on film in Merata Mita's long documentary, *Patu* ('The War Club'). The tour split opinion in the country, Māori as well as Pākehā; and it provided a nursery for those Māori radicals who questioned the very basis and justification of the Pākehā state.

Following the Springbok Tour and fuelled by its organizational and ideological lessons, the years from 1982 onwards saw a proliferation of Māori political activity. Some of its manifestations were captured in Michael Dean's TV film, *Maori – the New Dawn*. Protest and march continued to accompany the 'celebration'/'commemoration' of Waitangi Day. Most worrying from the Pākehā point of view was the publication of doctrines of Māori sovereignty in Aotearoa by Ripeka Evans and Donna Awatere in the early 1980s. In 1984 and 1985, hui and debates on the Treaty of Waitangi and the question of its inclusion in a Bill of Rights were widely publicized. The Māori presence in the political world was unmistakable. Then from the mid-1980s Atareta Poananga and the group of which she was a member, Te Ahi Kaa, continued the theme of Māori sovereignty in public (te ahi kaa was the ancient practice of keeping home fires burning on land that was lost but to which claims were not extinguished).

In 1987, three Māori of Te Ahi Kaa, including Poananga, visited Fiji and amidst great publicity proclaimed their support for the revolution there in which over half the population (of continental Indian descent) had been stripped of political rights by an aboriginal movement claiming permanent hegemony.

---

[17] Ranginui Walker, 'The Treaty as the Focus of Maori Protest', pp. 276–7.

Aboriginal inhabitants of Fiji, their rights in the place must override those of subsequent comers. The three looked to the day when the Māori, as the tangata whenua of Aotearoa, would reclaim similar rights of political domination. In the meantime, according to Māori custom, they would keep the fires burning on the place they claimed and from which they had been forcibly evicted. They would continually remind the interlopers that the land was theirs.[18] For though 'tangata whenua' may be innocently translated as 'people of the land', it meant in this context something like 'those whose racial descent and ethnic identification as Māori gives them a unique and overriding right of occupation and sovereign political power in Aotearoa, which, arrogating the Maori right of naming, others call New Zealand'. It was in pursuit of some such ideal that two other members of Te Ahi Kaa travelled in 1988 to Colonel Gaddafi's Libya in search of friends and aid.

In view of such developments, by 1985 Geoff McDonald, a right-wing Australian author, had discerned a communist-driven plot to destroy New Zealand by means of fomenting racial and ethnic disaffection.[19] His claim was mistaken. Left-wing[20] and feminist[21] circles, in fact, had serious problems coming to terms with a politics of ethnicity. They had their own commitments to analysis in terms of class and gender. In any case, few Māori argued so abrasively or with such a clear eye to Māori hegemony as Te Ahi Kaa; and it was hard to see what was *subversive* about the more moderate Māori claims – how, that is, they would tend to destroy the state.

Still, it was clear that many Pākehā had been hearing and learning of the Māori case. Many got scared and irritated; many thought the Māori claims an insult to justice. But some followed the Māori lead. At first left-wing, feminist and anti-racist groups, then with marked impact from the early 1980s, church groups collected especially under the umbrella of the National Council of Churches, began to speak of Pākehā injustice to the Māori. The government, especially the third Labour Government of 1972–1975 and the fourth Labour Government of 1984 to the present, was never far behind – though both main political parties (National as well as Labour) faced constraints that the pressure groups did not. Finally, the mass media by the mid-1980s were to catch up with Sir Arthur Porritt, the Governor-General who had spoken at Waitangi in 1977 of past injustices to the Māori. By

---

18 H3:1/9/87.

19 McDonald, *Shadows over New Zealand*, asserts this throughout. On McDonald, see Paul Spoonley's Chapter 5 in Jesson and others (eds.), *Revival of the Right*.

20 See Dennis Rockell, 'Understanding Racism. Response to ACORD', *The Republican* (Sep 1983), p. 10, and in other places in *The Republican*, e.g (May 1982), pp. 4–5 (July 1982), pp. 4–16, (Oct 1982), pp. 11–15; (Dec 1982), pp. 2–3, 7–16, (Feb 1983), pp. 2–3,16 (April 1983), pp. 15-18, (July 1983), pp. 2–12, 17–20; Chris Trotter, 'A Reply to Donna Awatere', *New Outlook*, 2, i (Winter 1983), pp. 8–9.

21 Camille Guy, 'Getting Away from Racist Guilt', *Broadsheet* (Sept 1986), pp. 30-2, and in other places in *Broadsheet*: Feb 1983, pp. 2-4; March 1983, p. 24; April 1983, pp. 2-3; June 1983, pp. 16-18, 37-9.

1985 it was routine for the large daily newspapers and for the TV channels to note that past grievances and current inequalities had been spoken of by the Māori 'loudly and justly over recent years'; and that 'now it is time for the pakeha majority government to respond'.[22]

By 1987 the conventional media response to the three who would make a Fiji revolution in Aotearoa was that of the Wellington paper, the *Dominion Sunday Times*: 'Nobody can deny the Maoris have genuine grievances whose resolution will require sweeping social and political changes'.[23] None of the newspapers or TV channels – and probably few people – supported the idea of the political hegemony of the 'indigenous'. But that did not mean they could not and would not recognize the feelings of injustice which might generate such a demand among the Māori. Indeed it may well be thought that it was precisely the threat of claims to Māori sovereignty and various degrees of independence from the State which moved the mass media to speak so sympathetically of justice for the Māori.

II

The Politicization of Disputes as to Names and Meanings

It will already be evident that in the midst of all this – indeed as part of the Māori challenge and the response it called up – names were disputed, substituted for each other and changed. Already I have had to speak of 'celebration'/ 'commemoration' of the Treaty of Waitangi and of 'Aotearoa/ New Zealand', adopting the hideous device of the slash to show a disjunction in understandings and purposes that would be hidden if one of the two words were to be used alone. The meanings (and sounds) of words were asserted, denied, shaped, and reshaped. Even the name New Zealand, given to the islands by the Dutch probably in the late 1640s (to replace the 'Staatenland' of Abel Janszoon Tasman in 1642) became what philosophers call an 'essentially contested' one. There were simply no grounds of agreement as to how one *could* decide what the right name was.[24] 'New Zealand' was seen to be laden with ethnic and political connotations. How, asked the challengers, could Europeans give a name to what was already Māori land? Why should a shameful history of colonization not be obliterated and the original name, Aotearoa, restored? 'Returning to this country's original name,' claimed one letter writer to a newspaper in 1984, 'is another small step in the process we Pakehas have to undergo to rid ourselves of our colonial and racist attitudes.'[25]

But on the other hand there was this response — how could the Māori

[22] AS6:8/2/85. See also H6:6/2/85; H6:11/11/85.

[23] DST2:6/9/87.

[24] See Connolly, *The Terms of Political Discourse*, Chapter 1.

[25] H6:7/5/84.

insist that the now-traditional name of the country be changed, to the hurt and confusion of the current inhabitants and the unnecessary puzzlement of the rest of the world?[26] Others asked what the point would be of calling New Zealand 'Aotearoa' ('land of the long white cloud'), when that name was a late nineteenth-century invention of Pākehā ethnologists romantically seeking to construct a name the original inhabitants neither used nor needed, though it was embodied in their cosmogonic myths.[27] One letter to the *New Zealand Herald*, the paper with the largest circulation in the country, said it did not matter either way: some Pākehā claimed they could not pronounce Aotearoa; both peoples pronounced New Zealand, 'Nu Zillan' anyway.[28] But mostly the question was debated with ferocious seriousness. In July 1988, the Returned Services Association wrote to the Prime Minister of the 'insidious and repugnant' spread of the name 'Aotearoa', complaining of a conspiracy 'especially in official publications' to introduce it. This could only 'precipitate a tendency among certain other individuals and groups to discard the name of New Zealand altogether'.[29] But whatever the objections to it, and whatever the outcome might turn out to be, the construction 'Aotearoa' had been successfully erected by the 1980s.

There were many other arguments about words, the nature of which revealed that they were essentially conflicts on policies and the power to implement them. Should it be 'Pākehā' or 'New Zealander'? Should it be 'Māori' or 'New Zealander'? (Should, that is, the distinguishing constructions of the Māori be used or the unifying and conflating construction of the Pākehā?) Should 'Pākehā' begin with a capital 'P', or should the 'p' be in lower case? Was 'Pākehā' a name as stable and clear as 'Māori', as first suggested by the more radical? Or was its usage disputed and unclear, not perhaps yet worthy of capitalization, as in the view suggested for example in *Hansard*, the parliamentary reports, and the main daily newspapers? (Oxford University Press, the impeccably moderate publishers of this book, changed to the upper case 'P' in the early 1980s.)

More will be said in the next chapter of disputes as to the correct naming of human groups in New Zealand/Aotearoa. There were, however, many that did not concern group names. To say 'Takaparawha' rather than 'Bastion Point' was as much to indicate political allegiance as to choose which of the nearby headlands after which to name the tent town occupation. There were very fierce arguments as to which should be used, of Mt. Egmont or Taranaki – the one denying the Māori name, the other denying the English name. A committee called the Save Mt. Egmont Committee threatened to

[26] In 1988 a typical letter to *The New Zealand Herald* read: 'There seems to be a conspiracy to change the name of our country to Aotearoa. Recently I purchased a garment marked "made in Aotearoa". How many people outside our country would know where Aotearoa is?' H8:16/4/88.

[27] H8:9/5/88, Letter from Senca Benzonio; H6:26/6/85, Letter from G. L. Pearce.

[28] H8:8/5/88.

[29] H10:12/7/88.

take the New Zealand Geographic Board to court if it dared, as it had been requested, to change its name. Two petitions, with a total of 11,000 names were got up. In the end the Board decided *either* name could be used. There were similar arguments as to Mt. Edgecumbe or Putauaki, and as to Mt. Cook (the country's highest mountain, in the South Island) or Aorangi or Aoraki (where Aorangi is the North Island Māori version, Aoraki the South Island idiom).[30] Pākehā were reminded that there were Māori names for the main towns, and of many others besides. In May 1988 it was finally announced that New Zealand Post would accept letters addressed to them: Te Whanganui-a-Tara for Wellington, Tamaki Makaurau for Auckland, and so on. Even common modes of greeting were at issue. Should it be 'good morning' or 'kia ora'? The Post Office, predecessor to New Zealand Post (est. 1987) *thought* it knew in 1984 and tried unsuccessfully, in the face of outraged opposition, to dismiss a telephonist for using the Māori greeting in the course of her work. But that was not the end of the argument. The mode of greeting remained a touchy matter. It was alleged for instance by an engineering firm's receptionist in May 1988 that she was dismissed for answering her employer's phone with the words, 'kia ora'.[31]

Personal names were changed, too, or varied according to the context in which they were being used. Many had long done this, as for instance, when Hirini Moko Mead, known to many as 'Sid', wrote in the 1950s under the name of Moko. But now the variation of names had a much more public history. Some were disputed and ridiculed, others accepted as registering separate uses in either culture: Rebecca/Ripeka Evans (indicating registration or not of Māori identity); Nicolle/Atareta Poananga; Professor S. M. Mead/ Sidney Moko Mead/Hirini Moko Mead; Eddie Durie/Chief Judge E. T. J Durie/Taihakurei Durie (depending on where or when); Joe/Joseph/Hohepa Hawke (casual English, formal English, Māori). During the 1970s, the Māori pronunciation of Māori words came to be insisted on more and more. The voice of a Denis Glover poking fun at earlier attempts in the 1940s was heard no more, asking that the Lord preserve us:

> From cinesound, and the reducer's ounces,
> From the meticulous Maori of announcers,
> From the assurance of him who walks and walking bounces.[32]

One recurring question was whether the 'Whanga' as in the town of Whangarei should be pronounced, as by the locals, to rhyme with 'Conger', hard 'g' and all. Or should it be 'Farnga', with (roughly) a bilabial fricative opening (either voiced or unvoiced), a long 'a' and a soft naso-glottal 'ng' as an ideal speaker of the te reo Māori would? And there were particular, one-off quarrels, as where, for instance, Judge Gillanders-Scott, first chairman of

---

[30] ASiv5:10/12/85; AS3:25/11/85; Hiii13:10/12/85; Courier 8:13/11/85.
[31] DST3:1/5/88.
[32] Glover, 'Prayers in Prejudice', in *Sharp Edge Up*, p. 44.

the Waitangi Tribunal, was criticized for pronouncing the 'tangi' in 'Waitangi' with the English short 'a' rather than a longer Māori one. The writing of Māori words was also contested. Was it 'hui' or 'huis' (the Māori or English plural form), Māori or Māoris? And occasionally there were echoes of the more academic arguments of the late 1950s and early 1960s: at times now more testy. Should one double the long vowels, put an accent (the macron) above them, or leave them as they had been in the early 1960s: Maaori, Māori or Maori? (In 1988 Oxford University Press decided on the macron.) Should one write 'the Te Reo Case', where 'te' translates as 'the'; or just 'Te Reo Case'? Should it be Lake Rotorua (lit. Lake Two Lakes) or should the lake be called simply Rotorua?

These issues were not simply questions of representational convenience. Often they reverberated with political meaning.

Most of all were disputes as to the meaning and force of the Treaty of Waitangi/te Tiriti o Waitangi, both overall and as to its detail; and perhaps more than any others, these disputes were self-evidently political. They were obviously to do with the organization of authority in society and the distribution of the material and mental goods it produced. The Treaty/te Tiriti had been signed by over 500 Māori chiefs in 1840, first on 6 February at Waitangi in the Bay of Islands in the Far North, but also over a period until September at a variety of other places.[33] All except 39 signed a Māori version, the textual content of which has never been disputed, though its meaning has. But there were also a number of English versions, four of which were sent overseas in dispatches – but not the 'official' English version signed by the 39 during March and April at various places around the mouth of the Waikato River and the south of the Manukau Harbour.[34] It is fortunate for the sake of simplicity in analysing the disputes – most of them, anyway – that the political arguments of the 1970s and the 1980s mainly swirled around the differences between the Māori and the official English version, and the ambiguities within each.

There were plenty of both. Both the English and Māori versions of the Treaty consisted of a preamble, three articles (the second in two distinct parts), and a concluding peroration. In the English version the preamble spoke of Queen Victoria's being 'anxious', in the light of British, European, and Australian settlement and continued immigration, to protect the 'just Rights and Property' of the 'Native Chiefs and Tribes' and 'to secure to them the enjoyment of Peace and Good Order'. This she proposed to do by authorizing Captain William Hobson to 'treat with the Aborigines of New Zealand for the recognition of Her Majesty's Sovereign authority over the whole or any part of those islands . . . with a view to avert the evil consequences which must result from the absence of the necessary Laws and Institutions alike to the native population and to her Subjects'. The English version then had it that the Māori (under Article 1) transferred 'Sovereignty' to Victoria:

[33] Buick, *The Treaty of Waitangi*, Chapter 5; Orange, *The Treaty of Waitangi*, Chapter 4.

[34] Ross, 'Te Tiriti', and 'Treaty on the Ground'.

namely, 'all the rights and powers of Sovereignty which the . . . chiefs . . . exercise or possess' ('or may be supposed to'). On her part (under Article 3) the Queen guaranteed the chiefs her royal protection and 'Rights and Privileges of British Subjects'.

But there was more in Article 2. And this is the article which was the primary textual locus of dispute in the 1970s and 1980s, spilling over into considerations of differences between the Māori and English texts and into questions as to how that article related to Articles 1 and 3. The Queen (under the first part of the article) also guaranteed the Māori the protection of the 'full exclusive and undisturbed possession of their Lands and Estates Forests Fisheries and other properties so long as it is their wish and desire to retain the same in their possession'. The second part of Article 2 gave the Queen an 'exclusive right of Preemption' over those 'lands' ('Estates, Forests Fisheries' are not mentioned) which 'the proprietors thereof may be disposed to alienate'. What the right of 'Preemption' was might conceivably have been clear in the English then, but it was very soon to become unclear – along with its rationale – whether the right of 'Preemption' was a right to have, over and against other potential buyers, the first option of buying, or whether it was the *sole* right to buy, exclusive of, and prohibiting, any other right to buy.[35] Nor, obviously, was it clear what was envisaged for 'Estates Forests Fisheries'. Could they, perhaps, be sold or otherwise alienated to *anyone*? But how would that stand with the English legal doctrine that the Crown had a dominion over the seas against which only very ancient rights could act as bulwarks against total control? And how would that stand with the Crown's feudal title to eminent domain which was, in the last analysis, a plenary power over the whole of a dominion? How would that accord with Article 1?

Not to pursue such matters further, the peroration to the Treaty talked of the Chiefs of the Confederation of the United Tribes of New Zealand, together with the 'separate and independent chiefs', 'claiming authority over the tribes and territories' which would be (but were not in the actual event of the signing) specified with their signatures, accepting and entering the treaty, 'in the full meaning and spirit thereof', 'having been made fully to understand [its] provisions'.

If the English text alone were at issue there would have been problems of interpretation. However to add to the difficulties then and since, the Māori version was significantly different.[36] It seems it was meant by its translator,

---

[35] *Johnston* v *McIntosh* (1823) the leading USA case on the rationale of the right of pre-emption as being based on a recognition of aboriginal title, was forgotten soon after 1847 and the New Zealand case *R* v *Symonds*. See McHugh, 'Aboriginal Title in New Zealand Courts', pp. 240–2 and following. But see the view that there may never have been any recognition of aboriginal rights, David Williams, 'Te Tiriti o Waitangi – Unique Relationship' in Kawharu (ed.), *Waitangi*, esp. pp. 84–9.

[36] See Kawharu (ed.), *Waitangi*, Appendix, for a useful parallel printing of the Treaty in the two languages, and for a translation by Kawharu himself. Also useful are the versions in the Appendix to Orange, *The Treaty of Waitangi*.

the Anglican missionary Henry Williams, as a fair but not literal rendering of the English version. Even so, a fair rendering would not have been easy, given the different vocabularies and conceptual apparatuses of the two peoples.[37] And it may even be that the Māori version was designed to play down what they would lose and exaggerate what they would gain – that there was an element of British fraud or at least missionary over-enthusiasm in the whole transaction. Certainly in persuading the Māori to sign the Treaty at various venues in 1840, such a British tactic was evident or can be inferred.[38] However that may be, there were significant differences between the texts. In the event, the Māori version spoke in the preamble of the Queen's wishing to protect the 'tino rangatiratanga' (full, true, chieftainship or authority) of the Māori, not their 'rights and property'. It spoke also of the hope that the chiefs would consent to the 'kawanatanga' (governorship) and not the 'sovereignty' of the Queen. The Articles of the Treaty were different too. They had it that (under Article 1) 'The Chiefs [here] and all the Chiefs who are absent' would cede 'kawanatanga' to the Queen, that (under the first part of Article 2) they would retain 'te tino rangatiratanga' (full and complete chieftainship or authority) in their lands, habitations and 'ratou taonga katoa' (all things highly prized), and that (under Article 3) in virtue of their acknowledging the 'kawanatanga' of the Queen, she would protect them and allow them 'the same rights as the people of England' (under Article 3). The second part of Article 2 in the Māori version did not look much like a right in the Queen or her agents to buy *first*, or much like a sole right in her to buy and thus the consequent disability of all others in that respect. It promised her indeed the 'hokonga' – 'the buying and selling' – of the land the Māori were willing to part with. But the conditions of priority or exclusivity did not come into the matter at all. Where in the English version 'pre-emption' was ambiguous as between those two conditions, the Māori version simply did not refer to either.

The peroration of te Tiriti was not markedly different than that of the Treaty, though it did not speak of the 'Confederated Chiefs' so as to distinguish them from others; nor did it speak of their claims to authority over territories and tribes. It was rather, simply, 'the chiefs of this assembly . . . perceiving the meaning of these words, take and consent to them all'.

Not for the moment to consider the understandings and intentions of the signatories, the English and Māori versions meant, and mean, different things. To take an example: in 1840 legal English, 'sovereignty' meant the absolute and indivisible power to legislate, judge, and interpret the law; the absolute power to administer it, and to back up its requirements by force; the sole power to engage in foreign relations and thus to appoint and control diplomats

---

[37] On William's motives, see Orange, *Treaty*, pp. 39-43, and, as to the linguistic difficulties, the best account is that of Biggs, 'Humpty-Dumpty and the Treaty of Waitangi', especially p. 306.

[38] See, for example, Orange, *Treaty*, pp. 46-7, 54, 82-3, 90, and Adams, *Fatal Necessity*. The point is made most strongly by Walker, 'The Treaty of Waitangi as the Focus of Maori Protest', in Kawharu (ed.), *Waitangi*. Also, see Chapter 5, Section I of this book.

and force of arms.[39] But in missionary Māori, the lingua franca of the Māori and missionaries, 'kawanatanga' did *not* indicate the status of having full sovereign rights of government. It rather indicated the delegated and limited rights of, say, the Roman Pontius Pilate in Israel – or of Hobson were he to become Governor: rights in Hobson's case delegated to him as much by the Māori as by his Queen.[40] Such rights as he thus acquired would clearly not be those of the sovereign of a state or of a rangatira among his tribe. They would be limited – the Māori at Waitangi may well have thought – to keeping the peace by the use of force if necessary: to something like the derived *merum imperium* or *ius gladii* of the ancient Roman magistrate.[41] Such peace-keeping activity they would have known about. Many Māori had travelled, for instance to New South Wales, and knew what governors were. Some had been the guests of governors and named their children after them. Many would have known what they were being offered because they had a concrete conception, derived from experience, of the kind of things governors did. But it is plainly impossible that they should have approached the abstract and magical conception of British legal sovereignty.[42] To get near to it they would have had to have been told that sovereignty was like 'mana', 'rangatiratanga', and 'kingitanga' – though impersonal, unlimited in its law-making scope and not obviously sacred. They would have had to have been told in the words of Thomas Hobbes, one of its greatest theorists, that the sovereign state was a 'mortal God': *Leviathan*, ruler of the proud, made by the proud to keep themselves in awe and to avoid *bellum omnes contra omnium* – the war of all against all.[43]

Thus disputes in the 1970s and 1980s could revolve around questions as to just how much of their authority the Māori *had* ceded (and how much therefore *stayed* ceded) to the Crown. And the many other differences between the texts and ambiguities within them were to be explored in the political debates of the 1980s especially. As to what was protected by Article 2 for instance: 'ratou taonga katoa' means, roughly, 'all things highly prized (spiritual

---

[39] See for discussions and references, Mark Francis, 'The Contemplation of Colonial Constitutions'; 'The Nineteenth Century Theory of Sovereignty'; and Francis with John Morrow, 'After the Ancient Constitution'. These sources should be compared with McHugh's New-Whiggish and anachronistic claims in 'Constitutional Theory and Maori Claims' in Kawharu (ed.), *Waitangi*, esp. p. 44 where he asks for the institution in New Zealand of pre-nineteenth century English notions of the protection of liberty and property from the sovereign.

[40] Williams, 'Te Tiriti o Waitangi–Unique Relationship' in Kawharu (ed.), *Waitangi*, p. 79; and his 'Te Tiriti', a contribution to both *New Hope* and to Arapera Blank *et al.* (eds), *He Korero Mo Waitangi, 1984.*

[41] This seems to have been Professor Kawharu's view of the matter in his evidence to the Waitangi Tribunal, contained in the *Kaituna Report* (1984), para. 4.9: 'what the chiefs imagined they were ceding was that part of their mana and *rangatiratanga* that hitherto had enabled them to make war, exact retribution, consume or enslave their vanquished enemies and generally exercise power over life and death'. On the Roman powers glossed by early European thinkers about the nation state, see Gilmore, *Argument from Roman Law.*

[42] See Salmond, 'On Sovereignty and "Kawanatanga" in the Treaty of Waitangi', p. 8.

[43] See Thomas Hobbes, *Leviathan* (1651), frontispiece, Introduction, and Book II. In *Job*, Chapter 41, one reads of Leviathan, the great sea monster, ruler 'over all the children of pride'.

as well as the more obviously material)' and this is clearly more than simply
the 'forests and fisheries' for which it may have been intended as a translation.
And as to 'te tino rangatiratanga', the bundle of rights the Māori retained:
it was then and is now the kind of bundle not easily conceivable as being
held of the Crown and was, for instance, to be given at least half a dozen
significantly different English translations by the Waitangi Tribunal.

Dispassionate foreign observers have spoken of the inherent unclarity of
the terms of the Treaty. The American anthropologist, Professor Marshall
Sahlins, remarked for instance that 'for sheer mystification, the curious
hieroglyphs the Maori chiefs appended to the Treaty of Waitangi could be
equalled only by its several provisions', and that 'the Maori text would be
enough to keep its own secrets'.[44] New Zealanders also remarked on the
difficulties of being clear as to the meaning of a Treaty contrived in two
languages. Mrs Ruth Ross, who first exhaustively traced the textual history
of the Treaty, remarked that it was 'hastily and inexpertly drawn up, ambiguous
and contradictory in content, chaotic in its execution.'[45] Professor D. F.
McKenzie and Dr H. B. Levine of Victoria University of Wellington
emphasized the very disparate understandings of the signatories at the time
when they signed. Professor Bruce Biggs of Auckland University asked himself
whether te Tiriti was 'in any reasonable sense equivalent to the Treaty',
and concluded: 'The answer has to be "no", not just because its language
is stylistically and grammatically awkward, but because the words chosen
to translate crucial terms in the Treaty are not equivalent, either because
they mean something else, or because the Maori words are more general
and less precisely defined than the English'.[46]

But questions as to the meaning of the Treaty were not, in New Zealand,
to be left merely to academics writing solely *as* academics. They were not
to be left unanswered in the way academics often leave questions, least of
all pronounced unanswerable. For Treaty questions were pre-eminently public
and political questions; and when academics well equipped to pronounce on
the Treaty's meaning (Dr Claudia Orange, Dr David Williams, Professor
Ranginui Walker, and Professor Hugh Kawharu in particular) did so, there
could be no mistake but that what they were talking about was as much
the contemporary arrangement of authority and property in New Zealand
as the past meaning of the Treaty. The texts of the Treaty and the context
of its signing were scrutinized in detail and with a fervour that almost never
accompanies historical research except when its purposes are those of the
living generation which undertakes it. These scholars thought for instance,
the Māori version to be the more important and now more worth following
than the English, and not solely on the legalistic grounds that the implications
of a bilingual treaty are to be construed in favour of the partner who did

---

[44] Sahlins, *Islands of History*, pp. 68, 69.

[45] Ross, 'Te Tiriti', p. 154; McKenzie, *Oral Culture, Literacy and Print in Early New Zealand*; Levine, 'The Cultural Politics of Maori Fishing'.

[46] Biggs, 'Humpty-Dumpty and the Treaty of Waitangi', *Waitangi*, p. 310.

not draw it up and offer it to the other. They were simply committed to the Māori version on the grounds that it better accorded with their notions of justice. Dr Orange's book *The Treaty of Waitangi* (1987) was unmistakably of this genre. So too were the essays of Kawharu, Walker, and Williams in Professor Kawharu's collection, *Waitangi: Māori and Pākehā Perspectives of the Treaty of Waitangi* (1989) which came out as this book was going to print. This is to say little of the quality of their scholarship. But it is to say that they unmistakably echoed and repeated, in fact *re-entered* the arguments that had been going on in the world of Māori-Pākehā politics, and in which they had played their parts in the 1970s and 1980s, not least as interpreters of te Tiriti.

Most notably they echoed the disputes which came to the Waitangi Tribunal. For it was partly to interpret the meaning of the Treaty in these conditions of radical uncertainty that the Tribunal was instituted, so that the course of Treaty arguments can be traced, as they will be later in this book, both in an examination of the proceedings of the Tribunal and of the context of contemporary polemic in which the Tribunal operated.

III

The Purpose and Plan of the Book

It will already be evident, and it will be shown in greater detail in the first section of Chapter 5, that in the main it was a growing Māori sense of injustice that fuelled the massively-publicized events and disputes that have been sketched so far. Dr Ranginui Walker, an office-holder on the Auckland District Maori Council since 1972, long proclaimed something of the kind, first as a matter of polemical consciousness-raising, later, as a matter of fact. Commenting in 1987 on the publication of a selection of fifteen years' worth of his articles on Māori matters for the liberal weekly magazine, *The Listener*, he described what the Māori had been doing since the late 1960s as 'eyeballing the Pakeha and saying, "Hey you guys, you shat on us, give us our fair share". Pakehas say to me, "What is it you Maoris want?" What they want is a nice simple formula which will get them off the hook from their past. I say to them: "If you want me to simplify it, I'll give you one word. Justice". Social equity and justice, and that's a big ball game'.[47] He called his collection *Ngā Tau Tohetohe: The Years of Anger*.

Walker's is a good description of how it has been: passionate talk of justice and equity *has* been the main form of Māori political language since the early 1970s. It does not really require the researches of modern psychology – though it has been demonstrated – to guess that 'the more to a man's disadvantage the rule of distributive justice fails of realization, the more likely he is to display the emotional behaviour we call anger'. People who

[47] NZL27:6/6/87.

think they do not get as much as they deserve, or who think themselves demeaned and denigrated, or who are not compensated for wrongs done them feel the wrongs deeply, and develop righteous anger. And they feel as it were in *groups* (as blacks, women, religious, and ethnic minorities), according to criteria shared among the group as to what is just.[48] I attempt in the remaining two chapters of this first part of the book to describe the conditions in which such angry talk of justice and injustice, equity and inequity, were possible: conditions in which there was enough division and dissension among people to make talk of justice necessary, but conditions too where there was enough of a sense of common membership of a political society to render such talk more than the empty rhetoric of enemies.

I also attempt to trace the lineaments of the leading ideas of justice for the Māori as they were to emerge through the 1970s and 1980s. I concentrate especially but not exclusively on the years from 1983, because 1983 was the year in which the Waitangi Tribunal made its first really important findings and recommendations on past and continuing wrongs to the Te Atiawa people of Taranaki. It was also the year when talk of 'social equity' began its career in official circles in New Zealand with the publication of the Planning Council's booklet, *Issues in Equity*; and it was the year when government departments, urged on by the State Services Commission and Māori activists, began a push towards 'biculturalism' in the design and provision of social (i.e. state) services to te iwi Māori (the Māori people). In sum, that year was the one in which the themes of injustice as consisting in unrepaired past wrongs and continuing current inequalities came together in a way that was to be characteristic of New Zealand political thought about Māori and Pākehā until the present day, 1989. And it was that combination of understandings of justice: justice as reparations for past wrongs and justice as an equalization of conditions – and both against a background of demands for a greater Māori autonomy and recognition of Māori ways of doing things – that made possible Ranginui Walker's simple summary of what the Māori was doing as 'eyeballing' the Pākehā.

The book separates as far as is possible the two kinds of justice claims. It takes as one idea basic to Māori demands, *reparative justice*: the idea that a thing wrongly taken or destroyed must be restored or that a substitute good be provided, and that compensation be made for the lack of the good in the period when it was wrongly absent. The idea is analysed (Part One, Chapter 2, Section II); then the story told is one of how reparations for past wrongs in general began to be spoken of in the early 1970s, were demanded for particular injustices during the 1980s, and found legally definitive expression in *New Zealand Maori Council v the Attorney General* (1987) when the Court of Appeal agreed that certain breaches of the Treaty of Waitangi could activate a 'right of reparation' (Part Two, Chapters 4–7). Most of all, it is shown that reparation for past wrongs has been one of the leading ideas that has

---

[48] G. C. Homans, quoted and glossed Mikula, 'The Experience of Injustice', p. 103. From a psycho-analytic viewpoint, see Jaques, 'Psychotic Anxieties and the Sense of Justice'.

informed the founding, reforms, and operation of the Waitangi Tribunal as it has dealt with claims to the restoration of Māori lands, waters, and fisheries – even of the Māori language and of Māori tribes.

The second kind of justice claim — the claim for *justice in distributions* — is also analysed in Part One of the book (Chapter 2, Section 1) and the story of the particular claims made is told in Part Three (Chapters 10-12). Despite international usage, which talks of 'justice in distributions' or 'distributive justice', this second kind of justice will mostly be called 'social equity' here so as to reflect the common usage predominating in New Zealand's public life. And in truth, the very vagueness and plasticity of the substitute name is highly appropriate. For the truth is that 'social equity' referred to many, sometimes contradictory, things. It referred to the ideals of equal opportunity, equal 'access' to institutions which benefit those who enter them, proportionality between contribution to society and reward, proportionality between hardness of work and reward, proportionality between need and share of social product, equal (or in other ways appropriately distributed) power to act in society. Etcetera. Even more productive of profusion of meaning and use, the phrase 'social equity' (we can obviously no longer think of it as a single ideal) was used to refer to much more than simply Māori and Pākehā in their relationships. Its scope of concern covered women in their relationship with men and institutions, other ethnic minorities, the physically and mentally handicapped, the gifted, solo parents and so on. In a word, 'equity' was claimed not simply for the Māori but for all those who were 'disadvantaged'.

Conceptual confusion was rampant, and it is the aim of the third part of the book not so much to sort out the confusions as to indicate them. It is also to show how Māori claims in particular were articulated in that milieu, and were also designed to transcend as well as to exploit it. As in the pursuit of reparation, so in the pursuit of 'equity', the Treaty/te Tiriti played its part in distinguishing the particular rights, powers, liberties, and privileges that the Māori ought to have and did not. Accordingly, and in that context too, the authority of that 'sacred document' was exploited or denied in the battle over 'special treatment' for the Māori. As Adelard of Bath truly observed in the twelfth century: 'authority has a waxen nose which may be twisted any way one wills'.

The historical point to be taken from the story which will be told is that very few of those who claimed either kind of justice claimed it fully. This is understandable in the case of 'social equity'. After all, *fiat justitia pereat mundus* is plausibly engraved on law courts and law schools. Let justice be done though the world perishes. But 'let *equity* be done though the world perish' seems to be overdoing it. Equity is too closely allied with the idea of ameliorating the rigours of the law (or of social justice) by adjusting for individual cases. In New Zealand it expressed as much policy goals which a government and other agencies might aim at as the inescapable duties of public agencies correlative to the rights of the disadvantaged. This might have been expected where there was such substantive disagreement over the wide range of ideals which the phrase referred to. But because reparative justice emphatically requires the restoration of rights as a duty it is perhaps more surprising that the demands for it have not often been made without stint or limit. Still, in fact the ideal of reparation was seldom pursued to its fullest extent *either*, and Chapters 7 through 9 of the second part of the book record this in the jurisprudence and practice of the Waitangi Tribunal, and then among the pronouncements of politicians and judges.

In the event then, neither of the two ideas of justice taken alone provided any notable number of the actors with an account that satisfied them of what justice required for the Māori. The usual tendency when people were arguing about justice was that they mixed considerations of equity and reparations in various combinations. And they also overrode considerations of justice with other considerations such as the desire for social peace and harmony (and its obverse, the fear of violence and discord) or for variety, or for the preservation of a threatened Māori way of life, or for the sake of a New Zealand 'identity' which would include Māori in it.

I develop a theory which suggests why New Zealanders were inclined to put up with injustice, or (to put it another way, and more judiciously) disinclined to think that justice was the only social and political virtue. It is a theory about the structure of the concepts of justice and equity in their contemporary New Zealand forms. It is a theory designed to show that in conditions of biculturalism, strict justice is actually impossible. And it is a theory whose application would *suggest* that New Zealanders/Aotearoans by and large felt this to be so – though I do not demonstrate that as thoroughly as it could be.

The inevitability of injustice is due in the case of reparations (Part Two, Chapter 6) to the presence of fundamentally distinct and competing ethnic conceptions of what things were (and are) wrong and as to how individual and group identity and responsibility for actions persist through time. Though Māori and Pākehā may (mostly) have recognized a common sovereign state, they did not recognize a common judge on questions of reparations. Nor, in distinguishing right from wrong, did Māori and Pākehā always recognize the same norms distinguishing right from wrong. Thus they did not recognize the same facts as to right and wrong in the past and present, and this condition of disagreement simply had to be, and largely was, recognized by the relevant institutions and public actors. As to 'social equity', the problems of seeing *that* as required by justice stemmed from the great variety of particular conceptions of what it was that gave people claims to things: whether their common humanity, for instance, or their needs, or their deserts, or their prior exclusive rights; and more, radical differences as to what it was to be equal, to need or to deserve or to have a right by virtue of some past fact. These differing conceptions of the nature and basis of distribution claims generated different prescriptions for the reorganization of society and politics, at which point the idea of a just society had transformed itself into a variety of competing conceptions of what a good society would be like. And as to much more besides: as to the nature of persons, and groups, and property, and authority, and as to the transmission of all these through time.

This is not surprising, because while (abstractly put) 'justice' seems to be the supreme political virtue, detailed practices of 'justice' in different societies are not so obviously good. The slave-owning gentleman of the southern USA thought that justice in accord with a hierarchy of honour demanded slavery.[49] Among the Council of Chiefs of Fiji, justice seems to be thought to consist in respect for a chiefly hierarchy, rule by ethnic Fijians of ethnic Indians, and the ownership of land being exclusively in the hands of ethnic Fijians. In Ulster it can be for Catholic to kill Protestant, and vice-versa; in South Africa, in the eyes of the Afrikaaner, it is for blacks to be ruled. The content of justice depends then on a prior valuing of freedoms and equalities, mutual obligations, disobligations, and mutual aid. But freedoms for who to do what and why? And equality in what respects and why? And equality of treatments in what respects and why? And aid (or repayment) for whom and why?

One thing that may be said about this temporal and geographic variation of the content of justice is to say it is 'relative' to times and places; another thing to say is that justice is 'dynamic' not 'static'.[50] Detailed justice in any place or time is a summary of the most important decisions made by a society about a large number of questions of how it wishes to live. Decisions are continually made; and though an essential aspect of the idea of a 'decision' is that it should stick (especially if it is a decision as to the just and the unjust), particular decisions do not. Justice for the Māori then is something that can never be done but is something to be continually discovered and aimed for. The search for justice is simply one of the ways of social living that New Zealand/Aotearoa's political tradition is exploring. Another way would be to attempt, laying aside all particular judgements of particular cultures, to decide what justice in the distribution of things really would be: to specify the requirements of transcendental justice. So far as I know no New Zealander has tried this. Nor shall I; mine is a record of justice as conceived within a particular political culture – and conceived separately at times by the two largest *ethnie*[51] who make it up.

My motives for this study are mainly intellectual and moral. They are to do with sorting out and describing the complicated ways New Zealanders have spoken about justice, and with showing the limits to the theoretical reach of the concepts they used. I also mean, at least implicitly, to commend those who, while understanding the imperative force of justice, have nevertheless argued that it cannot be attained. I have a lot of sympathy

---

[49] Ball, 'The Incoherence of Intergenerational Justice', at pp. 328–9, quoting Wyatt-Brown, *Southern Honor: Ethics and Behaviour in the Old South*.

[50] A theme pursued by Agnes Heller in her recent book, *Beyond Justice*.

[51] I use the French word *ethnie* as a technical term, rather than its closest New Zealand English expression, 'ethnic group'. The French term suggests a community, not necessarily physically grouped, but sharing a name, a sense of common past, a common myth of origins and other culturally specific beliefs. See for an extended discussion, Anthony Smith, *The Ethnic Origins of Nations*, Chapter 2.

with the saying of Bertrand de Jouvenel that: 'There is no once-for-all scheme of things to be established and preserved; our own conceits in this respect should be abated by our poor opinion of the different conceits held by our forefathers.'[52] But I should add that it is not hard to imagine that if the current injustices are not addressed more successfully than they have been, they will turn into the even more fundamental question: the question of the very legitimacy of the constitutional and democratic government of New Zealand. For the three from Te Ahi Kaa who went to Fiji were not talking justice and equity at all. They were talking the hegemony of the Māori in conditions where they thought justice and equity from the Pākehā to be impossible. They sought the rule of Aotearoa on Māori terms.

Leaving aside the many less sweeping Māori demands which will be covered in this book, it is not surprising that other academic and political writers – including Royal Commissions on the Electoral System, on Broadcasting and Related Telecommunications Communications (in 1986), and on Social Policy (in 1988) – have already come up with more or less concrete plans for the reform of thought and action to meet the Māori demands for justice and to rebut and avoid the Māori claim to absolute sovereignty.[53] For myself, I would rather say nothing as to the rectification of thought or policy in a book which sets out to be merely a history of arguments; but I shall have to say something about the moral inescapability of the sovereignty of the state because it relates to the endemic question as to what occurs where justice is not spontaneously done by members of a political society, each to each. That what tends to occur in fact occurred is the subject of the first two chapters of the fourth and final part of the book. Chapter 13 covers the nature of Māori claims to absolute sovereignty and their origin in disgust at the lack of justice they have had. Chapter 14 examines the response of the state not only to the claims of absolute Māori sovereignty but to the general messiness of the whole controversy about justice for the Māori: the assertion of absolute legal and practical sovereignty. At which point, in Chapter 15, I conclude for myself with some abstract reflections on how – where there is no agreement among persons on the content of justice – a sovereign state's enforcing an artificial, merely legal, justice is the best that can be done.

But legal justice must obviously come as close as it can to the two peoples' intuitions as to what is just and right. It is not enough that there simply *be* a legal sovereign and that it act. Its politics must be politics of peoples' justice. As I was writing in 1988, Hana Te Hemara, once Hana Jackson and

---

[52] de Jouvenel, *Sovereignty*, p. 165.

[53] e.g. Richard Mulgan: 'Aotearoa-New Zealand?' and *Māori, Pākehā and Democracy*; Raj Vasil, *Biculturalism*; Paul McHugh, 'Constitutional Theory', in Kawharu (ed.), *Waitangi*; Royal Commission on the Electoral System, *Report*, Chapter 3 especially; Royal Commission on Broadcasting, *Report*, pp. 310–20; Royal Commission on Social Policy, *The April Report* throughout as reported in Chapter 12 of this book.

an important member of Nga Tamatoa in the early 1970s,[54] was widely condemned when she was reported as saying that her habit was to advise young Māori men contemplating suicide in prison to 'kill a white and die a hero'. So she should have been condemned. However, that circumstances should be such that one human being, sane and pleasant as she is, should be brought to say such things to and about others is of much greater concern. That there are those Pākehā who simply refuse to consider that there could be *any* justice in the Māori claims is as bad: worse in fact, because they have the power to do more damage. My own hope is that my compatriots, seeing that there is justice on both sides and seeing also that there is more to life than doing justice, can continue to muddle and fudge along. I hope for a more enlightened, a more *principled*, a more cheerful muddle and fudge; and not just an instinctive reaction to uncomfortably recognized differences. Righteousness is easy; the sustaining of political society is not, and it is a much greater thing. It means really living with difference, hence living with injustice, and continually negotiating its distribution.

---

[54] For information on her political life, see Donna Awatere, 'Waihine ma Korerotia' in *Broadsheet*, July–August 1982, pp. 23–5.

Chapter 2
Justice and Reparations:
A Conceptual Analysis

I

The Difficulties with Justice and the Appeal of Contract

In September 1984 and in February 1985, two great hui were held at which Māori people discussed the Treaty of Waitangi and the issues of justice that it raised. The September hui was held at Turangawaewae Marae in the Waikato town of Ngaruawahia. The February hui was, appropriately enough, held at Te Tii Marae in Waitangi itself. There was a good deal of agreement among the participants that they suffered injustice at the hands of a Pākehā state, but they found it hard to see precisely what the detail of justice would consist of. The Chairperson of the workshop at Ngaruawahia called 'Moral Aspects of the Treaty of Waitangi', reported on both the confusion in detail as to what justice was, and on the overall agreement as to the nature of the injustice they universally felt. 'At the beginning of the first half of the session there was a real sense of getting at the basic issue of justice as a moral issue. This never quite emerged. Morality touches all aspects, whether legal, historical, or social, etc . . . [And] how *do* you see social justice in a dominating-dominated society?' The answer was obscure, but one thing at least was clear enough: 'That the Pakeha people, in view of the exploitation and oppression of the Maori people, have not honoured their moral obligation in fulfilling their part of the Treaty'.[1] This lay at the heart of Pākehā injustice. The issue was one of breach of contract. Justice would consist in its reparation.

This chapter seeks an abstract and philosophical understanding of the difficulties and confusions that seemed to the workshop at Turangawaewae to confound their attempts to define justice, and an equally abstract understanding of why the idea of injustice as breach of contract sits well with confusion about the details of morality. It then proceeds to clarify the idea of reparative justice and to say something about its appeal as well as its nature. The understanding provided is not perhaps *precisely* one that the workshop would have endorsed, and later chapters will corset and garb it in New Zealand/Aotearoan clothes: but the logic of the concept of justice and the contours of the situation suggest that it cannot be far from what was actually understood by the participants in debate.

It would be convenient to start by pronouncing on the nature of reparative justice, but that is impossible. For roughly speaking, reparative justice consists

---

[1] Blank *et al.* (eds.), *He Korero Mo Waitangi* (1984), p. 105.

in returning to people what is justly theirs and has been wrongly taken. So the first thing to understand has to be what justice is and who has a rightful title to what, because without knowing *that* we cannot know whether things have been wrongly taken, and thus whether reparation is really called for. But as the workshop on morality at Turangawaewae correctly recognized, it is difficult to say exactly what justice is, either as a matter of coherent theory or in the practical distribution of goods in a society. The 'real sense' of justice which they thought they were discovering, 'never quite emerged'. As the German philosopher, Wilhelm Leibniz, observed more than 250 years ago, 'everyone does not agree on a common concept of justice, with the result that everyone does not understand the same thing by the same name, and this is the cause of endless dispute'. Modern philosophers make the same observation and this colours their very different accounts of what justice is.[2]

Only one thing is certain. The rules of justice are not the same as the rules of law and the obligations, powers and liberties which the legal system distributes to us. Though we speak of the 'Courts of Justice', the 'Minister of Justice', even of the police as the 'arm of justice', we know that all these are capable of injustice and that the law lays unfair obligations or disabilities on some people and groups, and unjustly empowers others. The law ought to try to imitate justice; many think it succeeds quite well; but that is the best it can do.

It is not easy to go further. Some, like Leibniz, say that the virtue of justice is practised when the best is done for everybody in conditions of full knowledge and in a spirit of love. And this is the justice that God gives. But we are not gods; and we lack both total knowledge and much benevolence. In any case 'doing the best for everybody' is too broad a definition and confounds justice with benevolence or aroha (loving and forgiving solidarity). Justice is a duty that can be demanded *as of right*: love, forgiveness, aroha, benevolence, even the ministrations of friends, cannot be. Justice *must* be done; the other virtues lie beyond the bounds of rights and duties and cannot be demanded of people; they are supererogatory.[3] And justice distributes according to rules of strict fairness and proportion: but benevolence, love, aroha, patriotism and friendship are radically undistributive dispositions. They unify. They do not divide or distinguish. In a world governed by love we would still have difficulties deciding who would get what. We would busy ourselves insisting (against their loving objections) that everybody else should have things but not us.[4] In a country fired by patriotism, that patriotism would provide no clue as to how to distribute the national wealth.

Justice, on the other hand, can distinguish and separate. It is indeed founded

[2] Leibniz, 'Meditation on the Common Concept of Justice' (1702-3) in Patrick Riley (ed.), *The Political Writings of Leibniz*, p. 53. On modern disagreement, see for example James P. Sterba, 'Recent Work on Alternative Conceptions of Justice'.

[3] See, for example, Ewin, *Liberty, Community and Justice*, Chapter 4.

[4] Lucas, *Principles of Politics*, pp. 1-10.

in distinction. This is why, for instance, a policy of ethnic assimilation, though based on love and benevolence, can appear at once unjust and based on hatred and contempt. Assimilation seeks to unify and not discriminate; to deny difference and thus the different treatment due to different cases as of right. To deny difference and thus justice may seem to the recipient more like the hatred of an equal or contempt for an inferior.

Other philosophers, less ambitious for the scope of justice than Leibniz, have said that to treat people justly is to treat them *equally*, but this tells us too little. In any situation the language of justice as equality is a difficult one to use. The formal principle of justice requires treating equals equally (or the same cases in the same way) and other cases differently (but equally among themselves in so far as they are the same). However this formal principle, though necessary for justice, is not sufficient to generate any substantive principles of justice at all. For that one needs first of all to know who the equals are: one needs a definition of 'equality classes' and a way of distinguishing each class from others. Secondly one needs to know what kinds of treatment are right for those classes so distinguished: what is due each member of a class, or due the class itself. Without the two specifications it is impossible or unpersuasive to speak of people or groups as 'unequal'. Either it is not known whose condition is being compared or it is not known on what scale of good or evil comparisons are being made. Nor is either specification easy outside of the simplest situations (usually invented by philosophers), where for instance, it is thought that the sick because they need health care have it due to them, whereas those who are simply wealthy do not. In this case, need is the proper criterion distinguishing the equality class which must be treated, not wealth.[5]

At least simple cases show that if part of justice is to treat people equally, it must – except perhaps when it is punishment that is being distributed – mean treating them equally well, not equally badly. It is hardly 'just' to despise or harm people equally, or to subject them equally to a vicious legal system or set of moral rules. So the demand for equal treatment, when it is the demand for justice, is thus one that people should equally be given what is good for them, where what is good for them can be plausibly seen as theirs by right. However, it cannot be that all people should be given exactly the same things, because the same things are not good for different people (a crutch is good for those with broken legs but no good for those whose legs are perfectly good) and unequal distribution of things (like land, prestige, jobs and incomes) may well, depending on the society in question, increase overall good and the good of each individual.[6]

Let us say then that distributive justice is *giving to classes of people what is theirs by right, where classes are distinguished by characteristics that call for or generate*

---

[5] See Bernard Williams, 'The Idea of Equality'.

[6] See for examples from the vast literature on this: Flathman, 'Equality and generalisation'; Hart, *The Concept of Law*, Chapter 7; Rawls, *A Theory of Justice*; Dworkin, 'What is equality?'; Walzer, *Spheres of Justice*.

those good things that can be thought to be demanded for them as of right.[7] But even if it were agreed that that was true on a formal level, there would still be disputes. Rights belong to classes of people for reasons and on grounds, and the reasons and grounds – which are to do with what is good for people – may well be in dispute even though the formal principle of justice is not. Disputes about the grounds of rights to things have to be reconciled before there is agreement about particular conceptions of justice. More to the practical point, such disputes on conceptions of justice must be settled before there can be agreement about how things should justly be settled in particular cases.

But there *can* be no permanent settlement of particular cases or agreement on conceptions of justice. The content of justice is contingent on what particular societies take to be good for people and on what activities are being considered. This fact about the practice of justice is evident in academic philosophy and in practical life. Philosophers have made attempts to show that just rights to things (such as office and authority, education, security and welfare, money and commodities, respect, and honour) should depend on grounds such as moral entitlement, legal entitlement, need, and desert. Some have reduced the list to one qualification alone, arguing for instance that justice consists only in giving people what they need – or alternatively deserve, or what they are entitled to by law or by a moral code. Others variously combine and elaborate the qualifications in arriving at their conceptions.[8] In particular real world cases too, the claims of these various qualifications to have things are often reduced to one: to legal right, to desert, to moral right, or to need.

The problem is that to reduce the grounds of right-distribution to one requires an uncommonly coherent view of what is good for people; and the more coherent the view is the more it excludes competing conceptions of the good life. If people should get what they need, for instance, then legal rights and desert are not taken account of; and if people get what they deserve, then they would not always get what they need. Obviously too, different individuals, social groups and cultures have different ideas about what they, and other people need, or merit, or deserve or have a legal or moral right to. So often – more often in practical life than in the writings of philosophers who tend to seek a systematic understanding of things – the grounds of rights are compounded and mixed together.

Such a compounding and mixture characterized many of the claims made to the Waitangi Tribunal which, to put them at their most general, concerned rights to land, fisheries, the Māori language, to rangatiratanga (chiefly and stewardly authority), and to mana (which is at once a kind of authority and entitlement to unique respect and the ground of both).

Compounding and mixture, for instance, were very evident in the *Manukau*

[7] See Heller, *Beyond Justice*, Chapter 1.

[8] For example: Miller, *Social Justice*; Walzer, *Spheres of Justice*, especially Chapter 1; Heller, *Beyond Justice*, pp. 24–34.

Report of 1983 (and as it will later emerge they were in most of the other claims as well).⁹ In the *Manukau Report* it emerged firstly, that it had been argued by the claimants that the Tainui people of the Manukau Harbour and lower Waikato River areas were *legally entitled* to what they claimed: that, for instance, the land confiscations and losses which they suffered since the 1860s were legally void because they had proceeded without due process of law. One argument to this effect claimed that the fact that they had either been neutral or had been undertaking simply defensive wars from 1863 onwards against Pākehā aggression had been overlooked. Another argument was that the Treaty of Waitangi, valid in law, promised them that their possessions would not be alienated without their consent, yet they had had lands and waters taken by colour of statute, regulation and by-law without that consent. Secondly it was argued that in addition to having legal right (or even in the absence of legal right) they were *morally entitled* to what they claimed. One argument held this was so on grounds of the morally-binding Treaty. The Treaty might or might not be cognizable in domestic law because its provisions had never been incorporated into statute, but it was still morally binding. It had indeed been violated, but the rights it laid down remained, unextinguished, and the source of claims to justice. Another argument based the Tainui's moral rights on the grounds that they were the tangata whenua whose claims to land, fisheries, mana, and rangatiratanga were historically and morally prior to those of an alien law and the Pākehā who imposed it.

The third, fourth, and fifth sets of right claims made demonstrate much more clearly what is in fact also true of the first two sets: namely that arguments for just rights really depend on specific and varying conceptions of good human lives. It was argued (thirdly) that because they were better conservators of nature than Pākehās had shown themselves to be, the Māori *deserved* the office of kaitiaki (guardians) of the harbour. And (fourthly) there was a group of arguments from need. It was argued that the Māori *needed* control of their environment if they were to live lives which had meaning and value for them, that the Pākehā *needed* them to have that control because without it the harbour would continue to deteriorate to the loss of all, and that the environment *needed* their protection so that the balance and harmony of nature and the cosmos would be preserved. Finally (and fifthly) it was argued that the Tainui had a cosmically irreducible duty, as tangata whenua, to act as kaitiaki; therefore as a consequence they had a right to do so.

It was unjust, in brief, to deny the local Tainui their legal and moral rights, to deny their desert and to deny the needs of nature and both Māori and Pākehā. Most of all it was unjust to violate the dictates of a cosmic order in which the Tainui found the meaning of life and their own identity.

Doubtless this list of grounds of right is neither elaborate nor sensitive enough for many purposes. But the list will do for the moment because the only point that needs to be made here is that 'justice' appears in practical

---

⁹ See Waitangi Tribunal, Nganeko Minhinnick and others (*Ngati Te Ata and Tainui, re Manukau*).

life as a complex set of conceptions, not all – one may be excused for thinking in a preliminary way – reconcilable.

It is because of the complexity and irreconcilability of real world conceptions of justice that it is hard to say what justice is at the best of times. Should a wage, for instance, be based on desert? (And is that desert to be computed on grounds of ability, effort, long training, deferral of income during training, difficulty of the job, its dirtiness or danger, or what?) Or should a just wage be grounded on the need for an earner and family to survive? Or on a market or bargaining system, which, though imperfectly, reflects the gross sum of human wants and powers?

Such questions of just distributions were routine in New Zealand, and they were perfectly understood as *questions* – though debated as to answers – by all industrial (and ethnic, and gender) groups. But it was especially hard to find agreement on conceptions of justice at those points in life where the language of social anthropology and the perceptions of difference between cultures dominated. For where there existed two 'cultures' – and two *ethnie*, Māori and Pākehā – then there was a problem about justice. The cultures did not completely share the same views as to the substantive rules of law or morals, they differed on the claims of need and had different ideas as to who deserved what. There was too much vagueness, too much room for disagreement and misunderstanding and all the ills that travelled in their train. And much discussion of the relations between Māori and Pākehā did in fact take the form of disagreements between cultures about justice.

It was a form of disagreement that could lead to a politics of competing and starkly opposed epistemologies, for instance to the separatist and scarcely-negotiable politics which was the hallmark of much of Donna Awatere's extended essay, *Maori Sovereignty* (1982-1984),[10] and in many of the writings and sayings of Te Ahi Kaa. But for those who did not want a total politics of competing cultural conceptions – and this was largely the case among the Māori and Pākehā protagonists of the 1970s and 1980s – there was a way out of this condition. And it did not require arguing that the two cultures were in fact one and shared the same concept of justice. It was that the contents of justice should be thought of as constructed by way of formal contract or agreement and enforced by authority.

It is an ancient idea to think that in the absence of widespread agreement on the depth and detail of justice a thinner conception of justice can be constructed by two or more parties. This justice can now be enforced as justice must be if it is to *be* justice and not just an ideal of good conduct. It can be enforced because now justice consists in giving people their rights specified in contract rather than their rights according to the disputed conceptions of what justice is. A modern Norwegian, Professor Eckhoff, has celebrated the idea – doubtless too sanguinely as to its most extensive application – thus:

---

[10] On which, see Chapter 13, Section II of this book.

> Obligations determined by agreement will generally be better suited to organized enforcement procedures than obligations based on conceptions of justice. Agreements can be given in ceremonial or written form . . . Evidence can be more easily provided and the content of obligations can be defined more precisely.[11]

All that is required by way of preliminaries is that both the two parties have the right to oblige themselves by the contemplated promise. Private persons must be free from obligations which forbid them creating new ones; public persons must *be* persons (that is, be authors of their own actions) and have their (let us call it) 'sovereignty' similarly unencumbered. It may be that a contract thus entered into is artificial and not so complex in its provisions as are those detailed, often unspoken, agreements and shared norms which are the fruit of the long custom of living together. It is however a bond of union and source of specified obligations, the discharge of which constitutes justice between the parties.

This is a simple model of justice: simpler than the idea that justice is the administration of all the unspoken agreements and norms that exist in a complex society. It suggests something simpler too, than the idea that all wrongs in general ought to be righted. For where there is a contract and the contract is broken, then it is precisely and only the *specific* injustices done in breach of the contract which must be rectified. Finally, it is a simpler model in this respect. It insists that specific and contractual justice be enforced in a way that is impossible where justice is thought to be general and unspecified. It is much easier to see why contractual justice must be enforced than that all the norms of a society be enforced: if contractual agreements are not enforced, then, to quote Thomas Hobbes's *Leviathan* again: 'covenants . . . are but words, and of no strength to secure a man at all.'[12] And without the keeping of contracts human association would be impossible.

It was these ideas of justice in contract and reparation for breach of contract which provided one of the main approaches to understanding justice between Māori and Pākehā. They suggested themselves to the Pākehā mind, steeped in the Western tradition of contractual thinking. Equally, and for the same reason, they suggested themselves to the Māori. But the Māori had further reason to discourse of contract. First, the Treaty of Waitangi, its breaches and the demand for justice, had long been and continued to be a rallying point for kotahitanga (unity). It could stand for the preservation of their culture and kotahitanga in the face of disunity among tribes and Pākehā-imposed organizations, between the most traditionalist and the most reformist, between those who remained 'Māori' and those who had been disinherited by the processes of urbanization, industrialization, and the power of the nation state. Second, to claim justice-in-Treaty-contract against the Pākehā, as Ranginui Walker observed in 1987, was to take 'the morally high

---

[11] Torstein Eckhoff, *Justice*, p. 109.

[12] Hobbes, *Leviathan*, Chapter 17.

ground.'[13] The Pākehā – at least the Pākehā directive minority – believed in contracts. Treaty rights were being increasingly recognized in Canada, the USA, the United Nations, and even in Australia; breach of Treaty rights generated the right to reparation. Where there was a contract then the right to reparation could be claimed in a tolerably precise way.

II

Reparative Justice: Its Nature and Virtues

So what is reparative justice? What is its function and scope of action?

The idea of justice in reparation was very familiar *in use* to New Zealanders, as will be amply demonstrated in Chapters 4 to 7 and 13. But the idea itself was not in fact much discussed[14] until the Waitangi Tribunal made a start on it in findings in 1987 and 1988. So because of the paucity of New Zealand reflection, and because the practice of reparation is very widespread if not universal in societies, the answers to these questions are to be found mostly in the international scholarly literatures of philosophy, psychology, and anthropology. An internationalist model of reparation in fact provides a description of the way New Zealanders argued. They argued as if there were public acceptance of the abstract and internationalist reparatory model. Further, they argued as if they thought the model did not have descriptive power alone; they argued as if it also had moral force. In sum: they not only *described* things as 'unjust' when they did not conform with the model; they believed them to be wrong in that precise way that unjust things *are* wrong. The model then provides, in the language of philosophy, not only the New Zealander/Aotearoan's *descriptive criteria* of justice but their *moral sense* of it.

So this: *Reparative justice is a reciprocal exchange between two equal parties, recognizing the same standards of right, whereby one party having done wrong to the other, repairs that wrong by restoring the wronged party to his, her, their or its original position before the wrong. I wrongly take your land; I return it. I arrogate your authority; I restore it to you. I do not benefit from the transaction: your suffering is relieved; balance is restored and justice in transactions done. A debt – generated by the wrong action – is discharged in the reparation: what is owed is paid, what is taken is restored.*

But some questions have been begged here. Simple restitution of what was taken may not of course be enough to 'restore the balance'; and to 'return to an original position' is the more difficult the greater the complexity of the wrong and the longer the passage of time between the wrong and its rectification. The point is rather to try to put you in the position you

---

[13] At a public meeting in Auckland, 30 April 1987, quoting Thomas Berger's *Village Journey*.

[14] Hints that it should be are in Sharp, 'An Historical and Philosophical Perspective on the Proposal for a Bill of Rights in New Zealand', p. 33, and Brookfield, 'The New Zealand Constitution: the search for legitimacy', pp. 14–15.

would have been in had the wrong not been done by me, and to put me in the position I would now be in but for the wrong I did.[15] Legal thought complicates matters, for in contract law the idea is to restore wronged persons to the position they would have been in had the broken contract been kept, whereas it is only in torts that the idea is to restore them to the point they were at before the wrong was done. But the main thing is to wipe the slate clean as near as may be; to make it as if what happened never happened, at least as regards our mutual advantages and disadvantages. So as well as restoring your land and herds, I pay you in compensation something that is as equivalent as may be to the enjoyments you would have had during the time I arrogated your rights to them. I pay you (say) as near as may be the worth of the profits of the land during the time I used it. And if I arrogate your authority and now restore it: what else? It is hard to say. If authority brought perks with it: then the value of the perks; but if it brought only honour, fame, glory and praise it is a difficult matter. So also is it hard to say if the authority was rangatiratanga and its exercise both expressed and increased mana.[16] At these points the question is one of compensating for insult at loss of honour rather than loss of profits and the mundane comforts of life that can more easily be paid for in some equivalent valued thing. The history of Roman and more generally, western law, is partly one of decisions as to how to compensate insult as well as mere damage. Societies without written records have been recorded as wrestling with the same difficulties.[17]

There is another difficulty. What if the thing I took is now so changed – perhaps destroyed – or so much now entangled with other people's rights as to make it impossible to return it to you? Some jurisdictions, for instance the New Zealand, Canadian, and Australian, distinguish two kinds of reparation: 'restitution' and 'compensation'. 'Restitution' is the process by which things are restored to what they were. 'Compensation', so distinguished, admits failure to restore the parties precisely to their original position and comes as close as it can by returning not the good in question, but another as much like it as possible. I wrongly confiscate your land; I return to you an equivalent but other piece, or – more often – make monetary recompense. For obvious reasons this is a much more common form of the reciprocation for wrongs than pure reparation: the wrongly taken good may have been destroyed or else transformed to increase, decrease or transmute its value; or it might have subsequently changed hands legitimately and it might seem unjust to require it back from the third-party beneficiary. In these cases, compensation is a substitute for reparation. It may be thought of as second-best

---

[15] More or less, and without wishing to raise the complications due to the fact of events intervening between the original wrong and the moment of rectification – events which additionally change our conditions in a way which would make it wrong to put us back in the condition before the wrong. See Lyons, 'The New Indian Claims'.

[16] Read rangatiratanga (for the moment) as the status, rights, and responsibilities of a chief, and read mana as the highest kind of prestige there can be.

[17] See Beckerman, 'Adding Insult to *Injuria*'.

reparation. It has the same conservative aim and justification – to restore things – but it cannot entirely attain it.

It may be noted that the reciprocity in reparative justice is of good for evil over time, not as between the separate actions of the victim and the wrongdoer. The victim may indeed do nothing; the wrongdoer everything – though the wrongdoer may well need persuading, commanding or coercing by third parties who are interested in seeing that justice is done. So in what way are the two parties equal? The equality between them (let us call them W and V for Wrongdoer and Victim) is civic: the kind of equality that exists in well-organized societies. It necessarily requires that W and V are equally in subjection to the same normative system, the same rules distinguishing right from wrong; otherwise how could they – and the potentially enforcing Interested Parties (IPs) – agree that a wrong had been done, should be righted, and in virtue of what repayment remedy could be said to have been provided? The very idea of reparative justice can hardly be conceived of outside a society which recognizes common rules of right and wrong. Civic equality also – contingently and more or less – requires that each party has the actual ability to enforce the rights and duties of the agreed system. If V cannot, even with the help of the IPs, get W to do justice by persuasion or coercion, then justice will not get done. The truth of these propositions, the one to do with shared understandings and the other with the power to enforce them, may be felt in Lucy Mair's account of the relations among the Azende of North Africa. If reparative justice is to be done – as it often is – between sub-tribes, then (a) they must share the same rules as defining right and wrong and appropriate reparations for wrongs and (b) it must be possible for force of arms to be brought to bear if satisfactory reparations are not forthcoming.[18]

It will already be clear that reparative justice is not the whole of justice in distributions: it attends only to the breach of uncontroversial legal or moral rights, not (unless they are uncontroversially the grounds of settled rights) to needs, deserts or wants. Nor is it even the whole of reciprocal justice in exchange. There is also commutative justice which consists in a mutual exchange of good for good. Commutative justice looks to the future as well as the past. It may (like reparative justice) affirm and strengthen traditional arrangements as in societies where kinship structures largely dictate exchanges,[19] but it may also, notoriously in its market form, transform them as the parties seek precisely to change, by bettering, their positions – but end up in fact worse off than when they began. It is hard to tell what commutative justice ends up doing;[20] and this was a lesson that New Zealanders themselves were setting out to learn in the mid-1980s as their governments sought to regulate the economy rather less.

Reparative justice however is the pure form of conservative justice. If

[18] See Mair, *Primitive Government* (1982).

[19] Piddington, *An Introduction to Social Anthropology*, Chapter 7, Section 5.

[20] Most interestingly put in Lane, 'Market Justice, Political Justice'.

an appreciable tract of time has passed between the wrong and its righting it presents itself even as reactionary justice. Retrospection is essential to it and it contemplates the restoration of a past condition. It has less to say about what is to come. Where many conceptions of distributive justice would require a redistribution of social goods to bring about a more just future so that need is met, merit recognized, desert rewarded, or equality in some respect more nearly approached, reparative justice redistributes only to rectify past wrongs. It does not look to a better-patterned future distribution the way these modes of prospective justice can. Rather, the future must unfold according to just transactions among persons whose rights its purpose is to preserve. It can not contemplate the attractions of allowing a current unjust state of affairs to continue, whatever the overall consequential benefits of doing so. It is not conservative in *that* sense. Old wrongs cannot, must not, be allowed to provide the ground for any modern rights except rights to reparation. It rests on the idea that there are known and shared rules of justice which must be impartially administered with an eye to past transactions, and it is in this sense entirely legalistic.

One of its modern exponents in political philosophy is (sketchily) Robert Nozick. He embraces the idea of rectification for past wrongs, considering that rectification can be the only ground of state intervention in a social world otherwise completely, and rightly, constituted by private transactions. To intervene to redistribute for the sake of attaining some proportion between need, or desert and (say) ownership of things would be to wrongly violate individual liberty. To attempt to bring about other future states like equality, or some other 'patterned distribution' would be wrong on the same grounds: it would violate rights to liberty. Another (but more ambitious and optimistic) modern exponent of reparationism is Derek L. Phillips. Where Nozick stresses the difficulties in working out what would have happened had past wrongs not occurred, Phillips is less burdened by doubt and by the difficulties of constructing counterfactual but 'possible worlds' – worlds which might have happened but didn't. Where Nozick neither knows nor cares what the effect of redistribution on grounds of reparation would be, Phillips thinks that reparative redistribution would also be one which made the consequent future world one in which the ideal of equal distributions was better met, and thus the ideal of meeting the needs of all people better. He thinks that, different in theory as retrospective reparative justice and prospective distributive justice are, nevertheless both may in practice be pursued at once to yield the same, uncontradictory result.[21]

However used by philosophers, reparation is, it need hardly be said, one of the most basic concepts in the civil law. It is one of the main remedies for violation or infringement of rights. It is a right – some say a 'sanctioning right' – generated in the breach of rights. It is a universal feature of legal

---

[21] Nozick, *Anarchy, State and Utopia*, esp. pp. 152-3, 208-9; Phillips, *Equality, Justice and Rectification*, esp. Chapter 9 and 10. See also George Sher, 'Ancient Wrongs and Modern Rights.'

systems.[22] And it plays its part in wider, political, spheres too. Recent Indian claims in the USA and Canada have been based on the concept and pursued in law courts, in legislatures and with executive powers. In 1972, for instance, the Passamaquoddy Tribe of Maine set out to have the federal Government sue the State of Maine for the return of two-thirds of the land of that state to them on grounds of Maine's breach of the Trade and Intercourse Act (1790). The Federal Government instead undertook a long, delicate and sometimes acrimonious series of negotiations with them, and settled in an Act of 1980, on $25,000,000, plus 100,000 acres, plus long-term options on a further 400,000 acres. In 1980 too, the Sioux received $105,000,000 in compensation for the wrongful taking of the Black Hills of Dakota. Other particular Indian claims – the Sioux claims expanded, for instance – are under way in the USA; as they have been and are in Canada.[23] Philosophers, as well as statespersons (not least Māori ones) have found the claims fascinating both in their practical and theoretical implications.[24] But perhaps the most famous USA claim was made by James Forman in 1969, in the 'Black Manifesto'. It was the very general claim that the white Christians and Jews of the USA owed reparations to American blacks for their slavery and exploitation. The issue was hotly debated until the claim was largely given up by the blacks themselves in the early 1970s; but it is likely that Nga Tamatoa heard of it; and Boris Bittker, an eminent professor of law in New York went so far as to work out the kind of payment that might cover the tortious liability under such a case.[25]

Of course not everything that goes under the name of reparation is properly named. Nor is a reparative effect necessarily the only consequence, or intended consequence, of reparative justice. Often the motive behind claiming reparations is the desire to bring about current equality; this lay behind many defences of the 'Black Manifesto'. Often too, there are other motives. Hugo Bedau has rightly argued that German 'reparations' under the Treaty of Versailles, for example, might better be thought of as tribute exacted from a defeated enemy than as reparations for an unjust war. There was no civic equality on which to base them; and the reparation payments were certainly designed to have a punitive effect on the wrongdoer as well as compensating the victim of wrong. And punishment – like revenge, the exchange of an evil for a wrong – is not reparation. Reparation is the exchange of a good

---

[22] See, for example, Fried, 'Rights and the Common Law', especially pp. 216 and following; also Glanville (ed.), *Salmond on Jurisprudence*, Sections 34-6.

[23] See Taylor, *The Bureau of Indian Affairs*, Chapter 5; also Taylor, *American Indian Policy*, Chapter 2, which also discusses Sioux claims; and Becker and Kipnis (eds.), *Property: Cases, Concepts, Critiques*, pp. 39, 41-8.

[24] For example, Lyons, 'The New Indian Claims and Original Rights to Land'; Michael McDonald, 'Aboriginal Rights.'

[25] See Bittker, *The Case for Black Reparations*; Harrington and Kaufman, 'Black Reparations – Two Views'; Green, 'Reparations for Blacks? The question of effective equality through preferential treatment'.

for a wrong.[26] German reparations to Jews after the Second World War, complicated and difficult as they were to organize, meet the case more nearly. Here the successor regime recognized the wrongdoing and its citizens did not noticeably object.[27]

The general attraction of reparative justice comes to this: that it takes rights seriously. It takes them as seriously as John Locke, who was like Hobbes a seventeenth century English philosopher. Contemplating breaches of natural rights, he thought there must also therefore be an 'executive power in nature', the right not only to punish breaches of right but to take reparation of them.[28] For what is it to have a right if one may lose it and have no redress?[29] What indeed *is* a right, but a claim which will be enforced against the relevant persons by society, and what is reparation but a very common form of enforcement? As a practice it has commended itself both in face-to-face societies where people share a common moral code and a means of enforcing it – as for instance among the Nilotic people whom Lucy Mair studied – or in territorial states in which private citizens, who relate often impersonally or not at all to each other, expect political authority to protect them against tort and crime partly by the exaction of reparations from wrongdoers.

It is easy to think that wherever there is society among people there must be reparative justice. The justification of the practice could be either that it is a necessary condition for peace and co-operation: for who would remain at peace and co-operating in a society in which rights were continually violated without remedy? Or it could be that it is simply wrong to violate rights and that there must be remedy though the heavens fall. That the practice is well nigh universal would suggest that most people see these things. But despite the obvious attractions of the idea of reparations for past wrongs, there are difficulties, defects and limits to its proper application. And they are every bit as intractable as the problems that beset attempts to say what distributive justice is.

The attractions and the difficulties of both kinds of justice as New Zealanders saw them will be the subject matters of Parts Two and Three of this book. In Part Two they will be seen wrestling with the problems of constructing a shared view of reparative justice: not in its general outlines (they were as they have been described here), but in its particular applications to their conditions. In Part Three they may be seen debating distributive justice: 'equity', equality, fairness, the claims of need, desert, legal entitlement, the market, and so on. For the moment however, it remains in the final chapter of this first, introductory part of the book, to sketch the social conditions in which it has been possible for New Zealanders/Aotearoans to think of,

---

[26] Bedau, 'Compensatory Justice and the Black Manifesto', p. 32.

[27] See Nehemiah Robinson's accounts, recorded in the Finding List at the back of this book.

[28] Laslett (ed.), *John Locke: Two Treatises of Government*, II, Section 11.

[29] A recent attempt at the question is Judith Jarvis Thomson, 'Rights and Compensation', in her *Rights, Restitution and Risk*. A subsequent controversy is in the USA academic journal *Philosophy and Public Affairs* (1985).

talk about, debate, polemicize, squabble about, claim and disclaim justice of *any* kind. The conditions will be seen to be those outlined in the classical tradition of political thought. There was enough disunity to make claim and counter-claim inevitable; yet there was enough unity and common interest to allow the claims to be brought to the bar of law and reason, rather than to trial by force of arms.

Chapter 3
Distinction and Indistinction:
The Conditions for Justice

I

Separated Parties and the Conditions for Justice

This book will often speak of the 'Māori' and the 'Pākehā' as if each group were unproblematically a unit – an *ethnie* cohering by virtue of its members' sharing identity and interests. It speaks as if the members of each *ethnie* knew themselves to be so, found point and meaning in their lives in that identification, and saw that their group had interests specific to it. It speaks of the two groups as separate and in conflict. The very language of justice, which it reports as having been so vehemently used by the Māori, suggests these things. This is because justice is a virtue either of transactions between people (or groups) or of distributions among them; and both transactions and distributions require people or groups to have separate and often contradictory interests. So when the question is posed as one of *justice* between Māori and Pākehā then it is necessary to speak as though the two parties are separate entities, with separate interests and rights, continually in the business of the one making claims against the other and the other responding with counterclaims or evasions.

This is a conceptual and linguistic necessity, generated by the very concept of justice and the way people talk about it. Justice is a chilly virtue, one which deals with disputatious rivals separated by disagreement as to their rights. But it is not a conceptual or linguistic necessity that the language of justice should have been adopted. The language was *chosen* by the Māori. It was chosen to express difference, separate interests and rights. It was chosen to express the passions that the injustice of their denial arouses. It was also chosen because justice demands – it does not merely suggest – that its dictates be acted upon. The language of justice is imperative and divisive. So Māori 'radicals' and 'stirrers' were condemned during the 1970s and 1980s for dividing Māori and Pākehā with their non-negotiable demands; and their reply was simply that the divisions and imperatives were there already, and that they merely expressed them.

But justice *also* requires that something binds the rivals. If the rivals were entirely separate, if they were foreigners, even enemies, there could be no justice between them. As Hobbes put it, separate political communities are to be pictured as armed gladiators: 'having their weapons pointing, and their eyes fixed on one another', guarding their borders.[1] Between them there

---

[1] Hobbes, *Leviathan*, Chapter 13.

is no justice, merely the threat of force. If separateness is *all*, then the grounds of justice dissolve, because it is the rendering of *goods* that are at issue. Enemies do not wish good on one another; they may not even have reason, if their forces are not roughly equal, to be fair. At her most separatist, Donna Awatere reached this conclusion in *Maori Sovereignty*, depicting the relationship between Māori and Pākehā as purely and simply one of war for the past 140 years. Her demand was for a new unity to be enforced by a Māori hegemony in the absence of that justice which would have made a continued common life possible. Pākehā who did not like it must separate, secede, go back to where they came from. Justice can exist only where there is, or where people think there could be, a common life lived by the parties. With no common life, or no chosen prospect of it, there can be no talk of justice: only of the sovereignty of one contender over the other. Some few spoke like Awatere, but none, including her, argued continually that way. Most persisted in demanding justice on the assumption there was and would be a common life led by Māori and Pākehā.

Not just any kind of common life. If common membership in an enterprise is absolutely necessary for there to be justice, it is not in itself sufficient. It can deny otherness and difference in such a way as to constitute injustice. This from the Māori point of view was the danger of Pākehā hegemony. Justice requires the parties in transactions and distributions to treat each other as equals, not as subordinates. At least it does in New Zealand, where the reigning conception of Māori-Pākehā relationships has long been one of equality.

Yet there was one question of power, and another of the public ideology which complicated the treatment of Māori rights and interests as on a par with Pākehā ones. It is not only when *foreigners* confront one another that, as the Athenians are supposed to have informed the Melians nearly 2500 years ago: 'You know, and we know, as practical men, that the question of justice arises only between parties equal in strength, and that the strong do what they want to, and the weak submit'.[2] Confrontation can happen between friends and in families too.

The Māori do not have equal force in a democratic New Zealand. They are outvoted and outnumbered in most areas of common life, and are subject to what Koro Dewes successfully named in 1970 a 'Pakeha veto'.[3] Their claims to justice during the 1970s and 1980s were a way of protecting themselves and their rights, not against arms, but against the coercive votes and opinions of the democracy. They were trying to resist what Alexis de Tocqueville and John Stuart Mill called, observing the rise of democracy in the nineteenth century, the 'tyranny of the majority'.[4]

---

[2] Thucydides, *History of the Peleponesian War*, v, p. 89.

[3] Dewes, 'The Pakeha Veto'.

[4] See de Tocqueville, *Democracy in America*, ii, Chapters 6 and 7 on, 'a new kind of despotism', and Mill, Chapters 7 and 8 of *Representative Government* in his *Utilitarianism: Liberty: Representative Government*.

Pākehā numbers and democratic ideology could create that tyranny. With Pākehā at 90 per cent of the population controlling a single chamber Parliament elected on a simple majority system, the Māori, with no entrenched rights, were at their mercy. In July 1988, Matiu Rata, arguing for 50 per cent Māori ownership and control of sea fishing resources in New Zealand, was faced with the (TV interviewer's) question as to what he made of the fact that the vast majority of New Zealanders appeared not to favour the proposal. His answer was that this was an issue of 'justice', that New Zealanders should see this, and that the democracy should not prevail in that particular matter.[5] This was a recurring Māori tactic, and thought. That a thing is just is enough to put it beyond the reach of manipulation according to the dictates of public opinion. Three million New Zealanders *could* be unjust. To talk of justice was therefore in the interest of the Māori. And the tension between unity and difference was a necessary tension if there were to be justice between them and the Pākehā.

What then were the conditions in which the tension existed?

II

Unity, Mixture, and Mingling

The best attempt to describe 'Māori and Pākehā' from an anthropological point of view and in all their local variation, is Joan Metge's eighteenth chapter in her book, *The Maoris of New Zealand* (1976). Yet even she found the unities and the differences between Māori and Pākehā and their cultures difficult to describe: it was never simply a matter of describing what was the case, but of appraising present ways of life and prescribing future ones. And where the politics of *justice* were at issue – as they were among the population at large – the difficulties were still greater, because the object was to understand not so much the general and diffuse conditions of 'race' or 'ethnic' relations, but a more limited area of relations: one in which division and distinction reigned. In that more limited area, nothing as to separation and unity was non-political. Nothing could simply be described. Nothing was settled and clear. Nothing was non-controverted. Everything was connected with the distribution of material resources or of status and authority, mana and rangatiratanga. Although the tension between unity and difference was always likely to be resolved in a way which denied justice to the Māori people (by insisting on seeing them as so many separate individuals who were part of the New Zealand nation), yet they persisted in, and won, a propaganda battle with politicians over their separateness. Perhaps this is the best that can be said of the history of the conflicts of the 1970s and 1980s, with respect to justice. Even if the Māori did not convince the majority of Pākehā, they convinced at least the directive minority of the land that they were, and ought to be, a separate people.

There was much celebration of the unity of Māori and Pākehā among

---

[5] Eyewitness News, 5/7/88.

the politicians well into the 1980s in what Dr Pat Hohepa in 1978 and other Māori intellectuals and their sympathizers called the 'one people myth'.[6] The unity of the peoples in the nation was a common sentiment expressed especially after the Second World War. Politicians spoke of the shared blood spilt in battle, the famous victories and defeats shared in sport, and the continuous progress of the Māori in the adaption to Pākehā ways. Public opinion echoed them. Highly irritating to the activists, the myth was elaborated especially at celebrations of the signing of the Treaty of Waitangi. The habit at Waitangi was to quote Hobson's words on the day the Treaty was first signed: 'he iwi kotahi tatou': 'now we are one people'. Hobson may simply have been referring to the fact that Article 3 promised 'all the ordinary (that is Māori) people of New Zealand', 'the same rights and duties as the people of England'.[7] But the modern politicians meant to stress not only equality in rights and in subjection to government – equal citizenship – but also the growth of an indistinguishably common nationality constituted by shared blood, lives and beliefs.

The 'one people' school had in mind, and embraced, the proposition that racial and ethnic differences had faded (or soon would) as new (multiracial) bodies and a new mentality replaced the old differences. Sir Keith Holyoake, Prime Minister from 1960 through 1972, used to speak cheerfully of the day when there would only be 'light-brown-skinned New Zealanders'; and Sir Robert Muldoon, who was Prime Minister from 1975 to mid-1984, expressed the ideal of one nation of New Zealanders most eloquently for his generation. 'New Zealanders,' he said at Waitangi in 1984, are a 'mixed people' who had travelled 'vast distances to a new land', displaying 'courage and initiative' in doing so. That character was inherited; and the cultures they brought were melded: 'We take our culture from all the ancient tribes of Britain, as well as from the ancient tribes of Maoridom; but in addition, the Dalmatians who came to dig the gum and later made the wine; the Chinese who came to work the goldfields; the Dutch, post World War Two; the refugees, first from Nazi bestiality, and subsequently from communist terror in eastern Europe and in South East Asia. Modern waves of Polynesian migration have also washed on our shores. So, we are a mixed people.'[8] Also *one* people: later that year Muldoon spoke of the 'great achievement of New Zealanders in becoming one people – British, Māori and all others'.[9]

However, the insistence on national unity constituted by ethnic and racial melding had in fact become less confident and more edgy during the 1970s. The Māori rejected the description and the agenda. By 1980 it was no longer easy for politicians to be at all confident on the issue. In 1979, Hon. Ben

---

[6] Hohepa, 'Maori and Pakeha: The One-People Myth'; Walker, 'The Meaning of Biculturalism', p. 6; Mead, *Finding a Pathway to the Future*; Ballara, *Proud to be White?*, pp. 79–81.

[7] A translation by Professor Kawharu, quoted by Cooke P. in the *New Zealand Maori Council v the Attorney General*. See Government Printer, *Treaty of Waitangi*, p. 33.

[8] See the article, 'Waitangi Speakers Invoke Unity', H3:7/2/84. Also see AS2:7/2/84.

[9] H3:18/9/84.

Couch, the Minister of Maori Affairs, spoke of his being 'a New Zealander first and a Maori second'. There is no doubt at all that in speaking that way he echoed the sentiments of a great number of Māori; and in fact he was prepared to repeat himself in Parliament in 1981 (though note the subtlety about building, not being, a nation): 'I say we are all New Zealanders . . . We are here to build a nation.'[10] The implication could be taken that he thought being Māori was not such an important thing, and he was long attacked for the gaffe which was taken to indicate a disposition to Uncle Tom-ishness.[11] Couch was not the most rhetorically able of politicians but he could sense the way the wind was blowing. In 1981 he spoke on TV approvingly, but in a phrase embarrassingly redolent of South Africa, of 'separate development' (English for *apartheid*) for Māori and Pākehā. He could see that the Māori wished a high degree of self-determination and was beginning to reject what was now known as the policy of 'assimilation' – earlier 'amalgamation' – of the two 'races'. But he had not put it well. 'Apartheid', as official policy and common speech had ruled since the mid-1970s, was 'abhorrent'. There is a story that Sir Graham Latimer, Chairman of the New Zealand Maori Council, upon hearing the phrase 'separate development' issuing from the Minister's lips, buried his head under the blankets of the bed in which he was lying at the time. (Thus if he were asked by the media to comment he could truthfully say he had not seen the programme). Latimer's embarrassment was felt throughout the country by those who thought the Māori should be able to go their own way in affairs that concerned only them. For Couch's sentiment, if not the wording, was right. It was a sentiment approved by anti-apartheid church and secular reformist groups by the 1980s. The Māori were a separate people who should be free in *some* degree to go their own ways.

Other politicians were more adept at accommodating their language to the change in the climate of Māori sentiment. In 1981 Sir David Beattie, the Governor-General, suggested at Waitangi that 'we are not one people, despite Hobson's oft-quoted words, nor should we try to be. We do not need to.'[12] In 1982 he roundly proclaimed that there were 'two people, one nation': the very formulation suggested by Pat Hohepa when he had complained of the 'one people myth'. In 1985 though, Beattie modified his proclamation: 'We are not one people', he began, but he complicated matters by adding, 'we are a country shared by many peoples'. The issue was that of 'multiculturalism' as opposed to 'biculturalism', and the sensitivity of those who were neither Māori nor Pākehā at being left out of account.[13] But Sir Paul Reeves (Beattie's successor) was to simplify the complication again by stressing the existence of two, not many peoples. He told a group of Presbyterians at Palmerston North in the Manawatu: 'Claims that we are

[10] NZPD3:39 (31 July 1981), p. 2177.

[11] Ballara, *Proud to be White?* p. 165.

[12] Quoted as saying so by the Waitangi Tribunal in the *Te Atiawa Report*, para. 10.3.

[13] H3:7/2/85.

all New Zealanders were difficult to sustain . . . when few Pakeha spoke Maori and did not understand rudimentary aspects of Maoritanga or Maori spirituality. The Treaty of Waitangi offers us a different model of two people within one nation, each with rights and obligations towards the other'.[14] At the opening of the Auckland University Marae in early 1988, and echoing a common business-management phrase of the times, he spoke of the ideal of a 'Treaty-driven' society of two peoples. Only a few politicians, such as Robert Muldoon, remained absolutely staunch to the old ideal through the 1980s. In 1989 Muldoon was still speaking the same way.

Muldoon was a populist. Deposed as leader of the National Party in 1984 and relegated to the back benches during the period of the fourth Labour Government (1984-1987, and 1987 on) he retained the ability to speak for, and attract the support of the 'ordinary bloke'. Mr Winston Peters, a new generation National MP, emulated the master. In 1988 Peters emerged as the man second most preferred by New Zealanders as Prime Minister – Rt. Hon. David Lange, the PM, remained most preferred – and Muldoon was continually overhauling his party leader, Hon. Jim Bolger, to be third equal with him by September.[15] Muldoon and Peters were both proponents of unity-in-melding, and their popularity grew at a time when 'race relations', seldom of great public concern, was becoming a matter of very great concern, thought to be the 'most important problem' in the country by 11 per cent of the people.[16] The conclusion is inescapable that they expressed a powerful public ideology.

Nor was the ideology of unity-in-melding a fantastic fiction without a basis in concrete and sensuous reality. The realities of biological, social and cultural mixing between Māori and Pākehā and their ways of life made too clear a distinction between them impossible. Their relations were not only ones where justice and injustice were at stake. Many of their political relationships found them on the same side in Parliament, in local bodies, and so on; and often the questions were not to do with rights demanded but interests to be log-rolled and deals to be made. And then there were love relationships, family relationships, relations of friendship and mateship, and there were relationships of that indifference and acceptance that are born of living together, desegregated by law and largely also in practice.

As early as the 1840s it was reported by the colonizing New Zealand Association that there was no 'physical repugnance' between the Māori and the European.[17] Bishop Manuhuia Bennett observed in 1979 that 'in New Zealand, names such as Reedy, Mead, Bennett . . . can no longer be considered Pakeha names. They are now an intrinsic part of Maoridom. By the same token, when I look at the blue eyes and fair skins of the descendants of

---

[14] H13:4/11/86.

[15] *New Zealand Herald* – National Research Bureau Poll, reported H1:10/10/88.

[16] See the records of *NZ Herald*-NRB Polls from September 1983 to September 1988 at H3:20/ 5/87 and H1:11/10/88.

[17] Adams, *Fatal Impact*, p. 2, quoted also in *The April Report*, ii, p. 151.

people such as Puketapu and Parata, I am convinced that the day is not far off when those names will no longer be just Maori names.'[18]

Questions as to Māori genetic heredity are not easy to answer. Before 1974, when the Maori Affairs Amendment Act set in train a tendency to record and treat as 'Māori' those of *any degree* of aboriginal descent who identified themselves as Māori, people tended anyway to call themselves 'Māori' or not according to want they felt themselves to be, and differently for different purposes and at different times. In earlier years, when 'degree of blood' was a question, there were some complicated fractional answers; but by and large it was self-identification that really mattered then too, and not fraction of genetic inheritance.[19] According to Ian Pool and Nicholas Pole's 1987 study of censuses, 'the proportion of the Maori census reporting "full Maori blood" has always been far higher (usually above 60 per cent higher) than would be expected from probability'.[20]

It is difficult to quantify the facts of genetic intermingling because they are not recorded – they are precisely avoided – in official statistics. And it does not seem to be an issue with anyone. As to intermarriage, John Harré reported that in 1960 almost half the marriages made by Māori in Auckland were with Pākehā and that the proportion of mixed marriages to other marriages was 'increasing rapidly'. Of the mixed marriages, some ran Māori households. These were more extended than the Pākehā ones: more respectful of age, more relaxed often, and attentive to obligations at tangihanga (extended funeral obsequies for the dead) and other Māori events on their marae, in their houses and round town. Others lived as Pākehā families: more nuclear and attentive to the demands of market work and of Pākehā voluntary associations. Some marriages mixed their family styles. In general, Harré thought that relations between the races were much better than 'pub talk' might have led one to think, and that the stereotypes each group had of the other were not proof against closer personal relations in friendship and marriage.[21]

Figures taken in the 1981 census, and commented on by Pool and Pole, suggest that the high rate of intermarriage continued and that it had even further increased. They also suggest a good degree of interethnic mobility, 'in a plural society . . . where relations between the two major (and other) groups are rather fluid'. About 4 per cent of those of 'Maori descent' (people could choose between 'Maori' and 'Maori descent' on the census form) seem to have been lost each five years from the count of Māori taken in the national census. 'Category jumping' – changing one's identification for various purposes – was common too, and seems to have been a practice established well before the Second World War. Pool and Pole also thought the evidence suggested that it could well be that the direction of Māori jumping might

[18] Bennett, 'Te Kupa Whakamutanga', p. 73.

[19] Metge, *The Maoris of New Zealand*, pp. 39–42.

[20] Pool and Pole, *The Maori Population to 2011*, p. 7.

[21] Harré, *Maori and Pakeha*, p. 144 and throughout.

reverse in the future: the Māori renaissance with its attendant growth of pride in being Māori might well boost that tendency.[22]

Such fluidity of ethno-racial definition and merging allowed for very different reactions and predictions, often coloured by views of the proper relations between the races. For one thing, the figures afforded the thought perhaps that the larger the projected 'Maori' population and population of 'Maori descent', the better the claim to a proportionately greater share of resources. This could lead to an insistence on distinctness of Māori (plus Māori Descent) and Pākehā, and on a large predicted growth of the Māori population. Dr Edward/Te Kohu Douglas, intent on arguing the importance of preserving and sustaining Māori culture, argued before the Waitangi Tribunal in 1985 that projecting from the 1981 base of population of Māori descent, by the year 2000 a large proportion of the population (25-30 per cent and more) would be Māori or of Māori descent – more than 50 per cent from Lake Taupo to the north. His figures became a staple in Māori claims to a fairer distribution of resources, and the tribunal noted that 'many young Maoris, especially those whose political views usually find them being classed as "radicals" or "activists"', were 'excited by the prospect of being in a majority'.[23] Pool and Pole, more measured and deliberate in their policy proposals, projected Māori identification from the same base to 12 per cent by 2011; and they could see a 17 per cent, at most 19 per cent Māori descent population.[24]

That there would be separation and an increasing Māori and Māori descent population was one way of looking at it. But the figures could also suggest a racial and ethnic merging. Miscegenation tended to be thought an unmitigated blessing by those who would argue for assimiliation, or integration, or a continuous and peaceful co-operation between the groups until they became indistinguishable. Holyoake's hopes for a pale brown New Zealand, and such assertions that 'there are no pure-bred Maoris now', were the stuff of letters to the newspaper and politicians' pronouncements throughout the 1970s and 1980s. On the other hand those who were suspicious of too much dissolution of Māori ways and of too little Māori resistance to 'Pākehādom' viewed miscegenation with a colder eye. Certainly radical Māori women in the early 1980s vehemently protested against Māori men 'screwing the oppressor' – and they did not mean 'oppressing' the oppressor. To add to the confusion, their opponents might well have cited the Pākehā wives of such Māori leaders as Ranginui Walker, Manu Paul, and Stephen/Tipene O'Regan.[25]

As to friendship and mateship, the men mingle at work and at sports clubs, the women at sport, work and when shopping; the children at school. There is less intermingling in homes than would be expected if the groups

[22] Pool and Pole, *The Maori Population to 2011*, pp. 1, 6, and Chapter 3.

[23] Waitangi Tribunal, *Te Reo Report*, paras. 3.4.8 to 3.4.14. This was reported at AS7:2/10/85.

[24] Pool and Pole, *The Maori Population to 2011*, Chapter 3.

[25] Greenland, 'Ethnicity as Ideology', p. 98. And see Ripeka Evans's remarks in 'Aftermath of Waitangi', third page.

could not distinguish, and did not distinguish, between one another. Dr R. Chapple in his mid-1970s study of a central North Island forest town found the Māori women happy to admit that 'we Maoris around here live in each other's houses', suggesting a degree of Māori gregariousness and ethnic exclusiveness; for their part, Pākehā women and women more recently arrived from Europe were in general much less gregarious altogether, and when they did visit, they preferred visiting other Pākehā women rather than Māori, at a proportion of about 3:1. But inter-racial friendship and respect was perfectly normal; and the men, working together, kept up steady and permanent contact.[26] In general, too, working class Māori and Pākehā share many of the same beliefs and attitudes to, and in, the world of work: in 1977 they shared much the same low estimate of their bosses' interest in their ideas and welfare (workers recently from the Pacific Islands judged them more favourably). There were differences: Māori tended to have less of a 'work ethic' and to see in work less of an opportunity than Pākehā did to avoid boredom and make pleasing social contacts; and they worked in a way unthought of by Pākehā to support their kin groups. But the differences between the two were not nearly so great as those between them both taken as a single group and workers who lived as Samoans, Cook Islanders and Tongans in New Zealand.[27] This is not surprising, their work experiences were similar. So too were they both exposed to the same world of mass media in the 1970s and 1980s. Despite the great expansion of Māori language and Māori interest programmes on radio and TV after 1985, the percentage of these was still relatively small in 1988. All New Zealanders had no choice but to be bombarded by the same, increasingly USA-dominated, media messages. It was not until July 1988 that Radio Aotearoa began broadcasting in Auckland; and, wanting and needing an audience, it mixed Māori, Pākehā, and overseas modes of talk and music. Even so, far from all Māori watched or listened to the broadcasts aimed at them. English was and is the dominant tongue, and well-based fears were expressed throughout the 1970s and 1980s that if energetic measures were not taken, te reo Māori (the Māori language) could die, leaving the remains of the Māori way of life to persist only as ghostly presence in a Pākehā culture. Even though some measures were taken,[28] the fear justifiably persists.

At the institutional level the mixing and fusion of the people was reflected in the close ties between the National Party and the more conservative members of Maoridom. The party worked closely with the New Zealand Maori Council when it was primarily a mediatorial body until the late 1970s. It boasted Māori MPs and candidates elected by General and not Māori electorates (but in 1988 only one out of forty MPs, Winston Peters). It sustained traditional ties with such prominent Māori leaders as Dame Whina Cooper – leader of the Great Land March – and the chiefly leaders, Sir Hepi te Heuheu

---

[26] See Chapple, 'A Timber Town', especially pp. 193 and following.

[27] Nedd and Marsh, *Attitudes and Behaviour of the Multicultural Workforce*, pp. 3, 5.

[28] See Chapter 11, Section II of this book.

of Tu Wharetoa and Sir James Henare and Sir Graham Latimer of Ngapuhi.[29]
As to the Labour Party, it had had the Māori vote in the four separate
Māori seats solidly since 1943. Matiu Rata became the first Māori Minister
of Maori Affairs – other Māori had been Ministers before – in the third
Labour Government of 1973-1975. Hon. Koro Wetere was Minister of Maori
Affairs in the fourth Labour Government and Hon. Peter Tapsell was Minister
of Internal Affairs from 1984-1986 and became Minister of Police in 1986.
Sir Paul Reeves, once Anglican Archbishop of New Zealand, was the first
Māori Governor-General, appointed by the incoming fourth Labour
Government in 1984.

III

Being Māori

Much then may be said for the mixing and mingling of Māori and Pākehā
and of their consequent unification in a common society; and more will
be heard. But what of difference and distinction? What of there being 'Māori'
and 'Maoridom'? What of Māori being separate from Pākehā?

Māori invented – as the word suggests – Pākehā. They also invented
themselves and are continuing to do so. To speak of the 'Māori' as one people,
to speak of 'Māoritanga' as the Māori way of life, to speak of 'taha Māori'
as the 'Māori side' to things (or a 'dimension' of things or 'perspective on'
them), and to speak of tikanga 'Māori' (Māori custom) is to speak a
recently-invented tongue expressing a modern identity and modern customs.
The members of the aboriginal tribes thought of themselves as tribesmen.
'Māori', when the Pākehā arrived, meant 'normal, ordinary and of the usual
kind' – as the Pākehā were decidedly not when they first arrived. The 'ordinary
bloke' was not in the beginning a Pākehā but a Māori, and the Pākehā,
in what now looks like an irony, called the Māori 'New Zealanders'.

To call oneself Māori was to distinguish oneself from Pākehā. To say 'Māori
is my name' was, and is, to assert an identity over and against the Pākehā.[30]
As to 'Maoridom', the very etymology of the word (Māori, and English
from Old German) suggests its modernity; and the idea of a separate Māori
polity, like the idea of Māori people being separate, was and remains
recognizably a move in the politics of ethnicity: a move in the business of
claiming a share of the social product. The Māori are to be numbered with
other peoples of the world who this century have consciously, and for their

[29] Barry Gustafson traces some of the connections between the National Party and the Maori
in *The First Fifty Years: A History of the New Zealand National Party*, pp. 214-55.

[30] For the past, see Caselberg (ed.), *Maori is My Name.* On the present, for its mixture of
pride and shame, see Levine and Vasil, *Maori Political Perspectives,* pp. 108-18, 148-52.

own protection and benefit, constructed an ethnic identity out of numerous tribal identities.[31]

Many highly intelligent Pākehā were inclined in the 1970s and 1980s to write and talk of truth and falsity and to condemn falsehood when contemplating the large proportion of Pākehā 'blood' in leading 'Māori' activists like Ranginui Walker, Tipene O'Regan and Atareta Poananga. The activists' critics thought them factually wrong in claiming to be Māori, and insincere and self-seeking in proclaiming their Maoriness and denying their Pākehā ancestry and earlier ways of life. The critics did not like 'born again' Māori.[32] Less informed, and even less sympathetic, critics argued that the whole idea of there being a separate Māori culture was nonsense and a myth contrived by activists who hoped to benefit by it. The truth is that the Māori-Pākehā distinction of people and cultures, is, like any other distinction between groups of people, made, constructed, fashioned from a world of perceptions of similarity and difference which is far more complex than the distinction can express. The making of the distinction and the giving of a name cannot obliterate the more complex reality it only partly seeks, and anyway fails, to capture.

'Māori', like other names of identities, captures some things and obscures others; and who is to plumb the depths of the human heart when people choose what they are? It may have been brute ambition for power, or dislike of New Zealand mainstream society, or desire for the fruits of affirmative action programmes, or pity and fellow feeling for the dispossessed, or the need for the solace of a spiritual religion in a materialistic world, that led some people to call themselves 'Māori'. All of these explanations for the choice were suggested. On the other hand the Waitangi Tribunal expressed no more than an ordinary Māori belief when in 1986 it argued that while the 'Pākehā' view was that 'if a Māori has European ancestry then really speaking he is a European. The Māori looks at the same situation from exactly the opposite point of view. He says that if someone has a Māori ancestor, then that person is a Māori even if his ancestor was three or four generations back'.[33] Disinterested reason can find no principle on which to choose between the two views.

It does, too, seem wrong to deny people the right to define themselves ethnically if they should so wish, let alone to condemn those who are simply and unself-consciously Māori. For if 'Māori' is a modern construction for the use and benefit of its members – and abused by some – so is the democratic

---

[31] For a sympathetic view, see Royce, *Ethnic Identity*; and for a more hostile account, see Patterson, *Ethnic Chauvinism: The Reactionary Impulse*. A good summary of the modern political, moral, and historiographical issues at stake is Glazer, *Ethnic Dilemmas 1964–1982*, Chapter 12; and a good book on the matter over the long historical perspective is Anthony D. Smith's 1986 book, *The Ethnic Origins of Nations*.

[32] Most spectacularly Sir Robert Muldoon on *Frontline*, 17 July 1988. See also letters at H6:9/8/85; Courier 4:20/2/85; AS6:7/9/88.

[33] Waitangi Tribunal, *Te Reo Report*, para. 3.4.7. Compare Graham Latimer's words at DST16:17/7/88.

state a construction, made from an authoritarian governorship for the benefit and protection of its people. No less a focus of loyalty and commitment for being a construction, it also is subject to abuse.

And constructed or not, the Māori did have a separate culture and institutions to express it. The new style of confrontationist and separatist politics had a concrete base on which to build. The political and much of the social life of the Māori traditionally occurred – and still did – in tribal marae, in papakāinga (villages) and in enclaves of dense Māori population in the countryside. But Māori migration from country to town from the 1950s onwards had diversified the localities of their activity. In the cities and the large towns Māori life began to occur in church, school and community halls, and in private homes.[34] Urban marae – often multi-tribal – began to be built and filled with activity. In 1971, two were being planned; by 1986, 22 were built or in the last stages of planning.[35] Māori urban activity was a continuation and adaptation of older ways: the hui at which matters are discussed at great length according to a complex decision system in which the values of genealogical hierarchy, age, leadership qualities and consensus all play their parts; the tangihanga during which for three days the dead are honoured and accompanied on their final journey; the complex marae ceremonial in which the manuhiri (the visitors) are challenged then welcomed by the tangata whenua onto the marae and are then accompanied into the whare (meeting, eating and sleeping houses) for discussion, food and hospitality.[36] And then there were continued and adapted various customs and practices more obvious to the casual observer: the arts of whakairo (carving), tukutuku and weaving with other materials and techniques, the haka (action chant), whaikōrero (oratory according to tradition), the various modes of waiata (song), and the wearing of the distinctive dress of woven and dyed fibre. These were local institutions, arts, and practices. Each marae for instance, had its particular kawa (ceremonies and customs of proceeding) and te reo Māori was spoken as much as possible, in all its various idioms. But local procedures demonstrated a common style developed through intertribal marriage and communication.

By the late 1980s there were over 600 marae throughout the country.[37] A survey carried out in late 1987 for the Royal Commission on Social Policy, showed that of Māori people, 44 per cent had attended a hui or marae in the past six months. Of those, 29 per cent had been once, 20 per cent twice, 14 per cent three times and 36 per cent beween four and ten times.[38] These figures are not an unambiguous measure of Maoriness, but they certainly suggest the existence of family ties and a more than nodding acquaintance with the life of the marae.

[34] See the essays by Pieter H. de Bres and R. J. I. Walker in Kawharu (ed.), *Conflict and Compromise*.

[35] Hii3:5/11/86.

[36] Salmond, *Hui*; Metge, *The Maoris*; Sam Karetu, 'Kawa in Crisis'.

[37] *The April Report*, i, p. 280; iii part 1, p. 176.

[38] *The April Report*, i, pp. 397-700.

And even more people might have been ethnic Māori than the figures suggest. They shared *some* of the culture, and they certainly shared fellow-feeling with their people. Young Māori tended to reject the marae as being too formal, too stiflingly rural, old-fashioned and local; and they did not attend. Young Māori men, members of gangs, often described themselves as reacting in this way, or as cut off from their local and cultural roots by urban drift. But it is entirely possible to see their congregating in gangs as a traditional Māori response to the centrifugal and atomizing forces of urban life and underemployment; and when in the winter of 1988 the Mongrel Mob demonstrated outside Paremaremo prison for better conditions inside, they were supported by their arch-rivals Black Power, and by some of the traditionalist Māori leadership. For their part, young women often described the life of the marae as too male-centred in its ancient traditions of whaikōrero, which in most localities forbade them to speak, and it may be that they did not attend as much as they might have for that reason. Generally there is a wide variation in the degree to which Māori practise marae-based culture. But in their ordinary lives: living in their private homes, meeting people, eating, drinking, working together, going to school, or amusing themselves, Māori people tended to relate in a particular 'Māori' way which can be reasonably described as distinct from the Pākehā way. In their ordinary lives, as in the life of the marae, they valued rather more than a Pākehā could, meeting their extended families and tribal elders, and boosting their identity as Māori.[39] And they felt themselves to be te iwi Māori – the Māori people. In 1987, the Black Power gang began to publish a newspaper aimed at its people, *Te Iwi o Aotearoa* – the people of Aotearoa.

In 1988 *The April Report* of the The Royal Commission on Social Policy summed up what had increasingly been taught young Māori (and Pākehā as well) in both formal and informal educational settings in the 1980s: that the Māori particularly held to the values of Te Ao Tūroa (guardianship of the natural environment), Whānaungatanga (the bonds of kinship), Manākitanga (sharing and caring), Mana (authority and control among themselves), Kōtahitanga (commitment to a unified group rather than to individualism), Taonga-tuku-iho (cultural heritage), and Tūrangawaewae (a 'footstool'; a place to stand; a piece of land inalienably one's own).[40]

Irritating, unsubtle, simplifying, romantic, and naïve as such a summary gloss of any culture must be – manākitanga might well still be thought to connote 'respect' with a tinge of kindness rather than 'caring and sharing' – this statement of the official version of Māori ideology nevertheless does capture much of the way things were. Most of all, though many have physically left it, the Māori felt and proclaimed a profound attachment to their land, their 'whenua'. Many have described this academically,[41] but a novelist and

---

[39] *The April Report*, i, p. 435.

[40] *The April Report*, i, pp. 277-88.

[41] Most informatively in Douglas, 'Land and Maori Identity', and Asher and Naulls, *Maori Land*, Chapter 2 and pp. 52-3 esp.

a poet may do so here. Witi Ihimaera, writer and diplomat, in his didactic novel, *The Matriarch* (1986), has the young man of his story walk his ancestral lands in the countryside near Gisborne accompanied by memories of its inner tapu history imparted to him by the old kuia – the matriarch – his grandmother.[42] He knows the boundaries intimately, each fold of the land, each fishing and eeling hole, each house. He laments the present: 'Then the people began to leave the land, searching the lost cities for gold', 'gone, gone is the grandeur of the village', 'where has the mana of the land, and the tapu of the land gone?' But the ancestral past still permeates the present, and the connection of that singular locality with the totality of the universe remains. The kuia speaks to her mokopuna (grandchild: young relative), affirming in his memory as he walks, thus: 'E mokopuna, listen. The mana and the tapu still remain, in the land and in Waituhi and in the iwi of Te Whanau A Kai. It is in Rongopai also. It is not something that can be seen with the eye, e mokopuna, but with the heart and the soul and the intellect.'

In his poem, *Totara Tree* (1981), the poet and broadcaster Haare Williams, expressed that same attachment to the whenua. He plays on whenua's meaning 'land', 'mother' and (like 'pito') 'placenta'. The poem[43] begins as the manuhiri plant a totara tree to commemorate their visit:

> 'A totara' said one
> 'Has heart
> It'll be here for centuries'
>
> 'No!' replied Whenua
> 'It'll be here forever
> As part of the land
> The burying of the pito
> The sacred umbilical cord
> Is part of the living soul
> The implanting is the link
> To a new life.
>
> At death
> Body and soul are separated
> Soul returns to the pito
> The body of the land
> Life born, is reborn
> In the land'
>
> With these words
> The meaning came
> Land is sacred
> Communal
> Eternal
> Whoever understands its sacredness

---

[42] Ihimaera, *The Matriarch*, pp. 102–10.

[43] Haare Williams, *Karanga*, p. 29.

Can never forget
Nor violate it

To destroy it
Is to destroy a history
A people and a future

We planted
The totara tree
The ground freshly turned
Reminded us of a burial
Placing there part of us
Our umbilical link
With people and land —
Ancestors

Pākehā farmers felt an attachment to their land every bit as passionate as the Māori. Indeed the politics of New Zealand farming are largely a politics of this passionate and familial attachment not being understood by financiers and other 'townies'. Still, urban people often loved it for its refreshing qualities; environmentalists wished to preserve it with such a passionate intensity that they clashed with Māori owners who wished to exploit it; and some Irish still buried the placenta of their children in it. But the total idea, the idea of being tangata whenua – the people of the land, of particular pieces of land – was a uniquely Māori one. Land was their tūrangawaewae: their footstool, their place to stand, the source of their mana; it was what sustained their very being. These were ideals not always lived up to, but they had great unifying force and were powerful weapons in the political battle.

All this added up to the evident presence of Maoriness among the Māori. And as it became increasingly public knowledge during the 1970s and 1980s, there came to be public and not just Māori talk of taha Māori (the Māori way, side or perspective) and of Māoritanga (the condition in which there is Maoriness). During those years too, there remained, and were created, an array of institutions and practices which were very much instruments of the construction of a 'Māori' people, and were increasingly the instruments of Māori self-determination.

Some organizations were purely the creation of the Māori people. Most notable were the 3,000-strong Maori Women's Welfare League which was until the 1960s the leading national voice of Maoridom, the Maori Artists' and Writers' League, and the indigenous churches of Ratana (which have since the 1930s been the power base for the four MPs elected by those on the Māori roll) and the more localized Ringatu.[44] And of course during the 1970s many other pan-Māori groups for political and social action came into prominence: Nga Tamatoa, MOOHR, Te Matikite O Aotearoa, the Waitangi

[44] See Raureti, The Origins of the Ratana Movement'; Tarei, 'A Church called Ringatu'; Mead, 'He Ara ki te Aromarama', (*Finding a Pathway to the Future*).

Action Committee (WAC), Kotahitanga, and so on.[45]

But the most notable organizations of the Māori people were partly constructions of the State. The 1962 Maori Welfare Act had completed a Māori representative structure devoted to Māori concerns:[46] local Māori Committees with their executives; in 1972 nine, by 1986 twelve, District Maori Councils, the territories of which more or less (cities complicated the picture) coincided with those of the Maori Land Court districts; and a New Zealand Maori Council dedicated at the national level to improving the welfare of the Māori. Volunteer Maori Wardens worked more (and less) closely with that structure of authority, policing predominantly Māori venues and occasions; and, more successfully after the appointment of Judge Michael Brown (a Māori) to the bench in 1981, there were moves to extend the informal Maori Committee procedures for dealing with minor crimes and misdemeanours to the state court system.[47]

Then there was the Department of Maori Affairs in Wellington. It was devoted to administering Māori land and separate Māori welfare policies, partly in the service of the Maori Land Court, the Maori Land Board and the Maori Trustee. The Maori Land Court, administered by the Department and from 1981 chaired by Judge Edward Durie, a Māori, adjudicated on and administered a separate system of Maori Land ownership which the New Zealand Maori Council and other organizations spent the 1970s and 1980s trying to disentangle from Pākehā ideas of individual, exclusive and alienable ownership. Traditionally the locus of Pākehā attempts to get land from them,[48] the court was also a forum where Māori concerns about their land were aired and plans for it formulated. There existed throughout the period (though it changed its name from 1974–1982 to the Maori Land Board) the Board of Maori Affairs, with central authority in land development matters which it exercised on the advice of local Land Advisory Committees; and there was a Maori Trustee, separate from the Public Trustee, charged with administering Māori monies which had accumulated largely as a result of extinction of individual Māori titles under an unworkable system of infinitely-dividing ownership with partage on death.

There were still more distinctively Māori institutions which, not to labour the point, may be quickly indicated: there were four MPs whose electorates were exclusively composed of those Māori who choose to go on the Māori as opposed to General Roll;[49] from 1980 there was Mana Motuhake, the exclusivist Māori political party led by Matiu Rata. There were by 1987

---

[45] See Ranginui Walker, 'The Urban Maori'; 'The Maori People'.

[46] For a brief history of these developments, see Stokes (ed.), *Nga Tumanako*, pp. 1-5, 36-51. Fuller stories are in Metge, The *Maoris of New Zealand*, p. 210 and following, and Fleras, 'The Politics of Maori Lobbying'.

[47] See Brown's own account in his 'Equity, Justice and Maoridom'.

[48] Classically described in the works of M. P. K. Sorrenson, especially 'Land Purchase Methods', 'Maori and Pakeha' and 'The Politics of Land'. See also Asher and Naulls, *Maori Land*.

[49] See Sorrenson, 'A History of Maori Representation in Parliament'.

thirteen Maori Trust Boards set up under the Maori Trust Boards Act of 1955 to administer assets, most of which were generated by way of Government-paid compensation for the post-war confiscations in the 1860s. Others were in compensation for extinction of ownership titles to lakes and for land transactions of doubtful legality and worse morality. In July 1988, amid a process of devolution of Government functions from Wellington, five more were created by Parliament; and more were in the pipeline. There were – confusingly – other sorts of 'Trusts' too: 'section 438 Trusts', set up under the Maori Affairs Act of 1953 to administer land held in common as 'Māori land' and not subject to the law of General Lands. Both sorts of Trusts came together in 1985 into a loose Federation of Maori Authorities. Less visible, there was the Maori and South Pacific Arts Council; more visible, the Maori Education Foundation set up in 1962 to improve Māori education standards; and – by 1988 most visible of all – there was the Waitangi Tribunal, the dominating subject of the following four chapters.

'I make no claims to being a political scientist,' said Professor Robert Mahuta, of the University and tribe of Waikato, 'but several things seem obvious. New Zealand's political community consists of two ethnic segments – Maori and non-Maori – each totally separate and each with its own representation and regime.'[50] Total separateness is wrong as a description; but in the language of Political Science there is undoubtedly a Māori 'subsystem'. Indeed if demonstration of the existence of a subsystem is further needed, Professor Robert Chapman provided it in 1986 in an analysis of Māori voting patterns: though since 1943 the Labour Party has always had the support of the four Māori MPs, the vote in the Māori electorates has varied quite independently of the Pākehā vote in the general electorates.[51]

The language of Political Science is not however the right language to use if the unity of 'Māori' is to be grasped. In the language of the New Zealand Maori Council, whose important discussion paper, *Kaupapa – Te Whanga Tuatahi*, listed most of the Māori institutions that existed in 1983,[52] they were not spoken of as 'institutions' in a 'system' at all. Rather they were called 'modes of rangatiratanga'. They were said to be the vehicles by which the Māori people, 'after almost a century and a half of paternalism . . . define for themselves and for Parliament the rangatiratanga guaranteed them by the Treaty of Waitangi'. Modern rangatiratanga was the modern development of the old Māori chieftainship, 'where those who lead have obligations as well as rights, where, irrespective of lineage, they have to prove themselves in service, and where they are at all times accountable to those for whom they are trustees'. It is the 'working out of a moral contract between a leader, his people, and his god'. And the purpose of

---

50 Mahuta, 'Race Relations in New Zealand', in Stokes (ed.), in *Nga Tumanako*, p. 17.

51 Chapman, 'Voting in the Maori Political Sub-System, 1935–1984'.

52 NZMC, *Kaupapa: Te Whanga Tuatahi*, pp. 6–9. And for further lists of institutions see Stokes (ed.), *Nga Tumanako*, pp. 18–20. They are described in the greatest detail as at 1984 in Dyall, *Maori Resource Development*.

rangatiratanga was to preserve and sustain the 'mana' Māori – where 'mana' meant something like 'the identity, the right to self-determination, the authority over-and-against aliens of te iwi Māori'. The modern generation, concluded *Kaupapa – Te Whanga Tuatahi*, must fulfil those purposes, notably in a 'duty to keep faith with their people through seeking redress for past injustice'.[53] Such a description of the purpose and nature of Māori institutions was obviously not cast in the language of the modern democratic politics of the Pākehā world. It asserted a Māori identity and unity founded both in concrete institutions and in a common past. The description was undoubtedly that of the wide range of Māori with whom the New Zealand Maori Council had consulted in drawing up the paper. Te iwi Māori – the Māori people – was a fact.

The New Zealand Government too, tended to lump Māori together, as a people. There were for instance, the Maori Affairs Acts of the twentieth century, including the live Act of 1953 and its amendments of 1967 and 1974. In statute, the Māori were legislated for as a whole and not as separate tribes; and they were separated from non-Māori. The identity of Maoridom was asserted in 1987 in no uncertain terms by the Court of Appeal, in the *New Zealand Maori Council v the Attorney General and Others*. This was a crucial case, aspects of which will be discussed at many points in this book (Chapter 4; Chapter 9, Section II and Chapter 14, Section I especially). The fate of the state's plans to dispose by sale of 3.8 million hectares of crown land, including 'significant mid-town property sites', to State Owned Enterprises (SOEs) depended on the decision. One of the issues was whether or not the Government should have consulted 'the Māori people' before passing legislation that could have effectively deprived them of the opportunity, through the Waitangi Tribunal, of reclaiming Māori land by way of reparations. Crown land might be readily enough restorable, but it could be difficult to prize it from the hands of an SOE which had paid good money for it; and it would certainly cost the Government to reobtain it for restitution. As to consultation, one of the judges rightly observed that Government consultation on the matter would have been difficult in the 'absence of a single body able to speak for all Maoridom, and, indeed, the very elastic concept of "Maori".'[54] While the State, as respondent, put in a formal claim that the New Zealand Maori Council and Sir Graham Latimer could not represent the whole of Maoridom, yet it was allowed that they should. And the Council was allowed to speak for the Māori people considered as a whole.

Finally, the mainstream media saw and recorded what was uncontroversially said by all: Pākehā as well as Māori. There *was* 'Māori' crime; there *were* Māori gatherings, 'Māori' claims, 'Māori' protesters, 'Māori' elders', 'Māori' health'. There was even the 'Māori All Blacks'. There *was* the 'Māori people.' The people *looked* Polynesian, spoke New Zealand English in their own accents, had their own institutions and lived lives unlike those of the 'ordinary bloke.'

---

[53] NZMC, *Kaupapa: Te Whanga Tuatahi*, pp. 4–5.

[54] Government Printer, *The Treaty of Waitangi*. The judgment of Casey J. at p. 12.

So in everyday thought and practice and in law, 'Māori' was a kind of unity, 'Māori was separate from 'Pākehā', and 'Maoridom' existed.

Yet being 'Māori' and the existence of 'Maoridom' were not rock-solid constructions. They were in some ways as much a matter of political will and policy as descriptions of a settled form of group life or (from individuals' points of view) of an identity. What constituted 'Māori' was as much a matter of 'making' as of 'being'. Its construction occurred in the face of not only admixture with the Pākehā but also detribalization on the one hand, and on the other a continued, distinct, and rebuilding tribal identity.

As to detribalization, many who were (racially) Māori (i.e. looked like Māori) did not in their own eyes belong to the (ethnic) Māori people. Pākehā racial prejudice made it known to them that they were not Pākehā but brown-skinned Polynesians of some unspecified kind. In 1987 the Race Relations Conciliator discovered significant racial prejudice among Pākehā militating against Māori and Pacific Island people getting the housing they wanted. Equally cruelly, the more recently arrived Pacific Islanders often saw such Māori as non-Pacific: as brown-skinned Pākehās. And many young Māori did not identify themselves in any serious way as 'Māori', rather thinking of themselves as black, and victims of white rule, like blacks in the USA. This showed in graffiti. Uprooted, deculturated and alienated from both Māori and Pākehā society, they roamed the streets as 'street kids'; older, they joined gangs and perhaps began to construct a kind of Māori companionship not in the whānau (the extended family), but in the peer group. They did not turn easily to the ethnic Māori. As Rilke said of an earlier German generation: 'Each torpid turn of the world has such disinherited children/to whom neither what's been, and not yet what's coming belongs'.[55]

But there were attempts at reinheritance. The point of much of the Māori political renaissance was that of redeeming these young in the face of great odds. One of its academic and administrative leaders spoke to the Waitangi Tribunal in 1984 of the demoralization, detribalization and poverty of the Māori. 'The majority are urban, landless, often a dispirited and depressed minority in their own land.' The solution was to rebuild Maoridom.[56] In 1986 *Puao-Te-Ata-Tu/Day Break*, the report of a Ministerial Advisory Committee on a Maori Perspective for the Department of Social Welfare, referred to the fragility and non-existence of whānau (extended family) and hapū (subtribal) ties among the urban young. The report stressed that the Māori future was in danger and that the urgent necessity was not only to repair what was in danger of collapsing but to refashion the components, perhaps constructing urban substitutes for the endangered and mainly rural whānau, and for the home marae from which they had been separated. 'Though

---

[55] *Seventh Elegy*, quoted from Erich Heller, *The Disinherited Mind*, p. 138. Vasil and Levine, *Maori Political Perspectives*, note the concern of Māori people at this, pp. 108-18. And see Jackson, *The Maori and the Criminal Justice System*, for much evidence and argument as to the truth of the view.

[56] Douglas, 'Marine Resources and the Future, a Maori Alternative Strategy', pp. 22-3.

traditional resources survive – our elders, Marae, traditional communities and perhaps above all our language – these point the way back. The reality is that our future is to be built on today's youth, many of whom are alienated from their culture and identity'.[57]

It was on this understanding of things that the devolutionary policies that characterized the workings of the Department of Maori Affairs after 1978 were introduced. Before this time, though it was the scene of much vibrant Māori political life, the Department had been notoriously (among Māori) unresponsive to Māori demands.[58] Now, led by its new secretary, Kara Puketapu, the department instituted its Tu Tangata programme: 'standing alone', it was often translated. Tu Tangata was aimed mainly at improving Māori educational and vocational training standards and at involving the 'community' in both decision-making and delivery. By 1982 it consisted in kōkiri centres of devolved Maori Affairs administration and of kōhanga reo (language nests) in which the Māori people joined to immerse pre-schoolers in the Māori language and culture.[59] By 1983 there were mātua whāngai (extended family groups), funded by the Departments of Maori Affairs, Justice, and Social Welfare and devoted to the rehabilitation of delinquent youth outside the Pākehā 'bureaucracy' – as was the popular Māori name for the various Government departments. When informed of the difficulties besetting the policy, the department sent ten tribal teams into Auckland in an attempt to build urban tribal networks to which responsibility for Māori young could be devolved.[60] Devolution was the policy; the aim to 'deinstitutionalize Māori people'.[61] Make-work schemes and youth training schemes were devolved to 'iwi authorities' – tribes and quasi-tribes. By 1986 the Department itself was, as instructed by the Government, looking to devolve many of its social welfare and land administration responsibilities to the iwi.

Reclamation of the young to Maoridom thus pointed to the reconstruction of more local, tribally-based, Māori lives. The findings of the Waitangi Tribunal pointed in the same direction. In 1987 New Zealanders were reminded that tribal identity was the crucial, basic, constituent of Māori identity; and it was on this basis that the Tribunal criticized the Department of Maori Affairs for selling developed Māori land to a man whose claim was simply that he was 'Māori'. It would have been better to return the land on Waiheke Island in the Hauraki Gulf to the tribe whose ancestral land it was. This would give the young people of Ngati Paoa a place to 'stand tall, as Ngati Paoa, as Maori and as New Zealanders'. On this view, Māori and New Zealander were the more artificial constructs; Ngati Paoa, the people and their land, the reality.[62] Tribalism was indeed alive, and it was tribal claims that the Tribunal was hearing.

[57] *Puao-Te-Ata-Tu*/Day Break, i, p. 24.
[58] Levine and Vasil, *Maori Political Perspectives*, pp. 41–52.
[59] A sketch of the developments is in Fleras, 'Towards "Tu Tangata": Historical Developments and Current Trends in Maori Policy and Administration'.
[60] AS6:1/8/84; H2:8/8/84.
[61] Department of Maori Affairs, *Maatua Whangai Policy*, [1988].
[62] Waitangi Tribunal, *Waiheke Report*, p. 67. See also pp. 36, 37, 62, 69, 83.

Indeed an inherited tribalism divided Māori – as did urban versus rural living, traditionalist age versus less restrained youth, and many other ordinary things – and it is was the tribes as much as 'the Māori' who claimed justice. 'Maoridom', the polity of the Māori, was after all a largely twentieth century invention; it was constituted of separate and conflicting parts; it was sometimes hard to see as a unity at all. Despite the efforts of Māori leaders to produce a sense of common identity in their people, it was only after the Second World War that much consciousness of common Maoriness developed among their followers.[63] And in the 1970s and 1980s, as in the recent past, the separate forty-odd tribes had their own separate customs and their members found their 'terminal identity'[64] not as Māori but in more local groupings.

They found it in their canoe groups, tribes or sub-tribes (waka, iwi or hapū) – as in Tainui (a canoe), for instance, as in Ngati Kuhungunu (a tribe), or as in Ngati Whatua o Orakei (the sub-tribe of Ngati Whatua who live at Orakei, near the headlands of Takaparawha and Bastion Point). But these traditional groupings, though strongly associated with their own rohe (or territory), were groupings formed of multiple kinship relations, shared histories and current interests. At the edges they were fluid, ambiguous, a bureaucrat's nightmare, and no less a nightmare for Māori leaders wishing to put together representative institutions.[65] Matters were further complicated by the mainly twentieth century construction of tribal federations, some of them based on the nineteenth century Land Court Districts. Of those who reported themselves in the *Social Policy Survey* as having 'Māori ethnic origins'; 25 per cent reported tribal affiliations with Tai Tokerau (the tribes north of Auckland co-operating in the Maori Land Court district called Tai Tokerau); 15 per cent with Tai Rawhiti (the east cape North Island Maori Land Court District which extends north into the Bay of Plenty); 10 per cent with Tainui, the great canoe group centered on the valley of the Waikato River; 8 per cent with the east central North Island federated iwi, the Arawa; 8 per cent with the south-east coast North Island iwi, Ngati Kuhungunu. Smaller groupings included the South Island iwi, Kaitahu (3 per cent), as well as smaller North Island iwi. There were usually said to be forty-two tribes. Māori described themselves as 'affiliated' to such-and-such tribes, and the most effective operating group (at least in the countryside) was often the whānau, the extended family of perhaps thirty or forty relations. In the cities, to complicate matters still further, multi-tribal extended families, trusts, and authorities proliferated. Locality and genealogical propinquity, together with exclusively shared projects, often distinguished 'Māori' from 'Māori'.[66]

On the East Cape (of the central North Island) it was: 'Ko Hikurangi te maunga, Waiapu te awa, Ko Ngati Porou te tangata' (My mountain is

---

[63] See King, 'Between Two Worlds' at pp. 279, 299-300.

[64] A phrase from Epstein, *Ethos and Identity*, p. 101. 'Terminal identity, one that embraces and integrates a whole series of statuses, roles and lesser identities.'

[65] On the recent pre-twentieth century nature of these divisions, and for a part explanation of why they persist, see Cleave, 'Tribal and state-like political formations in New Zealand Maori society 1750-1900'. Also see Metge, *The Maoris of New Zealand*, Chapter 9.

[66] *The April Report*, i, p. 432.

Hikurangi, my river is the Waiapu; I am Ngati Porou').[67] At Ngaruawahia in 1978, it was (for the visiting Sir Robert Muldoon): 'Taupiri is the mountain, Waikato the river and the people, Queen Te Atairangikaahu is the person'. At the same conference Robert Mahuta, one of the tangata whenua, could speak approvingly of the argument of Professor Vine Deloria Jr., a Standing Rock Sioux, that each tribe must choose for itself how to act, depending on its group identity . . . 'its Tuhoetanga, Waikatotanga, Ngapuhitanga and so on'.[68] And the case is that on each local marae, separate and distinguishable stories were told of lineage (whakapapa), the exploits of ancestors, of tribal custom, and of wahi tapu — things sacred to those particular people whose places they were. The separate stories were the taonga (treasures) specific to the tangata whenua of the separate places. Each specific people of the land had an intimate and passionate contact with their land and its features.

It was only by a modern extension of the term that 'tangata whenua' could be applied to the general Māori relationship to all of New Zealand and used to declare their unity. And at times the traditional (and new) divisions were the despair of Māori leaders. Mrs Eva Rickard, Tainui Awhiro heroine of the Raglan Golf Course land claim, and a leader of the Kotahitanga (unity) movement which she helped revive in 1983, expressed some of the conflicts which beset 'Maoridom' in 1985. She was reported as saying after a hui that year that 'she believed the present Kotahitanga group was actually a "searching for Kotahitanga. I will always be a member of Kotahitanga, but which Kotahitanga?"'[69] She thus expressed the tension and difficulties of being part of a unified Maoridom. A Tainui submission to the Waitangi Tribunal explained *their* unity well enough: with a population of 120,000, 30 per cent of Maoridom, together with '120 marae and almost as many hapu within Tainui', their 'binding force' was their loyalty to Kingitanga, the King Movement, which found its origins in the 1850s.[70] But unified around the Māori Queen, Dame Te Atairangikaahu, Tainui was often to be found at odds with other groupings, almost systematically so against the Tai Tokerau Federation, the collection of five tribes of North Auckland which regarded itself as guardian of the Treaty of Waitangi – a treaty the Waikato did not sign. One member of Tai Tokerau, a Ngapuhi, wrote to a newspaper in 1981: 'It makes my blood boil' to see Dame Te Atairangi Kaahu called 'the Maori Queen'. A Waikato of the Tainui federation replied, maligning the fighting qualities and passivity of Ngapuhi, 'as is implied by the white-dominated names so common among Ngapuhi Maoris'. It is not unknown, either, for tribal sections of Tainui to be at serious odds, as Ngati Raukawa and the Waikato tribes have been for some years over control of the Tainui Trust Board which administers compensation funds for the region. Ngati Paoa, though Tainui, did not join the Trust Board at all because they did not agree with the quantum of compensation for which the federation

---

[67] Thus the report and translation in NZT2:21/12/86.
[68] In Stokes (ed.), *Nga Tumanako*, pp. 25-6.
[69] Hiv9:12/2/85.
[70] Douglas, 'Marine Resources', p. 2. Compare Mahuta, 'The King Movement Today'.

settled, nor the method by which it was calculated.[71] In 1982 clashes surfaced between Ngati Awa of the Bay of Plenty and Ngati Tuwharetoa of the central North Island over Mt. Edgecumbe/Putuake. They were to simmer on into 1988, the subject of a private bill and of claims to the Waitangi Tribunal.[72]

As the 1980s progressed and the policies of devolution to tribal authorities came into play, so did tribalist critiques of the New Zealand Maori Council itself as an artificial Pākehā imposition which ignored tribal boundaries and interests.[73] In 1984, the Tainui left the Auckland Maori Council (and thus the New Zealand Maori Council) to operate in future through the Huakina Trust. The Tuwharetoa and their ariki (Sir Hepe Te Heuheu, their paramount chief) had never belonged because the boundaries for the District Councils took no account of their existence. By 1987 firm proposals had emerged from a hui in the Waikato that a new, more tribally-based body representing Maoridom should be instituted, independent of government funding, and independent of the old division of District Councils according to awkwardly-fitting Maori Land Court divisions. But there were doubts as well as support for the proposal. Mrs Titewhai Harawira – one of the three members of Te Ahi Kaa who had gone to Fiji, and who had been a thorn in the side of compromisers of any kind since the early 1970s – attacked it as a 'vehicle for Bob Mahuta and Bert McLean'.[74]

To end this far from complete list of loci of Māori differences and disunity, most Māori live in the North Island. Kaitahu of the South Island (Te Wai Pounamu) did not often (because of the expense) get to intertribal hui in the North Island (Aotearoa: or better Te Ika o Maui, the fish of Maui to the South's Te Waka o Maui, the canoe from which the great ancestor pulled the fish from the sea) in large numbers. They have been intermarried longer and more widely with Pākehā than other Māori. The internal wars of the 1860s and 1870s passed them by. They got talked of in the northern idiom of te reo Māori as 'Ngai' Tahu rather than 'Kai' Tahu. It is an historical accident that the name of the Trust Board which represents their interests is Ngai Tahu. The name of their island was forgotten when the polemical point was made that New Zealand should be called Aotearoa. Indifference, feuds, factions, and local pride and prejudice, (often anciently-based) continue to divide modern 'Maoridom'.

Still, the feuds *were* family feuds and there is a distinct family resemblance among the practices of the tribes. An historian has recently written of the Tuhoe around 1900, that a man of that tribe would have regarded himself 'as being as far removed from a Waikato Maori as from a European': 'Tuhoe moumou kai, moumou taonga, moumou tangata ki te po' (Tuhoe extravagant

[71] NZL26:10/10/87. Recorded in Waitangi Tribunal, *Waiheke Claim*, p. 96.

[72] H20:14/11/82; H12:29/11/82. See too the submissions to Parliament on the Treaty of Waitangi (SE) Bill 1988), no.s 11A and 41.

[73] NZL24-26:10/10/87. See also *The April Report*, ii, p. 51.

[74] 10 p.m Evening News, National Radio Programme: 16/3/88. But it was defended by Ranginui Walker, GMNZ:2/10/87.

with food, with heirlooms and with human life) were a separate people.[75] But in the 1970s and 1980s, although the tribes remained distinct, they operated more as one, and against the Pākehā. They continued to insist on their differences; but at the same time the similarities that they acknowledged and built upon could be observed. In the 1970s John Rangihau wrote of his terminal identity as being Tūhoe. He was first, and overridingly, one of the 'children of the mist'; only secondly, and more artificially, a 'Māori'. But he *was* Māori. Pat Hohepa, spoke for all in 1987 when he said, 'There is a broad sharing of Maori ideals, but it only finds meaning in a tribal setting'. There *were* 'Māori ideals'. A Justice Department paper published in the same year made the same point.[76]

It would be possible to invent a form of words to express the 'opposition' yet 'unity' within Maoridom. Joan Metge did so, and in reproducing a model of social organization 'through Maori eyes,' she also diagrammed their occurence: opposition between families yet unity in hapū, opposition between hapū yet united in iwi, opposition between iwi yet united in te iwi Māori.[77] But here it is enough simply to insist that division and unity are not opposites, and were both present.

One thing remains to be said of the Māori view of social organization. They saw opposition between te iwi Māori and te iwi Pākehā – yet unity as New Zealand people. Their invention, 'Pākehā,' captured their experience and expressed their goals. It did not however much appeal to thePākehā.

IV

On Not Being Pākehā

Not many Pākehā identified themselves that way at all. Project Waitangi was a Pākehā movement confederated from church and political anti-racist groups early in 1986, in response to the suggestion of David Lange, the Prime Minister, that a 'dialogue between Maori and Pakeha' should begin. The Project decided that it had better ask its proposed clientele what its 'reaction' was to the word 'Pākehā'. Research was commissioned, and showed that only 4 per cent 'liked' it; and although most (69.3 per cent) did not 'mind', 26.7 per cent did not like it at all. Pākehā, the research concluded, revealed an 'ambivalent' or 'negative' reaction to the word.[78] And indeed most evidence points to the fact that, so-called because of their white skins, most Pākehā did not greatly welcome being identified in that way. Some few did (members of church, feminist, and anti-racist groups, and some liberals), but generally

---

[75] See King, 'Between Two Worlds', p. 279.
[76] H3:2/2/87; Jackson, *The Maori and the Criminal Justice System*, i, pp. 19-24.
[77] Metge, *The Maoris of New Zealand*, p. 315.
[78] Project Waitangi, *Resource Kit*, Part Two pp. 1-[12] with conclusions at p. 6.

they would rather have been called 'New Zealanders' or 'Kiwis', the latter a generic non-racial name taken from a native flightless bird. They felt New Zealander or Kiwi to be their identity; to be called Pākehā was to be grouped by others and did not express their commitments.

For one thing, 'Pākehā' could mean just *any* European,[79] and by the 1970s Pākehā mostly thought that they were not Europeans at all but New Zealanders, derived perhaps of European racial and cultural stock but now something different. Arguments were heard that most Pākehā were born in New Zealand, that they were indigenous – native to the place – and that it was their home. They had been for some time, as Sir Keith Sinclair made clear in his *A Destiny Apart* (1986), 'creole' nationalists, whose nationality they took to be created by the place where they lived (and were mostly born) rather than by shared race, ancestry, culture or religion. They would not see themselves as Europeans.

And then the issue was raised of those New Zealanders who were neither Māori nor Pākehā. For if there were to be Māori and Pākehā only, then what could be said of the Chinese, the Indians, the Vietnamese and the Filipinos who had migrated in succession since the gold rush days of the 1860s? And what could be said of the Pacific Islanders who had migrated in even more significant numbers in the 1960s and 1970s to constitute 2 per cent of the population by 1981, and 3.5 per cent by 1986: Samoans, Tongans, Tokelauans, Cook Islanders and Niueans? The Māori did not name *them* Pākehā.[80] Were they to be left out? Were the Māori simply racist and anti-white? It is likely that the 'Attitudes and Values Survey', commissioned by the Royal Commission on Social Policy, constructed 'European' and 'other' as categories of 'ethnic origin', firstly (in thus asking questions about ethnicity) to avoid a straight-out question as to racial type; secondly (in stressing origins) so as not to offend the white New Zealanders' strong sense of not (now) being European; thirdly to count as part of New Zealand those inhabitants who were other than Māori and Pākehā.

Avoiding 'Pākehā' on purpose no doubt, the Royal Commission on Social Policy itself adopted in the body of its *April Report*, the name Tau Iwi (roughly 'all foreign' not just 'white foreign') when it wrote of all non-Māori in the country. But even that did not go unremarked and uncomplained of. Who are they, it was asked, to call me foreign, and in a language that is not my own? A letter-writer to a newspaper complained of this in public, and what he said had the ring of truth. He had phoned the office of the Commission to complain: 'I was told that despite considerable unease over the use of Tauiwi in the Treaty booklet [which had been a basis for national discussion], staff were told it had to be used. I was also told that the use of Tauiwi instead of Pākehā had been discontinued.'[81] True or not, the story

---

[79] And note Paul Spoonley's attempt at a definition of Pākehā, made in the knowledge that any definition would be contested, in his *Racism and Ethnicity*, pp. xiii, 63-4.

[80] *The April Report*, i, pp. 104-5.

[81] DST10: 19/6/88. Letter of Colin Roberton, Wellington.

may stand as an emblem for the moral and political heat of Māori names for non-Māori things. They had to be handled with care.

Pākehā were suspicious too, about just how endearing a term 'Pākehā' was meant to be. The Race Relations Conciliator had to put out a booklet in 1986 reassuring them that their name just meant 'white' or 'white object rising from the sea' – not 'pig', 'bag of material goods,' 'fleabag' and worse.[82]

The unwilling 'Pākehā' also bore the burden, when the name was used, of hearing his or her way of life maligned, and forebears condemned. For it was one of the unsurprising strategies of Māori activists and their Pākehā sympathizers used to disparage what they identified as Pākehās and their 'culture', past and present. Their accounts of the Pākehā were mainly the product of the USA socialist-communitarian tradition, turned to the purposes of ethnic politics in the USA, and imported for the same purpose to New Zealand. They spoke of the Pākehā as individualist materialists, blind to the past, exploiters of the land which they regarded as a commodity, and heedless of the claims of future generations. 'Wanderers, you leave your fathers' graves behind you, and you do not care . . . One portion of the land is the same to him . . . as the next, for he is a stranger who comes in the night and takes from the land whatever he needs'. Ranginui Walker thus exploited the words of Chief Seattle of 1855 to describe the Pākehā of the mid-1980s.[83] And these words well expressed the ethnic stereotype of the Pākehā generated in Māori political activity from the late 1970s onwards.

The disparagement was not *entirely* an imported invention. John Harré, when he was studying Māori-Pākehā marriages in the early 1960s, found an informant who was criticized by an elder before her marriage: 'Who is this Pakeha you are going to marry? He is nothing. He has no ancestors, nor a canoe. He owns no land. He has no roots, no background. Who is this Pakeha'?[84] But that was for domestic consumption; and the politicization and moralization of the critique of the Pākehā was largely made outside New Zealand, and its partial fit was due to the fact that both Māori and Pākehā shared the culture of a universal metropolitan and capitalist society, some elements of which romanticized tribal pasts and denigrated territorial and liberal societies in that way: as hosts to possessive individualism and destructive greed.[85]

The disparagement was seldom accepted as just, no more than the history of past wrongs which it expressed. But perhaps most of all the Pākehā rejected the very idea of thinking of themselves as sharing a culture, and of being an *ethnie*. Lady Reeves, a Pākehā, and like her husband the Governor-General a firm supporter of Project Waitangi, encouraged Pākehā New Zealanders not to think of themselves as just 'normal, ordinary people' with no particular strange and bizarre customs, but as an ethnic group like other ethnic groups.

[82] Race Relations Conciliator, *Let's Work Together: Kia Mahi Tahi Tatou*.
[83] Walker in 'The Meaning of Biculturalism'.
[84] Harré, *Maori and Pakeha*, p. 115.
[85] See Mulgan, *Māori, Pākehā and Democracy*, towards the end of Chapter 2; and his 'Indigenous Rights'.

And this was a recurring theme in the arguments of those church and political groups – and academics – devoting themselves to improve race relations.[86] Their point was that for Pākehā not to see themselves as an 'ethnic group' with a unique 'culture' was undoubtedly for them to see themselves and their culture as normal and right – as providing the standards to be attained by those who are different. The denial of Pākehā ethnicity then, could – and it did – function as a way of ignoring or overriding Māori claims to separateness.

Yet it proved difficult to make the Pākehā think otherwise. Reformers testified to this. Mitzi Nairn, who as an officer of the National Council of Churches devoted a good deal of her life in the 1980s to anti-racist organization and consciousness-raising, was witness to that. Described in a newspaper interview of 1986 as 'a woman who has looked closely at her own culture', she was asked: 'So just what is Pakeha culture?' Her first response was that the Pākehā did not 'see their own culture alongside other cultures'. An 'arrogance about control and power and being okay' both precluded them describing their culture, and in fact could be taken as a description (from Nairn's reformist perspective) of it. But the description was not a Pākehā self-description. Asked 'What did your parents tell you was important to you as a Pakeha?' she replied 'I don't think Pakeha parents put any attention on being a Pakeha. They just say this is how to be'.[87] Maryanne L'Estrange, similarly in the business of reform as an officer of Project Waitangi, also noted the difficulty:

It is often difficult [for] Pakeha to express and realise the elements that make up our culture. We think easily of the arts, theatre and dance and the old cliches of rugby racing and beer. Beyond that, one of the aspects of our culture is to see ourselves as normal or right and others as ethnic, different and cultural . . . But Pakeha culture covers our whole way of doing things: the way we form relationships; bring up our children; the way we set up our homes, our workplaces; the things we value; what we wear, eat and drink; how we worship, make love et cetera.[88]

The Curriculum Review (1987), a report of an Education Department committee which researched widely among the people, irritatedly noted the same thing: that Pākehā *would* not adopt the language of social anthropology and apply it to themselves. It added, with an anti-intellectualism typical of much of the bureaucratic élite of New Zealand, that 'experiencing "culture" for many still means experiencing "art, music and literature from Europe" '.[89]

For the Māori it could be a point of pride and a matter of claiming political power to have a culture and ethnicity. The Pākehā had little reason to think

86 Project Waitangi, *Resource Kit,* Part 1, Section 2 on 'Pakeha Culture'. See Reeves, 'A Speech Given by Lady Reeves'.
87 See her 'Who are these Pakehas?' from *The Dominion,* 18/2/86, reprinted in Project Waitangi, *Resource Kit,* Part 1, Section 2. The academic, Paul Spoonley, agreed that Pākehā had difficulties seeing themselves as a 'culture', in *Racism and Ethnicity,* pp. 63–70, quoting the widespread recognition of the fact.
88 L'Estrange, 'Learning Anti-Racism', p. 24.
89 *Curriculum Review.*

in the same way. Those who would teach that there was a Pākehā ethnicity and culture had their difficulties because the fact is that it is not part of Pākehā consciousness to think of themselves as an ethnic group. Nor would it be easy for them to do so either, even if it were possible for them to conceive of their ways of life as a 'culture'. An outside observer would have little difficulty in accepting that what the Pākehā have is a colonial variant on British culture, yet notably unlike that of the *ethnie* who make up the UK. But if common ethnic identity requires common origins and ways of life then it is a non-starter for the Pākehā. They really are too diverse. Settler is their name, and together with Māori they are still, maybe, building an identity. They are of European racial origin perhaps, and may to the outside view, appear the same. Appearances are doubtless important to many, both Māori and Pākehā. But being of European origin with others is not to share common original languages, religious practices, political traditions, family organizations, and memories of motherlands and fatherlands. Being from Europe is just not an ethnic identity. It could only be seen as one, in origin and in most continued functions, as a construction of Māori thinking.

Pat Hohepa once remarked that 'the greatest difficulty . . . is that no one had any clear idea of what Pakeha society is and how it ticks'.[90] From a Pākehā point of view it was not a 'Pākehā' society at all, but a political society of divers national origins, of various (and no) ethnic identities, divided and unified in a great number of ways that merely being 'Pākehā' did not catch. In fact Hohepa was right. There have been few serious studies of the Pākehā mentality (and spirituality) in all its complexity. It is true that Keith Sinclair's *A Destiny Apart* traced some of its emerging lineaments as they expressed themselves in the idea of nationhood up until 1940, and it is also true that a literary movement of the 1930s began to sketch a New Zealand identity. But, like the literary movement whose work he partly discussed, Sinclair's interests focused on the building of a nation far distant from the centres of the civilization from which it mainly sprung. His was an attempt to write a history of an emerging New Zealand nation rather than a history of the Pākehā. And, attempt as it did to describe a nationalism awakening in the face of distance from the rest of the world and asserting its difference, it did not tackle the issues of the 1970s and 1980s where identity of *whatever* kind has been formed by the propinquity of metropolitan culture. Our nation, our Māori and our Pākehā are all indelibly marked by a shrinking world.

So while many do not 'mind' being called 'Pākehā', it does not capture their identity for them. Others, reflecting on the disparaging connotations of being called 'Pākehā', rejected it. Hence the Race Relations' Office defence of the term. In 1988, the right-wing Geoff McDonald, who had by then recently settled in New Zealand, was to organize a petition against white

90 Hohepa, 'Maori and Pakeha: The One-People Myth', p. 109.

New Zealanders being called Pākehā. The Lower Hutt Junior Chamber of Commerce and others joined in the objection.[91]

Yet 'Pākehā' just *could* be an identity constructed from New Zealand materials, and chosen by Pākehā. Some did choose it. Dr Michael King, author and editor of many books on Māori subjects until he became aware by 1983 of resentment in certain Māori quarters of his doing so, wrote with some pride of 'being Pākehā' in a 1985 book of that name.[92] And in general it was those Pākehā most sympathetic to the Māori viewpoint, together with those who wished to assert an identity over and against other people of European racial stock and cultural practices (especially over recent immigrants), who talked of themselves as Pākehā. But the fact is that in the 1970s and 1980s the available accounts – besides Dr King's – of the Pākehā today were mainly Māori accounts.[93] They were largely rejected as such, not simply because of their source, but because of their content, to which much of the rest of this book is devoted.

Perhaps I should say in closing this introductory part of the book that I often think of myself as Pākehā. But not always and for all purposes. A terminal liberalism insists with me that that is only one of my identities, not the sum and total of them all. Pākehā is a construction of human making, useful for some purposes, dangerous for others, often irrelevant too. For me, being Pākehā is to be measured against its purpose. But in regard to justice for the Māori, I do not see myself how a Pākehā can rightly escape the name and avoid addressing the issues at stake. Not to do so would be contempt of inferiors with no claims to make. And there *were*, as should now be clear, the conditions for justice: some separation and distinction of interest, some unity and common interest, claims of injustice and claims that the injustice should be repaired. It was not a land without the possibility of justice. But the question in the 1970s and 1980s was going to be whether there was a common standard by which the claims could be decided. It is to the claims for reparation of past wrongs and to the question of a common standard that we now turn.

---

[91] DST 12:15/5/88.

[92] See Chapters 8 and 9 of King, *Being Pakeha*. See also his remarks in NZT:10/11/85.

[93] But see Bruce Jesson, 'Race and Identity: Looking the Other Way', *Metro*, June 1986, pp. 150-1, for some signs of the Pākehā construction of a Pākehā identity.

Part Two
Reparative Justice and its Limits

Chapter 4
The Waitangi Tribunal: The History of a Growing Reputation, 1975–1988

The Māori made of the Treaty of Waitangi the standard of justice between Māori and Pākehā, Māori and the state. Tentatively during the 1970s, definitively in 1984 at the Treaty hui at Ngaruawahia, and from then on with increasing urgency and sophistication, they made of it a sacred contract, the clauses of which defined their rights. They elaborated many histories of past wrongs out of the written records and out of their tribal and local memories of past transactions. They also constructed and taught not merely local histories but a country-wide history of injustice, in which injustice was defined as Pākehā and Crown breach of Treaty rights. They looked to present laws, customs, procedures, and policies, and pronounced them similarly unjust: in breach of the rights secured to them in the Treaty contract. They demanded reparation of past and continuing wrongs.

The demands were variously totalistic. At minimum they were merely that the injustice should cease; at maximum that all that had been wrongly taken – and that was the whole of Aotearoa – should be restored. Mostly though, the Māori combined claims to reparative justice with a willingness to compromise and deal for the sake of peace and co-operation. But always at the foundation of the compromise would have to be a Pākehā recognition of the Māori right to reparations, that is, a recognition of their Treaty rights. Increasingly during the 1980s they took these claims to the Waitangi Tribunal and found there a response both friendly and equivocal. The Government (as it turned out, almost always the fourth Labour Government of 1984–1987 and 1987 on) answered in much the same way. But it responded even more slowly and at crucial times only because it was urged on by the law courts which reminded it of its legal obligations. It was not until late 1988 that it made available a systematic study of its own disparate and disorganized responses to the recommendations of the Tribunal.[1] The Pākehā public was divided about the developments, and from 1987 on to 1989 it clearly emerged as what it very likely always had been: largely hostile to the Māori demands. Many denied the Treaty and Treaty rights, asserted a different history, and repudiated entirely the Māori claims to reparations for past wrongs.

This is the story told in this second part of the book: a story of claims to justice, of their outright repudiation, and of negotiation on the basis of them. By the late 1980s the claims were argued about everywhere and by a great proportion of the population. What interests me is the way in which the arguments ended in disagreement and confusion because of the weakness

---

[1] In a work of the Parliamentary Commissioner for the Environment. See Helen R. Hughes, *Environmental Management*, November 1988.

of the reparatory idea in conditions of bicultural disagreement about the standard of justice and the history of injustice. My intention is to display the logic of disagreement as it emerged in the Māori demands and in the response of the Pākehā public and the Government. Most of all the logic will be traced in the jurisprudence and recommendations of the Waitangi Tribunal. This is because of the strategic role the Tribunal played in the politics of reparation. It is also because in mediating, first, the demands of the Māori, secondly, its own knowledge of public opinion, and thirdly, its expectations as to Government response, it developed two divergent lines of thought which perfectly expressed the disagreement it heard. It developed not only a retrospective jurisprudence of reparation but a prospective jurisprudence as to more just and better distributions of things in the future. In doing so it expressed, though with much more elegance and precision and with more sympathy to the Māori case, what New Zealanders/Aotearoans were also saying.

In a way it is surprising that the Tribunal should have come to stand dead centre in the politics of reparations and to have contributed so much to New Zealand thinking about justice. It was instituted in 1975 as a way of avoiding rather than confronting the continued Māori demand that the Treaty should be 'ratified', that is (in this usage peculiar to New Zealand), made by statute part of the municipal or domestic law. It was instituted too, as a means of negotiating, perhaps even evading,[2] Māori claims that many statutes – classically listed in a paper by Mr (later Sir) Henry Ngata for the New Zealand Maori Council in 1970 – were in breach of the Treaty.[3]

In examining its enabling Act (The Treaty of Waitangi Act, 1975), a lawyer would not have thought that it was much designed to dispense reparative justice. The Tribunal was, it was true, empowered to hear 'claims' of 'prejudice' (that is, hurt, damage, and injustice) by any 'Maori' or 'group of Maori' against 'acts or omissions' on the part of the Crown or its agents. But it could not do much in the way of reparative justice to those claims. It was to have three members, the Chief Judge of the Maori Land Court and two others, not necessarily lawyers. It was given no power of legal determination save that of the 'exclusive authority to determine the meaning and effect of the Treaty'; yet that power was limited in application. Any determination of meaning and effect would apply only to matters cognizable under the Treaty of Waitangi Act – the Act which constituted it. And in that Act its other powers were solely those of 'hearing and enquiring' into cases and of 'reporting and recommending' on them to the executive arm of Government. They were neither powers of determining distributions of legal rights and duties, nor powers of legal enforcement. It was not even

---

[2] See for example, Prof. R. Q. Quentin-Baxter to Hon. Matiu Rata, 12 Nov 1973, GAL: MA/19/1/55/1, vol 2, fols 388–4.

[3] See H. K. Ngata, 'The Treaty of Waitangi and Land: Parts of the Current Law in Contravention of the Treaty'.

the Tribunal was to specify Treaty *rights* and request the government to enforce them; it was rather to turn its attention to the 'practical application of the principles' of the Treaty. And 'the practical application of principles' is not the enforcement of rights. Legal rights are laid down in rules which judges and other public officials have no option but to respect and enforce; legal principles may be, as philosophers have shown,[4] weighed and balanced. They may even be laid aside if other principles outweigh them in the case in hand – and being laid aside, they have not been 'violated' – merely laid aside for the moment. When judges specify rules and rights they try to do so with the precision that enforceability demands; but principles may remain vague and imprecise. They guide rather than require action in the detailed, practical, circumstances of cases. Justice, it might be thought, could *not* be recommended by the Tribunal. It would not be able to define rights and recommend their enforcement; it would be able merely to recommend what would be best overall in the circumstances.

The odds against the Tribunal's being an instrument of reparation were further lengthened in that its powers of retrospection were limited to the time after its empowerment. 'Anything done or omitted' by the Crown between 1840 and 1975 escaped its jurisdiction altogether. Thus the great bulk of past wrongs of which the Māori complained could not (it seemed) be examined. It is true that the Tribunal did have some power to compensate. It could recommend to the Crown what action be taken to 'compensate for' as well as to 'remove the prejudice' caused Māori people by the Crown's breaches of the 'principles' of the Treaty. But this was as simply one among the practical measures it might take.

It was not a promising start. Matiu Rata and his advisors were hardly satisfied with what they had been able to obtain from their Labour Party colleagues. In any case the news of its birth was drowned out by the Land March from Te Hapua and the defeat of the one-term Labour Government.

The Tribunal continued to live on obscurity tempered by minor obliquity. The three-term National Party Government which succeeded the Labour Government and which was to remain in power until 1984, did not convene it until 1977 and never greatly supported it. It was underfunded and understaffed. Sir Graham Latimer, the only member of the Tribunal who served throughout its life until its reform in 1985,[5] said that it 'operated out of a billy can', and found difficulty in coping with its workload.[6] Just

---

[4] A view classically expounded by Ronald Dworkin in *Taking Rights Seriously*. See Chapters 2 and 3 especially.

[5] It was originally chaired by Judge-Gillanders Scott (as Chief Judge of the Maori Land Court) and, besides Sir Graham, its other original member was L. H. Southwick QC. After his retirement in 1979, Judge Gillanders-Scott was succeeded by Judge E. T. W. Durie. Judge W. M. Willis deputized for Mr Southwick on the Te Atiawa claim and Paul Temm QC, replaced Mr Southwick in 1983. In 1985, for purposes of the Waiheke claim, Mr W. H. Herewini, and after Herewini's death, Mr E. D. Nathan, deputized for Sir Graham Latimer, and Mr M. J. Q. Poole deputized for Mr Temm.

[6] *Nga Take Maori*, 24/11/86.

as importantly, the Māori people for whose benefit it was primarily designed did not like its manner of proceeding according to formal, legal, 'Pākehā' practice. Its first hearing was held in the glitzy surroundings of an Auckland tourist hotel. Looking back at its beginnings, in 1988 Ms Jane Kelsey of the Auckland University Law School was to deliver a verdict agreed upon by all observers who wanted justice for the Māori: 'When the Waitangi Tribunal worked along [established legal] lines – using lawyers, common law rules of evidence and procedure, alien physical surroundings, judges lacking taha Maori, it could not deliver decisions which reflected the spirit of the Treaty.'[7]

When Hon. Koro Wetere became Minister of Maori Affairs for the fourth Labour Government in July 1984 he found on his desk summaries of current and recently dealt with Māori claims. The Tribunal had hardly been active. It had received only 14 claims since its institution nine years earlier: three had been 'dealt with', three had been withdrawn, three referred back to the claimants for further information and five were in the pipeline.[8] In fact the Tribunal had made findings in February 1978 in its *Waiau Power Station Report;*[9] and in March it had made findings in a report on *Joseph Hawke and the Fisheries Regulations.*[10] Press reports had been scant and unrevealing, and in any case the issues were dead. The proposal for a power station on the Manukau harbour had lapsed anyway; and ordinary legal process had rendered irrelevant Joe Hawke's complaint against fisheries' regulations. Much more important were the nine other claims on Wetere's desk. None of them had been to the Tribunal, and they were claims with obviously more serious potential for political ramification than those with the Tribunal. They included the Bastion Point issue, where a statutory settlement,[11] reached by the Muldoon Government amidst public controversy in 1978, had not stuck. There was also the matter of restitution of and compensation for wrongful confiscation of Tauranga lands; there was the Raglan Golf Course Claim now in the public eye for the eighth year; there were Ngai Tahu claims to Otago fishing rights and a Ngati Awa claim to the return of land 'including Whale Island and Putauaki/Mount Edgecumbe'. The important claims had been taken to MPs, to Ministers, to Parliament by Petition and to the Maori Land Court. They had not been taken to the Tribunal.

---

[7] Kelsey, 'Te Tiriti o Waitangi and the Bill of Rights', p. 27. She is quoted with approval in Nadja Tollemache, *The Proposed Bill of Rights*, footnote 60 at p. 6 (second paging). And in substance the following agreed: M. P. K. Sorrenson, 'Towards a Radical Reinterpretation', p. 61; David Williams in a Memorandum to the Minister of Maori Affairs and others, 7 June 1977; ACORD at H1:16/4/79; Pauline Kingi at H1:30/8/79; Graham Latimer at H1:16/4/79; Ranginui Walker at NZT:11/7/82 and NZL76–77: 7/9/85. The point was made as generally accepted by Māori in NZL48:28/3/81 and EP4:30/3/83.

[8] Department of Maori Affairs, *A Brief Summary*, pp. 72–8.

[9] The naming of the claims has varied very much over time. In the text I use the names they were most commonly given in public. In the notes that follow and in the Finding List I give the names applied to them by the Tribunal from 1987. Thus the Waiau Power Station Claim is: *T E Kirkwood and others (Waikato, re Waiau Pa Power Station).*

[10] *Joseph P. Hawke and others (Ngati Whatua, re Fisheries regulations).*

[11] The Orakei Block (Vesting and Use) Act. No. 47 (1978).

Yet the Tribunal was the institution that was to become the central locus of reparatory demands and the institution which more than any other spoke to the issues they raised. It was never quite clear how many claims it had on its hands at any time. Lack of administrative facilities, the fact that it helped its clients shape their claims (and it took time to get them shaped), the overlapping and interlocking of claims: all this made counting difficult. But (always roughly), at Wetere's accession it was hearing two claims and had six awaiting hearing. From then on it was typically hearing two claims at a time and the backlog began – at first very slowly, then massively – to grow. By December it had 14 claims waiting.[12] In May 1986 it had a backlog of only 20; in December: 40. In July 1987 it had a backlog of more than 80; in December, about 140. In June 1988, scaremongering MPs believed there might be 'as many as 3,000 potential claims to come before the tribunal'[13]. But the facts seem to have been that in July it had a backlog of 160 and that by September it was 166. The following year, in March 1989, it was announced that 180 claims in fact awaited hearing.[14] The claims were clearly not in the thousands: but there were still an enormous number; and although some important claims – for instance the Ngati Awa ones – remained with the government and some were taken to the courts, the evidence clearly points to the fact that by late 1986 the Tribunal had attained a status and power with its clientele that could not have been dreamed of in 1975. Increasingly thereafter it magnetically attracted Māori claims.

How had this come about?

Partly it was a matter of the Tribunal's own doing, partly a matter of the activity of the Government and the law courts, and above all – but this will be discussed in the next chapter – it was a matter of the continuing and growing Māori demand for justice.

The Tribunal did part of the job itself. It reformed its procedure in 1979 to adopt a Māori way. It began to meet at marae and it tried to adopt appropriate kawa in each, proceeding in a way more familiar to its clients. When in 1981 E. T. J. Durie became Chief Judge of the Maori Land Court, the tribunal found itself in the hands not only of a Māori, but of a very capable judge, a brilliant and subtle advocate, and a man of marked political skill. This showed when in March 1983 the Tribunal announced its findings and recommendations on its first major case in *The Te Atiawa Report*.[15] With this finding on claims to prevent and repair destruction of reefs off the North Taranaki coast by pollution, it gained in prominence and authority. The Muldoon Government, demonstrating the irritability of its failing powers, at first tried to resist the Tribunal's suggestions. So the Tribunal added Pākehā partisan support to its already established Māori and conservationist support.

In 1984, 1985, and 1986 it continued to enhance its reputation on a broad

12 H4:27/9/84; NZT:23/12/84.

13 NZPD1:41, p. 4571 (21 June).

14 H20:14/3/89.

15 *Aila Taylor (Te Atiawa, re Motunui).*

front, publishing judicious findings and recommendations on three claims: in *The Kaituna Report* (November 1984), *The Manukau Report* (July 1985), and *Te Reo Report* (April 1986).[16]

The findings on each of these were greeted with a mixture of general content and some unease; but the Tribunal's 1987 cases were much more divisive of public opinion. The *Waiheke Report* of June[17] made suggestions in an attempt to settle an issue already well-publicized by occupation of the disputed land; the *Orakei Report* of November[18] was yet another attempt to settle the Bastion Point issue and was laden with party-political connotations. (The National Government had failed to make a settlement; this would stick.) The Tribunal was more direct in its approach in these two than in previous cases, or at least so it seemed to a public now notably disturbed by what it recommended: the restitution of ancestral land to Ngati Paoa at Waiheke and to Ngati Whatua at Bastion Point.

But the most divisive finding of all was to be the *Muriwhenua Fishing Report* of June 1988.[19] It inflamed the nation and Parliament for the remainder of 1988 and looked well set to do so for some years ahead. After that, though it was of great local interest, the Tribunal's findings and recommendations on sewage disposal at Taipa, the *Mangonui Sewerage Report* of August,[20] hardly attracted any attention at all. But perhaps only a year away lurked the Tribunal's Ngai Tahu findings as to the ownership of perhaps 70 per cent, it was often said, of the South Island; and in October it was announced that massive Taranaki claims against confiscation (extending southwards into Wellington) would be researched for the Tribunal by an eminent historian.

The Tribunal's own decisions then – both judicious and controversial – were part of the reason for its rise to prominence. Its rise was also due to Government actions and their unintended consequences, to the activities of Law Courts questioned as to the law by the Māori, and to the interaction of the Tribunal's work with both Government and Courts. The story is complex and legalistic in the extreme. But as law is the language in which the Government commanded its people, so it found itself commanded by law to rely on the Tribunal in ways it never seems to have contemplated when it came to power in 1984. This was not well explained to the public, and the lack of explanation in turn led to the Tribunal's power over the imaginations of the peoples in 1987, 1988, and into 1989 being very great: greater by far than its legal power (narrowly defined) would have suggested, but perhaps no greater than its strategic position in the politics of the times warranted.

Since the Tribunal's institution, Māori had continued to demand its reform,

---

[16] *Sir Charles Bennett and others (Te Arawa, re Kaituna River); Nganeko Minhinnick and others (Ngati Te Ata and Tainui, re Manukau); and Huirangi Waikerepuru and others (re Te Reo Maori).*

[17] *Hariata Gordon and others (Ngati Paoa, re Waiheke Island).*

[18] *Joseph P. Hawke and others (Ngati Whatua, re Orakei).*

[19] *Hon. Matiu Rata and others (Ngati Kuri and others, re fisheries).*

[20] *Mangonui Sewerage (Ngati Kahu).*

and that, taken together with its growing reputation after the *Te Atiawa Report*, persuaded the fourth Labour Government to set about amending the Treaty of Waitangi Act. In doing so it went some way towards providing for what the Tribunal and its clients wanted – reparatory justice. In legislation debated from late 1984 through 1985, important changes were made to the Tribunal's membership, its jurisdictional scope and its sheer capacity for work.[21] Its membership was increased from three to seven: at least four of its six ordinary members were to be Maori, and its Chairman was still to be the Chief Justice of the Maori Land Court. It was given greater administrative and research support as well as alternative members who could sit when the principal members were unavailable. Most controversially, its retrospective power to examine grievances was extended back from 1975 to 1840, thus opening an area of claims described by the Opposition as a 'can of worms'. They claimed that the power of retrospection was a 'potential time bomb that no-one wants'; they predicted land marches, disruption, despoliation, dispossession, and 'a pakeha backlash such as this country has, fortunately never seen'. The bill, one MP said, 'raises questions without answers . . . the questions of compensation and the righting of historical wrongs'. And at stake were 'claims going back to 1840 that will run into hundreds of millions of dollars'. It was not only money and land that was at stake: some of the more radical Māori, like the Rastafarians of Ruatoria on the East Cape, were already combining land claims with social revolution. Nothing (continued the Opposition) would satisfy such as them.[22]

The second, reconstituted Tribunal, began to operate only in late 1986, after a long period during which Judge Durie and a skeleton staff had battled on under both the old legislation and the new. Government commitment was not clearly evident, and the Opposition remained far from happy with the reforms. Perhaps the best that could be said at that time was that if it were not starved for lack of resources, the second Tribunal would prove to be a yet more potent force than the first.[23] Professor Keith Sorrenson, one of the second Tribunal's new alternate members, worried whether it would continue to be, like the first, at the mercy of its political masters in Parliament. It was after all, a mere statutory authority, and besides starving it of resources, Parliament could abolish it.[24] But the future proved to be quite the contrary; the Tribunal soon had Parliament at *its* mercy. This was

21 Compare The Treaty of Waitangi Act (1975), 1975, No. 114 as amended by the Treaty of Waitangi Amendment Act (1977), 1977, No. 178, with An Act to Amend the Treaty of Waitangi Act 1975 (1985), 1985, No. 148.

22 NZPD2:37, p. 5727; 3:37, pp. 4342-3, 4344, 4495, 4498, 5407; 1:41, pp. 2702, 2703, 2704, 2705, 2706, 2707, 2708, 2709, 2710, 2711, 5650, 6061, 6063-4, 6067, 6068-73, 6075-81.

23 The opinion also of P. G. McHugh, 'The constitutional role of the Waitangi Tribunal', p. 224.

24 Sorrenson, 'Towards a Radical Reinterpretation of New Zealand History,' *NZJH* version, last page.

due to not only the high calibre of its new membership,[25] but was also the consequence of two sets of circumstances and events which the Tribunal was involved in from December 1986. One set concerned Māori lands, the other, Māori fishing rights.

In that month the State Owned Enterprises Act was passed. The original bill proposed the transfer, at market price, of lands from the Crown to State Owned Enterprises (SOEs). This would have meant that governments would have had great difficulty in returning those transferred lands to Māori were there to be successful claims to the Tribunal in future. New property rights would now be at stake, and the expense of the Crown's reobtaining them might well be prohibitive. So in a letter of 8 December, the Tribunal, which was sitting on the Muriwhenua claims in the Far North, urged Parliament to rethink its position.[26] Heeding the Tribunal's advice, in passing the Act the Government established under section 27 a land title mechanism by which those Māori claims lodged with the Tribunal by 16 December were protected when transfers were made. It also made another provision which was to prove to have consequences of far greater significance. In section 9 it was laid down that: 'Nothing in this Act shall permit the Crown to act in a manner that is inconsistent with the principles of the Treaty of Waitangi'.

But why the Government made section 9 law was not clear (nor therefore its meaning), 18 December was too tight a deadline, and the Māori were not satisfied that a mere recommendation of the Tribunal to the Government would protect their right to reparation. So from March through June 1987 the case of the *New Zealand Maori Council* v *the Solicitor General* was fought, in which the meaning of the SOE Act and its section 9 was further explored.

One result of the case was that the Court prohibited the Government by injunction from proceeding with sales to SOEs without a Court-approved agreement with the complainants. The Government had no legal, and little political, choice. It was forced into negotiation with the New Zealand Maori Council, with the consequence that still further powers were proposed for the Tribunal in the Treaty of Waitangi (State Enterprises) Bill. Introduced into Parliament in December 1987 and made law by August 1988, the new arrangements were that some restitutory decisions of the Tribunal would now be *binding* on the Crown.

As these new powers loomed in prospect and then became fact, so the claims came in and the profile of the Tribunal became steadily higher. A *third* Tribunal in fact took shape in 1988–1989: the Treaty of Waitangi (SE) Act not only gave the Tribunal its new restitutory power. It further improved its administrative and research capacities. It got a director and was empowered to commission research. Partly also under the impulse of the SOE affair,

---

[25] The membership was to be: Professor I. H. Kawharu (Mr E. D. Nathan as his deputy); Rt. Rev. M. A. Bennett; Mr Monita E. Delamare (Mr Turi Te Kani as deputy); Georgina M. Te Heuheu (Emarina Manuel as deputy); Sir Desmond Sullivan (Professor M. P. K. Sorrenson as deputy); Professor G. S. Orr (Mr W. M. Wilson as deputy).

[26] Doc #A23: Interim Report of the Waitangi Tribunal [on the Muriwhenua Claims], 8 December 1986. Printed in the *Muriwhenua Fishing Report*, pp. 289-91.

further capacity was added. The Treaty of Waitangi Amendment Act of December 1988 allowed for the increase of the Tribunal's membership to a total of up to 16 people (17 including the Chairman who would continue to be the Chief Judge of the Maori Land Court) and it removed the Māori membership quota. The new members (five of the six it was insisted, were women; and now there were eight Māori, eight Pākehā, and Judge Durie) were announced in March 1989;[27] the Tribunal could now comfortably divide itself and hear as many as three sets of claims at a time. A new system was in place, and the third Waitangi Tribunal was ready for action.

It was, however, not simply the SOE affair that had brought about these enhancements of the Tribunal's power. Another series of primarily legal events parallelling the SOE issue had the same effect of enhancing the power of the Tribunal and revealing its strategic place in the New Zealand system of law and government. On 10 December 1986 – two days after the SOE letter – Judge Durie wrote to the Minister of Agriculture and Fisheries from the Tribunal's Muriwhenua headquarters expressing the Tribunal's concern about the Quota Management System (QMS) introduced earlier in the year for both inshore and offshore fisheries.

The proposed system meant an initial allocation to fishing interests of Individual Transferable Quotas (ITQs) of named varieties of fish. The amount of Quota each individual or company would be offered would be based on the volume of their past catches. An ITQ would define and limit an exclusive right to catch and market a species of fish, and in future the Quotas would be marketable by their owners. An ITQ was in fact a property right, not exactly in the seas, but in the activity of fishing. It was a right to catch and sell – a right that could now be bought, sold, gifted or willed, used as a basis of partnership with others or to provide an income. Though a rental would be due the government each year, it displayed many of the 'incidents' of modern private property.[28]

There was, warned the Tribunal, a problem. Article 2 of the Treaty had promised Māori the 'undisturbed possession' of their 'fisheries', yet many Māori – part-time fishermen – had not been offered Quota. They would lose rights which they were absolutely convinced the Treaty guaranteed. They would be excluded from the fishery. The Tribunal therefore told the Minister that: 'Considerable disruption may occur and very substantial compensation may have to be paid to Quota-holders if the Government were in due course to accept the recommendation of the Tribunal that certain quotas should not have been allocated and should therefore be purchased back by the

27 Dr Mary Boyd, Dr Ngapare Hopa; Mr John Kneebone; Joanne Morris; Dr Erihana Rupene Ryan; Dr Evelyn Stokes. Retired Chief District Judge Peter Trapski was also appointed but would not take up his position until the expected retirement of a sitting member in May. H20:14/3/89.

28 Influentially listed by A. M. Honoré, in 'Ownership'.

government'.[29] It was made clear that the issue of compensation for violated Māori fishing rights was as much on the agenda as the question of land rights.

This time – and from a legal point of view almost incredibly – the Tribunal's action brought no response from the Government. It may well be that Ministry of Agriculture and Fisheries gave it poor advice. Whatever the reason, inaction was the wrong policy: the Government was *again* forced to listen by the Courts.[30] In September and in November 1987, High Court interim injunctions were obtained first by the Muriwhenua people, then by Ngai Tahu, Waikato, and others, prohibiting the Government's further extending the QMS to other species of fish. The grounds for issue of the injunctions were not Treaty grounds at all. They were basically that section 88 (2) of the Fisheries Act (1983) – to which the QMS had been appended by an amendment of 1986 – held that 'nothing in this Act shall affect any Maori fishing rights'.

In fact 'Maori fishing rights' had been preserved in much this way in Fisheries Acts since the late nineteenth century. They were *there* all right, and according to the custom and practice of English common law that New Zealand had inherited, the judges were bound to uphold them. It was just that no one had defined their content. There had been fishing cases before, but they had turned on the relationship of fisheries with Māori land ownership, or else they had been claims under the Treaty. The Treaty was legally a nullity in regard to fisheries, and land sales were held to whittle away customary rights attached to customary ownership. Either way, the cases yielded no joy to the Māori.

However, by 1987, legal thinking had been informed by new research. Frederika Hackshaw and Paul McHugh, in writings of legal scholarship from 1984 onwards, had persuasively suggested the continued existence in New Zealand of 'aboriginal rights' in fisheries, if not in lands.[31] These were rights which aboriginal peoples retained even with their cession of sovereignty to the colonizing British. Aboriginal rights stood in common law as an encumbrance on the power of the new sovereign, and could be extinguished only by legislation which specifically named them as extinguished. Māori aboriginal rights in land had been so extinguished in 1908 (though it was proposed in the live new Maori Affairs Bill that they should be reactivated), but it was highly probable that aboriginal fishing rights had been preserved by the Fisheries Acts.

The recent case of *Te Weehi* v *Regional Fisheries Officer* (1986), while finding

[29] Memorandum from the Waitangi Tribunal to the Minister of Agriculture and Fisheries, signed Taihakurei Durie, 10 December 1986. Doc #A23. Published in the *Muriwhenua Fishing Report*, p. 292.

[30] The official version of how was given in Parliament by Richard Prebble on 21 September 1988: NZPD1:42, p. 6832.

[31] Hackshaw, *The Recognition of Native Customary Rights at Common Law* (1984); and a series of articles by McHugh up to that time, especially 'The Legal Status of Maori Fishing Rights' (1984); 'Maori Fishing Rights and the North American Indian' (1985); 'Aboriginal Title in New Zealand Courts' (1985).

for the Māori in breach – but for section 88(2) – of the Act, had found against the Crown on the technicality that it was up to the prosecution to define the rights it claimed the Māori did *not* have.[32] The Crown should have shown what the rights were. It had not researched the rights for *Te Weehi*, and in fact while the *form* or *mode* of the rights was known (there were common law 'aboriginal rights' preserved in the fisheries statutes), no one knew their *content*. No one knew exactly what the Māori legally could or could not do, did or did not own. So now in 1987, and predictably, the High Court issued injunctions against the extension of the QMS on grounds that the issue of further ITQs might well be in breach of the legal rights of the Māori. The Government would have to move.

It would have to move moreover in a way which relied heavily on the findings of the Tribunal. Why this should have been the case was in the nature of things not mentioned: it would have been too much a matter of arcane law, it would have infuriated those Māori who were intent on their *Treaty* rights, and it would have equally inflamed a Pākehā public which did not like to think of the Māori having separate legal rights. The logic of the situation pointed to relying on the Tribunal and drawing attention to its findings in a way that would, with luck, avoid the fundamental legal facts. These were that the Government could legally ignore Treaty fishing rights, but that it could not ignore aboriginal, common law, rights.

The Government was over a barrel. If the injunctions were to be successfully challenged, it would have to be shown that no legal rights had been or would be breached; and that was not an easy or pleasant prospect. If it were to pursue the matter through the courts it would need to find a definition of the content of 'Māori fishing rights' to show it was not abridging them in issuing extra ITQs. That might not be possible. And if the definition were further to show that the rights had been violated in the *original* ITQ issue, then the courts might well declare all the Government's proceedings to date outside the law and find that compensation was owed. And if the case of the *New Zealand Maori Council* v *the Attorney General* was anything to go by, the courts might then force the Government to negotiate with the Māori for rights it had mistakenly assumed it already had, but which were really the Māori's. The only other option was to extinguish the rights by rescinding section 88(2) of the Fisheries Act; but this was not politically, or in legal morality, on.

Legally speaking, none of this had anything to do with the Treaty or the Tribunal. Rather it had to do with the common law of the land, that is, that part of the law not laid down in statute but in inherited English custom and past New Zealand and Commonwealth judicial decisions. This was a law which governed the decisions of judges under the doctrine that they must follow precedent; it even perhaps limited the power of Parliament to legislate – for it was only a matter of custom that Parliament was supreme

---

[32] *Te Weehi* v *Regional Fisheries Officer* (1986), 6 N.Z.A.R., pp. 114–28. See Brookfield, 'Maori Fishing Rights and the Fisheries Act 1983'.

legislator, and Parliament might have to take the limits with the empowerments.[33] This was not the law with which the Tribunal was concerned. It simply had a statutory obligation to discover the 'principles of the Treaty' and tell the Government what they suggested.

But the Government's dilemma of November 1987 put the Tribunal in a powerful position. Though it was hearing claims of 'prejudice' to the Muriwhenua Māori consequent on contempt of the 'principles' of the Treaty, in trying to decide what the 'principles' *were*, it had to construct an account of the nature and extent of Māori fishing practices as they were at the time the Treaty was signed. Only in that way could it have penetrated the minds of the signatories as to what 'fisheries' meant and thus uncover the 'principle' on which they had agreed. But this reconstruction was exactly what the common law required too. The courts would not want to know what those rights were according to the 'principles of the Treaty of Waitangi,' but they *would* want to know what Māori 'aboriginal rights' were. It just so happened that the evidence as to rights under the Treaty was highly relevant as to the content of the aboriginal rights. Courts would be bound to preserve the customary rights of the Māori, and the nature of their customs would be indicated in studies of their activities around 1840 – the same studies that the Tribunal had undertaken to discover the content of the rights guaranteed by the Treaty. And for that reason the High Court consulted the Tribunal as a source of expert evidence.

The Tribunal's position vis à vis the Government was in fact still stronger. Since the Government wanted to issue more ITQs by the new fishing season beginning in October 1988, the Tribunal was in practice not only the best source of knowledge. It was in effect the only source of knowledge. The Government had under a year to get things organized. The Crown Law Office began to staff itself in 1988 to deal with 'Treaty issues'; and not till November was a competent lawyer appointed to help it full-time. Only Māori claimants and their sympathizers knew much about the rights at issue. The Tribunal would have to be listened to.

Finally, the Government probably thought it better to approach an unpleasant future on a definition of 'Māori fishing rights' taken from the 'principles' of the Treaty rather than from aboriginal rights, because the Māori's strict legal rights might well turn out to be much more extensive than the vague and negotiable intimations of the 'principles of the Treaty'. Already the High Court, in *Huakina Development Trust* v *Waikato Valley Authority* (2 June 1987) had shown the way, holding that the findings of the Waitangi Tribunal on Māori values and on the meaning of the Treaty must be taken into account in planning matters; and it might be better to take these into account, even give them priority, than to be forced by legal action to yield

---

[33] Cooke P's remarks to this effect, including ('some common law rights presumably lie so deep that even Parliament could not override them') are collected by Paul McHugh, 'Constitutional Theory and Maori Claims', p. 62, n. 144. And see L. J. Caldwell, 'Judicial Sovereignty' and P. Joseph, 'Literal Compulsion and Fundamental Rights'.

rights wrongly claimed by the Crown. It would be better too, to negotiate than to litigate; for litigation would be a long and expensive process. So the advice of the Tribunal would also from this point of view be a crucial factor in whatever the future might hold.

Thus the Government was forced to deal on the 'principles of the Treaty'. In December 1987, Crown representatives began a long train of negotiations with negotiators representing Māori interests. There was to be no rapid and fruitful termination to the business. In late September 1988, in the face of the breakdown of negotiations,[34] the Government unilaterally introduced a Fisheries Bill designed to make Quota available to Māori – but at a price unacceptable to Maoridom. Matiu Rata, one of the negotiators, was clearly furious. He spoke of the injustice of the proposals, and spoke of 'direct action': 'It is not a question of violence, it is a question of defending what is rightfully ours'. He seemed to speak of secession from such a state as could perpetrate them.[35] The bill was accordingly modified, and at the time of writing (March 1989) the new proposal lies before the Parliamentary Committee on the Maori Fisheries Bill. It is still a matter of heated contention and the outcome is uncertain. The matter may even be handed back to the Courts. One thing is certain however: both the negotiations and the final legislative solution have been, and will further be, markedly coloured by the jurisprudence of the Tribunal and by its *Muriwhenua Fishing Report*.

The Tribunal thus arrived, propelled by its own efforts and by the complex interaction of legal and political events. But that is really the outer husk of its history. What informed it – what really made it happen – was that it took centre stage as the institutional focus for a way of thought whose time had come. What vivified the Tribunal was the idea of reparation for breach of contract. It was the new importance given the Treaty as expressing Māori rights, the spread of indignation at the injustice of violating those rights and the demand for reparation that came together in the story of its birth, reformings and activity. The Treaty, injustice and reparations now demand attention.

---

[34] See further, Chapter 6 of this book, pp. 120–22.

[35] MR:28/10/88; H:29/10/88;H5:2/11/88.

Chapter 5
The Treaty of Waitangi and Justice in Contract

I

The Māori, the Treaty, Injustice Under the Treaty, and Reparations for Past Wrongs

It is fitting that in the 1980s the east wall of the Maori Affairs Committee Room in Parliament House, Wellington, was adorned with a huge facsimile of the Treaty of Waitangi. Many Māori had long seen the Treaty as a solemn contract which ought to define the relationship between Māori and Pākehā. It became a commonplace during the decade for historians and political reformers to insist that the Māori had uninterruptedly seen it that way: as instanced in attempts to have it 'ratified' by the Crown in 1882, 1884, 1924, 1981, 1983, and 1984; and by Parliament in 1939, 1963, and 1969.[1] In 1986 Dr Claudia Orange, by then the leading Pākehā historian of three important Māori conferences at Orakei in 1879 and at Kohimarama in 1869 and 1899, where the Māori debated and reaffirmed the Treaty, remarked: 'The Maori debate on the importance of the Treaty has continued throughout most of the 150 years since it was signed'.[2] She was to display this general point further in her book, *The Treaty of Waitangi*, published in 1987.

It would be equally interesting to have a history of the degree of Māori *non-support* of the Treaty, and *non-discussion* of it. Through most of the 1970s and 1980s, it is impossible to measure accurately the intensity and spread of Māori support for the Treaty. Contemporary New Zealand myth – spread by politicians, reformers, and Māori interests alike – probably much overstated Māori knowledge of and interest in the Treaty, at least until the summer of 1983-1984. The tribes of the Tai Tokerau Federation had always felt the Treaty rather more theirs than the southerners', for Waitangi lies in the heart of their territory. (Often the Treaty was said by southerners, especially from the Waikato, to be a 'Ngapuhi thing' or the 'Ngapuhi Treaty'.) Yet a member of Tai Tokerau reported in 1984 that the 'large majority of young Maori' were 'totally unaware of the significance of the Treaty of Waitangi . . . I think it would be true to say that in general the significance of the Treaty doesn't figure with the majority of Maori people in this modern and fast

---

[1] See the Letters to Queen Elizabeth II and to the Governor-General, 20 Jan 1984 in *Te Hikoi*, pp. 14-15. There were also attempts to petition Queen Victoria in 1882 and 1884, King George V in 1924, Elizabeth II in 1981 and Prince Charles in 1983. See in Blank *et al.* (eds.), *He Korero*, pp.26-8, 47-9.

[2] Project Waitangi, *Resource Kit,* Part 1, pp. 2-6.

living world of the Pakeha . . . Like a face behind a veil the Treaty remains an anonymous figure that we all feel within us but one that we are never allowed to touch or explore.'[3]

That said, it seems likely that interest in the Treaty had been growing from the early 1970s among the politically-aware Māori. Hana Jackson, then a young leader of Nga Tamatoa, read about the Treaty around 1970. Her doing so, and her reaction, were probably typical: 'I became like a raging bull. Only then did I see the full picture. My mother believed too.'[4] Given this perception, the Treaty was ripe to become the defining instrument of Māori claims and the injustice of their neglect.

There remained however a degree of contempt for the Treaty. Throughout the 1970s and early 1980s it continued to be regarded by protesting Māori as hardly worth the paper it was written on. It did not go unnoticed that the great central North Island tribe of Tuwharetoa and the federation of Te Arawa had refused to sign the Treaty in 1840. Nor that many of the Waikato-Maniopoto had also refused. The Treaty was the property (and burden) of only those iwi and hapū whose tūpuna (ancestors) signed it during 1840.

There was more to the story, the purpose of which was to scorn and demean the Treaty. It was said that many Māori were uninformed and uninterested in what they did in signing. Many had signed to obtain the blankets given by the Pākehā who hawked the Treaty around the land during 1840. The great old warrior Te Rauparaha signed twice. It was recorded that some, like the Ngapuhi chief Nopera Panakareao, came to regret their signing. Once believing that 'the shadow of the land goes to the Queen, but the substance remains with us', he came to believe that 'the substance of the land would pass to the European and only the shadow would remain with the Maori people'.[5] Such leaders, refusing to sign, or signing in ignorance of the consequences, could hardly be considered bound by the Treaty. In any case the colonial government never meant to stick to its part of the bargain. Certainly the land-hungry New Zealand Company thought it a trinket to 'pacify the natives'. The Treaty was 'a fraud' and a 'con-job'. It was unclear as to whether, and to whom, it mattered. This was the message of the protesters at Waitangi each February until 1984. And these arguments for rejecting the Treaty as worthless were still being heard well afterwards. Even in 1989, the slogan 'The Treaty is a Fraud' can be seen, newly-sprayed, on the concrete block walls and corrugated iron fences of Auckland.

Such cynicism was to be overcome by a new wave of pious respect for the Treaty by the mid-1980s. There is little doubt that much of the new respect for the Treaty is to be explained as the effect of the work undertaken from 1978 onwards by the New Zealand Maori Council. In that year the

---

[3] The words of Haami Piripiri, in *Te Hikoi* (a publication edited by the Waitangi Action Committee), p. 51.

[4] Des Casey, 'Hanna (sic) Jackson – Maori Activist', p. 12.

[5] Asher and Naulls, *Maori Land*, p. 13.

Council made submissions objecting to a range of features in a Maori Affairs Bill which had been designed to consolidate and refine the existing legislation. Ben Couch, Minister of Maori Affairs, ultimately withdrew the bill from Parliament in September 1979 and authorized the Council to 'prepare a draft Bill which in effect could become the new Act to take Maoridom into the 1980s'. The Council described itself as setting out to develop, in consultation with 'our people', 'an overriding philosophy with which we can advance into the new world'. The initial plan was set out in a 1980 Council paper which was to be the basis of consultation with the 'people as a whole', and the basis for new legislation;[6] by 1983 the 'overriding philosophy' – the kaupapa – had been developed, and it was presented to the Minister amidst much publicity.[7] The Council's work, *Kaupapa – Te Whanga Tuatahi*, placed the Treaty firmly back in Māori consciousness, interpreted both for Maoridom and officialdom.

It was nothing to the Council that the Treaty was 'drawn up by amateurs on the one side and signed by those on the other side who understood little of its implications'. This did not matter, for to both sides it 'was a symbol of mana'. It was 'imbued with the spirit of hope that sovereignty, so simply acquired, would solve all problems of ambition: the Maori would retain his rangatiratanga, and the Crown would add New Zealand to its empire'.

And the modern Māori? 'The present generation' had received the Treaty as a 'heritage and trust'. 'Ancestral initiative is tapu to the Maori . . . and lies at the heart of their mana and self-respect as Maori New Zealanders. None but their ancestors gave [the Treaty] to them and none will take it from them.' In more European terms, the Council put it that the Treaty was the 'origin and basis of British sovereignty and constitutional government in New Zealand', and that by it 'the Crown extends its protection over the Maori people and guarantees them their assets'. Thus, the New Zealand Maori Council proposed an 'interpretation of the Treaty from which we derive principles for determining codes of laws on Maori land and all other matters covered by the Treaty'. In this way the New Zealand Maori Council both recorded and shaped Māori views to the Treaty.

The unified respect for the Treaty was clearly evident by the summer of 1983–1984. In February 1984 a Kotahitanga (unity) movement assembled in the Waikato and marched north to Waitangi in a Hikoi, or Peace March, to attend the Treaty commemorations and to negotiate for the 'honouring' of the Treaty. All, from the most mediatory of the NZMC to the most disillusioned of activists, wanted the Treaty 'honoured'. As Pat Hohepa and Atareta Poananga noted: 'One theme was evident . . . There was a need to have the Treaty honoured legally or the celebrations would continue to be a sham and a fraud.' All could agree that what was needed was 'the kind of sovereign control which Maori people would have had if the Treaty

---

6 NZMC, 'A Discussion Paper on Future Maori Development and Legislation', pp. 1-3.

7 H20:21/3/87; AS3:21/3/87; H6:22/3/83; H20:23/3/87; and the largest report AS6:25/3/87.

had been properly honoured in fact and in spirit'.[8] Another participant expressed well the common idea that though evil had been done in its name (or in ignoring it) the Treaty should still stand with the Māori. He said: 'hold fast to it. Never let it go, because it was once our ruin as a nation but will prove to be our salvation as a people.' And no doubt with an eye to the Pākehā state, Bishop Whakahuihui Vercoe remarked: 'The Maori have always kept faith with the Treaty. And this is an invitation to the partner in that Treaty to be also a participant and to revive the spirit of the Treaty within our whole structure of life here in New Zealand.'[9]

Even the Waitangi Action Committee (WAC), formed in 1979 to oppose the 'celebrations' and since then a steady opponent of the Treaty, was by 1984 ambiguous about it. They still held it to be a 'fraud' and a 'con job', an event 'symbolically responsible for the oppression of the Maori people';[10] and they stressed the ignorance of the Māori signatories and the greed and duplicity of the Pākehā at the signing and since. But they now joined Kotahitanga in complaining more of the neglect of the Treaty than of its lack of intrinsic mana.

This was the mood that prevailed through the two great hui of 1984 and 1985. In line with a growing generality of Māori respect for the Treaty, the hui at Turangawaewae affirmed its importance as a solemn contract invested with the mana of iwi Māori as a whole. When Ranginui Walker spoke (in what had for the past fifteen years been a routine way) of the Treaty having been signed in circumstances of an 'irretrievable muddle' of misunderstanding, chicanery, and bribery with blankets, his remarks, once apposite enough,[11] were rejected. Rameka Cope could truly tell an enquirer that 'at no time had he heard any criticism of the Treaty itself nor any thought that Maoris were against the Treaty as such'. 'Care had to be taken not to confuse the protests against the "celebrations" at Waitangi ... [with] ... Maori opposition to the Treaty itself. Rather it should be seen in the light of the protests being for the Treaty in its truest sense.'

The Treaty was asserted to be a 'symbol which reflects Te Mana Maori Motuhake' at Turangawaewae. It was the outer and visible sign of the autonomous and unchallengeable existence of the Māori as a human society in Aotearoa. The hui held that the Treaty 'articulates the status of the Maori as tangata whenua of Aotearoa'. The Treaty reasserted – it did not create – Māori society's primordial and cosmic, uniquely intimate connection with

[8] See the report by Hawaiian visitors, 'Manuhiri No Hawaii – Report of the Hikoi', in *Te Hikoi*, p. 25. Hohepa and Poananga's account of the unity of the movement (pp. 27-31) is a bit exaggerated – it leaves out of account the non-participation of the Tainui kaumātua. See Hone Harawira of WAC, p. 34, and Hiwi Tauroa, the Race Relations Conciliator, pp. 49-50, and Hone Ngata, pp. 60, 64, for some divisions.

[9] *Te Hikoi*, p. 53. Cf. pp. 51-3, 56, 57.

[10] *Te Hikoi*, p. 18.

[11] Additionally on Māori ambivalence as to whether the Treaty should be ratified or declared a fraud from the late 1970s, see Greenland, 'Ethnicity as Ideology', in Spoonley *et al.*, pp. 90-1.

its habitations, its land, and its other treasured things: a connection which simply could not be severed. The Treaty was sacrosanct, not in and of itself, but by virtue of what it stood for: 'We declare that our Mana Tangata, Mana Wairua, Manu Whenua, supersedes the Treaty of Waitangi'. The mana of the people, the spirit, and the land was what informed the document and gave it its power. But power – derivative or not – it had: 'My ancestor's mark on that paper has made it tapu' said a speaker, directly rejecting Walker's remarks on its being a fraud.[12]

When the new Government, which needed still further guidance on the Treaty, facilitated a further hui, it heard similar statements. At Waitangi in February 1985 it was all respect for the Treaty, and through it there would be unity. Later that year, at an Auckland seminar on the proposal that there should be a Bill of Rights in New Zealand, Chief Judge Durie told a large audience, predominantly of lawyers, that before that hui he had continued to think that the Māori believed their rights were 'not dependent on the status of the Treaty'. (Nor was this surprising given the emphasis at Turangawaewae on the Treaty merely as a symbol of something deeper.) But after the Waitangi hui, Durie thought it worth emphasizing that, 'I have since learnt of the predominant view of some 1700 participants[13] . . . that the fraudulent approach was a temporary aberration. The Treaty has been re-established as a sacred document so that nothing short of its full recognition in unadulterated form can give satisfaction or restore honour.' Among the lawyers listening were Hon. Geoffrey Palmer, the Minister of Justice, and his close advisor Professor (in 1988, Sir) Kenneth Keith.[14]

The reports were true.[15] Only Hori Forbes expressed for the Tainui[16] a degree of exasperation with the common Māori obsession with the Treaty. Presenting a report on the future of the Waikato Valley tribes, he remarked: 'Any recommendations we have made on any of these issues could doubtless be related back by some exercise of logic or flights of rhetoric to the Treaty.' He added: 'We do not wish to waste our time or energy in futile bitterness on this matter or enter into semantic or legal debates as to what the Treaty did or did not mean.' Nevertheless, Tainui made their share of appeals to

---

12 Blank *et al.* (eds.), *He Korero*, Walker at pp. 44–51; direct rejection by Taipari Munroe: 'My ancestor's mark on that paper has made it tapu', p. 91; Cope, pp. 83–4; resolutions and submissions, pp. 2, 10, 56, 62, 63, 71, 72-3, 86, 87, 103. Walker's paper was also in *Te Hikoi*, pp. 7-11 and his 'The Treaty of Waitangi as the Focus of Maori Protest' was a development of it.

13 This may be wrong as an estimate of numbers. H3:7/2/87 says 1400 registered and about 700 attended.

14 See Sharp *et al.*, *A Bill of Rights for New Zealand?*, p. 190.

15 See also Ripeka Evans. NZT4:10/2/85.

16 In much the same way as Tuaiwa Rickards' similar case at Turangawaewae, Blank *et al.* (eds.), *He Korero*, p. 42.

it and to its spirit, and Forbes's remarks underline the centrality of the Treaty in the discussions.[17]

From 1985 onwards Māori expressions of reverence for the Treaty were legion. In February 1987, for instance, on the TV show *Nga Take Maori*, Sir James Henare, the distinguished kaumātua (elder) of Ngapuhi spoke of it as sacred because of his ancestors' tattoos on it and because they knew what they were signing; Shane Jones, a rangatahi (young tribesman) of Tai Tokerau – and not always Sir James's ally – agreed. He stated that 'all our Korero (discussion) needs some reference point. The Treaty is our reference point'. In 1988, Sir Charles Bennett, another 'Māori Knight', entered the fray as to what New Zealand should be called, saying that for his part 'Nu Tireni' would do, because that was the name it was given in that document. Mira Szaszy, ex-President of the Maori Women's Welfare League and a woman of great mana, told the Royal Commission on Social Policy that the Treaty was sacred.[18]

Sacred it might be. The Treaty was *also* a document which detailed Māori rights, which stood therefore as a measure as well as a sign of injustice, and which would be the basis of their claims to reparation.

Matiu Rata noted in 1975 during parliamentary debate on the creation of the Waitangi Tribunal that while the Māori saw the Treaty as 'a charter which protects their interests', they were even 'more conscious' of what had been lost by 'past injustices and accruing disadvantages'. He told the MPs that 'rightly or wrongly', Māori regarded the injustices and disadvantages as 'infringements or contraventions of the Treaty of Waitangi'. Injustice was defined in terms of the Treaty.[19] Pākehā might regard it as an unspecific contract, unspecific enough to operate as a symbol of harmonious racial association; the Māori knew its terms better, and saw that the Treaty had been dishonoured. At Turangawaewae in 1984 Rata put it more bluntly. The Treaty had been:

. . . long regarded by non-Maori opinion as a symbol, while our people have always regarded it as a reality. We are, after all, more aware of the losses incurred, lands alienated and the injustices. Much of which were in direct contravention of the spirit and letter of the Treaty. Were an individual or non-Maori group to suffer parallel wrongs and injustices, such would have been regarded as an infringement of their individual rights or an infringement of British justice. Little wonder that the Treaty has become a symbol for our discontent.

Eva Rickard talked of the Māori as seeing the Treaty as a 'symbol of the loss they have suffered since 1840'.[20]

---

[17] *Nga Korero Me Na Wawata Mo Te Tiriti O Waitangi*, pp. 153, 150. Contrast pp. 8, 9, 10-11, 19, 34a, 77, 125, 140, 150, 182-3.

[18] *Nga Take Maori*, 5/2/87. Cf. Mira Szaszy on the sacredness of the Treaty, *The April Report*, iii (1), 269.

[19] NZPD3:37, p. 4342. Compare the Caucus Committee Report of 5/2/74.

[20] Blank *et al.* (eds.), *He Korero*, pp. 25, 42.

The loss was an injustice, and it was this injustice that was expressed in the Waitangi Day campaigns, during the Land March, the Springbok Tour demonstrations, and the arguments about land and fishing claims. There was continued stress during the period of the first Waitangi Tribunal on the grief, anger, and feelings of injustice that possessed the Māori. Grief and despair for things irrecoverably lost, righteous anger – the feeling of injustice – because an equal had acted wrongly not only in taking particular things, but in doing so had arrogated power to itself at the expense of the mana and rangatiratanga of the tangata whenua. The Tribunal was not alone in pointing out the practical dangers of these emotions, how they could change to 'bitterness and resentment . . . suspicion and distrust; . . . contemptuous scepticism towards law and government'. Nor was it alone in seeing them not as blind passions, but as articulated responses to old and continuing wrongs. 'We saw such angry people giving evidence before us. They are no more than representatives of many others in our community. When one significant section of the community burns with a sense of injustice, the rest of the community cannot safely pretend there is no reason for their discontent. That is a recipe for social unrest and all that goes with it'. Paul Temm QC, a member of the first Tribunal, reported widely these sentiments too, in the press and to professional societies.[21] Mrs Tirikatene-Sullivan (Southern Maori) reiterated them in 1984 in asking the Parliament to 'appreciate that the sense of injustice has been considerable and is continuing'.[22]

If justice were to be done in these circumstances of solemn contract and passionate conviction that the contract had been broken, the justice would be justice in reparation.

Before 1975, Māori *take* (claims, grievances, demands) were typically local. But the first, and a continuing consequence, of the aggregation of Māori causes in the 1970s was to construct global and vague claims of 'Māori' against 'Pākehā'. There were suggestions for reparative payments en bloc from Pākehā to Māori, though the basis and quantum of the claims was never set out in much detail. In 1971 MOOHR (the Maori Organisation of Human Rights) proposed $800 million 'reparations for exploitation of the Maori race, taking our land, denigrating our culture, witholding all our basic human rights . . . for not holding to the Treaty of Waitangi'. In the same year Nga Tamatoa's demand to the Pākehā was: 'give us either the land that you confiscated or stole, or give us compensation equivalent to today's values'.[23] In 1974 a group of Tainui, considering arguments that the Treaty should be ratified,

---

[21] Waitangi Tribunal, *Te Reo Report* para. 6.3.9. See also 3.4.16-17; 6.1; 6.3.3; 8.2.3, as well as the *Manukau Report*, pp. 41, 44 (in para. 5.8), and 46-7 (para 5.12). Also Temm, 'The Treaty and Society Today', part II, EP:5/12/87. He delivered a longer version on this paper to the Auckland Medico-Legal Society and the Wellington District Law Society.

[22] NZPD41:1, p. 2706.

[23] MOOHR, Newsletter, September 1971; cf. Nga Tamatoa Newsletter, Ponsonby, March 1971.

told the Government that the Māori regarded it as sacred and binding and that it should 'offer compensation for all past transgressions of it'.[24]

As the protests continued, new (as well as old) local and precise claims were articulated. And the local and precise claims now took energy from the global and vague, and from the pan-Māori milieu in which they were discussed. The Land March of 1975 had as its global slogan that 'Not one More Acre of Maori Land' should be taken. Soon part of the leadership under Dr T. R. Sinclair of Hamilton began to work on the issue of reparations. They examined with much precision as they could muster a claim of Ngati Pukeko for the restitution of 20,000 acres wrongly confiscated for allegedly warring against the Government, a Tuhoe claim for compensation for 170,000 acres lost when they were moved inland from Opotiki on the Bay of Plenty, and a claim generated in 1975 when government contractors took a gravel island belonging to Tuwharetoa from the Tongariro River. Much of this was reported and commented on in the media.[25] Other claims surfaced. In November 1975, the tabloid paper, *Truth*, worried in a headline: 'Mt EGMONT . . . given back?'[26] The paper noted that the Government was in the process of 'giving the mountain back to its former owners because it had been wrongly confiscated'. From 1976 onwards there were the highly-publicized protests, arrests and court cases concerning the Tainui Awhiro claim to the Raglan Golf Course;[27] and from 1978 there was Bastion Point.[28]

By the end of the decade reparations were clearly a pantribal, pan group issue. In 1980, the New Zealand Maori Council articulated it; so did Mana Motuhake[29]. In 1981, its leader Matiu Rata, besides demanding again that the Treaty be ratified, now added: 'The New Zealand government must be made to pay their accounts to us. Whether by land or funds, or both, or by any other means, it must be paid'. Mana Motuhake, he said, 'wants the government to return all land wrongly taken'.[30] In 1981, 'Defiant kaumātua' of Northland were said to remember the prophesy that: 'What the Pakeha sought to disrupt the Pakeha will seek to restore; what the Maori has lost the Maori will seek to regain'.[31]

By the time of the Turangawaewae hui, the global demand for reparation was clear. One terse proposal said: 'Acts contravene [the Treaty]: Return

[24] AS8:19/5/74.

[25] P17:18/11/7; H5:11/6/75.

[26] T22-23:18/11/75.

[27] The cases are summarized in Maori Land Court, *Tai Whati*, pp. 225-8.

[28] A collection of Bastion Point material, notably copies of *Takaparawha*, the protestors' publicity organ, is collected in the unpublished R. J. I. Walker (ed.), *Bastion Point Tent Town*.

[29] NZMC, 'Discussion Paper', p. 5. Article 2 (c) of the Constitution and Rules of Mana Motuhake o Aotearoa (1980) had it as one of the purposes of the emerging party to 'foster and promote the lawful recognition and honouring of agreements and guarantees entered into in the Treaty of Waitangi, and to obtain reparations for past injustices. See Mana Motuhake in Finding List.

[30] H:18/6/81.

[31] *Tu Tangata*, August/September, 1981, p. 10.

all our whenua, fisheries and forests'; another, 'that the Churches return their considerable Maori land holdings to the Maori'.[32] A workshop recommended that the Churches undertake 'an enquiry into Maori land holdings, gifted, and where such land cease for the purpose of the gift, return the lands to the donors or the descendants of the original owners'.[33] Whanganui a Tara – doubtless thinking among other things of the city's Athletic Park which legislation prohibited them taking a decent rent from – asked that 'All Maori land, no matter of what category, be returned to the ownership of the original owners. Where leases exist these be allowed to run on unless the Maori owners wish to repossess the land because of special circumstances. In such cases equitable compensation be paid to the tenants.' Further, where complexity made the return of lands confiscated 'after War, etc' impossible, 'generous Compensation be granted'. It 'should run into hundreds of millions of dollars'.[34] Hikaia Amohia asked for the Wanganui River Tribes that the Treaty be ratified so that the Acts which contravened it would be thus voided and 'this will give our people power to claim for damage done to them'. He listed those statutes normally objected to, in effect updating Sir Henare Ngata's famous list of 1970. He mentioned, for instance, the Public Works Act (1931), the Soil Conservation Act (1941), the Rating Act (1967), the Mining Act (1971), the Town and Country Planning Act (1977), the Reserves Act (1977) and the Noxious Plants Act (1978). They encroached upon Māori rights to land by allowing it to be taken without consent for public works or to be mined, and to be rated when income was impossible to find; the Acts forbade the erection of buildings in a way appropriate to Māori lives, and they required expensive improvements and upkeep where the capital was not available; they allowed the pollution of waters with industrial and farm wastes. All these statutes were 'contrary to the Treaty'.

The hui resolved as a whole that 'not only should the beds of lakes and rivers be returned to the owners, but also all rights in respect to the water should belong to the owners'. And the Treaty was crucial to the claims. It was also resolved at Turangawaewae that the Treaty should be: 'the basis for claims in respect of land, forests, water, fisheries and Human Rights for the Maori people'. The Treaty was the measure of the wrongs that must be repaired.[35]

As a consequence of agreement at Turangawaewae that the various claims should be specified more precisely, most of the *take* at the Waitangi Hui of 1985 were demands – many of them demands with long histories – for reparations for past wrongs. There were reparatory claims to the bed of the Wanganui River, to Ninety-Mile Beach, to Owhata Road near Lake Rotorua, to lands at Whakarewarewa, to Te Reinga, to Parengarenga lands,

---

[32] Blank *et al.* (eds.), *He Korero*, p. 62.

[33] Blank *et al.* (eds.), *He Korero*, p. 86. See also pp. 88, 93, 94.

[34] Blank *et al.* (eds.), *He Korero*, pp. 74–5.

[35] Blank *et al.* (eds.), *He Korero*, pp. 1–5, 72–3.

lands at Pouto, at Stephenson's Island and in the Te Akau Block. There were demands that investigations with a view to reparation be undertaken into Tai Tokerau lands taken under the Wastelands and Surplus Lands Acts; and Tainui Awhiro asked that Governors' grants to churches of Māori lands 'should be investigated and this land returned to its rightful owners'. Te Maketu Action Committee reiterated a demand that the mouth of the Kaituna River be redirected to its old course so that the lagoon would again run clear and provide, as it used to, seafood for the local people. Compensation was demanded for undervaluation at sale of Māori assets in the Hokianga, and the reversal of an unsatisfactory exchange of land between the Government and the Hauai Trust.[36]

This was the reparatory passion that informed the demand that there should be an institution which would make reparations to the Māori. So when the Waitangi Tribunal was set up, it was universally argued by Māori groups and their supporters that it should have retrospective capacity. Redress of grievance was essential, and the grievances went back well before 1975. Parliament's committee on the Treaty of Waitangi Bill in 1975 was told that 'grievances concerning the Treaty relate to the past, and if the Bill is to be something more than window dressing its provisions should have retrospective application'.[37] To Rata's bitter disappointment, retrospective power was not granted.

However, in 1984 and 1985 the Government, with only some qualms, agreed to retrospection; for this was the demand of justice. The political pressure and the force of argument was too much to be resisted.[38] In 1985 Peter Tapsell had to admit that: 'there will be problems going back to 1840. This will be a difficult period to live through.' But what, he asked, was 'the option? The option is to turn our backs on justice and carry on as we are.'[39] Koro Wetere even faced head-on the argument that retrospection might reawake old grievances. 'That is a possibility, but we should note that the state of the law when those disputes were settled could well have been inconsistent with the principles of the Treaty. If that is so, should they not be re-examined in the light of those principles? . . . The Bill deals with deep-seated grievances that must be settled whatever the outcome, after having been dealt with by the authoritative judicial body in a Maori context.'[40]

Parliament had thus heard what its Select Committee on Maori Affairs was told when it considered the amendments to the Treaty of Waitangi Act.[41] It had heard too, the voices of the New Zealand Maori Council and every

---

[36] *Nga Korero*, p. 53-5 for a summary, p. 75 and following for individual *take*.

[37] GAL:MA/75/18, 24. See also especially documents 11/15/17/19/22 in the same collection.

[38] NZPD2:27, pp. 4342-3; 3:37, p. 4498; 1:41, pp. 2702, 2705, 2706-8, 5650, 6064-5, 6068, 6070, 6073-4, 6078-9.

[39] NZPD1:41, p. 6068. Cf. 2:37, pp. 5726, 5727; 3:37, pp. 4342, 4496-7, 4500, 5407; 1:41, pp. 2706, 6069-70, 6073, 6079-80.

[40] NZPD1:41, p. 6060.

[41] GAL: MA/85/2, 5, 6, 7, 8, 9, 10, 12, 16.

important hui calling for the power of retrospection.[42] It may have even heard that the Political Workshop at Turangawaewae chaired by Rata and Henare Davis had resolved that 'ratification [of the Treaty] be *defined* as "empowering the Waitangi Tribunal to survey and investigate land claims and issues retrospectively".'[43]

The other demand which the reparative passion informed was that the Tribunal should have powers of final adjudication and of requiring the executive to make reparations; and this was not so readily acceded to. The thought behind the demand was obvious. Justice is giving people their rights, not merely suggesting that they ought to be given them; and the legalism of reparation suggests that justice ought to be done by law courts not by legislators and the executive arm of government. After all, legislators and administrators have to consider things other than justice. Professor Hirini Mead argued the idea to the New Zealand Catholic Commission on Evangelisation, Justice and Development (the EJD Commission) and its audience in 1982.[44] It was also a theme of the hui at Ngaruawahia and Waitangi. There, various schemes were put forward for empowering the Tribunal or other quasi-judicial institutions. The case for a power of legal determination and control of the executive was summed up at Waitangi. Pat Hohepa held that the Tribunal's decisions ought to have the authority of an Appellate or High Court: 'The Government must never again be allowed to be the main arbiter.' It must simply 'satisfy adjudged grievances'. Tai Tokerau said, 'we see the Tribunal as the supreme authority in determining the rights deriving from the Treaty'; Manu Paul argued that the Amendment Act reforming the Tribunal 'should contain provision to correct injustices'; Ngati Awa as a whole agreed. In May 1985 Ripeka Evans conveyed the message of the two hui that 'the Waitangi Tribunal must be accorded Appelate Court status' to the Auckland seminar on a Bill of Rights attended by lawyers, academics, and the Minister of Justice (and Deputy PM) Rt. Hon. Geoffrey Palmer.[45] That justice should be done by the Tribunal itself was a dominant thought in the submissions to the Parliamentary Committees of 1975, 1985, and 1988.[46]

But the demand for adjudicative power was denied by the politicians (except when they were forced by the *New Zealand Maori Council* v *the Attorney General* to empower the Tribunal to cover land passed to SOEs). Nor was this result entirely disliked by influential Māori (except when it came to SOEs). The New Zealand Maori Council had avoided suggesting a power of final determination in 1983, and in 1986 Judge Durie endorsed the political, legal,

[42] *He Korero,* pp. 4–5, 35–6, 41, 86, 103; *Nga Korero Mo Te Tiriti,* pp. 23, 34a, 45, 51, 103–4, 114–15, 142.

[43] Blank *et al.* (eds.), *He Korero,* pp. 85–6. My italics.

[44] Mead, 'The Treaty of Waitangi and "Waitangi" '.

[45] At Waitangi, *Nga Korero,* pp. 44, 106, 140, 142. And at Turangawaewae, *He Korero,* pp. 4–5, 35, 103, 132. See Ripeka Evans, 'Is the Treaty of Waitangi a Bill of Rights?' in Sharp *et al.*, *A Bill of Rights,* p. 202.

[46] GAL:M/75/11, 17, 24; MA/85/2, 3, 10, 16; and others.

and bureaucratic establishment's continued view of the matter when he defended the Tribunal's lack of determinative power. He emphasized 'the political nature of most of the claims', and he thought it wrong that 'Maori claims should be constrained to fit the parameters of strict legal rights'.[47]

Political the issues may have been, and the Tribunal certainly dealt with them politically. Nevertheless it was the passion for reparation for breach of contract that was to face the Tribunal when it heard the claims. The treaty, the injustice of its violation, the demand for reparation. This was the recurring theme. It was well expressed in all its local and particular detail by Te Kaaho Wiremu Andrews, a young member of Ngati Paoa, when he spoke to the Tribunal in 1985 about land at Waiheke that had been lost to his tribe and which they now reclaimed. He stated that his tūpuna had been among those who signed the Treaty. Thus there could be no doubt that the Treaty was between 'US and THEM; our Tupuna and The Crown'. The Treaty indissolubly bound the signatories. It bound both parties because it was an oath in the sight of God, a 'witness . . . being the Supreme Being of all mankind; the Supreme being of Rangi and Papa (the Universe)'. God witnessed, blessed, and sustains this 'sacred agreement', this 'SPIRITUAL ACT OF MUTUAL TRUST'. The Treaty was an agreement therefore tapu and inviolable. But it bound Ngati Paoa in another and separate way: their tūpuna had 'honourably placed' their mana 'into the heart' of it. That mana, stated Andrews, still remained there, 'to this day'. That ancestral mana was binding on those who were their mokopuna – their inheritors.

The Honour of God, the Honour of the Crown, and the mana of Ngati Paoa were thus all invested in the keeping of the Treaty, Andrews stated; and to *keep* the Treaty was to 'honour' it. For their part Ngati Paoa had honoured the Treaty and kept their word; but 'the same [could not] be said of the other party (THEM)'. Through its agent, the Board of Maori Affairs, the Crown had acted in a manner contrary to the Treaty in regard to the land the return of which was at issue. More generally: 'Through acts of government, acts of law and acts of war, the Crown, time and time again', had 'acted contrary to the spirit (tapu) of the Treaty'. And '140 years of history showed that the Crown had NOT HONOURED THE SPIRIT OF THE TREATY; NOR KEPT ITS WORD'. It was 'GUILTY OF DISHONOUR TO THE TREATY' and thus 'GUILTY OF DISHONOUR TO GOD'. Andrews concluded with the demand for justice: 'WE DEMAND JUSTICE TO BE HONOURED'. The land should be returned.[48]

By the mid-1980s then, the Maori demand for justice for breach of the Treaty contract was an established one, so that when Joe Hawke heard in November 1987 that the Tribunal had recommended to the Government the return of sixty hectares and compensation of three million dollars to Ngati Whatua of Orakei, he responded that this was 'no more than justice'. 'The

---

[47] Durie, 'The Waitangi Tribunal: Its Relationship with the Judicial System', p. 236.

[48] Ngaati Paoa Whaanui, 'Submissions to the Treaty of Waitangi Tribunal', App. 6, no. 1, fols. 239–42.

wrongs . . . were not simple mistakes born out of ignorance. They were breaches of the Treaty of Waitangi'. 'So-called legal decisions' in the past were all of them unjust.[49]

II

The Pākehā Reformers and the Treaty

There was no doubt by 1987 of Māori participation in a Treaty culture. Between October and December that year the Department of Statistics carried out its 'Attitudes and Values Survey' for the Royal Commission on Social Policy. The findings of the survey indicated the degree and intensity of Māori support for the Treaty and its principles. Asked whether the Treaty of Waitangi ought to be taken into account by the Government when it was making economic decisions, 56 per cent of those describing themselves as of Māori ethnic origin thought it 'very important' that it should, and a further 21 per cent thought it 'fairly important'. Of those describing themselves as of 'Maori and European' ethnic origin, 26 per cent thought it 'very important' and 36 per cent 'fairly important'. The same two groups when asked the question of whether they would like to see the Treaty of Waitangi 'honoured', affirmed in even greater proportions that they would: 78 per cent of Māori agreed; 57 per cent Māori-Europeans. To the more precise question as to whether they would like to see 'Maori land returned', 64 per cent Māori agreed, as did 47 per cent Māori-Europeans. Clearly the Treaty, whatever its support among Māori in earlier years, was by 1987 firmly planted in their hearts and minds.[50] The tribunal thus lived its life in a burgeoning reparationary milieu. The milieu formed and sustained it. Without the milieu, it would have been a pointless institution, and it would have died.

The Pākehā public was much less convinced. Indeed it was on these Treaty and land issues, and these alone of the many researched for the Royal Commission on Social Policy, that Pākehā opinions differed significantly from Māori ones. The survey found only 8 per cent of those describing themselves as of European ethnic origin convinced that it was 'very important' and 26 per cent that it was 'fairly important' to take the Treaty into account in economic decision-making (compare the 56 per cent and 21 per cent Māori, and the 26 per cent and 36 per cent Māori-European response). Over half of them either thought it was 'not very important' (27 per cent: compare 10 per cent and 15 per cent) or 'not at all important' (26 per cent: compare 4 per cent and 18 per cent). Asked whether the Treaty ought to be 'honoured', many Pākehā (but not in nearly the same proportion as Māori) thought it should be: 44 per cent (compare 78 per cent and 57 per cent) agreed it should be, 19 per cent neither agreed nor disagreed (compare 8 per cent

---

[49] *Checkpoint:*26/11/88.

[50] *The April Report,* i, pp. 526, 530, 532.

and 21 per cent), 20 per cent disagreed (compare 6 per cent and 12 per cent). As to whether Māori land should be returned, only 20 per cent of Europeans thought it should be (compare 64 per cent and 47 per cent).

And what, after all, did the 48 per cent of Pākehā who would 'honour' the Treaty, *mean* by honouring? It may well be that many thought in a way long typical of Pākehā politicians and public commentators. As we have had Matiu Rata complaining, they had spoken of it as a vague 'symbol of unity' between the races, making of them 'one nation'. An editorial of the *Auckland Star* in February 1981 caught the general tone well when it commented adversely on the proliferating Māori view that the Treaty, 'far from being seen as a sacred article of our society, is taken to represent past injustices and grievances'. Trading symbol for symbol, the *Star* argued the Treaty to be a symbol not of injustice but of a unity projected into the future. 'In fact,' it said, 'the Treaty represents something a great deal more than injustice and grievance . . . It is a symbolic rallying point for racial cooperation . . . We cannot pin our failures past or present on an 1840 treaty, or make a scapegoat of Waitangi Day – the one day in the year when we should pledge ourselves to renew our endeavours as a nation'.[51]

Most Pākehā public talk about the Treaty during the 1970s and early 1980s was of this nature, asserting that the Treaty was a record and pledge of a good will which should continue to inform future relations. There was no question however as to whether or not the Treaty had validity or force in municipal law. Until the passage of section 9 of the SOE Act, requiring adherence to the 'principles of the Treaty', public comment followed the legal profession in thinking it did not; nor was there much interest in the legal profession (and even less among the public) as to its force in international law.[52] Only in so far as Parliament made its provisions law by statutory enactment would the Treaty have validity in municipal law; and no provision was currently valid law – except in the unlikely and obscure event that section 82(2) of the Fisheries Act, in speaking of 'Māori rights', meant 'Treaty rights'. And no doubt many could see the danger and the legal complications of thinking otherwise.

Māori accordingly thought the Pākehā gave the Treaty only 'lip service'; and so it might seem from the perspective of those who thought the Treaty ought to bind the Pākehā to past agreements, and that the agreements had been broken. The Pākehā however, had a purely symbolic and non-legalistic view of the Treaty – a mythology of the Treaty that ran parallel to and did not meet the Māori myth of te Tiriti. They simply had a different understanding of what the Treaty/te Tiriti required of the two peoples; and

---

[51] AS:3/2/81.

[52] See esp. Hackshaw, 'Nineteenth Century Notions of Aboriginal Title' (footnote 7 lists the authorities), in *Waitangi*, for an account of how domestic law treated the Treaty from 1840 onwards; on international law, see Kingsbury, 'The Treaty of Waitangi: some international law aspects'.

if challenged by te Tiriti (as Chapter 6 Section II will more amply show) the Pākehā proved capable of rejecting *both* versions.

The politicians though rejected it far less than the people; and then not seriously until 1987 when the Muriwhenua and Orakei issues began to bite. Their view in the 1970s and early 1980s was that of Matiu Rata who, when introducing the Treaty of Waitangi Bill in 1975, spoke for the Labour Party Caucus of the Treaty as 'an instrument of mutuality' between Māori and Pākehā. It was a 'contract of mutual respect and understanding' and the precondition of New Zealanders being 'one people'.[53] Government and Opposition alike agreed[54] with Hon. Whetu Tirikatene-Sullivan (Southern Maori) when she stated that the Māori had been treated as 'at least equals with Captain Hobson in 1840'. There was no outrage when she added that the Māori had 'tangata whenua status, [and thus] . . . prior proprietorial rights as a people with a certain sovereignty';[55] for nothing in particular hung on it, and she spoke also of the Treaty signifying 'the commencement of the nationhood of this country as we know it today'.[56] Typical of the Pākehā MPs, Mr Venn Young spoke of the Treaty as an 'unusual bond beween two civilizations', dear not only to the Māori but to other New Zealand citizens, 'who hold the obligations and the spirit . . . dear to their hearts and regard them almost as a human rights charter'.[57] The Maori Affairs Committees sitting on the Bills of 1974 and 1984 also heard this vague moralism, from Māori as well as Pākehā.[58]

What it did *not* add up to was the belief that the Treaty was a sacred contract whose every provision ought to have been respected, had not been, and that reparations were due for the violations.

There were, however, tendencies in this direction and they found some sympathy in Government circles by 1984. Echoes of the Māori view of the Treaty were picked up and amplified in the work of anti-racist – mainly church – groups in the mid-1970s. In the late 1970s the National Council of Churches, disgusted with the 1978 Bastion Point settlement, took up the theme 'that God's justice, and thus the making of laws which will obtain that justice, are major concerns of christian churches'.[59] In the early 1980s, largely inspired by the events of the Springbok Tour, a number of church groups came under the umbrella of the National Council of Churches[60] and

---

[53] NZPD2:37, p. 5728, quoting the Caucus Report of 5 February 1974, NA, MA/19/1/55/1, vol 2, fol. 382. Cf. NZPD3:37, p. 4496.

[54] Compare with the remarks of the Government's opponents, NZPD3:37, p. 434: 1.41, p. 2705.

[55] NZPD2:37, p. 5728; cf. 3:37, p. 4496.

[56] NZPD3:37, p. 4495.

[57] NZPD1:41, p. 2706; 3:37, pp. 4343, 5407.

[58] GAL: Box 10/1975, MA/75/10, 11, 17, 20.

[59] H6:8/2/81. Letter George Armstrong.

[60] See, for example, New Zealand Church and Society Commission, National Council of Churches, *What happened at Waitangi in 1983?* (Auckland 1983); New Zealand Church and Society Commission of the National Council of Churches, *The Pakeha and the Treaty: Signposts* (Auckland, 1986).

of the New Zealand Catholic Evangelisation Justice and Development (EJD) Commission,[61] and began a process of public education. In 1986 Project Waitangi was set up with government finance[62] and with Lady Reeves as its patron. It was in effect a coalition of existing groups and part of the continuing attempt to educate the Pākehā as to their 'responsibilities under the Treaty'.[63] At the same time, other politically active Pākehā – women and social workers, often in groupings like the Women's Transfer Fund – worked in various ways to discharge their 'obligations' and 'commitments' under the Treaty.[64]

This movement called in 1981 for a 'restudy of the Treaty' designed to lay bare past injustice. The Programme on Racism of the National Council of Churches spoke of Treaty dealings as 'an aspect of our history of which many of us are increasingly ashamed', and its Secretary wondered whether 6 February should be celebrated any more: 'Looking back, the Treaty of Waitangi was not a great event. We are celebrating something which the Maoris feel was an injustice'.[65] Besides the Salvation Army – who would not countenance not meeting at Waitangi, on grounds that the gospel was one of reconciliation – most mainstream churches came to agree. Church people dominated the protests at Waitangi in February 1983. Eleven were arrested and subsequently tried amidst great publicity. They asked their supporters to pray 'for all victims of past and present injustices. We recognise that for many things there can be no recompense: but we ask that you will make more demands of us for reparation than we would make of ourselves – and make us see through our excuses'.[66] After that, the theme of Pākehā reparationism was 'beyond guilt': the idea was that the Pākehā should *know* their guilt but then – because guilt was a 'negative' emotion which did not lead to action – transcend it and work to redeem the world. This was the theme of Project Waitangi's teachings, and of a series of National Radio broadcasts on such subjects as the destruction of Parihaka and the illegal imprisonment of its inhabitants. (But of course to go beyond guilt, one needs to feel guilty in the first place.)[67]

All this infuriated National Party politicians in their last years of office and it caused problems within the churches, which often found themselves divided into warring camps. Thus encouraged and fortified, by 1985 the Labour MPs were able to make the point about Treaty injustice much more emphatically than a decade before; and the Opposition could hardly disagree.

[61] GAL: MA/85/9, and see their Discussion Kitset, *New Hope for our Society* (1982-85).

[62] A52:21/9/88 sas $50,000 in 1987-88; NZPD1: 42, p. 5948 records $100,000 expenditure in 1988-89.

[63] See Project Waitangi, *Resource Kit*.

[64] 'Wanted: Your Money', *More*, May 1987, pp. 87-94.

[65] H1:3/2/81.

[66] Church and Society Commission, NCC, *What Happened at Waitangi in 1983?* (Auckland 1983), p. 95. See also the Baptist Union Submission on the Treaty to the Hikoi in November 1983: *He Korero*, p. 54.

[67] See for example, NCC, *Pakeha and the Treaty: Signposts*, pp. 18, 27, 57-60, 65-70; Radio New Zealand, *Beyond Guilt*.

Geoffrey Palmer, one of its main sponsors, was quite clear about the purpose of the Bill for the second Tribunal: it was 'to provide justice for people who have suffered from unredressed grievances'. Mr Noel Scott (Lab) argued that 'the basic problem of Maoridom is in many cases a feeling of resentment, a feeling that Maoris have not been well looked after and that they have not had justice'. His conclusion of the proposed second Tribunal was that: 'If we are looking for justice this is the way to get it'.[68] No Government MPs would disagree with Mrs Whetu Tirikatene-Sullivan that 'in the Māori world the fires still burn brightly', and 'justice denied must eventually be remedied'.[69]

But the politicians and reformers were far ahead of the people. Pākehā were probably just too individualistic and could not see what a Treaty made by a Governor 140-odd years ago had to do with them. When, in 1986, Mitzi Nairn of the NCC was asked what she made of the Treaty, she replied: 'For me the treaty is a basic document for this country with two sovereign people agreeing to share a nation. It was signed by my people by Hobson and on behalf of Queen Victoria.' But she noted a 'cultural thing' – a cultural difficulty – in Pākehā feeling bound by the Treaty. 'We are geared to be separate individuals and it's hard to think of myself as part of a people and being represented in some previous time. But I accept the treaty is a basic document for my people as it is for the Maori people . . . Maori people have always respected the treaty and put a lot of energy into hui and petitions and submissions. Now Pakehas have to understand what has been going on and get their act together'.[70]

Pursuing a strategy of persuasion that cut against the grain of a Pākehā tradition of individualist ignorance of the Treaty was a difficult task. Marianne L'Estrange noted the same problem as co-ordinator of Project Waitangi,[71] and Jane Kelsey probably did in February 1987 when she noticed among Pākehā a flagging of Treaty-centered reformist energy: a 'pervasive sense of exhaustion, lethargy and pessimism . . . Maori people continue to work just as hard or harder. What they have, and we lack, is a clear sense of purpose which is energising and which is moving forward'.[72]

If then there was a clear Māori reparationist view of the Treaty there was equally a powerful rejection of that view. Conflicts over the Treaty and its reparationary implications in fact accompanied the whole life of the Waitangi Tribunal, and provided the milieu of thought about reparations. The next chapter sets out to show how global Māori reparationism was rejected, and in doing so to show the logic of an ideological situation in

---

[68] NZPD2:27, pp. 4342-3; 3:37, p. 4498; 1:41, pp. 2702, 2705, 2706-7, 5650, 6064-5, 6068, 6070, 6078-9.

[69] NZPD1:41, p. 6073. Actually quoting Dr Evelyn Stokes of Waikato University, a submittant to the Committee of 1985. GAL:MA/85/6.

[70] *DST.* 18/12/86, reprinted in Project Waitangi, *Resource Kit*, Part 1.

[71] L'Estrange, 'Learning Anti-Racism'.

[72] Kelsey, 'The Treaty of Waitangi and Pakeha Responsibility'.

which it was impossible that reparatory justice should be done. This will set the scene for understanding the reparatory jurisprudence of the Tribunal – and its non-reparatory jurisprudence too. For it was the most notable characteristics of the Tribunal's activity that it neither fully pursued nor fully avoided either; and in this balancing act it expressed the real conflict of understanding in society at large.

Understanding the logic of the situation will also set the scene for understanding how the Tribunal, the Courts, the Labour Government, and elements of the bureaucratic élite came, from 1985 onwards, to erect yet another view of the Treaty: as an instrument of prospective justice and future-oriented policy, as containing not so much particular rights but as intimating rather a partnership between Māori and Pākehā. The Treaty was now held to express the wairua – the spirit – of partnership, and not the black letter legal requirements of a venerable, but outdated, document. This was a view of the Treaty starkly contrary to that which saw it as a repository of rights which, if violated, should be restored. It was the impossibility of reparative justice that brought about this remarkable ideological shift.

Chapter 6
The Difficulties with Reparations for Past Wrongs in the Case of the Māori v the Pākehā

I

Hard Cases in Reparation

The public debate about reparations in New Zealand/Aotearoa was mostly carried out at a very general and unspecific level. Despite the reasonable determination of the members of the Waitangi Tribunal and of those politicians who were knowledgeable and concerned to stick closely to particular cases and work them through one at a time in all their detail, the politicians and the people talked not so much about particular reparatory claims but about the very idea of there being these claims. It was as if there were, so to say, not *many separate* cases but *one big case*. When both claimants and respondents did debate particular claims, they related them to the overall picture. This reinforced the public presentation of the issues as one big case: as to whether 'the Pākehā' owed 'the Māori.'

This chapter shows how Pākehā perceptions were different from the Māori ones so far sketched, and it further seeks to evoke the milieu in which the Waitangi Tribunal operated to resolve not the one big case, but particular tribal cases. More immediately it shows what it was that made the one big case hard – even impossible – to decide. It was cultural difference. And it suggests how it is that if hard and impossible cases are actually decided, the loser feels that an injustice has been done and the authority of the decider may well be called into question. For as Voltaire once said: 'L'injustice à la fin produit l'indépendance.' (Injustice in the end produces independence).

But why was Māori v Pākehā a hard, even impossible, case? Because it departed so far from the conditions which make cases in reparation simple. Imagine a simple case. One morning William takes Vicky's bicycle in the sight of a group of small-town onlookers and runs off with it. He removes the bell for his own use and throws the violated machine into a nearby gully, where it is found at lunchtime by a passerby and returned to Vicky who has had to go to work in a taxi. Vicky naturally complains, and the next day William (who has attached the bell to his own bicycle) is brought before Judge Judex who pronounces him guilty of breaching a law against stealing and orders restitution of the bell in accordance with the normal judicial practice. The onlookers approve. They are also pleased that William is ordered to pay Vicky the price of her taxi fare to work in compensation for her not being able to use her bicycle while it was lost. Outraged at the breach of morals as well as law, they are delighted to hear Judex lecture William on his social responsibilities. Even William himself feels justice has been done, and thus shares the sentiments of all the other interested parties: judge, victim and onlookers. His greed and passion for bells had overcome him. Now he is ashamed and wishes to atone for his wrongdoing. He does not even mind paying a fine of 300 talens that Judex levies as a punishment on top of the reparations he has had to make by way of restitution and compensation.

That is a case in reparation for crime. In Anglo-American law there is also reparation for torts – roughly speaking non-criminal wrongs, as defined in law, done by one 'person'[1] to another. A simple case could be brought by Vernon against his neighbour Wanda for Wanda's absent-mindedly destroying Vernon's fruit tree when spraying her own garden. The idea would be to put Vernon back in the position he would have been in had the tort not occurred; so Judex orders Wanda to fix Vernon up with a new tree. The neighbours applaud and wonder at Wanda's eccentricity in insisting that Vernon had to take her to court to obtain such an obvious remedy. A final simple case in reparative justice may be taken from another area of Anglo-American (and New Zealand) law: contract. Wiremu has no particular relationship with Verity, but his firm enters into a contract with Verity, to create and tend a vegetable garden for her while she visits relatives in the Orkney Islands. Wiremu does not do what he has contracted to and is taken to court for breach of contract. He is ordered by Judex to bring Verity to the position she would have been in had the breached contract been honoured. He is ordered to provide vegetables and flowers to her in the abundance that could have been predicted had he kept his part of the bargain, and to prepare a garden plot for future use.

This case, it will be noted, differs from a case in tort or crime. In those cases the rule of reparation is to restore the Victims to their original positions before the wrong. In this case, the rule of reparation is that Wrongdoers should bring Victims to the position they would have been in at the time of trial, had the wrong not occurred, *and* the contract been kept. (Not the position the Victim would be in if the contract had not been made.) In some legal systems, notably in the USA and the Federal Republic of Germany, a doctrine of 'unjust enrichment' governs the nature and amount of reparation to be made. The basic idea is that no one should benefit from their wrong rather than that the victim should be restored to his or her rightful position. But perhaps the difference between that doctrine and the Anglo-New Zealand doctrine of reparation is one of the emphasis on one of the two basic elements of the wrongful transaction: the suffering of a wrong and the enjoyment of the benefit of the wrong. It is not so much that either element is ignored. In simple cases of crime, tort, and contract, wrongful benefit is certainly an element to be considered.

These simple cases share features which differentiate them from hard cases,

---

[1] By 'corporate' and 'artificial' persons as well as natural flesh and blood ones.

and to see why hard cases *are* hard it is as well to specify them. In simple cases of reparation the Interested Parties (IPs) are members of a unified society. It is unified in that everyone agrees on the rules that should govern their behaviour, and so it is a society where legal norms or laws (LN) and moral norms (MN) pretty much coincide. Again, in simple cases of reparation the Wrongdoer (W), the Victim (V) and the Judge (J) are all known and agreed to. There is no dispute as to the identity of V and W, and no dispute as to J's authority to hear their case. In simple cases too, sharing conceptions of what things are wrong, the parties to cases in reparative justice also agree on the fact of the wrong at issue's having occurred. Perhaps onlooking IPs (Os) saw the incident in question and W cannot deny it; perhaps there is no dispute as to its occurrence by W. In any case, there is no dispute as to whether, if the action alleged by V did take place, it was *wrong*, for all agree on LN and MN as providing the standards for recognizing wrong acts as wrong. Finally the IPs (W, V, J, Os and others of the society) also share conceptions of what it would be to right the wrong at issue. They agree, that is, on the rules of reparation (RR), hardly bothering to distinguish legally correct reparation from the morally correct remedy.

This analysis is evidently needlessly complex and cumbersome to express what are simple matters. It certainly lacks the grace and style of a good story. But it is undertaken, not to capture the essence of simple cases, but rather in an attempt to understand why hard cases are hard, and why, in particular, the One Big Case between Māori and Pākehā was to be plagued by vehement disagreement, and by uncertainty and hesitancy. The reason was that the further from being met any of these conditions are, the harder the case of compensation. But this is to get too far ahead of the argument. The conditions in which the issues of reparation are simple must be formalized still more, so that the hard cases can be dealt with according to a coherent system, and more precise reasons for their very hardness suggested. Here C1 to C10 will stand for the 'Conditions' I think are most important. This is not the only formalization possible, and I miss out excuses and countervailing considerations that might make otherwise simple cases *still harder*; but it will do:

C1. There exists among IPs (all interested members of society) an agreement as to the rules or norms (N) which should govern their behaviour.
C2. The IP's agreement is such that there is no difference between the content of legal and moral norms (NL and NM).
C3. A wrong is known by all IPs to have been done.
C4. The identity of the wrongdoer (W) is known.
C5. The identity of the victim (V) is known.
C6. W benefited from the wrong.
C7. V suffered from the wrong.
C8. There is an agreed court of morals or law with a judge (JM for morals: JL for law) armed with the authority to pronounce a verdict and have it enforced if necessary.

C9. There are rules of reparation governing the nature and quantum of remedies (RR).

C10. W is brought to the bar of law (JL) or of common opinion (JM).

C11. In these conditions, then W must make reparation to V of kind (K) and quantum or amount (Q). V has a right to reparation: a legal right if the decision was made in a court of law, a moral one if the judgment was made by the public in a 'court of morals'.

Leaving aside excuses, overriding considerations and so on, the pure logic of the practice of reparations would be (briefly and informally put) thus: *If Condition 1, and if Conditions 2 and 3 . . . 10 are met, then (C11) reparations of a certain kind and quantum are due.* The conditions, it might be thought, are individually necessary and jointly sufficient for reparations. But to speak of a pure logic of necessary and sufficient conditions is to get things wrong. Not all the conditions *are* necessary, and it is hard to say what combination of them is sufficient. If some condition is missing it does not follow that there is no case at all for reparations. It does not even follow that it is a hard case. Say (as is common and might well have occurred in Vicky v William) that W and V dispute whether a wrong was done and the onlookers are divided; but say also that J is quite clear. Then the full truth of C3 is not a necessary condition. Or say that (because circumstances alter cases so much) it will often not be clear that C9 exactly indicates the precise kind and quantum of reparation. Judex may have precedent cases of bicycle bells before; but what to make of William's repairing what turned out to be an originally faulty bell for his own use? Should Vicky pay for the repair job? Judex (say) decides confidently enough, and here the absolute clarity of the rule of reparation is not a necessary condition for reparation. (Though if it had been Vicky's useless computer which William had, brilliantly and with great pains, fixed?) Finally, say (though this would not be likely in the Vicky v William case) that many people doubt whether (or do not *really* think) a wrong was done, but that they suppress their knowledge and say publicly that it was. Or vice versa. These would then be easy cases, though only because of insincerity and bad faith.

There is not actually a pure logic of reparations at all. It is rather that there is a cluster of conditions that generate harder and easier cases according to their presence or absence (or degree of presence and absence) in various combinations; and as to deciding whether there is a right to reparation, it is a question of weighing the degree to which each condition is met and judging how far the absence of any condition alters cases. The point for the moment is simply this: that the further cases in reparation move from being ones where the rules for recognizing wrongs, the facts at issue, the identity of the parties, the right of jurisdiction and the rules of reparation are agreed to, the harder they are. And there are points at which reparative justice is impossible: if, for instance, it cannot be agreed that a wrong was done, or what authority should decide on the kind and quantum of reparation. This was the case that public debate revealed in Aotearoa/New Zealand.

II

The Impossibility of Global Reparation in Aotearoa/New Zealand

The hardness – actually the impossibility – of the one big case between Māori and Pākehā was, on the analysis given so far, undeniable. If 'the Māori' had a conception of justice in reparation, so did 'the Pākehā'. The conceptions were commensurable without difficulty; but what the one asserted, the other denied. An acquaintance with Pākehā argument in the 1980s would suggest as much; an analysis of that argument judged against the conditions for easy cases in reparation demonstrates it.

C1.   There exists among IPs (all members of society) an agreement as to the rules or norms (N) which should govern their behaviour.

There was no agreement as to the detailed rules and values which should govern New Zealanders/Aotearoans. Indeed the period saw attempts to provide accounts of a 'Māori' value system in stark contrast with that of the 'Pākehā'; and distinctions were (rightly) made between 'Pākehā law' and 'Māori lore'. But without a common set of standards (denied in the contrast) there simply cannot be justice. It was perhaps for this reason that the claimants, and to a degree the governing classes, turned with such vehemence to the Treaty of Waitangi. For here, whatever the differences in Māori and Pākehā norms and values, lay (it might be thought) a common set of rules. They could even be thought of as a fundamental set of rules, or at least a set of general principles of partnership which – because they had been mutually constructed in contract – should override all other values and rules in cases of conflict. The Treaty would allow both binding agreement *and* the diversity of morals.

The Treaty, however, simply did not deliver a common set of rules. It was not the source or locus of shared conventional understanding that the easy working of reparative justice required. Some embraced it, some rejected it, some did not know or care about it. It was in two languages. Its terms were porous, were capable of multiple application, and the interests of the protagonists led them to stress different interpretations.

It was in this context that the Waitangi Tribunal worked to construct a single, 'melded' interpretation. But the very circumstances which called for the attempt denied its success. For instance it was common for respondents to Māori claims to insist on Article 3 of the Treaty as the most important one. This was the article which gave Māori the 'same' rights as Englishmen, not 'special' ones. Mrs Hilda Phillips was a particularly indefatigable maker of this point from 1974 onwards. As the scales had fallen from Hana Jackson's eyes when she read the Treaty, so they fell from Mrs Phillips' when she read that the White Paper on Maori Affairs of 1973 proposed that anyone with any degree of Māori ancestry might choose for legal purposes to be

'Māori'.[2] She opposed special treatment as a violation of Article 3; she even opposed using the distinction of names.[3] And she was far from alone. Other opponents of Māori claims, especially after the publication of *The Muriwhenua Report*, argued that the English version of the Treaty that gave the Māori rights to 'forests and fisheries' as well as lands was simply a 'draft' – 'the original motion for discussion that was amended to become the final resolution as signed by the chiefs'. The Māori version, and the correct English one, did not include 'forests and fisheries' at all.[4]

Besides disagreement as to its detail, and despite what parliamentarians and other public figures kept saying about the symbolic importance of the Treaty, there was in fact no solid agreement on the Treaty's moral force: as to whether it *was* a contract, as to who had taken it and was bound by it, and as to whether it retained in current conditions its obligatory force. In 1983 the Catholic Commission for Evangelisation Justice and Development told a Parliamentary Committee dealing with the Waitangi Tribunal's findings in the *Te Atiawa Report* of 'culpable ignorance [about the Treaty] on a major scale' among the Pākehā populace. Other statements of the educational problem were common throughout the 1980s.[5]

On Waitangi Day, 6 February 1988, the New Zealand Maori Council put a full page advertisement in the main newspapers which printed the Treaty on the 148th anniversary of its signing. 'For most of you', it said, 'the Treaty has no meaning, you have never seen its text, nor do you believe that it has any impact on your lives . . . To help you to understand why the New Zealand Maori Council and other Maori bodies have recently successfully challenged the Government in the courts, using the Treaty, we give you this complimentary copy.' To little effect: reformers' contributions to the Royal Commission on Social Policy's discussions on 'Treaty issues' in late January 1988 noted a continuation of Pākehā ignorance and apathy. The Treaty was thought merely to be 'a Māori thing'.[6] Dr Mason Durie, a member of the Commission, noted that 'Maori submissions accorded much greater importance to the Treaty as a blueprint for national development in contrast to many other views which saw little in the Treaty as a guide to future social policies'.[7]

Though there is no doubt the reformers had made *some* headway, many Pākehā remained sceptical of or outright hostile to the Treaty. Accordingly, people who wanted to see the Treaty honoured made suggestions that it

[2] McDonald, *The Kiwis Fight Back*, pp. 168-70 and following.

[3] Besides her voluminous newspaper correspondence, see her pamphlet *Let the Truth be Known*.

[4] See also Hiii5:8/1/86. Letter, Nelson Blake.

[5] Archdiocese of Wellington Commission for EJD to The Secretary, Commerce and Energy Parliamentary Select Committee, 31 May 1983, p. 4. See, agreeing: Claudia Orange, 'The Treaty of Waitangi', pp. 2, 5; Archdiocese of Wellington Commission for EJD, Seminar 'Understanding Waitangi', p. 7; 'Understanding Waitangi II', pp. 2-3; MOOHR Newsletter, December 1970, p. 2, quoting Gabrielle McLeod, 'Race through Time', NZBC, 29 Oct 1970.

[6] *The April Report*, iii (1), pp. 234, 251, 253.

[7] Durie, 'The Treaty of Waitangi – Perspectives on Social Policy', p. 281.

should be renegotiated: Hiwi Tauroa (then the Race Relations Conciliator) tried in 1982; and Michael King in 1983 urged a 'new covenant' which would 'embody the principles that all parties believed were or should have been in the original treaty'.[8] But there were far less friendly reasons for suggesting a 'rethink' of the Treaty. In the high summer of 1987-1988, Mr Ralph Maxwell, a Labour MP and Under-Secretary of the Ministry of Agriculture and Fisheries, attempted to argue that it should be 'renegotiated'. No doubt expressing the anger and frustration of the Ministry of Agriculture and Fisheries, and of the commercial fishing industry, at the unforeseen complications of Māori claiming Treaty fishing rights, he stressed the vagueness and uncertainty surrounding the meaning and implications of the Treaty. The *Herald* reported him thus: 'He said he believed there was widespread acceptance of the need to redress legitimate Maori grievances. But efforts to resolve disputes had raised seemingly intractable problems with the interpretation of the Treaty of Waitangi . . . It would be helpful if Dr Gregory (MP, Northern Maori) or anyone could make a clear statement about what justice in this matter is.' Maxwell could see further problems too: even were agreement as to the meaning of the Treaty reached, 'then we would get into the problem of defining Maoridom and identifying who the applicants for rulings should be and who should benefit from them.' Maxwell even found himself having to deny in Parliament that he had urged the abolition of the Treaty.[9]

Others came at least close. In June and July, Mr Dover Samuels, the Māori representative on the New Zealand Council of the Labour Party, suggested a referendum as to whether or not the Treaty should be allowed to continue to play a part in national life. He clearly suspected many thought not. His party overruled his initiative, but in August Mr Bob Martin of the Commercial Fishermens' Association collected $300,000 and 5,000 signatures to support a process of education, renegotiation, referendum – and extinction.[10] In August the annual National Party conference was pretty much divided on a suggestion that the Treaty was outdated and should be renegotiated or abolished. Throughout the year, newspaper correspondents reminded the country that 'many chiefs did not sign the Treaty'[11], that there was indeed no full record as to who had and what tribes they represented, and (entirely wrongly) that the Treaty had never been taken for signing to the South Island.[12]

It was mainly Pākehā responses to Māori claims of the importance of the Treaty which included utter denial of its binding force because of the passage of time. 'Was it ever intended', asked the *Herald* 'that the Treaty should be inviolate, incapable of reform as new circumstances demanded?

---

[8] H10:21/9/83; AS2:20/9/83.

[9] H5:5/12/87. See also H1:4/12/87; H6:25/1/88; GMNZ:7/12/87: *Checkpoint*: 4/12/87; NZPD1:41, p. 4784 (28 June 1988).

[10] H1:3/6/88.

[11] AS10:15/2/88.

[12] AS10:15/2/88.

If so, it must be one of the few such compacts in history'.[13] It was a common argument in the 1980s that the treaty was 'ancient' and 'outdated'; and the point was merely reiterated in 1988 by Hon. Jim Bolger, the Leader of the Opposition, by Winston Peters, the emerging contender for his leader's mantle,[14] and by Sir Robert Muldoon, now a popular back-bencher.[15]

It must be concluded that even if piety required from politicians public expressions of reverence for the Treaty, there was at the very least no agreement that common rules of right were laid down in it. The IPs were not at one. An opinion poll of July 1988 found that 4 per cent wanted the Treaty to have the force of law, 24 per cent wanted it dealt with through the Waitangi Tribunal, 9 per cent wanted it renegotiated and then *not* given the force of law, 25 per cent wanted it renogotiated and then given the force of law and 28 per cent wanted it abolished.[16] R. J. S. Munroe (Opp) commented darkly on this poll in Parliament the following September, noting that '62 per cent of New Zealanders are not satisfied with the Treaty of Waitangi', and wondering what the 'real issues' were.[17]

C2. The IP's agreement is such that there is no difference between the content of legal and moral norms. (NL, and NM)

In these conditions of vehement moral disagreement among IPs there was disagreement as to whether or not, and if so then to what degree, the Treaty was or should become part of the law of the land. The combinations of belief were many. Those who said the Treaty *was* morally binding were inclined alternatively to lament its non-inclusion in law and demand its 'ratification', or else to think it should be supreme law overriding all particular laws that conflicted with it, or else to argue that even though morally binding, it could not become law because if it did then there would be 'one law for the Pākehā and another for the Māori'. On the other hand those who thought it *no* standard of justice at all were pleased that it had not been adopted as a whole into law, they lamented even the limited effect given it by judges and in statute, and they too, stressed the necessity of Māori and Pākehā being under 'one law'.[18]

In the event, a combination of legislative and judicial action (to be discussed in Chapter 9) retrospectively created a fundamental constitutional law for New Zealand which included the 'principles of the Treaty'. But the legalization of the Treaty, being a matter of state, progressed rather more than its being pressed to the bosom of the Pākehā. And if the provisions of the Treaty were to be taken seriously, and not its 'principles', legal and moral norms

---

[13] H6:25/8/88.

[14] DST2:18/6/88.

[15] AS2:20/9/88; H15:21/9/88.

[16] H1:26/7/88 quoting an *N.Z. Herald*-National Research Bureau survey.

[17] NZPD1:41 (15 Sept 1988), p. 6616.

[18] Hiii:24/3/88.

certainly did not coincide, leaving a tension between the two that made purely 'legal' solutions to questions of reparation out of the question. Very few Pākehā thought, for instance, that the Māori owned the sea; plenty of Māori thought they did;[19] the (legal) doctrine of aboriginal rights suggested one thing; the (quasi-legal) Treaty another. Hence faced with the High Court injunctions against the further issue of Individual Transferable Quotas (ITQs), Geoffrey Palmer stressed the need for a 'modern, practical approach by a process of negotiation' and he argued that litigation was not the way to go.[20] By mid-1988, the *National Business Review* was approving his finally having seen that a 'political settlement to Maori land, fish and devolution issues' was what was called for.[21] In a condition of high tension between the two sets of norms this had to be expected. When a 'political' solution was attempted in Parliament in September, it was attacked by the Opposition, not for being a *political* solution, but for being a badly engineered political solution.[22]

C3. A wrong is known by all IPs to have been done.

The conditions for the knowledge of wrongdoing are two: that (as per C1 and C2) there be agreed standards of right and wrong; and that agreeing on standards, witnesses (or uncontroverted records) attest to the occurrence of actions that unambiguously meet the standards of wrong. Neither of these conditions was attained in the public debate on the Treaty and on reparations.

Because the meaning of the Treaty was unclear and its obliging force doubted, the history of past wrongs as a history of Treaty breaches was beside the point for many Pākehā. As to whether it was wrong – besides the Treaty – that the Pākehā and their Governments should have taken Māori land and waters, gone to war against them, and the like: even these were denied to be wrong. A common argument was that if there was conquest and the imposition of rule and confiscation of territory, this was no more than the Māori in their times used to do to one another.[23] To the dismay of scholars as well as polemicists, many Pākehā letters to newspapers and contributors to radio talkback shows spoke of the Māori genocide of the 'Moriori' of the Chatham Islands. And in the same vein they spoke of the intertribal warfare, especially in the Far North, Auckland, Taranaki and Cook Strait areas in the 1830s.[24] It was also argued that even if Māori culture *had* been suppressed by the Pākehā and assimilation attempted, this was no more than was demanded by not only the facts of their warlike habits, but

[19] See later in this Chapter, in Chapter 7, Section II and in the *Manukau Report*, Section 6.

[20] GMNZ:3/12/87.

[21] Colin James in NBR7:19/8/88.

[22] NZPD1:42 (22 September 1988), p. 6888.

[23] NZL5:4/1/86. Letter D. J. Round.

[24] AS8:17/10/84, Letter Trevor Martin; AS6:7/1/85, Letter Recorder; H6:31/1/85, Letter 'Concerned Arawa'; H6:25/5/81, Letter F. E. B. Molesworth.

also Māori practices of slavery, paganism, subjection of women, and cannibalism.[25] If the Māori rebelled in the 1860s against the Government, then the Government was justified in putting down rebellion and confiscating lands as punishment. If there were lands the Māori 'owned' but did not use and left as 'waste', then the Pākehā settlers were justified in taking it and putting it to productive use, under the plough or mouth of the sheep. And why should 'unoccupied' land not be used? 'By the laws of nature and Maori customary law, the European had exactly the same right to occupy unoccupied New Zealand land as the Maori.'[26] And how much worse it would have been for the Māori, it was often argued, if the French or Americans, and not the British had annexed the place? 'Atareta Poananga [a member of Te Ahi Kaa and a protagonist for absolute Māori sovereignty] should be extremely thankful that it was a white race that colonised this country and doubly so that it was British', observed one of the less temperate correspondents.[27]

Some argued that it was a 'myth' that 'Maori problems can be laid at the white man's door'.[28] Some, equally brutally, suggested that the Māori should pay reparation for ancestors killed by them during peaceful negotiations and for other evils done.[29] Others argued that the Māori chose to lose their language: 'they had a language and they forgot it', and wrongly blamed the Pākehā for a choice they now regretted.[30]

Many, Māori as well as Pākehā, argued that, far from wronging the Māori, the Pākehā and Pākehā civilization had proved a benefit to the Māori. Peace was substituted for tribal war, and legal title to lands for a title based on conquest; a stable system of individual title replaced the unstable and now unusable communal one of old;[31] Christianity was introduced, and the benefits of prosperity and technology. One correspondent spoke typically of the 'immense material benefits that the indigenous (but not "original") race had derived from European colonisation'.[32] Many attested to the improvement in Māori living standards with the colonization of the Pākehā; and a private correspondent married a quasi-conquest theory of Pākehā domination to assertions of the spiritual as well as material benefits that the Māori had reaped: 'This country is gripped by a cold war instigated mainly by part-Maori activists who refuse to accept the verdict of history on a primitive stone-age culture in contact with a preferred European race. Religious apostasy has

---

25 AS12:5/12/86, Letter John F. Booth.

26 AS6:28/11/86, Letter M. Fraser. See also NZL5:4/1/89, Letter D. J. Round.

27 AS6:6/9/85, Letter J. Baker.

28 AS6:15/7/82, Letter J. R. Hooker.

29 H10:9/2/83, Letter P. M. Walker.

30 AS8:30/4/84, Letter 'Another New Zealander'.

31 AS6:24/8/81, Letter Kuku Karaitiana; SS6:24/7/88, Letter Jack Nicolson; Hilda Phillips, *Let the Truth be Known*, pp. 1-3 especially.

32 H6:8/8/85, Letter George Riddle. See also H6:22/2/84, Letter 'Demos'.

tended to obscure the verdict in recent years, making Polynesian paganism more acceptable.'[33]

These were extreme views, trenchantly put by a passionate minority absolutely convinced of the justice of their case. There is no doubt that some Pākehā did not know *what* to think and stuck with the New Zealand habit of therefore saying nothing to aggravate things. But no doubt, too, many more or less agreed with the articulate minority. It is not possible to give a measurement of adherence to what can only be *called* the 'Pākehā' theory of the past and its moral lessons. But over all the impression to be gleaned from the media, and what social surveys there were, was that around a fifth of Pākehā (with variations as to occupation and social situation) did in fact recognize that wrongs had been done, but were very unsure as to what they were and what might be done about them. About a half seem not to have recognized wrongs at all, and the rest did not know what to think.[34] The uncertainty of the few, combined with agreement of the many with the passionate denials of wrongs, did not provide that widespread and easy agreement that would be necessary for the Māori claims to be simple cases in reparation.

C4. The identity of the wrongdoer (W) is known.

Controversy as to the identity of the wrongdoer or wrongdoers was endemic. There were exceptions,[35] but most Māori Treaty argumentation suggested that it was the New Zealand Governments (and not the Pākehā) which had done the wrongs. This had the advantage, in naming a corporate and impersonal wrongdoer, of not only avoiding naming the 'Pākehā' as the wrongdoer and exacerbating ethnic conflict, but of overcoming problems of personal identity through time. For while individual Pākehā wrongdoers might perish, corporate ones do not – at least, not in the same way. In general too, the idea of the Crown as wrongdoer (but not the literal British Crown which was petitioned for help) suggested that only the Crown was liable to make reparation; and the Labour Government of 1984 onwards was at continual pains to suggest that the Crown, and not individual Pākehā, was the respondent.

However, the idea that it was 'the Pākehā' and individual Pākehā who were the wrongdoers, and therefore liable to make reparation, was never far from consciousness and was often raised. Māori racial prejudice, and sometimes political calculation, led some to blame the Pākehā for the past; Pākehā prejudice, and Pākehā calculation, saw claims against the Pākehā and individual Pākehā lurking behind every claim against the Crown. 'Mr Palmer assures us that the fear apparent throughout the country in respect of claims to the Waitangi Tribunal by Maori tribes was quite unjustified as the claims were not against individuals but against the Crown', reported one letter

---

[33] AS6:13/8/82, Letter G. F. Spencer.

[34] *The April Report*, i, p. 532 and the other tables on Treaty issues.

[35] *The April Report*, iii (i), pp. 229, 236.

writer, continuing, ' . . . that might be most reassuring if the Crown were some fairy Godmother but, as I understand it, the Crown is the Government of New Zealand – the people of New Zealand.'[36]

Reparations is a dish better served hot. When it is not, there are always incoherencies and contradictions consequent on the lapse of time and what has occurred in the interim. When the Waitangi Tribunal legislation was under contemplation in 1975, the Secretaries of Justice and Maori Affairs had thought for that reason that some sort of limitation to retrospection should be introduced: 'There must be a limit to the reopening of what has been decided and resuscitating the past.'[37] And hence, in legal systems, the doctrines of limitations in statute law and laches in torts. Common debate elaborated the core ideas. Politicians said that normally there was a six year limit 'in our law';[38] the wrongs were said to be 'ancient', thus hard to specify now, and anyway better forgotten.[39] And how could individual guilt be inherited? 'We may approve or condemn the actions of our ancestors, but we cannot be held responsible for them. To talk emotively of a Pakeha "heritage of guilt", is as silly as talking of a Maori "heritage of savagery".'[40]

Members of Parliament, editorialists and people joined in condemning the idea that present Pākehā should suffer for the sins of their ancestors – and to deny the existence of relevant ancestors. Ben Couch seems to have invented the tradition in 1979: he was reported as 'having a joust' . . . . at those Maoris who want the 'sins of yesterday's grandparents' to be visited upon 'today's grandchildren'.[41] A church submission on the bill for the second Waitangi Tribunal thought it would be wrong to 'visit the sins of the fathers . . . upon their children unto the third and fourth generations'.[42] And what of those Pākehā whose ancestors were not in the country when the Treaty was signed? What of those with Irish ancestors who could hardly be considered to have been bound by the act of a foreign government they hated and were finally successfully to resist? What of those who had genetically and culturally inherited from both peoples?[43] The underlying problem was this: if the actual responsibility was not to be sheeted home with precision, there could be 'little point in digging up the past in a sense of retribution, for if there is to be retribution, from whom will it be exacted, or to whom would there be benefit?'[44]

Only a few Pākehā joined Māori activists in speaking clearly and

[36] H3:30/7/88.

[37] Secretary of Justice to the Secretary Maori Affairs, 18 June 1975. GAL:MA/19/5/55/1.

[38] NZPD1:42 (15 Sept 1988), p. 6616.

[39] Sir Robert Muldoon at H5:20/6/88.

[40] H10:9/2/83; Letter G. L. Pearce.

[41] AS8:2/5/79; another example of many at AS8:7/8/85.

[42] GAL:MA/85/15. Submission of the Session of St. Andrew's on the Terrace.

[43] H10:9/2/83, Letter 'Bitzer'.

[44] GAL:Box 10, 1975. MA/75/13.

unequivocally of Pākehā guilt and the need to 'make amends'.[45] 'I, for one, will not be repented for by any member of any church or body', said a typical letter to a newspaper in 1983.[46] And repenters were lambasted by Winston Peters as 'sickly white liberals' in February 1988. In July Peters was to poll as the politician 'most New Zealanders would prefer as Prime Minister'.[47]

C5. The identity of the victim (V) is known.

As the identity of the wrongdoer was controverted, so was the identity of the victim. The crudest assault was simply this: that people who were not of pure Māori ancestry could not claim the fruits of reparation. There were letters to newspapers objecting to the idea that 'if you have an infinitesimal portion of the blood of those [first, Maori] arrivals you are completely acceptable to share the goodies'.[48] Reflecting on an argument from genetic inheritance, another letter-writer had it that: 'a half caste Maori, having blood equally of the oppressor and the oppressed parties should have no entitlement; and a quarter-caste Maori should be three times more liable to pay compensation than to receive it'.[49] The mixed blood theme was played endlessly in newspapers letters and talkback shows,[50] as was its corollary, that New Zealanders were all 'one people' and that 'extremists' should not be allowed to foment differences between them.

Since the opponents of reparations scarcely recognized the continuing importance of tribal organization, they did not, by and large, even address themselves to the question as to whether there had been wrongs done to tribes: to their existence, their mana, their rangatiratanga, their tikanga (values) and so on. Nor was the question much addressed as to whether, even if genetic inheritance were mixed, tribal identity persisted, damaged but intact, through time, and that it was the tribes who were owed reparation. When these issues were addressed by opponents of reparation, they were dismissed as displaying an atavistic romanticism best set aside in the face of the modern world.

C6. W benefited from the wrong.

No one argued that the Pākehā had not benefited from living in New Zealand. But many disputed that the benefits had come as a consequence of the

---

[45] For example, Dr Bruce Hucker, *Inner City News* 14:30/1/88, and other reformers discussed in Chapter 5, Section II.

[46] H10:9/2/83, Letter Winsome M. Rouse. See also H8:7/10/88, Letter D. Holm.

[47] H3:25/7/88.

[48] AS12:5/12/86, Letter John F. Booth.

[49] H6:9/8/85, Letter 'Real Maoris Only'.

[50] H6:9/2/84, Letter R. W. M.; H6:22/2/84, Letter 'Demos'; H11:2/7/88, Letter Braemar Anderson; Hiii3:13/2/88, Letter D. MacMaster.

exploitation and oppression of the Māori, and many praised the blood, sweat, and tears which the Pākehā (and Māori) had put into improving the country. There was no unjust enrichment. Mr Bob Jones, a rich and popular figure, who also founded and led the ultra-liberal New Zealand Party (August 1983 – July 1985), probably expressed a wide-spread sentiment when he claimed it was that, mainly the Pākehā – with their dedication to work, thrift, ingenuity and honesty in dealings – who had made the country great.

C7. V suffered from the wrong.

This condition was much controverted as per C3 and C5; and more will be said of it when the Pākehā idea of justice as equality is discussed in Chapter 10, Section I. Briefly, the very idea that the Māori suffered *now* as a consequence of past wrongs was condemned as self-seeking, self-defeating, and 'moaning'. Many espoused the ideal of equality of opportunity, and claimed that the Māori had long had it, had not used it sufficiently, and had only themselves to blame for the disadvantages they suffered. 'Every day,' a letter writer complained, 'encouraged by the media, the myth is repeated until it is hardly respectable to question it: Maori problems can all be laid at the door of the "white man's system". Canon Hone Kaa [frontsman on a TV programme] has said so, and he is echoed by an assortment of clerics, newspaper columnists, academics and social workers. On the day these people recognise the myth for what it is, the first step will have been taken to cure the ills that beset the Maori people.'[51] Radical clerics, irresponsible journalists, ivory-tower academics and wimpish social workers were among the most commonly ridiculed figures in New Zealand. They and the Māori had invented an intolerably wrong account of the sources of current inequality. In fact, the Māori themselves were to blame.

C8. There is an agreed court of morals or law with a judge (JM for morals: JL for law) armed with the authority to pronounce a verdict and have it enforced if necessary.

It scarcely bears saying that in the absence of common agreement there was no 'public opinion tribunal' – to use the language of the legal reformer Jeremy Bentham – to which the issues of reparation might be addressed. The only possible candidate for the role of deciding authority was the Waitangi Tribunal. But there was no agreement as to its authority with people, its mana, its right to decide. The Māori came, though always with reservations, to trust it and lament its lack of power of legal declaration. Governments, deciding in their own interests, had shown themselves not much to be trusted. Some, like Tipene O'Regan, thought quite early on that the predictability of a quasi-judicial process would have to be an improvement: 'Up till now the *take* (claims, concerns) of our people have been largely dependent on

---

[51] AS6:15/7/82, Letter J. R. Hooker.

the ebb and flow of the Parliamentary tide, the mood of caucus and the personality of the Ministers'.[52] Others came later to join him in that opinion. The Tribunal, far from perfect, was all there was.

The National Party was always leery of the Tribunal, the Labour MPs, while often seeming to defend it, nevertheless continually reminded the public of its severely limited powers. The Tribunal could recommend, they said continually in the debates from 1975 through the 1980s; but it could not decide.[53] And there were always objections to its hearing claims only from Māori, to the lack of provision it made for hearing opposing views and counterclaims, to the overbalance of Māori in its membership after the 1985 reforms, to its lax procedures in regard to the taking of evidence, and overall to its bias in favour of its clients. All this came to a head during the summer of 1987-1988 and subsequently, in the debates on the *The Muriwhenua Fishing Report* and on the two bills for reforming the Tribunal. For by then, besides Parliament, it was the most prominent institution in the country.

Opposition MPs began to wonder loudly about the wisdom of continuing with the Tribunal in its current form. The Tribunal 'should not be loaded in favour of one race when issues to be decided affect the whole population' said Mr Warren Kyd in December 1987, opening up a theme for his leader, Jim Bolger, to take up over the following months.[54] Mr Bolger himself spoke of the seeming 'lack of finality of decisions' beginning 'to gnaw away' at New Zealanders, and how decisions by 'legitimate authorities' should stick and not be relitigated endlessly.[55]

Objections to the Tribunal were aired in Parliament, on the Select Committee on Maori Affairs and in public. Letters to newspapers and speeches in Parliament described it as 'unrepresentative' and as a 'racist' tribunal; and the Treaty of Waitangi Amendment Bill (1988) was accordingly framed to make appointments not by quota but 'having regard to personal attributes, and the knowledge and experience of different matters likely to come before the tribunal . . . having regard to the partnership between the two partners to the Treaty of Waitangi'.[56] Fishing industry argument on fisheries organization had it that the Tribunal admitted oral evidence and 'legend' without stringent cross-examination.[57] Others noted that 'claims . . . are mere monologues by claimants, there is no questioning by sceptical people'.[58] The passage of the Treaty of Waitangi (SE) Act saw the same arguments, with Landcorp, Electricorp, and New Zealand Post presenting them to the Select Committee on Maori Affairs in place of the commercial fishing organizations. National MPs reiterated them, stressing too the injustice of those who might be

---

[52] In Ngai Tahu submissions on the Treaty of Waitangi Bill 1975: GAL:MA/75/12 (20).

[53] See Chapter 8, Section II of this book.

[54] NZPD1:42, p. 1732 (8 Dec 1987).

[55] H5:4/12/87.

[56] H11:2/7/88, Letter S. Gillespie. NZPD1:42 (15 Sept 1988), p. 6611.

[57] H1:17/6/88.

[58] Dr Bernard Gunn in H8:1/7/88.

disadvantaged by the Tribunal's decisions having no rights to be heard by the Tribunal, nor any right of appeal against them.[59] Newspaper editorials agreed, liberally quoting Jim Bolger and other Opposition MPs: 'The Tribunal must be constituted in a fashion which is democratic, fair and seen to be so'.[60]

Throughout 1988 Sir Robert Muldoon talked of the Tribunal's work as a 'recipe for racial disharmony', asserting that 'the vast majority of Maori do not want claims to the Waitangi Tribunal to continue'. He even suggested that it should be abolished.[61] South Island nervousness about Kai Tahu claims surfaced in a newspaper report that New Zealand's economy could be 'ruined if liberal compensation was awarded for Maori land claims'.[62] Mr Peter Clark, leader of the One New Zealand Foundation, bracketed the desirability of eliminating the Tribunal with abolishing all 'racist privilege' and bringing about 'one law, one people, one New Zealand'.[63] Hilda Phillips, indefatigably campaigning against the Tribunal, found, she reported, 'enthusiastic audiences' for her message. She taught that the Tribunal was deeply implicated in the hydra-like evil of racism and racial injustice originating in the separate treatment of Māori land from the 1860s onwards; that the Maori Land Courts had perpetrated many of the injustices against Māori and Pākehā alike in its corrupt, fraudulent, and incompetent proceedings; that the Department had an interest in perpetuating them, together with the greatest injustice of all – the continuing and artificial distinctions between 'Māori' and other people, and 'Māori' and other land; that they were distinctions which masked the fact that many Pākehā owned Māori land, and that most Māori owned general, not Māori land; that when Judge Durie became chairman of the Tribunal as President of the Maori Land Court, that the Māori were not only judging in their own cause, but were doing so by means of the head of the very court which lay at the root of the problem.[64]

The Parliamentary Opposition, the newspapers, and campaigners seem either to have spoken for a large constituency, or to have created one. It was in this context of hostility and suspicion that a *National Business Review* poll of April 1988 showed that 67 per cent of the total population believed the workings of the Tribunal 'threatened racial harmony'. There did not seem to be much difference between Māori and Pākehā on the matter: 69 per cent Pākehā believed in the threat; 60 per cent Māori. The Tribunal was far from an 'agreed court of morals or law', as required by the conditions for easy cases.[65] In March 1989, when the new members of the Tribunal (added

[59] NZPD1:42, pp. 1722, 1728, 1731-32, 1733. 8 Dec 1987; 1:41, pp. 4570, 4575-8, 2584 (21 June 1988); 1:42, pp. 4779-80, 4782-3, 4787-8, 4789-91 (28 June 1988).

[60] H16:13/2/88; H5:11/12/87. Also H8:11/12/87; AS10:28/1/88; H5:3/2/88, etc.

[61] H1:9:2/7/88; SSi14: 19/6/88; SSii2:2/10/88.

[62] H18:1/7/88.

[63] SS7:13/11/88.

[64] Hilda Phillips, *Let the Truth be Known*, pp. 2-9 especially, and personal interviews.

[65] NBR2:14/3/88.

to bring its membership up to 17) were announced, it was clear that nothing had changed. All the Opposition accusations were heard once more, and the Government (even Judge Durie himself)[66] had to once more defend the Tribunal carefully against accusations of bias, racism, unwarranted raising of expectations, and clogging of the proceedings of good policy.

C9. There are rules of reparation governing the nature and quantum of remedies. (RR)

There were no agreed rules of reparation regarding what current goods would amount to restitution, or could otherwise be taken to be equivalents to what past wrong. Governments laid down no rules and none were accepted. They simply, as a consequence of the Muriwhenua findings for instance, made offers on which they would negotiate with the claimants. Agreement between claimants and the Governments as to proper reparation was a matter of making deals from positions of disagreement as to rights, wrongs, and justice in reparation. Nor was settlement ever evidently permanent, on grounds of expressing mutually-acceptable equivalences. Robert Muldoon often bitterly observed this when his 1978 settlement of the Ngati Whatua of Orakei claims was overturned in 1988; and it was evident in the 1988 renegotiations of the 1981 Tauranga settlement, as it was in the claims of various Maori Trust Boards that the quanta of their compensation monies, typically set in the early 1940s, should be updated to fit the circumstances of the 1970s and 1980s.

Most negotiations for reparations were private and between the parties alone, though much detail as to disagreement can be gleaned from the documentation surrounding the two Ngati Whatua settlements. But, fortunately for the record, on 7 July 1988, one set of negotiations *was* made public, in the *Reports of the Joint Working Group on Maori Fisheries*.[67] They were made public probably because they had failed, and were an educative device designed to show the problems that were being faced. Hon. Richard Prebble foreshadowed the bill in Parliament on the issue by saying euphemistically that 'the Crown and the Maori have agreed to disagree'.[68] The record of the negotiations perfectly illustrates difficulties which the parties continually found in pitching upon restitutory and compensatory settlements thought by both sides to be just.

The Joint Group (Māori and Crown) was set up in November 1987 as a consequence of the High Court injunctions against the further issuing of Individual Transferable Quotas. The Government, unwilling to explore the legal situation too fully, instructed the Group to report on 'how Maori fisheries may be given effect'. But the Joint Group could not agree. Informed to differing effects by the Waitangi Tribunal's *Muriwhenua Fishing Report* which

---

[66] H20:14/3/89: Durie noted that 'Anglos can hear Maori cases and will not be accused of bias, but Maori cannot (hear Pakeha cases without being so accused).'

[67] Wallace, *Reports of the Joint Working Groups on Maori Fisheries*.

[68] NZPD1:42, p. 6922 (21 Sept 1988).

they received in the last weeks of their deliberations, the Māori and Crown components published two separate reports. The reports differed markedly on the questions of original entitlement to fisheries and therefore rights to restitution, as well as on what would be proper compensation for past sufferings as a consequence of violated rights.

The Māori Group, backed by a pan-Māori hui held on the issue, asserted its live Treaty right to the 'full, exclusive and undisturbed possession of the fisheries of New Zealand . . . asserted by our ancestors', who 'never recognised any seaward boundary . . . ever since the Treaty was signed'. The Māori and only the Māori had property rights, 'full and exclusive', in the fishery. The Māori and only the Māori had, in addition, a rangatiratanga over the fisheries, which would deny the Crown many of the rights it claimed to regulate the ownership of things. The rangatiratanga of the Māori denied the Crown any sovereign right to 'interfere' with their fisheries except 'in the national interest and subject to appropriate safeguards'. The Crown certainly had no current rights to income from the sale of Individual Transferable Quotas and from resource rentals.

For their part, the Crown negotiators, directly contradicting the Māori claims, spoke not at all of the Treaty's affirming Māori property rights in fisheries. They declined to follow the jurisprudence of the Waitangi Tribunal in that respect. Fisheries were (as in English common law) a common property and to be exploited according to rules laid down by the sovereign Crown. Nor could the negotiators contemplate a settlement which would last more than twenty-five years: 'for Treaty-based arrangements may require to be reconsidered by Crown or Maori as a result of changes which take place in our society'; and they spoke not of Māori 'rights' but of Māori 'interests' in the fisheries. But they were willing to speak of the Māori now participating in management – hitherto an 'Article I function' – by virtue of the tino rangatiratanga the chiefs were guaranteed in Article II. Thus an 'Article II function' could be seen as entailing an 'Article I function'. This way of looking at it would 'meet the two Treaty concepts of kawanatanga and tino rangatiratanga'.

But what of reparations in the absence of agreement as to what, precisely, the violated rights were? Or a settlement of any kind? Non-committal as to rights violated, the Crown negotiators nevertheless produced proposals which in *some* ways suggested recognition of them. They thought 29 per cent Māori ownership of the fisheries would be the right split. They also suggested a 'new institution' to control and take profit from the fisheries – a State Owned Enterprise. It would have share capital, owned 75 per cent by the Crown and 25 per cent by the Māori; it would have seven members: three appointed by the Crown, three by the Māori, and a chairperson appointed by the Crown after consultations with the Māori.

The proportions of Māori ownership (there were separate issues of control which had best be left aside for simplicity's sake) were argued thus. The Māori could have 100 per cent of the inshore fisheries out to the twelve mile limit, 'OR 100 per cent of the fish species generally caught by Maori, both of which produce a figure of 19 per cent of the total fisheries'. The suggestion was perhaps restitutionary; it restored what the Māori used to have. But there was more. An element of compensation for past wrongs was added, compounded with considerations of distributive justice according to the Māori proportion of the population. In addition the Māori negotiators were offered 12.5 per cent of the deep water fisheries, which represented 10 per cent of the total fisheries. This 12.5 per cent was 'reasonable and logical' because it reflected the fact that 12.5 per cent of the New Zealand population was Māori. The offer denied prior Māori rights to the offshore fisheries, and divided on grounds of distributive justice. In fact (because Māori individuals benefited also from Crown ownership and control) it distributed *more* than would have been required on strict population grounds. Thus the offer contained within it a 'real element of compensation for past wrongs'. Thus the Māori had a 29 per cent overall share: restitution of inshore fishing, and proportional and compensatory division of offshore fisheries.

This was complex reasoning. The Māori proposals were simpler. They declined to require full restitution of what was nevertheless 100 per cent (inshore and offshore to the 200 mile limit) theirs. Eager to reach a just settlement, they claimed only 50 per cent ownership of the resource and would make 50 per cent available to the Crown. Their offer stated that they should have 'an equal say in management and control of the fisheries . . . and would receive 50 per cent of the resource rentals'. As to compensation for past wrongs, the Māori Group would leave that to individual tribal claimants to take to the Waitangi Tribunal. The settlement they proposed would not include them.

Obviously there could be no reparative justice on the grounds given. There were no shared conceptions of the rights at issue. There could be only bargaining. And so there was for the remainder of the year and into the next amidst no less contradictory claims from commercial fishing interests, politicians, and public.

The Joint Working Group at least agreed that in doing justice, no injustice should be done to a third innocent party. And this was the one commonly-accepted rule. At the Waitangi Day observances of 1988, it was reported, that '24 farmers staged a silent protest. . . . Banners carried messages such as, "We don't want more land, let us keep what we have," "Farmers have land rights too".'[69] They need not have worried. Only a very few Māori claimants or their representatives suggested otherwise. The Waitangi Tribunal itself made it abundantly clear throughout its findings that only as a last resort, and only after fair agreement, would private land and other interests ever be used as a form of restitution or compensation. Governments were always at pains to firmly deny any suggestion that compensation would entail loss of private lands, and the Opposition said so – if that were possible – even more firmly. National MPs, bureaucrats and corporate executives joined in arguing that if retrospection and reparation were introduced, many a *bona*

[69] H4:8/2/88.

fide private landowner would lose his land, and even that the whole Torrens system of registration of private landholdings would be threatened.[70] In 1985 and in 1988, when retrospection was in prospect and when the Tribunal was being given extra powers over lands and waters that it was proposed should be sold to SOEs, it was argued that reparation would undermine contracts entered into in good faith by, for instance, large forestry, electricity, telecommunications, and property interests.[71] In its briefing papers to the incoming Government of 1987, Treasury announced that the Māori had no right to 'tax revenue' (that is, money as compensation) 'on a no strings basis'. This was because the Treaty was between the Crown and the Māori rather than between Māori and Pākehā peoples, so that it would be 'difficult to justify' the use of 'general taxpayer funds' (extracted from Māori and Pākehā alike) for reparations.[72]

Although these arguments can be seen to be expressing agreement as to the proper confines of reparatory settlements, they were actually a serious challenge to the very ideal of reparation. They came to this: that where there were private rights and interests, then these settled rights and interests as a matter of justice should not be disturbed in the name of reparatory justice. They also tended to come to this: that included in private interests were those of each individual citizen in the state's ownership and control of public assets. Certainly this is what the Government was told about any proposed Muriwhenua settlement which would 'give away' fishing rights to the Māori. At the heart of the rules of reparations therefore, lay a contradiction in the form of the rule that justice to settled private interests should override justice in reparation; and the question of what private interests were was at least unsettled – it seems to have been thought that private persons had private interests in the state ownership of things.

Just as the details of equivalences were unsettled, so was the very core conception of reparation in its relation to settled rights which might well have originated in past wrongs. What if the rule were to be that *no* settled rights were ever to be disturbed by a reparatory settlement? Then assuredly reparation would not be possible.

C10. W is brought to the bar of law (JL) or of common opinion (JM)

This is the one condition that was thoroughly met. But to bring the one big Māori v Pākehā case to public attention was, as will now be evident, far from having it decided as an easy case. And as for being brought to the bar of law, some cases were: to the Waitangi Tribunal and to the Court

---

[70] GAL:MA/85/14. Submission of Federated Farmers. Winston Peters on Torrens system, NZPD, 1:41, p. 2706, 5649; Doug Graham on it 1:41, p. 2704.

[71] See Submissions to the Select Committee on the Treaty of Waitangi (SE) Bill 1988: nos. 5a, 6w, 7a, 10a. See NZPD3:37, p. 4500 for Departmental advice to this effect; and MR:18/2/88 for publicity on the issue.

[72] The Treasury, *Government Management*, i, p. 324.

of Appeal especially. It is to these that we now turn to see how they dealt with cases, which, whatever their particular simplicity, were set in the context of the hard and controverted – even impossible – general claim. The jurisprudence of the Tribunal, no less than that of the highest court in the land,[73] was a political jurisprudence concerned to reach and explain decisions in a way that would actually work.

[73] The Privy Council was in fact the highest court but was not called on.

Chapter 7
The Waitangi Tribunal and the Jurisprudence of Justice in Reparation for Breach of Contract

I

The Waitangi Tribunal and the History of Past Wrongs

It will be evident that the Waitangi Tribunal lived its life in conditions that made doing reparative justice difficult, and in fact it took great cognizance of the difficulties that its clients would face in attaining it: even to the extent of developing a non-reparationary, forward-looking jurisprudence which concentrated not on past wrongs but on future goods. Nevertheless the Tribunal also developed a reparatory jurisprudence. It was a jurisprudence devoted to the careful detailing of the histories of past wrongs that its clients had suffered, and one devoted to finding in the Treaty those strict rules of right necessary to be discovered if their breach was to trigger the right of reparation. Even the first Tribunal, in the absence of retrospective powers entitling it to look back before 1975, was to develop by 1985 a jurisprudence that displayed a tendency to interpret its powers in a reparationist direction. Whatever the legal limits to its retrospective power, and however much emphasis it placed on the imperative that it itself should act within its lawful powers, the Tribunal was clearly also of a mind that if Treaty justice were to be done, then it would be better if it could retrospect. Nor was this surprising given the context in which it operated. Retrospection of past wrongs was asked of it by its clients, and the Tribunal did that as much as it could within the bounds of legal plausibility. The second, reformed Tribunal, armed with retrospective powers, proceeded from late 1986 with much more ease down the same path.

In all its findings the first Tribunal necessarily had to look to the past in order to understand the Māori grievances currently at issue. But the point, given the context in which it worked, was not simply to understand the injustice of the present; it was also to recover to the gaze, and to condemn as such, past arrangements and activities. This was evident enough in embryo from the beginning, and especially in the Te Atiawa and Kaituna findings;[1] but it was in the Manukau findings of 1985 that the Tribunal most clearly came to enunciate a jurisprudence of retrospection that would get a grip on the past - even though its retrospective power seemed limited. Here it held that past legislation of Governments, if still in force, was 'current' law.

---

[1] See *Te Atiawa Report*, paras. 4.6-8, 8.1-7; *Kaituna Report*, para. 6.3.

Its retention was a contemporary 'policy' of the Crown, and to see what it was that was being retained, the Tribunal would have to retrospect. In its findings the Tribunal also told the story of the 'prejudice' of Māori interests in a long chronology of broken Treaty guarantees to the use, ownership and enjoyment of lands and fisheries. In particular it dwelt on the way in which the Tainui people of the southern Manukau shores had been in effect forced into war and suffered, therefore, unfair confiscation of their lands. This history including war, confiscation, and legal policy was, the Tribunal suggested, (my italics): '*reflected* after 1975 from whence our jurisdiction begins'. That was why it could be brought to light; and that was why, for instance, while it could not in the case of land at Pukaki 'adjudicate upon the taking of the land' in various ways from 1865 to 1972, the Tribunal could nevertheless (my italics) 'make a finding on the *keeping* of it.' It concluded its recommendations with a summary and justification of its proceedings: 'The enormous losses sustained by the Manukau tribes must be looked at, although they are for the most part beyond our jurisdiction to examine in any detail. The policies that led to the land wars and confiscations are the primary source of grievance although they occurred last century. It is the continuation of such policies into recent times that has prevented past wounds from healing.'[2]

A similar jurisprudence of retrospection was evident too, in the Report of the first Tribunal on Te Reo claims and the Waiheke Claims of 1986 and 1987. In those reports, a pleasing and prosperous past was contrasted with a disastrous present; and past and present were linked by a history of past 'errors', 'mistakes', 'wrongs' and 'injustices'. In *Te Reo Report* the history was of the 'breach of the promise made in the Treaty of Waitangi' to protect the Māori language. The story was told in a section called 'Te Reo Maori in the Past'. The breach was largely a matter of misplaced goodwill, but breach it was. In the mid-nineteenth century, te reo Māori was not in danger, though the numbers of Māori were to decline from 100,000 in 1840 to their lowest of 41,200 in 1896. 'Many settlers were bilingual . . . . Missionary instruction was given in Maori, Governor Grey recorded the myths and legends of the Maori in the Maori language. Church authorities often recorded their proceedings in Maori although many of the clergy were pakeha.' But as the population rose again to 385,000 in 1981, the language declined. Kaumātua told the Tribunal that in the first quarter of the twentieth century they were forbidden to speak English at school, on pain of punishment. Sir James Henare, a former Commander of the Maori Battalion in the Second World War, told the Tribunal that he heard a school inspector saying, 'English is the bread-and-butter language, and if you want to earn your bread and butter you must speak English'. He related how he was once sent into the bush to cut a piece of supplejack with which he was to be whipped for speaking te reo within the school gates. 'It was not realised,' commented the Tribunal, 'what a destructive effect this emphasis on English speaking would have on te reo Maori and ultimately on the culture.'

---

[2] *Manukau Report*, para. 8.4, esp. pp. 96-9. See also pp. 122, 134.

In the second quarter of the century, when the generation of Henare's children were growing up, they were brought up by their bilingual parents to speak mainly English; by the third quarter, Māori parents themselves were agitating to have their children taught solely in English. In 1913, 90 per cent of Māori schoolchildren could speak Māori; in 1953, 26 per cent; in 1975, 'less than 5 per cent'. The evils antedated 1975, but because they explained the present condition, the Tribunal had no difficulty in bringing them out into the open. Nor could the long-settled (1858) prohibition of te reo being spoken in the law courts escape the Tribunal's jurisdiction: 'the law as it exists is a policy of the Crown.'[3]

In the Waiheke Case, a similar history – a retrospection on past wrongs – was related in two chapters;[4] and a similar jurisdiction over the past was claimed.[5] As in *Te Reo Report*, the accusation was not so much, as in the Manukau case, of dark and purposeful misdeeds. Nevertheless it was again an indictment of evil and wrong, though evil and wrong suspected rather than clearly known. When they signed the Treaty, Ngati Paoa had behind them a chequered past both of prosperity and of exile and misery at the hands of warlike enemies; in 1840 they stood under imminent threat from Ngapuhi, and signed the Treaty partly to counter that threat by gaining protection from the 'white tribe'. But if it was a chequered history, at least it was their own. They were a substantial power on the lower Hauraki Gulf and on Waiheke Island which dominates the gulf at its entrance to the Waitemata Harbour, on which Auckland was to be built. Markedly prosperous as traders in food supplies in the early 1850s, by 1858 they had nevertheless alienated the greater part of their lands to Crown Land Purchasing Officers, in circumstances the details of which were unknown. 'This claim,' commented the Tribunal, in a passage which illustrates well its tendency to retrospection:

. . . was filed before our jurisdiction was extended. It was beyond our authority to review these early transactions in any detail except as here to provide a background to the Ngati Paoa people. As part of that background however we refer to the research of some modern historians doubting that at this early time the Maori understood that a deed of sale meant they were giving up their right to the land for ever, and postulating that they often seem to have believed that they were granting only rights of occupancy.[6] We would add that customary settlement arrangements had no affinity at all with sales as the settlers knew them . . . . Occupational arrangements . . . or customary land gifts both involved a sharing of the land, not a conveyance of ownership or vacant possession. They each required too a commitment from the recipient to honour the mana or authority of the benefactor.[7]

---

[3] *Te Reo Report*, para. 1, at p. 4; para. 3.2.0 ('Te Reo Maori in the Past') at pp. 13–16; para. 4.3.11, at p. 32.

[4] Chapters 2 and 3.

[5] Mostly in Chapter 8.

[6] The Tribunal quoted the work of Ward, *A Show of Justice*, p. 29; and Ann Parsonson 'The Pursuit of Mana', p. 148.

[7] *Waiheke Report*, p. 13.

The point was that on Māori understandings of the 1840s, 'sales' were not sales at all. Worse had followed: a foolish attempted raid by Ngati Paoa on Auckland in 1851 may have led to forced sales in reprisal; or it may have been that in the face of settler pressure for land, Ngati Paoa had alienated most of their Waiheke land in somewhat suspicious circumstances; or it may have been that it was Ngati Maru land which Ngati Paoa disposed of to the Pākehā. 'We have no record (as yet),' noted the Tribunal in a masterly piece of suspicion-inducing rhetoric, 'of the large tribal meetings that were normally associated with customary land transactions . . . The historical events and internecine disputes described, cloud the clear wording of the Deeds of cession and question whether the Waiheke sales were freely and willingly entered into, and then with the assent of all the right people'. The hapū retired to lands on the Firth of Thames. Some fought for the Waikato tribes to whom they had obligations when 'Imperial forces invaded', demonstrating the 'true intentions of the [Treaty] partners'; others remained 'loyal' (the Tribunal's quotation marks) to the Crown. Loyal or not, their lands were confiscated: Ngati Paoa said 50,000 acres were taken; the Tribunal's staff thought the amount 'difficult to quantify, and while the loss would not amount to 50,000 acres, yet in modern terms it would appear substantial'.

Land loss led to poor nutrition, ill health, lowered resistance to disease, and lowered fertility rates. Lacking leadership, Ngati Paoa lost still more lands on the Firth of Thames and at Waiheke, ignorant victims of the mechanics of a Maori Land Court, first established in 1862 and designed to individualize titles and encourage 'economic' uses of land. In 1865 they still owned – in common and as a tribe – a quarter of the Island (about 5,700 acres) and 16,000 acres on the Firth. But that year the Court awarded the ten Waiheke blocks 'to the few to the disinheritance of the many'. By 1900, nine blocks, averaging 400 acres and awarded by the Court to an average of only two persons, were sold. The last block was vested in five persons, then sixty-five, then, in 1897, divided among the sixty-five into thirteen parts. Further subdivisions and alienations occurred. In 1986 there were just over ten acres left. A similar process occurred on the mainland. 'For the moment,' concluded the Tribunal, 'only the humble hamlet of Kaiaua on the Firth of Thames is home to the seeds of Ngati Paoa now scattered throughout Auckland and Waikato'.

These histories thus retailed by the first Tribunal registered what its clients had said and what the Tribunal had additionally been able to find out. They were also designed as part of a pattern of moral persuasion aimed at the Government. They were – whatever else they were – *arguments* and not simply stories. The idea was to persuade the Government to make amends for a present state of affairs inseparable in its reality from the past wrongs which formed it. And whatever the legal power the Tribunal may (or may not) have had to enter upon such histories of error, mistake and wrong going back well before 1975, its rational cause was clear. It was the Tribunal's concern for justice: a concern based on a knowledge that the Māori claimants felt that breach of contract on lands, fisheries, mana and language had occurred, and consequently suffered an 'enormous sense of grievance, injustice and outrage'. The Tribunal had been told endlessly of the injustice that its clients had suffered and it recognized the force of a 'moral obligation' to remedy it.[8] In the light of its knowledge and commitment, despite the Tribunal's lack of legal powers to remedy past wrongs, the feeling of injustice obviously had to be taken into account as a massively present fact. It had at the very least to be brought to light.

For its part the second Tribunal was under no legal disability in viewing past wrongs, and it had a research staff at its disposal. Its histories were accordingly undertaken in a more confident and lengthy vein in the *Orakei Report*, and in the *Muriwhenua Fishing Report* and the *Mangonui Sewerage Report*. We need not follow them at such length here as the earlier ones, because the main mode of exposition had already been set. The history of Ngati Whatua was told in much the same way as that of Ngati Paoa, though in much more detail and with greater technical expertise. It began at the beginning, before the journeys from the Pacific Polynesian homelands, sometimes called Hawaiki: 'Ngati Whatua begins before the journeys to Aotearoa. Some say the tribal ancestor, Tumutumuwhenua, came from the Gods, not human kind'. But basically, it was the story of a tribe with its tūrangawaewae on prime lands near Auckland: in this case precisely where Auckland was to be, on the isthmus between the Waitemata and Manukau Harbours. It was a story of scandalously cheap land sales in the 1840s; of land taken by the Crown for public purposes it would not be used for; of how the Land Court's individualizing of land titles from 1865 onwards led to further alienation in the 1890s; of how the remnant of a once proud people were expelled from their papakāinga as recently as 1951 and their meeting house torched; of how Ngati Whatua thus 'inherited a legacy of bitterness, division and defeat', the result of which Auckland was to see in the events of 1977 at Bastion Point; of how the settlement of the Bastion Point Controversy struck in 1978 was satisfactory (and then very doubtfully so) only if strict legal claims were taken into account, but not if the real rights and wrongs of history were taken into account.

Muted, but evident throughout, were implied criticisms of Mr Justice Speight's dicta as to past dealings in the *Bastion Point Judgment* of 1978. There Speight had refused to dismiss charges of trespass against four protestors who had pleaded that in equity the Crown did not have 'clean hands', and that therefore the prosecution should lapse. He had held that despite every 'sinister innuendo' cast by the protesters on the agents of the Crown who had bought the Orakei lands, he could find no evidence of chicanery or illegality. Rather he had found evidence of the utmost 'good faith' in the Crown's dealings with Ngati Whatua.[9] The Tribunal's story told otherwise,

---

[8] *Te Atiawa Report* para. 4.9. at p. 17; para. 7.3 at p. 34, para. 10. 1 at p. 53; *Kaituna Report*, paras. 3.11-13, 3.17, *Manukau Report*, pp. 8-9, 12 (quoted from p. 9), para 5.12 at pp. 46-7; *Te Reo Report*, paras. 6.1.1-3. at p. 38.

[9] *Bastion Point Judgment*, p. 15 and see pp. 10, 17, 24, 25.

and the chronicle of wrongs was accompanied throughout by reflections on the consistent loyalty to the Crown and peaceful demeanour of the people in the face of continued injustice.[10]

The history of the Muriwhenua fisheries recurred throughout the largest (370-page) report of the Tribunal. Less evidently recording the indignation and suffering of its clients, in four considerable chapters the Tribunal marshalled evidence of the rise and decline of Māori fishing in the Far North. It described the fishing technology that at first compared well with – even outstripped – that of the Pākehā. It recorded from 1840 through 1870, even into the 1880s, the highly developed Māori trade and industry in fishing, stressing the Māori emphasis on conservation and marine hygiene and the co-operation of the Muriwhenua tribes with the Pākehā. It then recorded the wrongs. From 1866, with the first conservation restrictions on oyster fisheries and exclusion of the Māori from them, the state-aided development of an inshore fishing industry excluded the tribes despite the Fisheries Acts which spoke of reserving rights to them. Then, from 1900 to 1987, there was the utter commercialization of the activity of fishing; first inshore, then from 1987 when a 200 mile Exclusive Economic Zone was declared, offshore; and there was the sale in 1987, against the Tribunal's advice, of Individual Transferable Quotas which excluded the Māori from an occupation, income and way of life they had enjoyed from time immemorial.[11]

This history, without dwelling on the wrongs done, and the sense of wrongs done, nevertheless recorded them. It recorded the existence of 92 Māori fishing petitions from 1869 to 1986 complaining of the Crown's contempt of Māori fishing rights in ponds, lakes, rivers, bays, harbours, estuaries, and seas.[12] It recorded Māori distress at overfishing and pollution, and at the presence of foreign – Japanese, Russian and Korean – boats near their shores. Above all, it recorded all these things against the yardstick of Article 2 of the Treaty, in which possession of fisheries was guaranteed. It was against that standard that the history was to be read; and it was clearly a history of past wrongs.

The Tribunal's findings then, produced a history patterned on the narration of past wrongs: each pattern illustrating both different and recurring kinds of wrongs. And its last findings in 1988 were no different, though as part of a larger claim yet to be reported on, they were briefer and less complete. There, in the *Mangonui Sewerage Report* it was related how Ngati Kahu, wedged between aggressive Ngapuhi and Te Rarawa and suffering in the 1790s from the ravages of European diseases, had their lands 'sold' for them by others – much as Ngati Paoa may have sold Ngati Maru's Waiheke land as a sign of their domination over their weaker neighbours. Soon after the Treaty, Hobson himself, to solve the consequent disputes as to ownership, had indulged in an unwise 'purchase', and left Ngati Kahu by 1843 in the midst of tripartite war-like contention. This was not the 'protection' as promised in the Treaty.

---

[10] *Orakei Report*, paras. 3-7. Quotations from pp. 11, 89.

[11] *Muriwhenua Fishing Report*, Chapter 3-6.

[12] *Muriwhenua Fishing Report*, App. 8.

Nor were the activities of the Land Claims Commission of 1843 and then in the 1850s just. The Commission extracted 'surplus lands' from pre-Treaty buyers who had not paid a fair price to the Māori. This was fine, and in accord with the purpose of the Treaty to protect the Māori from unscrupulous buyers; but then the Crown *kept* those lands and did not return them to Ngati Kahu. 'The Maori', commented the Tribunal of its clients, 'could not get past the fact that surplus lands, amounting to many thousands of acres in the Far North, had been retained by the Crown.'

There was more. In the 1850s Commissioners stepped up their buying programme in Northland, breaching in the process the instructions of the Chief Land Purchase Commissioner, Donald McLean, to purchase only 'subject to [creating] ample reservations for [the Maoris'] own present and future wants'. So that by the time of the Native Land Court which stripped most other Māori of their lands from 1865 onwards by individualizing titles, most of the harm had already been done.[13]

In sum, by 1988 the Tribunal had compiled a significant history of Pākehā wrongs to the Māori. This was an essential element in its reparative jurisprudence.

II

The Treaty Interpreted as Stating Strict Rights

There was then, a history of past wrongs. Another essential element in the Tribunal's reparationism was the interpretation of the Treaty as containing rights, the breach of which had constituted those past injustices. For without the precise specification of wrongs according to some rules there could be no reparation.

The Tribunal was given power to compare the Māori and English versions appended to the Treaty of Waitangi Act and 'for the purposes of this Act' to 'have exclusive authority to determine the meaning and effect of the Treaty . . . and to decide issues raised by the differences' between the two. Professor Eckhoff's remarks about the clarity and uncontroversiality of contractual justice being potentially clearer and easier to administer than the often unspoken agreements on justice at large in a society, emphatically do not apply to the Tribunal's proceedings in declaring the 'principles' of the Treaty. In fact the Tribunal interpreted the Treaty in two distinguishable, even contradictory, modes: the first, as if the issue were reparation for the past wrongs it had uncovered, the second – the subject of the next chapter – as if the issue were not retrospection and reparation, but prospection and the amelioration of future relationships between Māori and Pākehā.

In its reparationist mode the Tribunal not only interpreted the past as a history of injustice. It also tended to define the content of injustice by

---

[13] *Mangonui Sewerage Report*, Sections 3.3–3.4.6.

reference to the rules of action laid down in the Treaty as if those rules laid down what are called in legal philosophy 'strict rights'.[14] These are those kinds of rights which, when some people have them, 'correlate' with duties that others have, so that to say that A has a right to have, or be or do X *is the same thing* as to say that B had a duty (to A) that A should have, or do or be whatever X specifies. Where strict rights exist there is in principle no room for negotiation, no room for evasion of duty. 'Rights,' as has been observed, 'are trumps.'[15] They bar the consideration of other reasons for acting, for example acting according to the greatest happiness of the greatest number, or for general convenience. Goals of public policy and the public good cannot override the rights that people have. And the Tribunal, arguing in this way, spoke the language of rights in the Māori and duties in the Crown. Less harshly, it spoke of rights and 'responsibilities'. But whatever the language, the tendency of this way of arguing was towards the idea of reparation for breach of contract, and thus the precise definition of the terms of the contract.

This intellectual procedure was not an easy one, given the nature of the Treaty and the conditions in which it was signed. And it was indeed largely thanks to the work of the Tribunal and its informants and supporters that New Zealanders learned of the conditions of signing and the differences between the different language versions. It was the Tribunal in the Kaituna claim that marshalled the evidence to show that the 'kawanatanga' that the Māori agreed Queen Victoria should have did not indicate full sovereign rights of government but rather a right limited to keeping the peace by violence if necessary.[16] It was the Tribunal in the Kaituna, Manukau, Te Reo and Muriwhenua reports that again marshalled the evidence as to what the Māori had thought was to be protected: that 'ratou taonga katoa' meant roughly 'all things highly prized (material as well as spiritual)'; and it was the Tribunal which showed that *that* obviously covered more than simply the 'forests and fisheries' for which it may have been intended as a translation.[17] The Tribunal also glossed 'te tino rangatiratanga' that the Māori was to retain over those things that it was guaranteed they should keep as meaning something like 'full chiefly authority of a customary kind' – minus in the case in point, the element of kāwanatanga.[18]

---

[14] Hohfeld, *Fundamental legal conceptions*, well summarized in an article by Thomas Perry, 'A Paradigm of Philosophy: Hohfeld on Legal Rights'. But compare Flathman, *The Practice of Rights*, pp. 48-51 esp. whose 'strict rights' I prefer to Hohfeld's 'claim rights'.

[15] Philip Pettit, 'Rights, Constraints and Trumps', discusses well this pre-emptive nature of rights as most influentially put forward by Dworkin, *Taking Rights Seriously*, pp. 90-4, 364-8, and Nozick, *Anarchy, State, Utopia*, Chapter 3.

[16] *Kaituna Report*, paras. 4.6-10. Useful scriptual references in David Williams, 'Te Tiriti o Waitangi,' *New Hope*, p. 10, also printed in *He Korero*. Compare Professor Kawharu's gloss on te Tiriti reported in the *Kaituna Report*, paras. 4.9-10; and *Te Atiawa Report*, para. 10.2 (b).

[17] *Te Atiawa Report* para. 10.2 (a); *Kaituna Report*, para. 4.7; *Manukau Report*, para. 8.3; *Te Reo Report*, paras. 4.2.3-4; *Muriwhenua Report*, para. 10.3.2.

[18] *Te Atiawa Report*, para. 10.2(b); *Kaituna Report*, paras. 4.9-10; *Manukau Report*, para. 8.3; *Orakei Report*, para. 11.5.

Sovereignty/kāwanatanga? 'Full, exclusive and undisturbed possession of their lands, forests and fisheries'/'te tino rangatiratanga o o ratou wenua o ratou kainga me o ratou taonga katoa'? In fact no single interpretation of what the Treaty/te Tiriti meant then or means now can be given. It has multivalent locutionary force because it is in two languages, in at least five versions in English; and though it is only in one version in te reo Māori, Māori is a language which plays on multivalence. Its illocutionary force – what people intended and intend in referring to its words – has and has had no less a range, the more so since it is such a potent symbol. And the point of symbols is that they *should* be richly ambiguous. So even if, as is doubtful, the English and Irish (Hobson was Irish) authors of the Treaty really intended a precise translation into te reo Māori, there would have been difficulties in providing one. And if the Treaty was intended as a deception, it must have been the deception of the blind by the blind. It is unlikely that Hobson, who signed it for the Crown, understood the meaning of the Māori version. It is not even clear that Hobson and his amateur helpers knew much about English law: whether, for instance, they might have been thinking of sovereignty in the absolutist terms most influentially put forth in their generation by John Austin in his *Province of Jurisprudence Determined* (1823), or whether, against the trend of the thought of colonial governors but in tune with the jurisprudence of the USA, they might have known of 'aboriginal rights', and recognized them as an incumbrance on sovereignty.[19]

As to the Māori signatories, it is unlikely that all of them placed much reliance on their reading of the Māori version (not to mention the 39 who signed an English language version). Most seem to have been persuaded by word of mouth to sign. And word of mouth, including an alleged 'fourth article', based on a report that Hobson was said to have promised freedom of religion and Māori customs, doubtless varied from the texts.[20] Nor is it clearly the case that anything like all the signatories *were* persuaded at all, if being pursuaded means having understood and judged arguments that had a bearing on the content of the Treaty. Many signed out of belief in the goodwill of their missionary advisors; others so that they might collect the blankets that were distributed to signatories; still others, Tainui and Arawa most notably, simply refused to sign.

So the difficulties in the way of construing the Treaty as containing

---

[19] I refer to two separate scholarly positions now taken by Mark Francis (that contemporary thought was rooted in absolute sovereignty) and Paul McHugh (that it was conceived that the rights of earlier, 'aboriginal' occupiers of colonized territories constituted *prima facie* limits to the scope of the exercise of sovereign power). See their names in the Finding List, and see also Frederika Hackshaw in Kawharu (ed.), *Waitangi*.

[20] See McKenzie, *Oral Culture, Literacy and Print in Early New Zealand: The Treaty of Waitangi*. Judith Binney, reviewing the book, is not so convinced of the lack of literacy that the thesis of orality seems to suggest. See her 'D.F. McKenzie, *Oral Culture*'. And she claims that 'there is a Maori text, which was debated, and which was probably substantially understood . . . The problem would lie in the fact that the British did not fully grasp what *they* had ceded.'

strict rights were formidable, and the Tribunal itself noted the unclarity of the document drawn up by amateurs. Nevertheless, in accordance with the idea of justice in contract and its statutory duty to discover the 'principles' of the Treaty, it did pronounce on what rights the Treaty/te Tiriti contained.

It did so tentatively in its second case in 1978, in the report on the proposed Auckland Thermal Power Station, and it continued with increasing sophistication in the *Te Atiawa Report*, and the reports on the Kaituna River, the Manukau Harbour and Te Reo Māori. By the end of that process Treaty rights were held, under the concept of 'taonga', to include the right to the protection of Māori 'cultural and spiritual values',[21] rights to 'equality in education as in all other human rights',[22] and the right to guaranteed protection of te reo Māori – the Māori language. In the Waiheke findings and recommendations of 1987, the last under the old legislation, the Tribunal next found that in the Treaty the Crown guaranteed, in protecting rangatiratanga, the tribes' rights to continued existence. This doctrine was to be re-emphasized by the second Tribunal in the Orakei and Muriwhenua reports. And in the *Muriwhenua Fishing Report*, the Tribunal, as well as equating rangatiratanga with 'dominion', and arguing rangatiratanga to be an exclusive right, turned its attention to the question of what rights the relevant part of the English version of Article 2 of the Treaty might yield: the right to 'full and undisturbed possession' of 'their . . . fisheries'. It advised the government that that meant an exclusive property right to the places where fish were in 1840 (and are now) caught, to the fish that were (and are) found there, and to 'the business of fishing' as it was then (and as it had developed).

There is plenty of room to doubt the persuasiveness of such findings, though some of them could be right. But the thing to see is that even in the face of what must have been severe doubts, the Tribunal sought to find strict Treaty rights where it might be thought they were not to be found. Many of their interpretations of the Treaty seem to me to run counter to the rules of treaty interpretation (and historical reconstruction), which are that the contents of treaties (or any documents) are to be understood not only in terms of linguistic usage at the time the treaty (or document) was made, but also in terms of what meaning it *would in fact then have had in the minds of those who signed (or authored) it*. The distinction is between what people *could have by virtue of the conventions of word meaning meant*, and what they *actually intended to mean and therefore meant*. The legal test is probably – the rational

---

[21] *Kaituna Report*, para. 9.33, at p. 40.

[22] *Te Reo Report*, para. 6.3.8 at p. 51.

test is certainly[23] — one not only in regard to conventions of meaning but to intentions in signing. Of course the intentions can only be understood by reference to the conventions of meaning – and acting – then available, so the two things are always at issue. But it is unlikely that protection of the language and cultural values were *intended* in 1840 by the Māori signatories. There would have been no *point* to it in the case of the language. While clearly (then as now) a 'taonga', te reo Māori was equally clearly not under threat, so how could it have been in anyone's mind as a thing needing protection? It is even more doubtful that anyone could have had in mind the necessity for protecting 'Maori cultural values'. Taonga now, without doubt, the very idea of 'cultural values' generated in twentieth century sociology and cultural anthropology, can only have been the merest gleam in our forefathers' eyes. As to the signatories envisaging a guarantee of 'equality in education and other human rights', that is simply a stark impossibility: an anachronism. One might as well say (some people did in 1988) that the Treaty prohibited pornography! Those conventional extensions of the meanings of 'taonga' were simply not available in 1840. They were not yet there in English, or in any language in the world. 'Equality in education and other human rights' are distinctively post-Second World War ideals.

In *Te Reo Report*, to examine an example of these anachronistic extensions of intended meaning more closely, the Tribunal, considering that the word 'taonga' could extend to te reo Māori in 1840 was led to say[24] that 'the right to use the Māori language would have been one of those rights expected to be covered by the royal guarantee'. The Tribunal proved this by citing what would (counterfactually) have happened if an antecedent conditional had occurred: 'We think it is unlikely that many Maori signatures would have been obtained if it had been said by Captain Hobson that the Royal guarantee of protection would not include the right to use Maori in any public proceedings involving Maori.' But it is as hard to imagine Hobson thinking about disallowing the language – and thus making the antecedent conditional true – as it is to imagine the Māori signatories perceiving a threat. It is surely truer to the facts to imagine that the question of language never crossed anyone's mind, and that 1840 (when the language was not under threat) is not 1985 (when it was).

The Tribunal was not alone in arguing this way. Dr Richard Benton had

---

[23] This may be pushing it a bit. But 'normal and natural meaning in the context in which they occur' seems to me to *limit* the possible extensions to things which the intensions of the words (conventional meaning) would otherwise allow. Also, 'declared and apparent purpose' would exclude some conventional meanings; ditto, and most strongly, 'meaning which they possessed, or which would have been attributed to them, and in the light of linguistic usage; is either impenetrably repetitive, or 'would have been attributed to' means 'would in fact have been thought to mean in the circumstances'. The tribunal developed its view of the law regarding all this mainly from I. M. Sinclair, 'Treaty Interpretation in the English Courts', quoted in *Te Atiawa Report*, para. 10.1 at pp. 56–7 and see the Tribunal quoting Lord McNair together with USA, English and Australian cases *Manukau Report*, para. 8.2 at p. 88; *Orakei Report*, paras. 11.31–33 at p. 127; *Muriwhenua Fishing Report*, para. 10.4 at pp. 188–9.

[24] *Te Reo Report*, esp. paras. 4.2.3 and 4.2.4 at p. 28, and para. 4.3.6 at p. 31. Also paras. 4.3.8–9.

produced exactly the same counter-factual argument in 1983 and repeated it at Te Reo hearing. Others spoke of the broad meaning of 'taonga' and modernized its applications.[25]

Perhaps there was some arcane and technical legal reason for pretending that people had something in mind in 1840 which they did not. If so, it is a reason that defies common sense. But certainly an impulse behind the extension of the concept of 'taonga' to include the language, culture and education *in 1840*, was not so much one to rewrite (wrongly) the history of the signing of the Treaty for its own sake, but rather that of bringing injustices to the Māori under the aegis of breach of contract. It might have been enough to argue the importance of the language for the survival of a unique culture at home only in New Zealand, or the unfairness of an educational system which systematically failed Māori children, or the value of the Māori conservation ethic in a land careless of pollution, or the dependence of particular hapū on the unpolluted wairua (spirit) of their own lands and waters. But it seems to have been felt that the Treaty must be brought into account so that it could be demonstrated to express the content of justice, and so that it could be shown that breach of Treaty principles was an injustice.

Similar construals of the Treaty as yielding strict rights which could then be shown to have been violated were made in the Tribunal's reports after Te Reo. In the *Waiheke Report* (Mr M. J. Q. Poole dissenting), Judge Durie, while unhappy with what he called a 'tortious'[26] approach – an approach which sought for, to rectify past wrongs – to settlement of the claim, nevertheless found that Ngati Paoa had a strict Treaty right. Recognizing a lack of jurisdiction to 'compel the Crown to adopt policies that would relieve Ngati Paoa', arguing also that 'we are not concerned in this case with compensation for past wrongs but with the significance of the Treaty in the formulation of modern policies',[27] he nevertheless found that the Crown's right of pre-emption of 'lands, forests and fisheries' implied in the Crown 'a duty to ensure that each tribe maintained a sufficient endowment for its foreseen needs'.[28]

In the *Orakei Report* the word 'guarantee' was made, echoing Te Reo findings, to yield the idea of an active protection amounting to 'affirmative action'.[29]

---

[25] Benton, 'The Maori Language, the Treaty of Waitangi, and Race Relations in New Zealand', p. 10; Ross, 'The Treaty on the Ground', pp. 20-1, argues from the meaning (sense: extension) of 'taonga' that: 'It could be argued that . . . the Treaty . . . guaranteed the Maori language, for is not a people's native tongue something highly prized?' But if the issue concerns the intention of contractees in using particular verbal formulae this needs some proof, and is probably wrong anyway.

[26] *Waiheke Report*, Chapter 8 at p. 65.

[27] *Waiheke Report*, Chapter 8, at p. 70.

[28] *Waiheke Report*, Chapter 8 at pp. 77-8.

[29] *Orakei Report*, paras. 11.6. 2-3 at pp. 135-6. Compare *Te Reo Report*, para. 4.2.7. at p. 29, quoting the New Zealand branch of the International Commission of Jurists and the *Shorter Oxford Dictionary*, together with 'various law dictionaries'.

The Tribunal also reiterated, this time on the authority of all seven members, that the Crown, bearing in mind the context of understanding in 1840, did have a duty to ensure a tribal endowment 'sufficient . . . for its foreseen needs', even though the 'plain terms' of the Treaty did not state exactly that. This conclusion was reached by glossing at length the 1839 instructions of the Colonial Secretary, Lord Normanby, to Hobson, to stress Normanby's recognition of Māori sovereignty and the humanitarianism of the times, and to dismiss the idea that the power of pre-emption was insisted upon simply as a way of obtaining cheap land for the settlers. Had that been the British intention, and had it been communicated to the Māori, the Tribunal argued in its counter-factual vein, 'the likelihood of the chiefs agreeing to such a proposal would have been remote'. The right of pre-emption was not to extend to land needed by the Māori.[30]

This is not an implausible interpretation. Nor is it certainly true beyond the shadow of doubt. It is rather an interpretation that seeks more knowledge of human motivation and understandings of things than is available, especially after the passage of a tract of time has obscured the evidence.

The same over-interpretation of 1840 understandings was evident in the *Muriwhenua Fishing Report* where it was found that the Māori had a strict Treaty right to fisheries: the places, the fish, and the industry as it would develop in the future. The understanding that 'fisheries' meant more than the site of fishing activities was derived from English dictionaries and international law, but not from English law as it has ever been, and was not in 1840.[31] The idea that Hobson and his helpers may have been confirming simply aboriginal fishing rights and not guaranteeing the development of fisheries into the future was dismissed. The tribes in 1840, held 'dominion' over the seas. This is what rangatiratanga meant, and like Adam's 'dominion' over all creatures – translated as 'rangatiratanga' at *Genesis*, 1, 26 in Māori bibles – it included an exclusive property right in the seas and the taonga they contained. But it was not *limited* to being a property right; for property rights are guaranteed by, regulated by, and held of a sovereign legal power, whereas this 'dominion' was held of no sovereign at all. It was an underived 'right to control'. It was authority over the seas; and it was an authority not, like an aboriginal right, extinguishable by Crown action. Rangatiratanga/dominion over the seas could be waived only by the consent of those who had it. And such consent had never been given. It had on the contrary, been continually denied in the long chain of petitions.[32]

Finally, even if rangatiratanga were to be limited in its scope of activity, it was clear that it implied a far wider range of activities than aboriginal rights. It was not simply a right to continue unmolested in the old ways.

[30] *Orakei Report*, paras. 11.9.1–26; pp. 137, 143 quoted.

[31] *Muriwhenua Fishing Report*, para. 11.3.2–3, pp. 203–5.

[32] *Muriwhenua Fishing Report*, para. 10.3.3, at pp. 182–4. Appendix 8, pp. 330–37.

It was a right to development. For the purpose and function of rangatiratanga was, among other things, 'the maintenance of the tribal base for succeeding generations'.[33] Thus the guarantee of rangatiratanga given by the Crown was a guarantee to that maintenance and consequently to the support of changes and developments that would support it. Again, counter-factual arguments were used: 'A Treaty that denied a developmental right to the Maori would not have been signed',[34] and again, suspiciously modern-sounding claims were made. UNESCO was quoted saying that 'if a group claims that the realisation of its rights to development requires a certain type of autonomy, such a claim should be considered legitimate'; and the Tribunal spoke for itself in holding that 'it is the inherent right of all people to progress and develop in all areas'.[35] Again, as with the case for te Reo or against pollution, plenty of *other* good reasons could have been given for the Māori having the right and resources to develop fisheries: but the Tribunal found the right to be a Treaty right.

In the face of all this inflation of the idea of 'fisheries', the ancient English habit of proclaiming sovereignty over as much sea as it could (subject only to the exigencies of an international politics which restricted it to a claim to sovereignty of three miles from its shores in the early nineteenth century) was not examined.[36] Nor was the idea that Hobson and his masters at the Colonial Office might have thought that sovereignty in the Crown could potentially obliterate all encumbrances on title whatsoever examined. But the Tribunal *did* find that if a modern critic were to think so, and to argue that the Māori had 'irrevocably ceded rights, or parted with exclusive powers', *that* would be to 'assert a claim against the sovereignty of the Crown'. It would be wrong to dispute that it had recognized 'the independent authority of the Maori', because it *had in fact made* that recognition in 'right of sovereignty'.[37] That the Crown had been *entitled* to recognize the Māori right was taken as an argument that it had in fact done so. Where, in the *Waiheke Report*, the Tribunal had found that the Crown's pre-emptive right to buy 'lands, forests, and fisheries' generated a duty of preservation of the tribes, it was now pointed out that in the English version of the Treaty, the Crown had no such pre-emptive right regarding fisheries *at all*: 'a literal approach to the Treaty suggests only Maori would have had the right to fish in Muriwhenua'.[38] They might sell or lease that right, or give licence for its use; but the whole of Pākehā law and practice had not recognized this and had breached Treaty rights. (That, not recognizing the seas as Māori property, the Crown had not had reason to treat for a right of pre-emption, was not considered.)

---

[33] *Muriwhenua Fishing Report* paras. 10.3.2-3 at pp. 181, 183.

[34] *Muriwhenua Fishing Report*, pp. 235, 236, 237.

[35] *Muriwhenua Fishing Report*, para. 11.6.5. at pp. 234-5.

[36] Fulton, *The Sovereignty of the Sea*, throughout.

[37] Substituting 'in right of' for 'as a right of sovereignty'.

[38] *Muriwhenua Fishing Report*, p. 208.

There is no doubt that these Muriwhenua interpretations, like the others reflected and extended a long-standing Māori understanding of the terms of the Treaty. Claudia Orange's *Treaty of Waitangi* leaves no doubt of that: the Māori did not think they were ceding sovereignty, and they thought they retained their rangitiratanga over most of what mattered to them. But there is equally great doubt however as to whether they reflected the Pākehā understanding, past or present. And great doubt *was* expressed, especially on the issue of fishing rights, because valuable commercial interests were at stake. The difficulty lay in this, that the attempt was – had to be by the Tribunal's empowering Act – to find one single and applicable understanding to a document not amenable to that treatment. And the overall tendency of these controvertible and controverted findings was to confound current purposes with old ones and to distort and make uniform the multiform past understandings of things. All this was in the service of the search for injustice, so that it might be rectified. Modern standards of what was right and wrong, just and unjust, were read back into the intentions of the Treaty's signatories, and into the meaning of what they said.

A recent American Indian legal historian has recently criticized 'white-man's law' for doing just this to the detriment of Amerindians and their rights in the USA. White man's law constructs a mythical past which it now claims binds the present.[39] But *anyone* can invent a false past; many have, many do. Often it is a benign and harmless activity. But a criticism of one aspect of it may be applied to the reparative jurisprudence of the Tribunal in the words of the German philosopher, Friedrich Nietzsche:

The 'purpose of law', is absolutely the last thing to employ in the history of the origin of law: on the contrary . . . the cause of the origin of a thing and its eventual utility, its actual employment and place in a system of purposes, lie worlds apart; whatever exists, having come somehow into being, is again and again interpreted to new ends, taken over, transformed, and redirected by some power superior to it.[40]

European history is full of attempts to reconstruct the past to provide a guide for the present: the reconstruction of the 1000-year history of Roman law during the Renaissance, and the reconstruction of biblical times during the Enlightenment are two famous examples. In each case, too much reconstruction demonstrated the impassable gap between what used to be the case, and what was currently wanted. The idea of anachronism had been

---

[39] See Robert A. Williams, 'The Algebra of Federal Indian Law: The Hard Trail of Decolonizing and Americanizing the White Man's Indian Jurisprudence', pp. 219-99.

[40] Quoted by Williams, 'The Algebra of Federal Indian Law', p. 219. See Nietzsche, *The Birth of Tragedy and the Genealogy of Morals*, p. 209.

discovered.[41] In the case of reconstructing the meaning of the provisions of the Treaty of Waitangi, it is likely that a faithful historical reconstruction simply would not talk ('speak' in the language of the law) to New Zealanders. It would not be a usable history. But for legal and moral purposes the Treaty had to be made to talk. Not like a ventriloquist's dummy – that would demean a serious fact about New Zealand's past – but rather as a founding oracle.

In fact it was in this direction that the Tribunal's second line of jurisprudential development tended, as did that of Government and the courts. The oracular jurisprudence was, it should be said, no more (or less) accurate as regards what actually happened in 1840. The point about oracles is, above all, that what they say should be little, and should be ambiguous: capable of many interpretations. And the oracular jurisprudence was as much concerned with the present as the jurisprudence of past wrongs. Its concern was with a present in which future co-operation between the two peoples was the main point at issue and goal to be sought for. Its concern was indeed, besides pursuing that goal, to minimize dark broodings on past wrongs. The jurisprudence of reparation co-existed with jurisprudence of moderation, negotiation and an eye to the future.

---

[41] See the classic account of the diminishing confidence of European scholars (legal ones especially after the work of Jacques Cujas) in their ability to apply the lessons of the past, in Myron P. Gilmore, 'The Lessons of History' in his *Humanists and Jurists*: 'For about two hundred years – roughly the period between Petrarch and Erasmus – the humanistic tradition . . . was able to combine a deep historical knowledge of the classical past with an undiminished confidence in the relevance of the lessons of that past. But by the time Cujas gave his response this phase of the Renaissance was over' (p. 37). Compare, on the doubts about the relevance of biblical history to contemporary Christian belief encouraged by the work of Richard Simon, in Hazard, *The European Mind 1680-1751*, Part Two, Chapter 3.

Chapter 8
The Waitangi Tribunal and the Political World: Moderation and the Eye to Future Prospects

I

Mildness and Conciliation in the Tribunal's Findings and Recommendations

In reparative justice it is violated rights that are at issue. Though compensation must obviously sometimes be negotiated as a substitute for or in addition to restitution, the negotiations concern current, live, rights and duties. And undoubted rights and duties cannot be too readily bargained over and traded. The normal point about rights and duties indeed is precisely that they are *not* open to be made mere commodities in the political market-place. There is something shabby, something seedy – not to say immoral – about compromising principles where principles concern rights and obligations. Negotiating and bargaining do not sit well with adherence to the demands of justice. Not everything can be bought, sold and traded. Market justice works only within limited areas of activity.[1]

Yet despite the reparationist tendency in its jurisprudence, over the whole period of its existence the first Tribunal's patent desire was not to enforce the rights that backward-looking justice might discover to have been violated. It was rather to make practical arrangements for a more peaceful – and just – future. Armed indeed with the power to recommend compensation to the Government, it recommended this weaker form of reparation in only a few minor instances. Instead it concentrated on practical measure to address the claims. It adopted what Keith Sorrenson, reviewing its work just before he himself became a member, called 'mild and conciliatory', 'mild and compromising', 'mild and accommodating' instead of 'potentially radical' recommendations. For which, read also (and mainly): 'based on a non-reparatory concept of justice and social policy' and 'based on a non-reparatory jurisprudence'.[2]

The second Tribunal was scarcely different, and Sorrenson has similarly

---

[1] See for a brilliant exposition of this: Luban, 'Bargaining and Compromise: Recent Work on Negotiating and Informal Justice'. And see Walzer, *Spheres of Justice*, pp. 95-103 for a USA list of the things (government office, acquittal in courts, exemption from military service, the murder of an enemy, etc.) that 'money can't buy'. New Zealand's might be different. As to why money isn't enough for workers (who want something else) see William M. Reddy, *Money and Liberty in Modern Europe*, esp. Chapter 6.

[2] Sorrenson, 'Towards a Radical Reinterpretation', pp. 164, 168, 171.

written of its 'restrained and achievable' recommendations in the *Orakei Report*.[3] But, especially in the Muriwhenua findings, it placed rather more emphasis on showing that there were *grounds* for rightly demanding reparation, and though it came to see that its legal duty did not require it to make 'practical' suggestions, it never actually recommended more than a mild form of reparation as a remedy for past wrongs. Instead, like the first Tribunal, it recommended negotiations and compromise as the method of attaining settlement, and it looked to justice as an ideal to be attained in the future, largely independent of the wrongness of past transactions.

In sum: in both its first and second forms, the Tribunal always considered what would, for the future, be the best thing to do; and it recommended what would be practical and what would be good for reasons other than reparative ones. The fact is that the Tribunal practised another mode of thought than the reparative, one which nevertheless co-existed with it on easy terms – in the same minds, the same speeches and the same texts. The other mode was one not of retrospection for the reparation of past wrongs but of prospection (forward-looking) for future, just distributions. It looked to distribution in terms of need, especially, and of equalization of opportunities to lead satisfying lives. Sometimes it was simply prospection with a view not to justice at all, but to other ends like the avoidance of violence and discord, and like the attainment of peace, tranquility, concord and the maximization of fulfilment for individuals and groups: prospection was for policy goals. Whether aiming at justice or other policy goals though, prospection was the mode that made *possible* moderation, compromise, accommodation, conciliation and mildness. It was their conceptual foundation.

This foundation will be explored in the next chapter, together with its elaboration in a non-reparative Treaty jurisprudence by the Tribunal, the Court of Appeal and the Government. But it will be best first to examine the practice of prospection, conciliation and negotiation so that the weight it bore may be properly felt, and thus the need appreciated for a new, non-reparatory Treaty jurisprudence. For, the question will now be seen to be, how *could* the jurisprudence of the Treaty as specifying strict rights possibly be maintained in the face of such proceedings?

The first Tribunal almost always eschewed suggesting retrospective justice and plumped for prospection. The record is clear. During its first hearing in 1977, on a breach of fishing regulations by Joe Hawke and others, the Tribunal was – rather to its surprise – asked to recommend that the Government restore to Ngati Whatua of Orakei all the reclamations on the Waitemata Harbour made since 1840 without the consent of the hapū. If the Government could not restore, it should compensate. The Tribunal declined to consider these claims on grounds that they were irrelevant to the matter of the breach of fishing regulations, which Hawke, also embroiled in the Bastion Point

---

[3] Sorrenson, 'Towards a Radical Reinterpretation', p. 173 – in a section added to the original 1986 version of his essay.

controversy, was appealing.[4] Off the hook on that case, the Tribunal was then spared making any recommendations at all on the following two claims by the lapse of Ministry of Works plans to construct a thermal power station on the Manukau Harbour.

However it did make findings on the next claim it heard, the Te Atiawa claim that Petrocorp was about to join the town and freezing works of Waitara in piping still further pollution into the sea near its fishing reefs at Motunui. But the Tribunal avoided reparationist conclusions. It praised – as did the press –[5] the 'commonsense and accommodating approach by the Maori people to the application of the Treaty', and it commended their 'reasonable and practical approach'. It agreed with Te Atiawa's view that it would not be in the 'spirit' of the Treaty to claim the 'full, exclusive' fishing rights that the letter of the Treaty contract guaranteed. It spoke of a Māori approach to the Treaty as implying that its 'wairua or spirit' was 'something more than a literal construction of the actual words' and putting a 'narrow or literal interpretation out of place'. Quoting and glossing the preamble and section 6(1) (c) of its enabling Act, it noted (its italics) that it was required to determine 'whether certain matters are inconsistent with the *principles* of the Treaty' (rather than 'with the *provisions* of the Treaty').[6] Accordingly it suggested forward-looking administrative and statutory reforms to planning and public objection procedures so as to ensure that the Māori people would in future have their special rights to fisheries recognized; and it suggested practical measures in regard to the disposal of the industrial waste and sewage at issue. The only compensation suggested was an *ex gratia* payment to Aila Taylor as representative of his hapū, to help meet the costs of their battle for their reefs – a sum of $8,000 which his hapū regarded as derisory was finally offered by the Government.[7]

The first Tribunal found and recommended along similarly non-reparationist lines on the Ngati Pikiao claim which opposed the piping of sewage direct into the Kaituna River. It sympathized with the damage which that hapū of Te Arawa had already suffered from sewage pollution under the current system – in which pollutants were piped into Lake Rotorua, flowed sluggishly into Lake Rotoiti and from there out to Maketu via the Kaituna. It even found that 'cultural rights' guaranteed in the Treaty had been thereby violated: tapu against pollution had been ignored. But it spoke of Lake Rotorua as a 'national' asset and not simply a Māori one; it spoke of 'common sense' (as well as the Māori sense of things) requiring the preservation of Rotoiti, the Kaituna River and the Maketu Estuary; it said the proposed discharge of sewage into the river not only offended Māori values but was 'out of date and needlessly expensive';[8] and it made no powerfully reparatory findings.

---

[4] Waitangi Tribunal, *Joseph P. Hawke and others (Ngati Whatua, re Fisheries Regulations)*.

[5] EP4:30/3/83.

[6] *Te Atiawa Report*, para. 10.1 at pp. 55, 58.

[7] *Te Atiawa Report*, para. 4.9. at pp. 17-18, para. 9.2 para. 12.1 at p. 66 para. 12.5.

[8] *Kaituna Report*, paras. 7.11-12, 7.18.

Instead it commended Ngati Pikiao's patience and reasonableness and suggested action for the future. Despite the very strong local Māori feeling that sewage should never be released into water, it recommended (as well as consideration of land-based disposal of the city of Rotorua's sewage) the exploration of biological systems of treatment such as the badenpho system of stripping minerals from the waste before it entered the water.[9] This was indeed an alternative to the proposed disposal of sewage direct into the Kaituna River. But the badenpho system was certainly not on the locals' agenda – who in 1986 were to say they would rather 'die' (in battle if necessary) than see it introduced[10] – and no compensation for damage to and destruction of culturally valued things was suggested by the Tribunal.

In the *Manukau Report* the first Tribunal came the closest it ever did to recommending reparation. Though the formal claim made no mention of reparation, there was ample evidence that during the hearings the ownership of the harbour was (re)claimed.[11] And while the Tribunal recognized that compensation for land and fishing losses might be the only 'practical option' available, it did not actually suggest that option. It insisted instead that it was free to make recommendations or not, '*having regard to all the circumstances of the case*', (its italics) and equally emphatically noted that it was required to have regard to the '*practical application*' of the '*principles*' (its italics again) of the Treaty. The 'jurisprudential point' it concluded, was 'that although a claim may be well founded according to our interpretation of the Treaty, we have still to consider whether in all the circumstances of the case it is practicable to apply the principles of the Treaty to it'.

Dealing with the general claims before it as to the ownership and control of the Manukau Harbour, the Tribunal, asked to 'return' the harbour to its 'rightful owners', briskly distinguished between ownership and control, denied the claim to restored ownership and wondered whether some minor control might be revested in them. Exclusive control was out of the question, it argued, because of changed conditions since the 1860s. 'We cannot accept that Maori experience alone is sufficient to deal fairly with the complexities of a modern reality and with water uses beyond the experience of tribal forebears.'[12] Neither could the Tribunal see its way to recommend the return of the Treaty right to 'exclusive' use of the Manukau fisheries to the tribes. Remarking on the obvious conflict between Māori, commercial, and private recreational claims to the use of the fisheries, it suggested that 'a genuine search should begin to define the options available for the recognition and protection of Maori fishing grounds and securing compensation for Maori fishing losses'. For: 'We think it would be unfortunate if Maori fishing rights fell to be determined solely on a literal interpretation of the Treaty which guarantees an *exclusive* use of *all* Maori fisheries, for Maori fisheries are extensive

---

[9] *Kaituna Report*, paras. 9-10.

[10] *Nga Take Maori*: 24/11/86.

[11] Noted in the *Muriwhenua Fishing Report*, p. 185.

[12] *Manukau Report*, para. 9.2.3 at pp. 102-4.

indeed.'[13] When it came to consider the question of compensating the Tainui people for the adverse impact of industrial development in general on their lands and settlements as well as fisheries, it suggested that 'compensation' could take the form of the diversion of existing development levies – available because of the development of the New Zealand Steel plant at Glenbrook – to fund a programme of 'affirmative action to fund and assist tribal authorities to establish a new economic base for their people'.[14] But it did not find that any compensation was due.

It was as leery of suggesting precise reparative settlements in the particular claims as it was on the general ones. On only two of the particular Manukau claims did the Tribunal seriously approach reparation; but in both cases, plenty of space was left for negotiation. On lost Pukaki lands it suggested the return at least of wāhi tapu (sacred sites) by way of their compulsory acquisition from private owners by the Crown; but for the rest it urged simply 'that the Crown negotiate with the current owners and lessees for the acquisition of Pukaki marae, urupa and lagoon'.[15] On land and fishing right losses of the people of the Makaurau, Pukaki and Te Puea Marae, it did not assess for compensation. But it did suggest some form of (highly negotiable) compensation for the people of Makaurau, those whose lands and waters had suffered irreparably from the construction of the Manukau Sewage Works: 'The claimants do not want compensation. They want things restored to what they were. Regrettably, that is unrealistic'.[16] 'The Makaurau people lost more than most. Compensation has not been assessed but even if it were to be assessed under existing laws, the tribal and fishing loss is not compensatable. This most unsatisfactory state needs to be remedied. Any compensation payable ought to be payable not to individuals but to the various marae. Although compensation was not sought it provides the only practical alternative.'[17] On the Crown's past compulsory acquisition of the Waiuku forest it suggested 'that the search for a settlement be continued'; on mining of iron sands at Maioro, it indeed required that damage to the Tangitanginga burial reserve be repaired, but otherwise spoke of compromise and future co-operation; on the non-return of found Māori artefacts, it recommended a change in legislation and in administrative policy to assure that these taonga would be returned in future.[18]

Its most arresting suggestion for continued negotiation rather than reparation was made on the question of the heating of the waters of the Waikato River and the mixing with them of Manukau waters. The heating of the waters occurred as, transported from the river in a slurry pipe, they passed through the steel mill; the mixing occurred as they were discharged into the Harbour.

[13] *Manukau Report*, para. 9.2.8 at p. 112.

[14] *Manukau Report*, para. 9.2.12 at p. 120.

[15] *Manukau Report*, para. 9.3.1-2, pp. 120-2 and following.

[16] *Manukau Report*, para. 5.6 at p. 39.

[17] *Manukau Report*, p. 134.

[18] *Manukau Report* paras. 9.3.3-8, pp. 122-8.

It was a long-standing grievance and can be numbered with a series of a similar kind in the Waikato region where the issue was the pollution of the wairua (spirit) of rivers and streams, often by the discharge of animal waste, sewage or waters used for cooking and cleaning. The Māori view, now expressed again, was that each body of water had its own wairua and no body should be unnaturally mixed with any other; that waters were spiritually polluted by mixing, by discharge of wastes, and by heating; that the local people were irrevocably bound to protect the familiar spirits (the taniwha) who inhabited bends in rivers and other notable parts of the waterscape.

Such non-negotiable beliefs about water had been at issue with the Tribunal in the Kaituna claim and in the Motunui case. In the legal system at large they had recurred most famously in a 1981 Planning Tribunal case on the Steel Mill, at which the Principal Judge had decided that the conflicts between Māori belief and development programmes were not justiciable, partly on the grounds that they were conflicts of 'metaphysical beliefs'. 'Because they involve value judgments', the sceptical Judge was further to remark in 1985, 'there is no final indisputably correct answer'.[19] Now the Huakina Trust, wishing to protect the Manukau, told the Waitangi Tribunal that the mixing was offensive to their beliefs and thus to their culture, which was their 'taonga' as defined in the Treaty. But whereas in *Te Reo Report*, the Tribunal would see its way to saying the language was a taonga and therefore guaranteed by the provisions of the Treaty, and whereas it had already in the *Kaituna Report* identified 'cultural rights' as taonga, it chose not to do so here. It went so far as to say that 'the ultimate test may be not what is right, if that is capable of determination, but what is acceptable to the community', and that therefore the best that could be suggested was that Māori values, different from Pākehā in the respect that they found the mixing offensive, be given an 'appropriate priority' in 'a search for a practical alternative if there is one, or a reasonable compromise'. It might have been thought impossible to distinguish te reo as a taonga and cultural rights as taonga from the wairua of waters as taonga; but the Tribunal did.[20]

In these first Tribunal cases then – and despite Manukau publicity to the opposite effect[21] – there was little mention of reparation from the Tribunal itself. It was mostly negotiation and an eye to the future. The Tribunal did not consider its function to blame, apportion fault or to judge others, be it the Crown, an agency of the Crown, or any person. 'We were concerned', it stressed in its *Te Atiawa Report*, 'to identify problems but only for the purpose of seeking solutions.'[22]

Of course this approach was not unmixed with reparative considerations,

---

[19] See the Judge's account in A. R. Turner, 'The Changing Basis of Decision-making. Is Reason Sufficient?', at p. 181.

[20] *Manukau Report*, para. 9.3.5, pp. 123-5. See also paras. 7.1-2.

[21] As in *Metro*, April 1986.

[22] *Te Atiawa Report*, para. 9.2 at p. 46.

and from Te Reo case onwards the Tribunal was to make recommendations much more obviously rooted in considerations of reparation for past wrongs. But it did so in Te Reo not unmixedly, and in the *Waiheke Report* only to mention the possibility as an alternative to a better, future-oriented policy that it really preferred. It was only with the Orakei and Muriwhenua reports that the (now reformed) Tribunal came to make the serious proposition that reparations were, strictly speaking, owed. Even so, in the Muriwhenua case it made the suggestion in much more muted tones than its clients would have wished – if their highly reparationary claim to the return of their seas was anything to go by – and the suggestion was anyway supposed to be taken not as decisive but as a preliminary to hard negotiation with the Government. Still, the Tribunal did undoubtedly become more reparationist under the new legislation. What had happened was that, from being an institution that mediated between Māori claims and Government final decisions, it came to take up rather more the role of an advocate on its clients' behalf and left it to the Government to mediate between the demands of the tribes and a hostile public opinion. All the same, while the retrospective and the reparatory played a greater role in these post-Manukau reports especially after retrospection to 1840 was introduced, they were still greatly modified, even overridden, by considerations as to better future distributions of things and by the desire to change the present in a mode of political negotiations rather than juristic enforcement of rights.

In *Te Reo Report* the Tribunal, in line with its finding that the Māori language was a taonga guaranteed by the Crown and that it had not been actively protected and sustained as promised in the Treaty, recommended reparation of a sort: 'We have recommended that te reo Maori should be restored to its proper place by making it an official language of New Zealand with the right to use it on any public occasion, in the Courts, in dealing with Government Departments, with local authorities and with all public bodies.' It also recommended making the language available as of right in schools and favoured the appointment of a Maori Language Commission to 'watch over its progress and set standards for its use'.[23] But the language of restorationism was accompanied by the language of justice as fairness for the future, and justice itself was tempered by practical considerations of what the population would put up with: 'What the claimants seek . . . is fairness and equality of opportunity. We think that no fair-minded New Zealander would deny them what they ask for.'[24] Pupils at schools would not be under a duty to learn the language, 'for we think it more profitable to promote the language than impose it'.[25] Nor would it pre-empt the findings of the Royal Commission on Broadcast Communications by making recommendations at all on the matter of te reo on radio and television.[26]

23 *Te Reo Report*, para. 1 at p. 5.

24 *Te Reo Report*, para. 9.1.7 at p. 70.

25 *Te Reo Report*, para. 1 at p. 5.

26 *Te Reo Report*, Chapter 7.

It was all circumspection: the Tribunal correctly noted that 'to do justice' to the claim they had 'looked at the past . . . looked at the present situation and . . . tried to see what lies ahead in the future'.[27]

The arguments for and against reparation, the uneasy balancing of retrospective with prospective considerations of justice and policy, the hesitations as to whether to inform the Government that it had a strict duty to act or whether it would merely be a very good thing if it did: all these elements in the findings and recommendations of the Tribunal from then on are best illustrated in the Waiheke case. The claim put, and the claim answered, was 'that Crown policies fail to support the tribal groups that were parties to the Treaty of Waitangi, and in particular, those tribes like Ngati Paoa now so lacking for land or other endowments that they are threatened with extinction'. It was the present and future at issue; and the Tribunal roundly declared: 'We are not concerned in this case with compensation for past wrongs but with the significance of the Treaty in the formulation of modern policies.'[28] Nevertheless the Tribunal did retrospect both for 'background' to the land losses[29], and also to gloss the Treaty. It had to put the Treaty in its historical context because that is what it was required to do to discover the 'principles' that informed it; and Judge Durie examined subsequent Imperial Government policies up till 1852 when the colony got a constitution, to demonstrate the settled concern that the Māori not be rendered landless.[30] Throughout the findings the moral imperatives of 'duty' and 'obligation' recurred, intertwined with the optatives 'ought', and 'should'. That the Crown was 'in honour bound' to do what it ought was a recurring thought, hovering uneasily between the imperative and the simply strongly recommendatory.[31]

The Tribunal found that Ngati Paoa had no legal interest in the land at issue; their tribal connections in that respect had been severed with its sale in 1852. Nevertheless it was still 'ancestral' land[32] and this was the first time since development schemes had begun to be administered in 1929 by the Department of Maori Affairs that there was a chance to return to it. Even though it was neither Government policy nor a legal obligation, the Department ought to have given them first option to settle when it became vacant. For this was what Treaty 'principles' would suggest; and the Tribunal insisted that the 'principles' and not the 'provisions' of the Treaty be adhered to. For one thing the approach via the provisions of the Treaty would have

---

[27] *Te Reo Report*, para. 3.1.6 at p. 12.

[28] *Waiheke Report*, Chapter 8, p. 70.

[29] Chapter 8, p. 70. And see this book, Chapter 7, Section I for the history of past wrongs that was provided.

[30] *Waiheke Report* pp. 75-7.

[31] See, for example, *Waiheke Report*, pp. 81-2.

[32] Land no longer owned perhaps, but with which the hapū retained strong ties through the mode of tradition. See Holland J. in *Royal Forest and Bird Society* v *W. A. Habgood Ltd and others* (1987).

required 'the identification and proof of some wrong, like land confiscation'. It would have been 'the "tortious approach"as we call it'. For another thing, it would have required a Parliamentary petition to activate any suggested remedy as it lay outside the Tribunal's retrospective competence.[33] It was better anyway to think that the Government ought to have a policy of seeking a 'better and proper land base for the tribes in tribal ownership'. Hui since 1980, the New Zealand Maori Council in 1983, and the Maori Economic Development Commission set up in 1984 had suggested the provision of such bases without avail. The Government had not properly addressed the issue, and the Tribunal found that 'while the land development provisions of the Maori Affairs Act undoubtedly provide considerable benefit to the Maori people, they do not assure their equitable development in accordance with their tribal divisions'.[34]

Still, the issue was more than a question of what the Government, all things considered, *ought* to have done. It also had Treaty obligations. Strict rights violated were at issue as well as future goods in contemplation. The Tribunal glossed the Treaty to demonstrate the 'parentalism' of Queen Victoria's Government shown in her 'anxiety' to protect the natives, and in Lord Normanby's instructions to Hobson to acquire only 'unsettled' and 'waste' lands. A Government 'duty to protect the tribes in the acquisition process' must be presumed to correlate with its right of pre-emption. If not, Victoria was not a true parent.[35] All the signs of reparationist jurisprudence were there, then, despite the Tribunal's pronounced, and genuine, concern only with 'modern policies'. Judge Durie concluded the train of thought (the two other members of the Tribunal could not follow him in this) by arguing that the Crown had 'a duty to ensure that each tribe maintained a sufficient endowment for its foreseen needs'. It was not just that the Māori, before the Crown could buy under Article 2, should display a willingness to sell. They should *not have been allowed to sell* if it would have destroyed their land base: for this was part of the 'just rights and property'; that the preamble to the Treaty promised protection for. The duty had clearly been neglected.

What then of reparations? The Durie finding combined considerations of reparation with recommendations as to future policy in a way that will not now surprise the reader. The language of imperative duty alternated with the language of strong suggestion. Past wrongs and future goods equally played their part in the reasoning:

The Tribunal is established 'to make recommendations on claims relating to the practical application of the principles of the Treaty'. . . . [And] 'practical' denotes in this context, that a degree of adaptation of principles to meet changed circumstances is envisaged as well. . . . The claim may . . . be seen as contending, and properly so in my view,

[33] *Waiheke Report* pp. 61-5.
[34] *Waiheke Report*, pp. 65-9.
[35] *Waiheke Report*, pp. 70-3.

that a policy to prevent Ngati Paoa's landlessness, in 1840, when Ngati Paoa had all and the settlers none, becomes in 1987, an obligation to restore when the original policy has lapsed and the position in land ownership is reversed. It seems then a reasonable expectation today, and in keeping with the spirit of the Treaty, that the Crown should not resile from any opportunity it may have to provide at least part of those endowments that it ought to have guaranteed, and to ensure, that proper policies to that end are maintained. There is little Crown land left in Ngati Paoa territory . . . with which to make amends. . . . The Waiheke Scheme was surplus to the Crown's requirements. . . . Thus there was the opportunity to reaffirm in a modern way the Treaty with Ngati Paoa . . . I hold the view that the omission to seek a land base for Ngati Paoa, when the opportunity presented itself, and although a substantial gift of equity would have been involved, was contrary to the principles of the Treaty having regard to Ngati Paoa's landless state. I am therefore of the opinion that the claim is well founded.

Judge Durie concluded by arguing that while this would in terms of the Treaty of Waitangi Act 'compensate for or remove the prejudice', policy steps should also be taken by the Crown to 'prevent other persons from being similarly affected in the future'. The Treaty was 'not just with Maoris. It was a Treaty with tribes': a Government policy to enable Māori tribes not only to keep but to recover lands was called for.[36]

Retrospective or prospective justice: which was it to be? The policy of tribal restoration 'raises', said the Judge, 'the most profound issue to have come from the Waiheke claim. Need the resettlement of the landless tribe depend upon the proof of some past wrong or is it more equitable to apportion assistance having regard to need? Does the reparation approach in any event create more problems than it solves?'[37] Reparative justice would require the assessment of damages according to settled rules of quantification. This might mean those tribes which suffered 'atrocities' might 'recover handsomely', while those, 'perhaps "loyal" to the Crown in the wars, may expect little if anything at all. Yet, in the same historic process, tribes in both categories have somehow lost a reasonable land base. It is difficult to see that a tortious approach serves best to provide equity amongst them, or that it can ever deal adequately with those consequences of social dislocation that call for an assessment of the particular needs of each.' There were other problems too: the state, if the USA example was anything to go by, might well not be able to afford the monetary compensation that might be decided upon in the many impending cases. Worse perhaps, the impending policy of the privatization of Crown lands would make it very much harder for the government to return lands and waters to those tribes which wanted *their own things* back rather than money, which they could see only as an unsatisfactory substitute. And finally, while 'an exposure of past wrongs may be necessary and will no doubt bring new understandings to help heal old wounds', it might also turn the Treaty into a *casus belli* – a cause of and occasion for war.

---

[36] *Waiheke Report*, pp. 82-3.
[37] *Waiheke Report*, p. 84.

Thus Judge Durie, mixing reparative with ameliorative considerations, advocated that the best way to proceed was to transcend the idea of reparations, to 'move beyond guilt and ask what can be done now and in the future to rebuild the tribes'. This, he proclaimed, 'releases the Treaty to a modern world, where it begs to be reaffirmed, and unshackles it from the ghosts of an uncertain past'. 'In this way, the Treaty may yet be given new life and the honour of the Crown restored, not upon the assessment of past wrong, but upon the Crown's concern to promote the survival of the tribes in the years ahead.'[38]

And it was on this note that the findings of the Tribunal on the Waiheke claims ended; and not surprisingly. Mr M. J. Q. Poole, the second member of the Tribunal did not agree with Judge Durie. He explicitly rejected reparation. He could not find in the 'plain words' of the Treaty that the Crown was obliged to do anything other than to ensure that it had willing sellers on its hands, arguing against the Chairman that 'the provision of the Treaty expound the principles and we are limited . . . to what the Treaty states'. He could not find a duty on the Government to 'guarantee an endowment for the tribe's present and future needs'. He argued it to be just as persuasive (which was not very) to think that the chiefs, in having been accorded the right to alienate land at will, had *themselves* undertaken an 'obligation to retain sufficient land to constitute a resource base'. He noted that the Crown's exclusive right to buy Māori land had been 'abolished' in 1862, and that the various other measures replacing it (Land Acts, Maori Affairs Acts and so on), while they might well have been prejudicial to Māori people, nevertheless lay outside the retrospective ambit of the Tribunal. All this occurred before 1975. And if the third member of the Tribunal, Mr E. D. Nathan, did not explicitly reject the strict reparative approach, he did so implicitly, preferring to think of policies that would revive the ihi (life force) and wana (feeling of wellbeing) of Ngati Paoa.

Nevertheless Mr Nathan did add that the restoration of land to Ngati Paoa would be a particularly 'worthwhile exercise', 'because of their past history and the suffering endured of 150-200 years'.[39] And Mr Poole did not disagree with *that*. He dwelt on the loss of Ngati Paoa lands in the confiscations under the New Zealand Settlements Act of 1863 – a loss brought about by their loyalty to their Waikato relatives. The Board of Maori Affairs could not have been 'expected' to re-establish Ngati Paoa, but because of their history, he thought it 'worthwhile to find relief for this particular tribe'.[40] In the end, all three members of the Tribunal concluded that the four relevant parties – the Crown, the Board of Maori Affairs, the new owner to whom the Board had unfortunately sold the land, and the Ngati Paoa Development Trust (Inc) – should negotiate. Failing agreement, the Crown should seek some other 'endowment that involves a land base' within Ngati Paoa's territory.

---

[38] *Waiheke Report*, pp. 84ff.

[39] *Waiheke Report*, pp. 87-90.

[40] *Waiheke Report*, pp. 91-8.

Negotiation and conciliation had prevailed once more. But it had prevailed against a backdrop of serious, if inconclusive, reparatory considerations. 'Equity' – a projected good future distribution of things – had prevailed. But it was equity not only for its own sake; it was an equity made more urgent, more imperative, and less simply recommendatory, by considerations of past wrongs. Guilt and reparations may have been transcended, but they were transcended in the way Georg Wilhelm Friedrich Hegel, Karl Marx and other German dialecticians used to think ideas and activities transcended themselves.[41] They were *still there*, transformed to become of the substance of forward-looking considerations of equity.

Less need be said about the *Orakei Report* of November 1987, the first report from the second Tribunal and one which (successfully) recommended that the government should restore the claimed lands, pay $3,000,000 compensation, and remit debts of $200,000. The Tribunal found that 'as a consequence of the many breaches of the Treaty of Waitangi which we have recorded, and the serious loss and deprivation . . . incurred as a result, . . . appropriate relief should be granted' Ngati Whatua.[42] The Waiheke claim had established the principles of restoration of a tribal base at issue, and the Tribunal repeated the considerations of reparative justice and prospective justice and policy which buttressed those principles. The way was now cleared for a less modified reparationism if necessary.

In earlier cases the Tribunal had dwelt on the practicability of remedial measures. Now it looked more closely at its empowering statute and reiterated with a powerful new emphasis what it had already found in the Waiheke case, and what had also been suggested from a different perspective by the judges in the *New Zealand Maori Council v the Attorney General*: that the remedies proposed need not be 'practical' at all. Following the Court of Appeal, the Tribunal now held that the injunction to be 'practical' related only to the preambular instruction on how to interpret the wording of the Treaty in current conditions, not to the kind of recommendations it should make. The Tribunal was 'to make recommendations on claims relating to the practical application of the Treaty', that is, it was to interpret the Treaty for modern times and make recommendations that would bring things into line with the Treaty so interpreted. But as to the *recommendations* themselves, the Tribunal now argued that the remedies under Section 6(3) could include 'full and just compensation untempered by the convenience of the result. We depart in this respect from an earlier opinion of the Tribunal that it is obliged to make practical recommendations (*Manukau Report* . . . 8.1)'.

Still, it was not as if the Tribunal had lost sight of the practicality of remedy it had so insisted upon only five months earlier. 'The effective settlement' of claims, it thought, would rest with the parties' seeking 'reasonable compromise'; Ngati Whatua had made compromises in not seeking

[41] See Avenieri, *The Political and Social Thought of Karl Marx*, pp. 36-8, and (for an example of how the idea worked on practical problems), pp. 202-4.

[42] *Orakei Report*, p. 184.

the restoration of the full 700 acres it might have; it would share in the control of the public spaces that would be placed again under its mana; 'options for mediation' were and should remain open; 'the restoration of land taken may not be the necessary consequence of proof that it was taken wrongly. It may need to be asked for example, whether it is contrary to the principles of the Treaty to dispossess an innocent landholder who bought in good faith'. Considering whether it might calculate the 'host of variables' as to damages for injuries, 'lost use and missed development opportunities' so as to make reparation, the Tribunal emphatically rejected the approach: '"what might have been" is highly subjective'. A better approach was 'to re-establish in modern context an objective in the Treaty appropriate to the case . . . surely, the duty on the Crown to ensure the retention of a proper tribal endowment'.

All this flow of argument back and forth between the now familiar sets of considerations followed the pattern already set. So what was the point of the Tribunal's insisting that it was not bound to propose 'practical' measures at all? It was so that the tribes and not the Tribunal itself would have 'the mana to propose a compromise'. The Tribunal was divesting itself of its earlier mediatorial role and becoming an advocate, where it felt the facts of past wrongs justified it, of the Māori cause.[43] The mix of prospective and retrospective justice remained as before; the difficulties of reparation stood still acknowledged; practical politics still played a part in deciding what should be done.

So it was, too, in the *Muriwhenua Fishing Report*. Here, the lack of necessity to recommend 'practical solution' was again reiterated;[44] but this time with the effect that this left the negotiations not precisely with the Muriwhenua people, but with the Joint Committee on fishing already set up by the government and working towards agreement even as the Tribunal reported. Otherwise the Report – standing at the end of the unfolding process of balancing reparative justice with future-regarding justice and good policy – kept the balance hanging even, and also added weight to both the sets of considerations on which its recommendations hung. It did not pause to imagine that they might conflict. Rather it used each to buttress the other.

The first few pages of the Report, in the *Summary*, show this well. Balancing and trimming in a typical passage which mixed the modes, the *Summary* talked of 'developing a partnership' between Māori and Pākehā. It argued that this would require that they should, firstly, 'understand one another', and secondly, should 'repair some mistakes of the past': 'some', not 'all'; 'mistakes', not 'injustices' or 'wrongs'. In a similar balancing of considerations, it held that any 'impracticality' in giving the Māori what was rightly theirs by Treaty stemmed 'not from the Treaty but from our failure to meet its terms'; but it insisted that 'there was, and still is, room for an agreement to be made'.[45]

---

[43] *Orakei Report*, Sections 14.1, 14.2 at pp. 183-7.

[44] *Muriwhenua Fishing Report*, pp. 212, 219, 227.

[45] *Muriwhenua Fishing Report*, pp. xiii, xix.

Putting even more weight into both sides of the balance, the *Summary* spoke even more forcefully of 'numerous and serious breaches of the Treaty' and of the Quota Management System being in 'fundamental conflict with the Treaty's principles and terms, [in] apportioning to non-Maori the full, exclusive and undisturbed possession of the property in fishing that was guaranteed to Maori'. Yet there was great force to the other side: 'A new agreement or arrangement is essential . . . Rightly or wrongly, new circumstances now apply and a number of private interests, honestly obtained, must be weighed in the balance. It is out of keeping with the spirit of the Treaty . . . that the resolution of one injustice should be seen to create another'. And in its concluding sections, the *Summary* spoke the language of tribal restorationism which mixed reparative and backward-looking concerns with views as to the justice and policy of current and future distributions of social goods. 'It is the restoration of a tribal base that predominates amongst the Muriwhenua concerns. Any programme would be misdirected if it did not seek to re-establish their ancestral association with the seas, providing for their employment, the development of an industrial capacity, the restoration of their communities and the protection of their resource. Their own current programmes directed to those ends are grossly under-funded and much assistance is required'. The *Summary* concluded by endorsing a Canadian view that it was better to 'enhance the ability' of indigenous peoples to support themselves, than to 'spend increasing amounts of [government] revenue supporting them on social assistance'. It thus married reparationism, future-orientation and the common New Zealand prejudice against state 'handouts' with its fundamental view that, 'somewhere in this great scheme of things, in the changing economies and technologies of our day, there must still be a place for tribal communities'.[46]

Such balancings recurred throughout the Report. The Tribunal noted the difficulty 'in maintaining the "just rights" ' of one important sector of the community without prejudicing another's, and it lamented the fact that 'both Maori and non-Maori have been driven to more extreme positions to the prejudice of reaching arrangements to the mutual benefit of both'. It would not 'follow that if the Treaty [was found to be] breached, the whole [QMS] scheme must be jeopardised provided a reasonable agreement can be made'.[47] Restoration of tribal position must be the aim of the Crown; *perhaps* it was even a duty. The ways and means, however, of attaining it would need careful study, then negotiation. In re-allocating fishing Quota to tribes it would be necessary, for instance, to consider 'the number of Maori who have alternative employment, or who already hold fish quota, and who would opt to remain in the general regime'.[48] The language was never purely that of reparation, though the implicit reparationism of the recommendations was clear enough: 'It is consistent with the Treaty that agreements or arrangements

---

[46] *Muriwhenua Fishing Report*, pp. xx, xxi.

[47] *Muriwhenua Fishing Report*, pp. 227, 150. See also pp. 3, 137-9, 148-50, 184, 193-5, 211, 227.

[48] *Muriwhenua Fishing Report*, pp. 228–31, 237.

on fishing should be sought. In the light of changed circumstances, new agreements or arrangements are now essential. It is in the interests of both sides . . . . The Quota Management System need not be in conflict with the Treaty, and may be beneficial to both parties, if an agreement or arrangement can be reached . . . . Very substantial relief to the claimants is required in respect of past breaches and to restore their fishing economy to what it might have been.'[49]

Overall, it may be concluded, the Tribunal had consistently moderated the demands of reparative justice. And this too it did in the Taipa case in which it held in the end that though manifest wrongs had been done Ngati Kuri, all local interests in an efficient and cheap sewerage system must be weighed and the good of all considered. Ngati Kuri must on this occasion bow to the public interest. Thus from 1977 through 1988, ever more powerfully making the case for reparations, the Tribunal nevertheless continued to insist that reparations were not the whole of justice, and that a balance must be kept.

II

The Tribunal's Clients and the Politicians

Some of the political motives of the Tribunal's careful activity will already be obvious. While the one big hard case of *Māori* v *Pākehā* was being heard in public it was doubtless advisable to proceed with caution. The public view would be coloured – even clouded and obscured – by the global case, so that even local and limited cases for reparation might not be sympathetically received. There were other practical political motives too. The Māori constituency of the Tribunal, as well as wanting reparations, also *wanted* prospection and negotiation. Most also wanted moderation of reparatory claims. And the politicans of both main parties kept speaking of the importance of not dwelling on past wrongs but on constructing a better future. Living in the real world of politics, the Tribunal had to react to these stated positions.

The Tribunal's Māori constituency wanted at base, as well as reparation, something else. They wanted redistribution of rights (especially) to property, employment, and education; they wanted the liberty and power to practise their culture; they wanted more (and more independent) political authority both nationally and in their tribes; they wanted more resources on the grounds of the current injustice that Māori wants, needs, and rights were being denied more than those of the Pākehā. They looked forward to a better future when the redistribution had occurred. This was all expressed awkwardly but clearly, hampered often by the rhetoric of reparative justice in contract which they also continued to use; and they continually mixed considerations of reparation with forward-looking policy. Perhaps they could not escape

---

[49] *Muriwhenua Fishing Report*, pp. 239–40.

the mixing of modes because they were always aware that it was in their past that they found their identity not just as a *wronged* people, but as a people, so that for them the prospect for the future could not exist independently of their continued retrospection. Whatever the explanation, they mixed the modes of retrospection and prospection; and it was this that gave the Tribunal room for manoeuvre out of the ambit of reparatory justice.

The mixture of modes was evident for instance at Turangawaewae and during the Hikoi. At Turangawaewae, Te Runanga Whakawhanaunga i Nga Hahi o Aotearoa (The Maori Council of Churches of Aotearoa) indeed wanted reparations for confiscated land. But it also argued for 'greater equality of access to material resources', greater Māori participation in the financial system, the recognition of Māori values in the legal, governmental, and educational system, and better policies to preserve Māori land, to ameliorate Māori unemployment and to improve Māori housing. Wanganui a Tara, demanding reparations, also looked to Māori housing conglomerations, and to insurance and finance companies staffed by Māori who would have learned the skills to manage them. Others recommended that the Tribunal itself have a power of forward-looking 'positive discrimination', as well as the power to repair past wrongs. Locating the current Māori-Pākehā problem in Pākehā breach of the Treaty, the Moral Aspects Workshop called nevertheless for a 'realistic approach to the problems of our street kids, unemployment, the problem of crime'. It called for a return to the past, not for purposes of determining reparation, but for the purpose of restoring ethnic identity: 'Our young people have a dislocated past, a dreaded event in the future, or a huge question mark, and are disoriented in the present. Therefore one of the problems that needs to be addressed is how we restore them to their identity and self-esteem through restoration of their past, the offering of options for their future and rediscovering themselves in the present.'[50]

'Hey Pakeha' exclaimed a broadsheet put out by Kotahitanga supporting the Hikoi: 'You signed the Treaty too! If you want a just future for all the people of Aotearoa – then expose the unkept promises!' But Kotahitanga also looked to the present: 'Hey Maori! What have you got to celebrate! No land! No language! NOTHING! Wise up now & join the march for a better future!'[51]

Kotahitanga's policies as well as their slogans were forward-looking, though set against a background of past injustice. Their aim was 'to gain for the Maori people for the first time the opportunity to make decisions for themselves independent of the New Zealand Government'.[52] Hilda Halkyard-Harawira typically looked to the future: 'The Treaty has a lot to do with the future of the children of this country';[53] and Nick Tangaroa expressed well in 1984

Blank *et al.* (eds.), *He Korero*, pp. 69-70, 75, 85, 105. Compare p. 8 with p. 79, and p. 88 with p. 95.

51 *Tautokotia te Hikoi ki Waitangi*, in WAC (ed.), *Te Hikoi*, p. 21.

52 WAC (ed.), *Te Hikoi*, pp. 7-20.

53 WAC (ed.), *Te Hikoi*, p. 57.

the mixture of justices demanded by Kotahitanga: 'A challenge has been mounted against the present Pakeha system which does not recognise Maori needs and Maori values – taha Maori. The demand for the return of ancestral land, traditional fishing grounds, action in areas of unemployment, housing, health, education and justice.'[54] Justice was Janus-faced, looking both ways.

The Tainui were clearest of all as to the future they wanted in early 1984, and it was their speakers who in a range of fora, while supporting Treaty debate and requiring the government to address the various *take* arising from it, thought it a mistake to forget the future and motives other than justice in contract. 'We believe', said Mrs Eva Rickard – also a leader of Kotahitanga – 'that it is time to present to this country the "hurts" our people have suffered since that fateful day in February 1840.' But the purpose of this, argued the veteran leader of the Raglan land claim, was not to get into debate about the Treaty; rather it was to argue that the 'hurts'. . . . 'strike at the very heart of this country's perceptions of fairness and moral principle. We believe it is still possible to build a good relationship between all the people of New Zealand provided that Government and Crown take notice of these *take* and in the light of these "hurts" make a new and real attempt to bring to fruition the promise of the Treaty'. She saw that 'political will' was needed 'to initiate a grand and meaningful debate to examine all outstanding grievances. Even greater political will is called for to resolve those grievances. We believe these issues can be resolved through goodwill rather than confrontation, through negotiation rather than litigation, and through *whanaungatanga* rather than *factionalism*'.[55]

Robert Mahuta and Hori Forbes said much the same for Tainui at the Waitangi hui: 'We want you to see how concerned we are with particular issues that are also of great national moment – people developments in the Waikato, the push towards Maori economic development by way of young people who are living on their lands to become self-sufficient, the past detailed operations of the Waitangi Tribunal and its vastly more significant future. Any recommendation we have made on any of these issues could doubtless be related back by some exercise of logic or flights of rhetoric to the Treaty. We go to the spirit of the Treaty which we interpret as meaning that the Crown would be concerned with the welfare of the people and that it would respect Maori rights to self-determination.'[56] And similar (but non-Tainui) Māori sentiments may in fact be found throughout the life of both Tribunals wherever the question of reparations for past wrongs arose, though the Treaty was never questioned in that forum. They were perhaps best expressed in the 1983 Report of the Advisory Committee on Youth and Law in our Multicultural Society:

There is the continued focus of attention by some on the dishonouring of the Treaty

---

54 WAC (ed.), *Te Hikoi*, p. 33.
55 Blank *et al.* (eds.), *He Korero*, pp. 41-3.
56 Department of Maori Affairs, *Nga Korero*, p. 153.

of Waitangi. Others make claims concerning the injustices of land deals; still others' claims refer to the broken promises relating to the food resources of the sea, the rivers and the lakes. All . . . [these] . . . ultimate judgments, provide a haze that obscures areas that could be more immediately resolved. Many claims do reveal injustices and do need corrections. Nevertheless . . . [and so on.][57]

In sum, the Tribunal's Māori constituency did not see reparative justice in contract as the sum total of justice and good policy. Nor, even more emphatically, did the politicians, who were at once the Tribunal's masters and the registrars of public opinion.

This was evident from the beginning of the Tribunal's career in the public eye. In 1975, debating its creation, the Government stressed its future role as a means of attaining agreement as much as they argued for it as a means of repairing past wrongs. Dr Gerard Wall admitted the Treaty of Waitangi Bill would not provide much by way of retrospective justice, but praised the Māori people, as being above all 'essentially realistic'; Matiu Rata spoke of the Bill as preserving the 'spirit of the Treaty and provid[ing] practical guidelines affecting Maori interests'.[58] In 1984-1985, debating primarily the question as to whether or not the Tribunal should have retrospective powers, both sides of the House stressed the need for moderation, conciliation and an attention to principles rather than to the strict letter of the law. The Opposition's main concern was to show how the increased power of the Tribunal would lead to an unhealthy reparationism, the Government's to concede a growth in *healthy* reparationism against a background of willingness to compromise and reason. Mr Doug Graham (Opp) talked of the complexity and difficulty of reparatory justice and the 'tact' necessary 'if a solution beneficial to all New Zealanders' were to be found. Mr W. R. Austin (Opp) spoke of the need to work 'sensibly' and 'sensitively' and how the Tribunal's success would depend 'on the wider community accepting its findings as fair'. And they and their colleagues in Opposition worried about compensation claims spreading hydra-like to destroy the land. Winston Peters showed himself to be particularly skilled in that area of argument.

Government MPs for their part spoke of the necessity that justice be done. Indeed: 'If we are to maintain peace, good order and good government in New Zealand it is essential to provide for the redress of grievances', said Geoffrey Palmer. But their *other* message was that the Māori, like the Pākehā, were a reasonable people, prepared to settle. It would not be easy but it must be done, and the Tribunal had shown, said Whetu Tirikatene-Sullivan, 'the patience of Job and the wisdom of Solomon' – no precipitation, no insistence on the strict requirements of justice. Mr Noel Scott held that 'utu [meaning 'revenge' here] is quite different from the justice and conciliation

---

[57] Tauroa, *Report of Advisory Committee on Youth and Law in our Multicultural Society* (1983), p. 59.
[58] NZPD2:37 (8 November 1975), p. 5727; (10 September), p. 4342.

the government is trying to achieve', and the fact that Maoridom was prepared to leave the decisions to government was an admirable 'act of faith'.[59]

Other parliamentary debates through the 1980s showed this same tendency to balance reparationism with conciliationism. But never more so than in those following the *Muriwhenua Fishing Report*. The Report, impinging as it did on the private interests of those fishermen and fishing companies who had bought ITQs from the Government, raised by far the greatest outcry of any of the Tribunal's pronouncements. It raised, said Hon. Colin Moyle, Minister of Agriculture and Fisheries, in the parliamentary debate in mid-June 1988[60] on the matter, 'fears and expectations'. He admitted injustices had been done in the past and that the Government 'had not fulfilled its obligations under the Treaty'. Indeed there was injustice as recently as 1985, when local Māori were denied ITQs by his own party's Government because of the small scale of their activities. This was 'unjust, and an error'. But he admitted that 'scepticism' as to the 'reliability' of the oral evidence on which the Tribunal had relied was 'inevitable' and he wondered how, having mainly confined themselves to inshore fishing in the nineteenth century, the contemporary Māori could now lay claim to fishing rights to the full extent of the 200 km limit now – since 1986 – by international agreement under Government control. He assured Parliament that it was not right to create further injustices in rectifying those of the past. Nor should the sins of the parents be visited on the children. And, he said, echoed by all the politicians, 'time', 'calm', and 'reason', would be needed to reach a 'fair and workable compromise'. Inflammatory words, from either side, but especially from those who opposed the Tribunal's findings, were 'disappointing'. He spoke in tones of some confidence about the work of a joint Government and Māori working party on fisheries which would report at the end of the month.

This pattern: the admission of past wrongs, the casting of doubt as to their precise nature and extent, reflections on the practical and moral difficulties of reparation, and the pleas for restraint and compromise on both sides was the dominant one in Parliament. Mr John Banks, Mr Ross Meurant, Mr John Carter (the MP whose constituency included Muriwhenua) and others liable to opposition extremes were not put up to speak in debate. Jim Bolger called for a 'calm, rational, fair' settlement, though he noticed that Mr Moyle had provided no 'principles' on which one might be founded. He spoke against 'violence and extremes'. For his part, he wanted 'one law' to apply to all, and a consideration, not of the past but of 'the real facts of the current situation'. He described the Tribunal's (reparationist) interpretations as partaking of 'fantasy', and he stressed, quoting the Tribunal, that the Treaty was 'hastily drawn up and ambiguous', and thus that a 'broad approach' was necessary. He thought it 'inconceivable' that all fishery resources should pass 'absolutely into Maori ownership', as the drift of the Tribunal's findings

---

[59] NZPD1:41, pp. 2704, 2706, 2708, 2710 (18 Dec 1984); 1:41, pp. 5649; 6060, 6063, 6065-7, 6070-1, 6073, 6076-7, 6078-9 (6 Aug 1985).

[60] NZPD1:42, pp. 4384-4407 (14 June 1988).

seemed to suggest. He noted that Matiu Rata, considering who would be eligible for any possible benefits from the claim, had thought it might include any Māori on the Māori electoral roll in the Far North, and commented how far *that* criterion of membership was from those of 1840. In brief, 'the solution must be a political one', it must be 'acceptable', there must be 'accommodation'. The Treaty could 'guide' but not 'impose'. Māori were 10-12 per cent of the population; 'others' in the high 80s. *That* was the fundamental fact on which distributions must be based – and any future arrangement 'to be accepted by all New Zealanders must be seen to be fair by all New Zealanders'.

Similar speeches were made by the others, all of whom – in ways modified by party allegiances – stressed the 'historic importance' of the issue, and how it would be best approached 'gently, quietly and with respect'. They talked of Māori fishing 'interests' rather than 'rights', of the need for 'negotiation' and 'mediation', of the fact that the Tribunal could only suggest solutions and could not bind the Government. They were told by Mike Moore (Minister of Overseas Trade) that the Tribunal had found not that the Māori 'owned' the fishery, but that the Muriwhenua 'business and activity of fishing' had been guaranteed by the Crown and could not be 'impinged upon without some agreement'. Mr Wetere reminded his colleagues that the *Muriwhenua Report* was an 'interim' one, not even a 'finding'. All respect was paid to the Treaty as a charter of 'fundamental human rights'; and it was said to be 'all about . . . charting the way forward', the source of an 'obligation with the future'. Mr Simon Upton (Opp) spelt out the meaning of this in criticizing too 'legalistic' an approach to the Treaty. Wondering why, so obviously outdated as it was, the Treaty still persisted, Upton thought it was because its 'spirit persisted' and it was *that* that people were prepared to acknowledge. But 'that will continue only if there is a political conviction that the treaty will still speak.' And: 'For that conviction to have legitimacy, and for negotiations to stick, the Government must have a mandate'. So the solution would have to be a 'compromise' – 'I take no pleasure in saying that'. In a peroration that reminded listeners that 'the Crown is the people', Upton concluded that the results of negotiation would need to satisfy not just the Government and the Māori claimants. It would need to satisfy the rest of the people too. On a similar naming agenda, Bruce Gregory insisted the Treaty was between the Māori and (represented by the Crown) the 'many people' who were not. And he too came to a similar conclusion about the necessity for a popularly acceptable settlement. Hon. Ian McLean, Deputy Leader of the Opposition, argued that the 'principles' not the 'letter' of the Treaty were what counted. Only Winston Peters spoke slightingly of the Treaty and of any tendency to a retrospection that would be balanced by conciliation: 'the path to partnership is constantly hampered by a Treaty that was signed 148 years ago when the mixture of our races on such a scale as (now) could scarcely have been conceived'. For him the future was all important and 'rhetoric, cliches and platitudes' were not enough. But Peters' was not the normal parliamentary view, at least as regards the Treaty.[61]

If peace by negotiation was one theme the Tribunal heard from the politicians, the other was that of the greater importance of distributive justice than reparations. Voices of those who said they wished to minimize reparation and maximize equalization of condition, often spoke like Mr Bruce Christopher, an Auckland journalist, in 1980: 'I certainly don't feel guilty about anything people of the same race as I might have done to the Maoris or anything the Maoris did to them. On the other hand, I am concerned that Maoris today should get their fair share of justice.'[62] Or, opposing too much reparation, they spoke like the *Star*, editorializing in 1985 on the idea of the retrospective powers of the Waitangi Tribunal being extended to 1840: 'Instead of pressing on with this potential hornet's nest, the Government would perhaps be wiser to concentrate on the cycle of deprivation so many Maori families face today.'[63]

While either opposing or supporting the Tribunal and reparations, politicians routinely emphasized the importance of prospection for the sake of equalization and meeting Māori needs, and they minimized the importance of retrospection to seek a justice that was unattainable – and the contemplation of which was not an unmixed good. Mr Venn Young, National's Social Welfare spokesman in 1985, set the tone of that party's commentary on the Labour Government and the Waitangi Tribunal: 'Re-examination of the early land deals will not alter Maori prison rolls, the 70 per cent of Social Welfare boys and girls who are Maori or the clients of the courts, or the homelessness and unsupervised Maori youth.'[64] Ian McLean spoke that way too on the Treaty of Waitangi (SE) Bill: 'The youngsters at Murupara will not wake up on Monday morning with jobs, skill, and free of crime because of the Bill. The Bill will give them hope and opportunities for the future, but it will not solve the economic and social problems of the Maori people or the pakeha people of New Zealand.'[65] Winston Peters in 1987 through into 1989 combined the pleas for more jobs and better education for the Māori with attacks on the idea for reparation; and the National MPs always spoke of the 'false hopes' and 'dangerous fears' raised by the prospect of reparation through the Tribunal. Social justice was to be attained less by reparations than by better distribution of goods; and the pursuit of peace was endangered by reparations.[66]

Labour politicians naturally stressed rather less the prospective elements in what they did when they strengthened the Tribunal and defended its recommendations, and when for instance (in July 1988) they proposed creating

---

[61] NZPD1:41 (15 June 1978), pp. 4384-4497.

[62] AS16:29/3/80.

[63] AS8:7/8/85. Similarly, H6:7/5/81.

[64] AS5:3/6/85.

[65] NZPD1:42, pp. 1726-7 (8 Dec 1987).

[66] NZPD1:42, pp. 4565-6, 4569 (21 June 1988).

more and strengthening the existing Maori Trust Boards to administer, among other things, compensation monies. But prospection was not absent. It was during the debate on the *Muriwhenua Fishing Report* that Mike Moore – quoted in Chapter 1 – contrasted Māori and Pākehā figures on home-owning, unemployment, education and health, asking 'How can any of us be proud of two nations?' Bruce Gregory spoke of the Maori Trust Boards Amendment Bill as dealing with 'some . . . injustices' and helping to 'rocket Maoridom into the modern era as a member of the brotherhood of mankind'. Mr Jim Anderton spoke more soberly of confronting not only a history that had 'good and bad actions on all sides' but of a duty on Parliament to 'redress imbalances in the New Zealand community in creative ways'.[67]

The practice of political argument from 1975 through 1988 was, it may be concluded, far from solely reparatory. We have seen the foundations of reparatory thought, so the question now must be as to the foundations on which the Tribunal's arguments and recommendations were – if not on reparationism – based. Why did it insist on prospection as well as retrospection; and why was not all its prospection a prospection aimed at the attainment of distributive justice, but rather at whatever could be negotiated to improve the Māori condition? Why did its clients and the politicians argue in the same ways? These questions cannot be answered merely by reference to the political conditions just described, because it was the very foundations that made those political conditions intelligible and therefore possible. Without the foundations, the politics of moderation and negotiation would have been pointless and unconvincing. Nor, in fact, can the questions satisfactorily be answered in the language of the Tribunal itself, though many of its particular arguments and recommendations suggest the answers. The Tribunal indeed developed a new Treaty jurisprudence designed to answer to its practice of prospection and negotiation. But that served as much to obscure as to clarify its proceedings. Without the foundations, the new jurisprudence would have been gibberish.

The foundations lay in some conceptual truths about justice and political morality, as well as about reparative justice itself. If never stated, they nevertheless seem to have been accepted as true not only by the Tribunal but by the political nation of New Zealand/Aotearoa. They were rather used than consciously addressed; and they were garbed in the new Treaty jurisprudence of New Zealand/Aotearoa. The foundational beliefs about justice and the new jurisprudence now demand attention.

Chapter 9
The Foundations of the Politics
of Compromise and the Jurisprudence
of the Wairua

I

The Foundational Beliefs about Justice

It will be emerging that the particular arguments made by the Tribunal, by its clients, and by most of the New Zealand/Aotearoa population were informed by some certain foundational beliefs. These seem to have been: that justice is not the whole of political virtue, that the unmitigated pursuit of justice (especially reparative justice) is indeed a vice, and that in any case reparative justice might well not bring about the distribution of social goods that other ideals of justice required and that other ideals of a good future suggested. Equally, these same beliefs must have informed the 'Treaty jurisprudence of the wairua' that was developed by the Tribunal and the courts and which is the subject of this chapter. It is not that the three sets of beliefs were ever fully articulated. It is rather that if they (or something very like them) were *not* believed to be true, then the argument used by the practical men and women of a proudly untheoretical and unintellectual nation would not have been thought at all convincing by anyone.

How may these foundations of arguments be articulated so that they may be understood?

Firstly: reparative justice suffers along with all ideas of justice from the defects of justice itself as a practice. It shares with them the unalloyed insistence that relations between people are to be seen as ones of rights and duties. And there is more to political – and even more obviously personal – life than that. Justice insists on dividing and distinguishing people; and not all politics and life is like that. Politics fudges differences and compromises rights. It is the kind of activity characterized by log-rolling, horse-trading, compromise of principles and principled stands.[1] It features equivocation, insincerity, bombast, hypocrisy and slyness. It is seldom what it appears to be. If justice should be seen to be done, politics probably should not. Politics does not thrive (like justice) where things are settled and where rights and duties are clearly understood. Politics is (to use definitions from all parts of the political spectrum) *precisely* the 'field of the unsettled'.[2] It is the activity of 'attending to the arrangements of society'[3] so as to adjust or change things;

---

[1] See Luban, 'Bargaining and Compromise: Recent Work on Negotiation and Informal Justice'.

[2] Connolly, *The Terms of Political Discourse*, conclusion.

[3] Oakeshott, 'Political Education', pp. 112–13.

it is the activity of looking to the future in a legislative frame of mind, acting and arranging things with an eye to the consequences;[4] it is the 'authoritative allocation of resources', where the business of allocation never ceases.[5] Politics is a process, never finished, something (unlike justice) which can never be 'done'.

If there is something seedy and seemingly immoral about the practice of politics, then so too is there something wrong with justice. The vices of politics consist in giving too little regard to established principle, treating people and their interests with arbitrary favour and disfavour, and a tendency to multiply production of things out of a desire to do well by everyone and thus to avoid complaints of unjust distributions in conditions of scarcity. The vices of justice are to regard only established (or sought-for) principle and not to allow affection or personal interest to count in making decisions. Justice concentrates too much on the distribution of what there is rather than on the enjoyment of production, or on trying to produce more, or instead of simply forgetting the whole boring issue of distributions when it *is* boring. And justice is too straightforward and uncompromising where things are complicated. Politics recognizes complexity and seeks to fudge and unify; justice tries to simplify by dividing and distinguishing.

To stress the vices of each practice is perhaps to miss the main point: that each – politics and justice – covers a different segment of morality. They are differently concerned about the way people do and should live. There is of course a politics of justice and rights – a 'hot' politics which is couched in terms of claims to justice.[6] But hot politics is not the whole of politics, and when it occurs it is a symptom of ill-health in the political system. Thus the politics of contemporary Ulster, South Africa, or Far West Asia (the 'Middle East' to Europeans) are to a large degree of this kind. Such politics shows marked dissatisfaction with current arrangements of rights and duties. Though he might have been factually wrong in arguing that the Jews invented the ideals of rights and justice to combat their powerful oppressors, one can see what Nietzsche meant in arguing that the 'genealogy of morals' was to be found in the resistance of the weak against their rulers.[7] And where justice-talk occurs it can be a sign of trouble in the state.

Secondly, as well as sharing the defects of justice in general, reparative justice suffers defects peculiar to itself. The basis for claims of reparation lies in a wrong having been done; the process of repair is painful and burdensome to those with the duty of reparation. The victims of the wrong feel resentment and a sense of grievance at their past treatment and are likely to consider any compensation they receive inadequate to their loss; the beneficiaries are likely to resent making recompense, especially if they do not consider themselves personally guilty of the wrong. Both resentments

[4] Held, 'Justification, Legal and Moral'.

[5] Easton, *The Political System*, Chapters 4 and 5.

[6] See the introduction to Maier, *Changing Boundaries of the Political*.

[7] Nietzsche, *The Genealogy of Morals*.

create and feed a feeling that injustice is being done.[8] And feelings of injustice are no basis on which to build that common life which exhibits a warm solidarity and identification of mutual interests – a life, as the Māori might put it, of aroha. At worst, even a settled system of reparations can break down, leading to cycles of revenge and civil war. Revenge, the exchange of an evil for an evil, normally occurs when reparations owed are not payed. The thirteenth-century *Njal's Saga* amply demonstrates this process occuring in Iceland over the centuries;[9] and it is a common pattern in human history. The Māori concepts of utu and muru illustrate well the close connection there can be between reparation and revenge. Utu and muru (roughly justice in transactions) demands reciprocity through time: good for good between parties, good for evil from one party to another, evil for evil if the utu of proper exchange is not done. The imagery – utu is repayment, returning, satisfying, rewarding, replying etc., and muru is wiping off, rubbing out, plundering, forgiving, etc. – is archetypically that of transactional justice.[10]

So that, essential as reparation is, where cases in reparation are hard cases then it had best be avoided – if it can be.

Thirdly: reparation is not the whole of social justice. It is simply – like market justice – part of justice in transactions; it is not justice in distributions. Though, like the results of just market transactions, the results of reparations *might* turn out to conform with people's ideas of just distributions, then again they might not. Like market justice, reparative justice might turn out rather to contradict what is thought to be a just (or otherwise better than current) arrangement of things.

The literature on positive discrimination and affirmative action aimed to aid women, and blacks and other minorities in the USA and the UK displays a definite rift on the question of justice – a rift that illustrates the point that there *is* a distinction to be made between reparative and distributive justice. There are those who argue that 'disadvantaged' groups should have public resources 'paid back' to them as reparation for the past wrongs that have caused their disadvantage; and there are those who argue that the disadvantaged' should now be 'compensated', that is advantaged, for future-oriented reasons.[11] Future-oriented compensation was made famous by President Lyndon B. Johnson in the image not of compensation or payment for past wrongs, but of the granting of helps and handicaps on, as it were, competitors in the race of life. People and groups were to be 'compensated' for their current disadvantages so that the race would be made more even when the starter's pistol fired. The (complex) core idea was to provide equality

---

[8] Day, 'Compensatory Discrimination'; Montague, 'Rights and Duties of Compensation'.

[9] Magnusson and Palsson (eds.), *Njal's Saga*.

[10] H. W. Williams, *A Dictionary of the Maori Language* (7th ed., Wellington, 1985). See also Biggs, 'Humpty-Dumpty', p. 304 on muru and for an implicit warning as to my perhaps too easy translation of concepts from one culture to another.

[11] See, for example, Thalberg, 'Reverse Discrimination and the Future'; Wasserstrom, 'Preferential Treatment'; Richards, *The Sceptical Feminist*, Chapter 4.

of opportunity, not to repair past damage. With the competing conceptions of compensation in mind, Bernard Boxill, a contemporary American philosopher, suggested that 'compensation' always be regarded as forward-looking, and 'reparation' as backward-looking.[12]

That suggestion could not have been adopted in New Zealand. New Zealanders, following legal usage, saw 'compensation' as a weaker form of 'reparation' and mostly spoke of distributive justice as 'equity'. But the difference Boxill insisted upon was observed even if his distinction was not. Reparation was retrospective, and there was also a distinguishable form of prospective justice and policy. The question then was whether reparations would bring about equity.

There is no general and theoretical answer to that question. It all depends on the circumstances. Professor Phillips, in his book on reparations, argued that were reparative justice to be carried out in the USA then those who had wrongly suffered, blacks in particular, would have goods distributed to them in such a way that a just distribution would emerge. And it *may* be that reparations would in some cases bring about a just distribution of opportunity, property, power, esteem and so on. Everything however would depend on the details as to who would get the reparations, in what form and from whom, and on the particular conception of distributive justice that was being answered to. In general, reparative, like market justice, might well deny the claims of merit through hard work or dirty work or excellent performance, or the needs of those who suffer poverty or illness or old age or cultural deprivation; or the claims of expectation grounded in an accepted way of life; or the claims of those whose work – whose very being perhaps – is simply not paid for in the currency of money, honour or even of minimal respect. Reparations may even give to those who do not need and take from those who do.

The facts as to what making reparations would turn out to do for future distributions are contingent on the way things happen to be.

All these three sets of thoughts are consistent with the arguments of the Tribunal, its clients and the Government. The weight of each set was undoubtedly felt, though their articulation and separate development were not much evident. And perhaps because of that theoretical inarticulacy it was never said that the arguments for doing reparative justice were arguments for simply that, no more or less; and that if it was a better and more just distribution of things that was wanted then arguments ought to be made for *that* and policies framed to attain it. Rather the Treaty was continually dragged in to complicate matters, conflating questions of the duty to keep promises and the duty to repair breach of contract with questions of the justice and good policy of current distributions of social goods – and both of these conflated with the question as to whether the descendants of the aboriginal inhabitants of the land ought to enjoy a special status by virtue of original occupation.

---

[12] Boxill, 'The Morality of Reparation'.

But the agendas of the Waitangi Tribunal, the Court of Appeal and the Government were rather more complex than analytical clarity might require. The Treaty was – whatever else it was – a fact. They were dealing with passionate and competing convictions as to justice and they had to accommodate as many as possible. They recognized that some reparations in clear cases were due and the difficulties in delivering them; they recognized and lamented Māori inequality of condition; they recognized and sympathized with Māori claims to a degree of independence of, but independence within, the Pākehā state; they recognized and resisted Māori separatism. Recognizing all of these things, they developed the jurisprudence of the wairua, a peculiarly New Zealand/Aotearoan statement of (and an attempt at a solution of) the problems of justice between two peoples.

II

The Jurisprudence of the Wairua of the Treaty

Alongside its reparationist jurisprudence the Tribunal first led, then joined, the judiciary and legislature in developing another jurisprudence to which it is hard to give a name: oracular, and oriented to the future, yet a jurisprudence which sought retroactively to construct a 'fundamental law' for New Zealand based on the transactions of 1840. This fundamental law, which stated that all other law and policy should be 'consistent with the principles of the Treaty of Waitangi' was vague in content: vague enough for the courts to begin to proceed along common law lines. They could now start to decide what precise (legal) 'rights' the Treaty *might now be taken to have implied* in speaking of 'sovereignty' and 'rangatiratanga' for instance. In line with the normal proceedings of the common law, what was really the invention of legal rules and precise rights could appear to be a discovery of what was already there.

This fundamental law would now stand as a test and measure of all existing laws. It would better protect both the rights of the Māori in general as tangata whenua o Aotearoa and it would protect, too, the rangatiratanga and mana of particular iwi, hapū and whānau in their own places. When it seemed important to concentrate on the 'principles' of the Treaty and to override particular items of 'black letter' law, the fundamental law would allow it. But it was also a fundamental law the force of which was enough to override any currently undesirable right-and-duty implications that might be discovered in the *detail* of the Treaty itself; and it was a fundamental law the detail of which was not so much known as yet to be discovered. Like the 'fundamental law' of the English seventeenth century over which battles were fought and which was so sincerely loved by men of all descriptions, it could secrete many, contradictory, things.[13]

---

[13] Gough, *Fundamental Law in English Constitutional History*.

The Treaty was, in a word, negotiable. In te reo Māori, the point was to find an interpretation of the meaning of the Treaty which captured its Wairua – its living spirit. For the Wairua, while insisting on the non-negotiable fundamentality of mana Māori, could yet allow the scope of rangatiratanga and sovereignty to vary through time and place; and it could allow for negotiation and compromise in a way that adherence to rigid rules could not. This Māori and Pākehā jurisprudence was, let us say, a jurisprudence of the Wairua.

The jurisprudence held that the 'principles' of the Treaty were to be found not so much in the provisions it contained as in the still-living 'spirit' in which it was signed. This, for the Pākehā, was the 'spirit' mentioned in the final peroration attached to it, following the three substantive Articles. There the chiefs had accepted and entered into the Treaty 'in the full meaning and spirit thereof'. The content of the Treaty would be interpreted in accord with the general intentions of the signatories and not with the precise details of their agreement. This idea of 'spirit' accorded well enough with the Māori interpretation of the *force* of the Treaty though not (always or necessarily) its *content*. For the Māori view was that the Treaty's particular and binding 'wairua' inhered in it because it was signed by the Māori ancestors. Their mana constituted the Wairua or spirit of the Treaty. That was why it bound their successors. But as to the content of the Treaty: as in the Pākehā interpretation of the 'spirit', the wairua could speak in many tongues. And while in some Māori interpretations of the wairua the Treaty should be interpreted broadly and accommodatingly, on others it could be held that what was required was that the strictest Māori-favouring interpretations possible should be given to te tino rangatiratanga, kāwanatanga and taonga.

In this ideological context, the jurisprudence the Tribunal developed was, to say the least, complex and richly ambiguous. It built on both Māori and Pākehā materials, appealed in its different formulations and intimations to different groups and institutions, and issued in a variety of doctrines some of which were starkly contrary to others. Yet in the Tribunal's case, the motive in developing it was most likely that of forwarding negotiation and conciliation. It was soon to be imitated by – perhaps it was advised by – the Government and the judiciary – and the new jurisprudence, matching well with the already-existing moderating rhetoric of most politicians, was almost universally adopted, much to the irritation, of those few who saw it as a move away from a jurisprudence and policy of reparations for past wrongs, and who saw that an appeal to Treaty principles might not award the Māori so much an appeal to Treaty rights.[14]

The Tribunal's alternative jurisprudence was expressed in a variety of ways, all of them stressing the importance adhering to the 'principles' and not the 'provisions' of the Treaty. The formulation in *Te Atiawa Report* was the

---

[14] For example, Kia Mohio Kia Marama Trust, *Jaws Unmasked* p. 2, which was Submission 37a on the Treaty of Waitangi (State Enterprises) Bill (1987). See also Submissions 17a, 40a., pp. 11-12. Also a report on Jane Kelsey's view, H16:10/3/88.

most quoted and approved. There as elsewhere it made the Treaty a basis for future-oriented policy rather than backward-looking rule application.

> The Treaty was an acknowledgment of Maori existence, of their prior occupation of the land and of an intent that the Maori presence would remain and be respected . . . The Treaty was . . . more than an affirmation of existing rights. It was not intended to fossilise a status quo, but to provide a direction for future growth and development. The broad and general nature of its words indicates that it was not intended as a finite contract but as the foundation for a developing social contract.
>
> We consider . . . that the Treaty is capable of a measure of adaption to meet new and changing circumstances provided there is a measure of consent and adherence to its broad principles.

Soon after, in the *Kaituna Report*, the Tribunal interpreted its jurisdiction as suggesting exactly this kind of jurisprudence: 'Our statutory authority is to make a finding whether any action . . . is inconsistent with the *principles* of the Treaty. This wide power enables us to look beyond strict legalities so that we can identify where the spirit of the Treaty is not being given due recognition'. And in the *Manukau Report*, considering the differences between the Treaty and te Tiriti and that the Māori might be disadvantaged by a strict interpretation of the English version, it insisted that the 'spirit' in which the Treaty was drawn up must be taken into account – where 'spirit' seems to have meant something like 'general understanding of it in the circumstances as to what it might help attain for the future'.[15]

In this formulation, the Treaty did not so much specify rights as suggest a continuing process of discovery and elaboration fundamental to the New Zealand constitution.

But, as it was also argued, any process of discovery and elaboration would have to occur in a context of recognizing a unique and permanent Māori presence. The importance of that way of putting it cannot be overestimated. For it suggested that it was possible to see the Treaty as one of the moral (and perhaps legal) cession of sovereignty and yet not of rangatiratanga. 'The Treaty,' the Tribunal further held in its Motunui findings, 'represents the gift of the right to make laws in return for the promise to do so so as to acknowledge and protect the interests of the indigenous inhabitants. . . . The gift of the right to make laws, and the promise to do so so as to accord the Maori interest an appropriate priority'. It was notably not clear in these formulations – 'Maori presence would remain and be respected'; 'appropriate priority' – what the detail of rangatiratanga might be. The Māori were owed *something* special into perpetuity, but exactly what it was might be negotiable and its content might change from time to time and from context to context. The wairua of the Treaty, as well as taking the emphasis off strict Treaty rights and reparations, preserved state sovereignty and

---

[15] *Te Atiawa Report*, para. 10.3, pp. 61-2; *Kaituna Report*, para. 5.11 at p. 24. Similarly in the *Orakei Report*, para. 11.4 at p. 130: ('we are not confined to strict legalities. We believe that the essence of the Treaty . . . transcends the sum total of its component written words and puts a narrow or literal interpretation out of place') and 11.8 at pp. 136-7.

sustained rangatiratanga while leaving the latter open to constant renegotiation as to its content and application.

Geoffrey Palmer was impressed enough with these formulations to mention them approvingly in the second edition of his constitutionalist tract, *Unbridled Power* (1987). More importantly, he and his friend Professor Kenneth Keith, architects of a proposed Bill of Rights for New Zealand, quoted them with approval in the White Paper of 1985 in which they laid down and defended the proposal, including the proposition that the Treaty of Waitangi should be included in the Bill of Rights as 'part of the supreme law of New Zealand'.[16] What clearly appealed to the two constitutional lawyers was what has already been noticed: firstly, the combination of legal sovereignty in the state with a rangatiratanga in the Māori, the details of which would be a matter of negotiation and judicial decision in particular exigencies; secondly, the de-emphasis on reparations.

The new official doctrine of the wairua, the White Paper told its readers, would 'help put to rest any fears that to affirm the Treaty in a Bill of Rights would be to put the clock back to 1840 or any other date'. A Bill of Rights incorporating the Treaty would on this doctrine, 'look forward to the future'; it would not 'require the reopening of past transactions or disturb in any way lawfully acquired rights and interests'. As to the Waitangi Tribunal, it would indeed continue to look to the past. It *could* 'reopen and examine past grievances'. But it would continue merely as an 'investigating body with responsibility for making recommendations' – a voice to be listened to with respect, but of no legally determinative effect. This doctrine as to the legal powers of the Tribunal accorded much better with the idea of the wairua of the Treaty than with the idea of its being a legally valid document, the provisions of which must bind New Zealand Governments and provide the basis for lawful claims against it. The Government assured its people that questions of reparation for past wrongs would be treated, under this doctine of the wairua – as they had been all along by the Tribunal – not as questions of rights and duties under law, but as questions as to what might best be done in a bicultural society.

For his part Judge Durie expressed his view of the flexibility of the new jurisprudence in various public places during the period between the imminent lapse of the first Tribunal and the start of operations of the second. In August 1985 he told a seminar on the Bill of Rights in Auckland that the Treaty lacked 'the precision of a legal document and is more in the nature of an agreement to seek arrangements along broad guidelines'.[17] In September 1986 he told the Wellington District Law Society: 'We can read into the Treaty what we might modernly call the heads of agreement for a bi-cultural

---

16 Palmer, *A Bill of Rights for New Zealand. A White Paper* pp. 35-9. Commented on in Sharp, 'An Historical and Philosophical Perspective on the Proposal for a Bill of Rights in New Zealand' at pp. 31-3. And compare Palmer's remarks in his *Unbridled Power* (2nd ed. 1987), p. 20; and the remarks of the Royal Commission on the Electoral System, p. 112.

17 Durie, 'Part II and Clause 26 of the Draft New Zealand Bill of Rights'.

development in partnership'. At about the same time he told an Auckland University History Department seminar: 'as a constitutional document it must always be speaking. To speak in our time it must be stripped of its old law clothing, and . . . its essential body exposed to view'.[18] And he spoke to the legal profession again of the Tribunal's work as 'experimental' – a process of discovery, the results of which could not be predicted, something not to be undertaken in the spirit of applying known rules but of reaching new arrangements.

It was this understanding of the Treaty that had made, and was to continue to make, possible the Tribunal's search for practical solutions and its retreat from the legalism which sustained the idea of reparation for breach of contract. As the Tribunal summed it up: 'In our view it is not inconsistent with the Treaty of Waitangi that the Crown and the Maori people should agree upon a measur of compromise and change.'[19]

The new jurisprudence found approval – interpreted indeed differingly but always expressed in Māori idioms – among the Māori. This is not suprising. It echoed *Kaupapa – Te Whanga Tuatahi*, the New Zealand Maori Council policy paper of 1983. There it had been argued that from the Treaty could be derived the 'principles for determining the codes of laws on Maori land and all other matters'. And Māori often argued that the 'principles' of the Treaty were precisely its wairua or spirit. Its dead and outmoded letter did not matter so much. At Turangawaewae the lawyer, Koro Dewes, provided a formulation later to be used by the Tribunal itself; a 'Maori approach to the Treaty would imply that its wairua or spirit is something more than a literal construction of its actual words can provide. The spirit of the Treaty transcends the sum total of its component written words and puts a narrow or literal interpretation out of place.'[20] Others agreed with Dewes and the Tribunal, saying 'our belief is that the proper way to look at the Treaty . . . is to consider its spiritual significance and to consider it in the way our Tupuna did when they signed.'[21]

The jurisprudence of the wairua thus captured what many Māori felt – a perfect willingness to compromise. Yet it stressed also their continuing status as tangata whenua. It expressed their conviction that the Treaty merely confirmed and did not create what European jurisprudence recognized as 'aboriginal rights' and what they called (denying their origin and continuing force to lie in common law or their scope to be defined by it) mana and rangatiratanga. For the many with a taste for it, it confirmed their teachings that separate Māori institutions should be built and that the Māori should share much more in the deliberations of the sovereign state. And for a few it reaffirmed the basis for claims to an absolute Māori sovereignty that had

---

[18] Sorrenson, 'Towards a Radical Reinterpretation', p. 163.

[19] *Te Atiawa Report*, p. 62.

[20] WAC (ed.), *He Korero*, p. 19. Compare *Orakei Report*, p. 130.

[21] Hikaia Amohia on behalf of himself, Titu Tihu, and the people of the Wanganui River in WAC (ed.), *He Korero*, p. 72. Cf. pp. 74-5, 98.

never been relinquished entirely and which might well have to be reconstituted in its old fullness . . .

But for the moment (though see Chapter 13) the Māori claims to sovereignty and areas of autonomy must be disregarded, because the appeal of the Tribunal's formulations to the Government and in legal and political circles was as *respondents* to these demands. It was an appeal located in the possibility of Māori and state co-operation in the problematic circumstances where the Māori were asserting various degrees and combinations of separate status, rights and sovereignty, as well as claims to reparations for past wrongs. Generally those who served the state were more interested in the 'responsibilities' than the 'rights' of the Māori. Entirely happy to give an 'appropriate priority' to the tangata whenua, even to accede to some rights-claims, they were not about to relinquish the permanent right and power continually to negotiate the terms on which Māori and the rest would live. While, for instance, the Government from 1986 onwards was happy to make arrangements to 'devolve' some legal authority and even financial resources to iwi and other locally-based Māori authorities, it was to be devolution, after negotiation, of the existing and unchallengeable powers of government from Wellington. It was not to be the recognition of a prior right in the Māori to autonomy. Less theoretically interesting perhaps, but practically much more important, the Government also came to decide that the rights it *would* devolve would certainly not be derived from the 'provisions' of the Treaty, nor would its policies be constrained or trumped by any such rights. The rights the Government created and allowed to constrain its activity would rather be in accord with the 'principles' of the Treaty.

And the jurisprudence of the wairua, stressing negotiation, partnership and mutual exploration of a future, had the effect of avoiding too much assertion of state sovereignty. It gilded the pill – a pill which the Government in any case thought would benefit the Māori and give them much of what they sought. It was the analogue of the politics of moderation, compromise and future-orientation. As it avoided too strict a concentration on rights violated and a too strict interpretation of rights which must be protected, so it avoided as much as might be recourse to the authority of the state. It was (very likely) for those reasons that the jurisprudence of the wairua and the principles of the Treaty was elaborated. This was very likely why, for instance, a celebrated Cabinet Minute of 23 June 1986 instructed Departments to draw to Cabinet's attention in future any implications for the 'principles' of the Treaty in legislation they proposed: not the 'provisions' of the Treaty.[22]

Judicial explorations of the intimations of the doctrine of the wairua were soon invited in legislation. Statutes were passed, which included, in authorizing

---

[22] Cabinet Office Circular, CO (86)10. Jane Kelsey of the Auckland University Law School is currently writing on the Government's general retreat from an intention to introduce the provisions of the Treaty into various laws and (from early 1986) policies, to a more sparing intention to consult its principles.

activity, the requirement that the activity so authorized should not be contrary to 'the principles of the Treaty of Waitangi'. This was the phrase, it will be recalled, most notably included in section 9 of the State Owned Enterprises Act. A similar phrase was included in the Environment Act (1986), which laid down that in the management of physical and cultural resources, 'full and balanced account is [to be] taken of . . . the principles of the Treaty of Waitangi'. It was soon also to be included in the Conservation Act (1987) which required that that Act itself 'be so interpreted and administered as to give effect to the principles of the Treaty of Waitangi'. And further statutes were promised. Judicial elaboration of what the 'principles' and allied notions meant came most importantly with the Court of Appeal's *New Zealand Maori Council* v *the Attorney General* but also in High Court: for instance in *The Royal Forest and Bird Protection Society* v *Habgood Limited and others* (1987) and in the *Huakina Development Trust* v *Waikato Valley Authority and Bowater* (1987).[23] It is the Court Of Appeal case that matters most here.

The legal issues hung on what the Court would make of the constitutional force and the meaning of section 9 of the SOE Act: 'nothing in this Act shall permit the Crown to act in a manner that is inconsistent with the principles of the Treaty of Waitangi'. As to its constitutional force, the judges agreed with the appellants that 'the Treaty is a document relating to fundamental rights; that it should be interpreted widely and effectively as a living instrument taking account of the subsequent developments of human rights norms; and that the Court will not ascribe to Parliament an intention to permit conduct inconsistent with the principles of the Treaty'. It found, in brief, that the 'principles of the Treaty' were fundamental to the SOE Act – they had 'the impact of a constitutional guarantee within the field covered by the State Owned Enterprises Act' – and hinted that they should be applied as 'fundamental law' in interpreting *any* ambiguous legislation that seemed to contravene the Treaty, even though the Treaty was not mentioned in the relevant statute.[24]

As to the meaning of the 'principles' of the Treaty, the Court noted the difficulties which lay in the path of deciding what the particular provisions meant, partly because of the difficulties in interpreting rangatiratanga, kāwanatanga and taonga. It declined to specify the content of the principles further than the case in hand required, holding however that 'what matters is the spirit' and that 'this approach accords with the oral character of Māori tradition and culture'. The Treaty, observed Sir Robin Cooke, the President of the Court, was 'an embryo rather than a fully developed and integrated set of ideas'.

The President held that what the treaty 'signified' was 'a partnership between races'; and partnership implied that each partner had the duty to

---

[23] On the Forest and Bird Case, see Rick Shera, 'Section 3 of the Town and Country Planning Act 1977: Adjudicating the Non-Justiciable', at p. 454.

[24] Government Printer, *The Treaty of Waitangi in the Court of Appeal*, Cooke P. at pp. 15, 21, 24, 44; Casey J. at p. 13. Henceforth this title will be called TWCA.

act towards the other 'reasonably' and 'in good faith'. The partners had 'responsibilities analogous to fiduciary duties' towards each other: not narrowly-defined, pre-set and passive duties, but broad-ranging and active ones, the substance of which should be decided by mutual discussion as to the common benefit. Thus, said the President quoting the Tribunal, ' "the duty of the Crown is not merely passive but extends to active protection of Maori people in the use of their lands and waters to the fullest extent practicable" . . . (and) I take it as implicit that, as usual, practical means reasonably practicable'. Where, for instance, Māori views as to how they wished to use their communally-held lands had apparently markedly changed since the McCarthy Commission on Maori Lands of 1980, then so should the Crown vary its policy in response to 'today's philosophies and urgings'. So that if assimilation of Māori uses to Pākehā ones by individualization of title had in 1980 been the ideal but now no longer was, then the Crown should act appropriately.[25]

The other judges broadly concurred in four other separate, differently reasoned, but in the event converging, judgments. Concurring, they joined in the construction of a jurisprudence of prospection rather than retrospection; and they too, dwelt on the idea of partnership. Mr Justice Casey, agreeing that the Treaty set up a 'partnership', even managed to assimilate that idea to Hobson's saying 'now we are one people'. The words pointed, he said, to Hobson's appreciation of partnership 'rather than to the notion that with the stroke of a pen both races had become assimilated'.[26] The bench thought that what mattered would be the detail of future arrangements, not past ones. A partnership for mutual benefit implied an ongoing relationship. It was the 'principles' not the 'terms' of the Treaty that were the issue. Not that it could 'be said that there is broad general agreement as to what those principles are . . . the way ahead calls for careful research, for rational positive dialogue and, above all, for generosity of spirit'. All that could be said for the moment was that the Treaty was a solemn compact which required the two parties to act 'reasonably and in good faith' towards each other, 'no less than under settled principles of equity as under our partnership laws',[27] or with the 'sincerity, justice and good faith' that 'civil law partners owe to each other'.[28] And while 'good faith' did not *require* consultation, 'it is an obvious way of demonstrating its existence'.[29]

The meaning of the spirit of the Treaty then, made it possible for the Court to find as it did: that even though section 27 of the SOE Act provided a mechanism to restrain the Crown from alienating lands which were already

[25] TWCA, Cooke P. at pp. 28-40, 44. At p. 36 he quoted the Royal Commission on Maori Lands (1980) as to how feelings as to competing Māori and Pākehā uses of Māori lands were mixed among Māori, and he observed a change since then.

[26] TWCA, Casey J. at p. 16.

[27] TWCA, Richardson J. at pp. 13, 14, 34-9. Casey J. at pp. 14-23; Bisson J., at p. 2027.

[28] TWCA, Somers J. at p. 21.

[29] TWCA, Somers J. at p. 23.

by 18 December the subject of reparatory claims made to the Waitangi Tribunal, section 9 required more. It required the Crown and the New Zealand Maori Council to agree on a 'scheme of safeguards giving reasonable assurance that lands or waters will not be transferred to State Enterprises', whether claims had already been made to the Tribunal or whether they might 'foreseeably be transmitted' to it.[30]

Rights to reparation were not denied by the Court; indeed it was the threat by the Court that it might enforce just such rights that sent the Government into negotiation with the Council. But negotiation in reasonableness and good faith with an eye to the future was the key to the new jurisprudence of the meaning of the Treaty. Whether the negotiations would bear fruit was a matter for the future, and in any case 'outstanding points of disagreement' could be settled by the Court.[31]

Bound from that time on to the Appeal Court's interpretation of the 'principles' of the Treaty as they related at least to the SOE Act, the Waitangi Tribunal was to follow its lead in refusing to exhaustively specify the full complement of the 'principles it contained' – and indeed followed it in somewhat obscuring rather than clarifying things. In the *Orakei Report*, the Tribunal cited Mr Justice Casey with approval to the effect that to find what was inconsistent with the 'principles' rather than the 'terms or provisions' of the Treaty meant the 'adoption in legislation of the Treaty's actual terms understood in the light of the fundamental concepts underlying them'. 'It called for an assessment of the relationship the parties hoped to create and reflect in that document, and an enquiry into the benefits and obligations involved in applying its language in today's changed conditions and expectations in the light of that relationship.' Anything and everything, perhaps, was open for negotiation. In the *Muriwhenua Report* too, the Tribunal noted again that the Court had declined to specify all of the principles of the Treaty; it quoted Mr Justice Richardson as to the 'overarching principle' that the Treaty was a 'solemn compact between two identified parties'; and it quoted the bench as a whole on the necessity for 'reasonableness and good faith' in their mutual dealings. They stood in 'partnership'. Indeed, the Tribunal held, adding judicial authority to its own, 'the key to defining the principles of the Treaty is to be found in the idea of a partnership between Pakeha and Maori . . . and cooperation is at the heart of the agreed relationship'.

Still, certain other principles *could* be laid down, broad and conflicting as they might sometimes be. The 'principles' the Tribunal discovered in the English version were that the 'just rights and property' of the Māori were to be protected; that 'peace and good order' was to be preserved and that 'Her Majesty's sovereign authority' was to be be introduced. In the Māori version the 'intention' was reported to be much the same except that it 'upholds tribal authority, which is wider than ownership and includes . . . control over persons in the kinship groups and their access to resources'.

---

[30] TWCA, Cooke P. at p. 42.

[31] TWCA, Cooke P. at p. 41.

'It was the basic object of the Treaty that two people would live in one country.' It was, 'in Maori eyes', the basis 'for a continuing relationship between the Crown and the Maori people'. They 'acknowledged' that they entered the Treaty in the 'full knowledge and spirit thereof'. 'On examining the verbal promises' made at the signing, said the Tribunal, 'we find . . . the principle that emerges is the protection of Maori interests to the extent consistent with the cession of sovereignty.'

The 'provisions' of the Treaty might, and did, conflict. But they could be reconciled because they followed from – they were derivative of – the 'principles' and 'intentions' of the signatories. This meant among other things that the Crown was bound by the 'principle of protection', expressed in its working out as the 'problem' (and here the Tribunal quoted Richardson J.) 'of balancing or blending the competing philosophies of protecting Maori as equal citizens, or upholding their distinctive heritage'. It lay in balancing Articles 2 and 3. The problem was one to be solved by negotiation and conciliation. The 'principles', the Tribunal again quoted the judges, 'must . . . be the same today as they were . . . in 1840. What has changed is the circumstances in which those principles are to apply'. The point was to find the 'fundamental concepts underlying the Treaty, and applying them in today's changed conditions and expectations'. And President Cooke was quoted too, saying that the Treaty was a document 'relating to fundamental rights', and should be 'interpreted widely and effectively and as a living instrument taking account of the subsequent developments of international human rights norms'.[32]

When in 1988 the Parliamentary Commissioner for the Environment came to list the 'principles of the Treaty', she made an excellent collection of the dicta of the Tribunal, the Court of Appeal, the Royal Commission on Social Policy and (in evidence to the Court of Appeal) the New Zealand Maori Council and the Crown.[33] She did not perhaps succeed as well as she might have wished in reducing them to a system, and quoted Mr Justice Richardson: 'Regrettably, but reflecting the limited dialogue there has been in the Treaty, it cannot yet be said that there is broad general agreement as to what those principles are'. She noted that while 'partnership' was at the heart of it, 'yet the practical meaning of this partnership has yet to be fully explored'.[34] And that, in the autumn of 1989, was still how it was.

The jurisprudence of the wairua thus emerged, distinct in form and implication from the jurisprudence of strict Treaty right.

In many ways it was as unsatisfactory an intellectual construct as was the jurisprudence of rights. Though its gist was clear and its political philosophy not to be mistaken, strictly conned, its intellectual foundations and its expression were historically dubious and philosphically contradictory. It spoke unselfconsciously of the 'reasons' and 'motives' for signing *being* the 'principles'

---

[32] *Muriwhenua Report*, pp. 190-4.

[33] Hughes, *Environmental Management*, p. 19 and Appendices J, K, L, M.

[34] Hughes, *Environmental Management*, pp. 17-18.

of agreement. Recognizing mixture of motives on both sides at the time, it nevertheless clearly and unequivocally distinguished the meaning of the Treaty 'in Maori eyes', from what it might have meant judging from British 'policy' in the 1830s; yet having distinguished so clearly at the expense of strict accurancy as to actual motives and reasons, it sought to meld the two disparate views. And where the disparate reasons and motives of people in the real world of 1840 are 'melded' into one set of overall reasons and motives it is hard to see what 'reason' or 'motive' means any more. Dubious historical reconstructions were made, certainly reaching beyond the proper limits of real and possible knowledge and the great silences on which the writing and telling of history relies. A philosophy of morals and action was used too, which conflated 'motive', 'reason', 'principle' and much else besides – the separate performances and conditions of developing a policy, signing a Treaty, orally agreeing, needing to live together now, and so on. And on the level of simple dogma, it taught on the one hand a doctrine of partnership, on the other a doctrine of state sovereignty.

But such criticisms would be quite beside the point. The jurisprudence was neither history nor philosophy. It expressed a modern, 1980s, legal understanding of a developing institutionalized relationship between 'Māori' and 'Pākehā', and a modern decision that the Treaty would be used as its ideological and legal foundation. The question for the Treaty jurisprudence of the wairua was no more and no less than what the Treaty could best mean in the 1980s. It was a jurisprudence that mirrored the difficulties facing reparative justice, and it was a jurisprudence which also attempted to set a framework – and limits – to the discussion of that other kind of justice at issue between Māori and Pākehā: distributive justice. This was the kind of justice that Ranginui Walker called 'equity' in his *Listener* article of 1987, to which we now turn. The language and the practice of equity, it will emerge, proved unsatisfactory to many Māori, who accordingly developed their own arguments from the nexus of wairua Māori. Equally, the state, always alive to disaffection, elaborated doctrines of state sovereignty, drawing on the full implications of the jurisprudence of the wairua of the Treaty.

Part Three
Equity, Equalities, and Māori Independence

Chapter 10
Inequalities and Government Policies, 1960–1988

'Social equity' was not discussed in the streets, on the beaches, and in pubs the way 'justice' and 'rights' were. The words were used to invoke so many and conflicting ideals as to the distribution of things, and with so many varying emphases as to their prescriptive force, that it would have been hard for the ordinary man or woman to say what they meant. Yet from 1983 onwards, especially after July 1984 when the new Labour Government came to power, the phrase was often heard. 'Social equity' – so vague, so flatulent – became an element in a meta-language invented by professional policy-makers, administrators, and mainly non-parliamentary politicians to order and to discuss public policy. And it was in his role of politician-cum-bureaucrat that Ranginui Walker spoke in 1987 of the Māori demand for 'equity', secure in the knowledge that his educated *Listener* readers would have known what he was talking about.

In plainer language, the issues that 'equity' covered were of two sorts, both of which in fact attracted much and passionate public attention. First, they were issues generated in Governments' undertaking special policies aimed at helping the Māori to overcome their relative deprivation of the goods of life – in health and housing, in education for fulfilment and for employment, in employment itself, in the status and income derived from employment, in power and influence in the state and in society, and in receiving proper respect from fellow-citizens. Secondly, they were issues generated in Māori attempts to retain, regain and expand their independence of Pākehā control of their lives, especially in those areas precisely where the goods of life were at issue. So that at those very points where the Māori were demanding a fairer distribution of goods from the state and the Pākehā, they were also demanding various degrees of independence from the state and from their fellow citizens. The two issues – equality of condition and Māori independence – were scarcely separated in public debate. Thus in the 1980s the scene was set for some fundamental arguments about distributions of social goods and of human freedom – the central concerns of distributive justice in modern western societies.

From the point of view of the purist who might want to follow arguments about justice, the scene was not played in the most desirable way. It was partly that the issues between Māori and Pākehā were fudged in the polysemic jargon of 'social equity' which also had to cope with the demands of many other sectors of society wanting incompatible things.

Even more, the issues were partly avoided in the invention of a Māori code. For that code translated demands for justice in distributions into the language of ethnicity. In the code, justice in distributions was translated into talk of justice as fidelity to a Treaty contract between Māori and Pākehā; or else it was translated into talk of justice as pertaining only to Māori-Pākehā relationships and no others. It was not commonality of need, or want, or desert that constituted classes of persons in the code. It was ethnicity.

In the Māori code the Treaty contract was not that with which the reader will by now be familiar. It was a contract neither confined to the strict rights of the reparationist model nor so diluted by the prospectionist interpretation of the wairua of the Treaty as to mean nothing in particular but only a general agreement to act in friendly concert. Combining elements of both models in a way that defied abstract logic but accorded with the flow of debate about 'equity', the Māori code spoke of a more just future to be attained in an indissoluble but ill-defined 'partnership' between a separate Māori and Crown (or Māori and Pākehā) in a bicultural society and polity.

However, despite the consequent unclarity of things overall, the Māori demands for equity (for equality in the goods of life and for independence) were recognizably demands for justice. They demanded what they took to be theirs of right; and when those things were not delivered, the non-delivery was interpreted as injustice. When neither reparative justice, nor justice as equality was done, *nor* justice as fidelity to the Treaty, then there was the thought of radical independence – of absolute Māori sovereignty.

It is this movement towards the idea of absolute Māori sovereignty that this and the following two chapters trace, through a consideration of Government equalization policies and the reactions to them, and then through a consideration of the language of equity and the Māori code. The movement, it should be said, was not chronological. The old idea of absolute Māori sovereignty was revived in 1981 during the Springbok tour; the languages of equity and the Māori code came later; and all this was preceded by argument as to whether or not there should be special treatment – and some independence – for the Māori. And by 1985, all ways of arguing and thinking co-existed, competing and intertwining. So the movement traced was not a chronological one, it is one in the logic of ideas: away from the ideal of equality in a homogeneous political society where there is wide and detailed agreement as to the goods of life, towards the ideal of there being two different homogeneous societies within the same land whose judgements as to the goods of life are so greatly different that there can be no living in the same polity. Nor, finally, was the movement one, necessarily, towards effective polarization of the country. It is hard to say if that is what it will turn out to have been; but it will likely not. However that may be, at either pole of insistence on homogeneity and on difference there were those who came to think political society possible only among those who shared beliefs about what the goods of life are; but the great majority of New Zealanders/ Aotearoans seem to have been more or less liberal, believing or hoping it possible for difference to co-exist with living in political society. In brief, it is the *pattern* of thought that will now be traced, rather than the detailed occurrence of its elements and the political attraction and force of their use in practice.

In New Zealand for half a century before the 1980s there had been widespread agreement on the undesirability, if not the injustice, of some kinds of inequality. Equality as to the receipt of social welfare benefits as between similarly qualified Māori and Pākehā had been official policy since the first Labour Government of 1935. And vague equality-talk had been the common coinage in race relations discussions in New Zealand since then. So that when the Māori came to the towns during and after a World War in which they had greatly distinguished themselves and when, as a consequence, the facts of inequality of condition presented themselves for urban as well as rural dwellers to see, it was clear something would have to be done. The inequalities were measured with as much precision as possible. Māori were compared with Pākehā on scales of health, housing, education, employment, and suffering at the hands of the criminal law. They were found to be worse off on all those dimensions of welfare. Steps were taken. Policies were especially introduced by governments to aid them.

The first comprehensive measurements were in the *Hunn Report* of 1960; and by the late 1980s New Zealanders had been contemplating statistics of inequality for nearly thirty years. The figures were in the New Zealand Official Year Books and in many official publications of the 1970s and 1980s; and they were endlessly rehearsed in the news media. A few examples will do: in 1975 there was a report of the Joint Committee of the Departments of Social Welfare and Justice on Young Offenders. In 1980 there was a report (publicized in unfinished form in the late 1970s) on Māori health by Dr Eru Pomare. In 1982 the State Services Commission put out its *New Zealand's Multicultural Society: A Statistical Perspective*, drawing on the census returns of 1981. Soon after, the best known and most quoted figures on social inequality in the mid-1980s were published by Hiwi Tauroa, the Race Relations Conciliator, in his booklet *Race Against Time*. In 1986 the Ministerial Report on the Department of Social Welfare, *Puao-Te-Ata-Tu/Day Break*, collected the overall figures on 'deprivation' from the 1986 census. In the same year, the Board of Maori Affairs published *Fading Expectations: The Crisis in Maori Housing*, showing continuing discrepancies in Māori and Pākehā enjoyments of that convenience.[1] In the same year, the Department of Statistics drew on the 1986 census to produce its *Maori Statistical Profile, 1961–1986*. In 1987 a Planning Council report on the institutionalization of Māori recorded that in 1984, 50 per cent of the Department of Social Welfare's clients were Māori, that they made up over 50 per cent of those in Education Department special residential schools for learning difficulties, and that they made up 30 per cent of those in Health camps.[2] Also in 1987, the Treasury undertook a detailed study of Māori education in its advice to the returning Government – the two-volumed book, *Government Management*. In 1988 the Royal Commission on Social Policy produced its *April Report*, which quoted all these

[1] *The April Report*, iii (2), p. 11 (and p. 25 for other refs. quoting Douglas, *Fading Expectations*, 1986).

[2] H3:15/6/87.

sets of figures and findings as to inequality, plus others. In September 1988, the Justice Department publicized its latest figures on criminal offending, imprisonment and recidivism – all of which much concerned the Māori and told the same story as before.[3]

The measurements given were routinely quoted in arguments as an incantation to action. It was not so much the precise statistics that mattered. It was rather that they showed what everyone conceived to be important inequalities, not easily justifiable (if justifiable at all) and therefore to be addressed in some way. *Race Against Time* let the figures speak for themselves. They showed that Māori and Pacific Islanders made up 10.6 per cent (Māori 8.6 per cent) of the population, compared with 86 per cent Pākehā. Yet they made up 64 per cent of those employed in factory, production and labouring work. Only 4.7 per cent of them were in the professions compared with 15.2 per cent of Pākehā. They were vastly under-represented in occupations like law, medicine, education, and Government, which dominated New Zealand decision-making. Specifically Māori educational achievement was shown to be unequal. In 1978, 67.1 per cent of Māori school leavers left with no qualifications, compared with 28.5 per cent of Pākehā. Only 6.9 per cent of Māori attained at school the University Entrance qualification, compared with 31.7 per cent Pākehā. And Māori were over-represented in the courts and prisons. Under 9 per cent of the population, in 1975 they accounted for nearly 50 per cent of all criminal cases heard in the courts and they made up 46 per cent of the prison population.[4] By February 1980, one result of rising unemployment was that while only 4 per cent of the Pākehā population was unemployed, 7 per cent of Māori were.

Later figures only showed that while on the dimensions of measurement adopted some things were improving – education, health and housing especially – they were not improving as fast as for the Pākehā. And other things were getting worse: unemployment, institutionalization in welfare homes, and imprisonment especially. Treasury's 1987 figures, for instance, showed some of this: they showed a continuing imbalance between Māori and Pākehā passes in School Certificate, the crucial sorting mechanism for 15-year-olds in New Zealand schools. In 1985, 37.5 per cent of Māori passed English as against 60.9 per cent non-Māori; in Mathematics the figures were 40.6 per cent and 65.8 per cent; in Science 39.5 per cent and 64.8 per cent; in Geography 35.2 per cent and 62 per cent. Only in Māori Language and Culture did the Māori do better, and then not by much: 60.4 per cent as compared with 56 per cent. The same report reaffirmed unemployment and imprisonment differences as at 1986. By that year recession had bitten deeply compared with 1980. This accentuated the Māori disadvantage: 14.9 per cent of the Māori workforce were unemployed; only 5.8 per cent of the Pākehā workforce were. And while Māori now comprised 12 per cent of the population they

---

[3] The Treasury, *Government Management*, ii, pp. 215, 228.

[4] Race Relations Conciliator, *Race Against Time*, pp. 35–42.

made up 47.4 per cent of the male prison population (where males made up 95 per cent of the total).

No one ever doubted that the Māori should enter what Hunn, following Gunnar Myrdal's discussion of negro and white race relations in *The American Dilemma* (1944), had called the 'magic circle'. 'Better education', said the *Hunn Report*, 'promotes better employment, which promotes better health and social standing, which promotes better education and thus closes the circle'. But Government action did not seem to be bringing it about.[5]

Indeed looking back at it, things had not been so bad in the prosperous fifties and sixties. The Māori were foresters, farm labourers and an urbanizing proletariat, competently earning good money and often enjoying the status that comes with being 'good with machines'. But in the late sixties and then especially after 1974 when problems began to get serious as a consequence of the OPEC producers first massively raising their oil prices, New Zealanders were made increasingly aware by the news media of 'problem' types of Māori: the aimless and anomic drifter; the street kid; the violent gang member; the destitute solo mother; the drunken, bingo-playing South Auckland parent; the criminal. And then there was the 'stirrer' and protester: often university-educated and probably the catspaw of foreign, communist states. By the mid-1980s, with rural recession and the running down of state involvement in forestry, rural Māori were in poor shape too, and the forest towns which had provided examples of Māori-Pākehā mixing and mingling were threatened with extinction. Country towns were the locus of bickering about race: in Pukekohe, south of Auckland, squabbling divided the town; around Ruatoria on the East Cape, law and government did not fully extend.

In sum: inequality in the goods of life seemed increasingly, from the late 1950s through the 1980s, to be the problem. Certainly, it was on that understanding that Governments acted (or did not act), providing the materials for an ideological battle in doing so. For there were those who disapproved of their aid to the Māori; and there were those who thought that neither enough was given, nor that what was given was properly under Māori control for Māori purposes.

Only the barest outline of what was done can be provided here – and that for the sake of understanding the debates rather than to provide a basis of judgement as to who was right. In the early sixties the National Governments set up the lightly-funded New Zealand Maori Council, and they remodelled the tribal committees of the localities and replaced them with the 'Maori committees' that were now to provide the electoral base for the national Maori Council. They established and partly funded the Maori Education Foundation which, together with separate tribal committees unwilling to join a national scheme, provided scholarships to schools and tertiary institutions. They reorganized and partly funded apprenticeship schemes designed to equip

[5] See Howe, *Race Relations, Australia and New Zealand*, pp. 79-80; and Kenworthy and others, 'The Hunn Report. A Measure of Progress on Aspects of Maori Life', on this aspect of the Hunn Report: neither very fully.

young Māori for the skilled workforce; and they organized and partly funded hostel schemes which were designed to house and keep young country Māori on their arrival in the cities. The Department of Maori Affairs continued to be equipped and funded to carry out special social welfare work over and above that carried out by the main Government departments; and the Department especially devoted itself to providing Māori housing, purposely scattered – 'pepper-potted' – among Pākehā housing. Though the houses were supplied ultimately on much the same financial terms as Housing Corporation houses, the Department was able to help its clients with administrative and legal advice, and it was allowed to provide more flexible terms for repayment of loans. Most importantly, it had at its disposal a set quota of state houses that it could distribute in any year to its Māori clientele, so that they could avoid the queues that plagued others wanting state housing. In the meantime the Department sustained – it did not intensify as the *Hunn Report* had recommended it should – its policy of taking over and improving Māori land for its joint owners, then returning it and retrieving its costs over an extended period.

These schemes and arrangements were continued and extended in the 1970s: the hostel scheme, for instance, was extended to take in urban as well as rural youth; the Maori Education Foundation expanded its reach as its capital – predominately derived from the Maori Trustee who gathered the proceeds of 'uneconomic' Māori lands – gradually grew.

Governments were also impelled into further action to ameliorate the lot of the Māori as prospective and then actual parties to the United Nations Conventions[6] – on the *Elimination of All Forms of Racial Discrimination* (passed by the United Nation in 1965: ratified by New Zealand in 1972) on *Civil and Political Rights* (UN 1967: NZ 1978) and on *Economic, Social and Cultural Rights* (UN 1967: NZ 1978). They took special measures to help eliminate invidious discrimination against the Māori, as well as to help them determine their own lives equally with other citizens and in accord with their right, as an ethnic group, to do so. 'Human Rights' legislation was passed. In 1971 a Race Relations Act continued and extended a statutory trend in forbidding – now across the board – discrimination on grounds of 'colour, race or ethnic origin'. The Act also prohibited 'incitement to racial disharmony' and set up a Race Relations Conciliator to mediate on race problems, including problems of incitement. In 1977 the Human Rights Act amended the Race Relations Act, section 9a of the amended Act now providing for complaints against those who used 'threatening, abusive or insulting' language, 'likely to excite hostility or ill-will against, or bring into contempt or ridicule any group of persons' in New Zealand. A mediatorial procedure might, if it failed, lead to enforcement by an Equal Opportunities Tribunal.

There was also to be – what there had obviously been under another name – 'affirmative action'. This was provided for in the Race Relations

---

[6] Some of the background is in Jagose, 'Section 9a of the Race Relations Act'.

Act, in accordance with the International Convention on the *Elimination of All Forms of Racial Discrimination*, which allowed 'special measures to be taken for the sole purpose of securing adequate advancement of certain racial and ethnic groups';[7] and The Human Rights Act set up a Human Rights Commission empowered not only to combat invidious discrimination in the workplace, but to initiate and assess affirmative action programmes designed to provide for equal opportunities. The Equal Opportunities Tribunal was accordingly provided as an arm of the Commission.

Educational institutions took steps to introduce equality of opportunity in the 1970s, and 1980s. In the 1970s the universities introduced 'Polynesian Preference' schemes, making provision for quotas of academically qualifed Māori and Pacific Island students to be enrolled in their medical and other schools where, in the absence of open entry, competition for priority might otherwise have excluded them. Waikato University went out from Hamilton to visit marae to inform Māori of their opportunities.[8] Teachers' Colleges were given by the Minister of Education a 'three Ms' quota of students to fill: Māori, Males and Mature students. And through the 1980s universities, technical institutes (mostly called polytechnics from 1987) and teachers' training colleges (some of which came to be called colleges of education) elaborated, extended, and initiated a variety of plans to increase the throughput of ethnic minorities. Even the Department of Education, long hostile to too much Māori in the school curriculum and in the running of the school day, began in 1984 – in response to a Maori Development Conference Hui's strong suggestion that the Māori would rather have a separate educational system – to support the introduction of taha Māori into schools.

The central bureaucracy was not far behind the educational system in the seventies, and soon came to lead the drive to affirmative action. In 1978 the State Services Commission, in consultation with the powerful union, the Public Service Association, began. It funded departments to mount a Cadet scheme for Māori and Polynesians wishing to make careers in the Public Service. Policy developments followed, first in the State Services Commission itself with the establishment of an Equal Opportunities Unit in 1983,[9] then – and with highly variable degrees of alacrity[10] – in other departments and offices. To the fore was to be[11] the Ministry of Women's Affairs, set up by the new Labour Government in 1985, and answering to women's demands for affirmative action long coinciding with and often supporting those of the Māori. By 1987 the Equal Opportunities Unit of the Human Rights Commission introduced its Equal Employment Management Plan: 'done as

---

[7] See on the Act, Keith, 'The Treaty and the Race Relations Act, 1971'.

[8] H2:9/2/80.

[9] The history of State Services Commission policy may be consulted in *Appendices to the Journals of the House of Representatives*, G3, 1979 onwards especially.

[10] See State Services Commission, EEOU, *Departmental Equal Employment Opportunities Monitoring Report* (31 March 1986).

[11] See Te Aroha McDowell, 'Tokenism in the Ministry', mentions some early problems.

an aid to departments/organisations in developing their plans' in that direction. And in 1988 the State Sector Act made affirmative action programmes mandatory in the State Services.[12]

The basic idea behind all this activity was that Māori would have jobs, education, housing and status to the same degree as – equally with – the Pākehā. But the questions were, and were increasingly to be: on what dimensions, and using what scales, were the degrees of inequality to be measured? And who would administer the achievement of equality? For the different cultures at times seemed to have whole ranges of different dimensions and scales of appraisal along those dimensions which they thought relevant to human flourishing; and where the dimensions *seemed* the same (as in housing, health, education), they might not be, or ideas of how to measure better or worse on each significantly differed. Houses for nuclear familes and away from ancestral land, no matter how well appointed, did not always seem good to the Māori. Counting flush lavatories seemed not to be counting what mattered. Nor did the techniques and practices of western medicine always seem good – or the slow-moving and painstaking system of coroners' decision-making which held up the tangihanga for the dead. And where there *was* cultural difference, could it be that the failure of the state to achieve equality was a consequence of the Māori people's not having the power to act in groups for themselves?

In contemplating equalization, the *Hunn Report* had wrestled with precisely this range of problems. But he had not taken as seriously as later commentators were to (and some contemporaries did), the proposition that Māori might choose to live different kinds of lives from Pākehā: lives whose success could not be measured on the same dimensions. Besides providing the statistical base against which the progress of the Māori was measured, the *Hunn Report* had also proposed the 'integration' of the races as the goal of policy, in contradistinction to other alternatives: 'assimilation', 'segregation' and 'symbiosis'. The immediate aim – and the ascribed meaning[13] of the verb 'to integrate' – was 'to combine (not fuse) the Maori and Pakeha elements to form one nation wherein Maori culture remains distinct'. But in the longer term it was rather a process of 'assimilation' – '[becoming] absorbed, blended, amalgamated, with complete loss of Maori culture' – that was contemplated as the wave of the future; and Hunn regarded 'Maoris who resent the pressure brought to bear on them to conform to what they regard as the Pakeha mode of life' as a bit of a problem. Because the distinctions between the four forms of race relationships were not easy to apply in the face of the concrete and sensuous real world, and because Hunn himself rather slid between

---

[12] The State Owned Enterprise Amendment (No.5) Act. No. 20. 1988. Section 58, mandated policies on 'equal employment opportunies' and opposed 'inequality in respect to employment of any person or groups of persons'.

[13] It is not a very natural meaning and was the cause of much confusion.

two of them, the *Report* was the occasion of much Māori criticism as an assimilationist document aimed at continuing an old policy under a new name.[14]

And so equalization policies were always tempered by considerations of ethnic difference and Māori claims to independence. The Year Books after Hunn always talked, as well as of equalization, of consulting the Māori people through the New Zealand Maori Council as to the formulation and execution of policy. But it was never enough; and Māori complaints about the insensitivity of the centralized Pākehā bureaucracy in Wellington – especially the departments of Education and Maori Affairs – were never stilled. Accordingly, but slowly and from mixed motives, steps were taken to further consult and to devolve. The third Labour Government of 1972–1975 tried hard to consult. Matiu Rata's *Maori Affairs Amendment Act* of 1974 was, according to an observer, 'hammered out on the maraes'; but consultation failed to stem the Great Land March of 1975.[15] With National back in power, the late 1970s saw more devolved governmental schemes for the Māori. Devolution answered to Māori complaints against Wellington and Pākehā centralism; it responded to their desires for a greater control of their own destinies in their localities and through their tribes; it was supported by many senior officials within the Department of Maori Affairs; and it accorded with support in at least some sectors of officialdom – social and community workers in particular – for creating a more 'representative bureaucracy' and for devolution of decision-making powers to the local 'community'. Led by its new secretary, Kara Puketapu, Maori Affairs introduced its Tu Tangata programme in 1978: 'standing alone' in kōkiri centres, kōhanga reo (language nests) and in programmes like maatua whāngai.[16]

Over a hundred kōhanga reo were to be established between 1982 and 1984; by 1987 there were nearly 500.[17] In 1983, maatua whāngai (extended family groups) were added to the Tu Tangata programme. They were funded by the Departments of Maori Affairs, Justice and Social Welfare, and devoted to the rehabilitation of delinquent youth outside the Pākehā 'bureaucracy' – as was the normal Māori name for the various government departments.

Devolution and consultation were the policies of the day, though Government retrenchment in general and (an inflation-adjusted) decline in spending on Maori Affairs from 1975 to 1984 militated against any activity being too energetic.[18] Maori Affairs indeed fought (and won in 1984) a battle[19] against the State Services Commission to keep its housing programme out of the clutches of the Housing Corporation, but policies of devolution otherwise prevailed in the department itself. Its social welfare division was allowed

[14] Biggs, 'Maori Affairs and the Hunn Report'; Presbyterian Church, Maori Synod, *A Maori View of the Hunn Report*; Metge, *The Maoris of New Zealand*, pp. 306-8.

[15] Trlin, 'Race, Ethnicity and Society', p. 208.

[16] See Puketapu, *Reform from Within*.

[17] The Treasury, *Government Management*, ii, p. 219.

[18] Fleras, 'Towards "Tu Tangata" '; Historical Developments and Current Trends', p. 36.

[19] AS2:3/11/83; H3:11/4/84.

to lapse and its social workers were redeployed to other Departments, or were sent into the field as 'community officers'. Maori Leadership Conferences (Tu Tangata Wananga Whakatauira) were called in Wellington to inform the government further of Māori views. Tu Tangata's recent historian summed up the policy thus: 'Promotion of socio-economic equality, particularly for those at the bottom end of the ladder, lay at the heart of this philosophy. But compared to earlier policies which conflated social equality with cultural conformity, Tu Tangata advocated retention of Maori cultural values as intrinsic to their advancement'.[20]

As the depression bit still deeper, and as the dismal ideology of the market and of self-help took a stronger grip on New Zealanders, the busy entrepreneur and the demoralized (and dangerous) unemployed came to figure in the Māori world as they did in the Pākehā. But they figured much more largely because of the Māori world's *lack* of entrepreneurs, professional financiers, and managers; and because of that world's increasing abundance of unemployed manual and skilled manual workers. Separate business and commercial initiatives by Māori, along with separate schemes of social engineering for the Māori, became the order of the day.

The Wananga Whakatauira of 1982 advocated the institution of a Maori Development Finance Corporation. The same year the first Maori Development Conference was held. The Minister of Maori Affairs told it that his department had funded twenty young Māori to take Bachelor of Business Studies degrees at Massey University.[21] In 1983 Kara Puketapu spoke with enthusiasm of the coming times in which Māori would 'go to university to take business studies rather than anthropology or Maori studies';[22] and soon after, he himself left Maori Affairs to manage Maori International Inc., financed, it was originally hoped, by Māori money alone.

Maori International, aiming at the development of Māori tourism, crafts and farming in particular, did not thrive; but the trend to devolution and to preparing the Māori people to hold their own in the 'market place' accelerated with the coming to power in 1984 of the new Labour Government. In October that year, a Maori Economic Summit, the Hui Taumata, was held in Wellington. Faced with a briefing booklet outlining the statistics of inequality,[23] it condemned the 'negative funding' that had been spent on Māori victims of the economic and social system as breeding an 'unhealthy dependence' on the state. It insisted instead that the Māori people, properly funded, should not only administer their own lives but create new ones in the world of finance and business. The next decade would be 'a decade of Maori development', devoted to expunging the inequalities between Māori and and Pākehā.

After the conference, separate tribes held their own Economic Conferences,

---

[20] Fleras, 'Towards "Tu Tangata" ', p. 27.

[21] H1:4/2/82.

[22] Hii1:1/10/83.

[23] H2:27/10/84.

and from Hui Taumata also sprang the Maori Economic Development Commission and its progeny: the Maori Enterprise Development Scheme (1986), Mana Enterprises (1986), and – 'to trade at the top end of the commercial sector' and possessed of members of the great conglomerates of Fletcher Challenge and Brierley Investments on its Board – the Maori Resource Development Corporation (1987).[24] By 1987, Sir Graham Latimer was speaking of the need for more Māori to understand 'taha commerce'; and he may have been reflecting not only on the obvious, but also on the various financial and management scandals, which by then had begun to plague the Department with the appearance in the news media of the Hawaiian Loan Affair in December 1986.

From the Hui Taumata also sprang an attempt to unite the Maori Trust Boards – those that managed land once developed by the Department of Maori Affairs, and those subsisting on compensation monies – in the Federation of Maori Economic Authorities. Initially, in 1986, this effort at reorganization was made under the Chairmanship of the Ariki (high chief) of Tu Wharetoa, Sir Hepi Te Heu Heu: such was the importance accorded the matter. The discovery, creation, and legal formalization of further 'iwi authorities' accompanied the efforts at federation. This was (manifestly) in line with the Government's devolving economically profitable departmental functions in general to SOEs – to Landcorp, NZ Post, Forestcorp, etc. It was also (less manifestly) in line with its general policy of cutting expenditure on social welfare while putting up a smoke-screen of talk about reducing dependence on the state to disguise it. It accorded too, with the ideals of self-management of those tribal, waka and other Māori organizations with the most developed administrative and financial capacity: Ngai Tahu, Ngapuhi and Tainui especially. Nor, when for either Māori or Pākehā to argue against self-help was to commit rhetorical suicide, could the weaker or unorganized tribes argue with the general gist of the policy.

Finally, devolution, 'transferral of resources' to the Māori – with proper financing – accorded with the whole continuing Māori attempt to combine a parity with the Pākehā in the goods of life with a degree of independence. Ripeka Evans, for instance, after her time in 1985 with the Maori Economic Development Commission, commented in 1986 that the Enterprise Development Scheme was 'the first time a practical application of the arguments for autonomy and equity has been attempted'.

I see it as . . . applying the arguments: first of autonomy, and second of equity. When we talk of autonomy we are talking about self-management or delivery within our own system. Put the other way round: first we extract what we think is our equity, even though at present it's not sufficient, and secondly we apply the resource by delivering it through our delivery system. So that is really the whole argument for autonomy; it's no use pulling a resource out for Maoridom to use if it's going to be put through a pakeha system.

[24] AS3:1/7/87; H5:2/7/87. It was 'launched' in Parliament on 1 July.

Hers, noted Evans, was 'a very simplistic interpretation of the whole autonomy and equity argument'. Perhaps what she had in mind was that she had put the argument into the language of business management and administration, and that that could provide only a very crude translation of Māori ideals of mana motuhake. Otherwise she was too modest. It was a good description of the case Māori groups made to the Government from the Hui Taumata onwards.[25]

But the concrete detail of devolution was always a live issue. In July 1986 the Government appointed a committee under Bob Mahuta to oversee changes by which the 'Maori Affairs Department [would] give rangatiratanga – authority and dignity – back to the people'.[26] That committee was disbanded for unstated reasons. Its successor, consisting of government servants, came up with a Green Paper on devolution. Dr Tamati Reedy, the Secretary of Maori Affairs was enthusiastic about the paper: 'It is a reaffirmation of that principle of the Treaty of Waitangi . . . It is giving Maoridom a sense of true partnership'.[27] But there were doubts. At a series of fifty-five hui, Koro Wetere heard well-grounded Māori suspicion of the cost-cutting motives of the two most powerful control departments of government – Treasury and the State Services Commission – of the organizational unreadiness on the part of iwi authorities, of a certain Māori affection for 'their' department, and of the difficulties of constructing urban Māori authorities to devolve functions to. The reforms were therefore slowed down, and projected to be substantially complete by 1994.[28] But the constructions of Māori authorities proceeded still; and in 1988, five further Trust Boards – now called tribal rūnanga and joining the existing thirteen set up to administer compensation monies – were created by legislation.[29] The new Boards were now empowered to contract with and act for the Government on matters of employment, education, health, housing, and 'enterprise development'. The Act would provide the legal capacity for the rūnanga to act in 'partnership' with the Government, Wetere explained.

A parallel devolutionary trend in job-creation and training schemes also strengthened after the Hui Taumata. At the outset of the 1980s such schemes had existed, funded and administered in an ad hoc manner by the Departments of Maori Affairs, Labour and Social Welfare, and by the Technical Institutes.[30] But other schemes developed as part of the Tu Tangata programme. The Rapu Mahi scheme was put together by Maori Affairs over the summer of 1981–1982 to provide summer work for unemployed school leavers and to train them in job search and work skills. Government funding was then

25 Ripeka Evans, 'Maori Economic Development', at p. 20.

26 AS6:25/6/87.

27 H4:27/6/87.

28 See Department of Maori Affairs, *Te Urupare Rangapu/Partnership Response* of November 1988, which addressed itself to the problems.

29 NZPD1:42 (26 July 1988), pp. 5460-77.

30 H1:6/1/81;. H3:1/3/84 will give the reader some idea.

found to extend the scheme for a further year; and again administration was devolved, notably to urban organizations such as the Auckland pan-tribal groups, Te Whanau O Waipareira and the Tamaki Makaurau Employment Agency.[31] Under Labour, Māori employment schemes were further articulated. Mana Enterprises and the Maori Enterprises Development Scheme were designed as business – and therefore job – creation schemes. And Māori Access schemes were introduced to train Māori youth for employment. Existing Polytechnics and Community Colleges shared the training with a variety of new growths, and where general Access schemes were precariously administered by Regional Employment and Access Councils, Maori Access schemes were equally uncertainly managed by a variety of iwi authorities. Starting on a modest ($4 million) scale in 1986, the Access schemes in 1987 were budgeted at $40 million.[32] Mana Enterprises was also greatly expanded in 1987.[33]

All of these programmes, specially aimed at Māori citizens, augmented the normal social welfare benefits available to them through the Departments of Health, Education, Social Welfare, and so on. In sum, New Zealand Governments were becoming committed to policies devoted to equalizing the condition of Māori and Pākehā.[34] Whatever the questions as to the directions and strength of that commitment – and there were many – at least *that* was clear. And Governments were also committed by the 1980s to devolution of at least some resources and authority to the Māori people operating in their tribes and quasi-tribal structures.

When placed alongside a tendency to reparation under the second Labour Government, the equalization policies took their place as part of an overall policy of systematic differentiation of Māori from Pākehā. This is how it seemed universally to New Zealanders by the mid-1980s and had for some time previously. The question was: were these policies the right ones or not?

---

[31] H10:22/4/82; WL27:19/7/83.

[32] AS5:22/6/87.

[33] H3:19/6/87. Compare, Note to Minister of Trade and Industry from Maori Affairs, 17 February 1987.

[34] At least this is the way it was put. A more plausible description of their activity is probably that they were moving to control the damage consequent upon the end of full employment.

Chapter 11
The Pākehā Ideology, Distributive Multiculturalism, and the Cloudy Rhetoric of Equity

I

The Pākehā Ideology of Equality

The programmes were always at issue, and were – except when Kara Puketapu was at his ebullient best – invariably dourly defended rather than celebrated. In 1980, the *Herald* reported that, 'Professor [Colin D.] Mantell [of Auckland University], himself part-Maori and keenly interested in Maori education, said the work ethic was still something Maoris had to learn . . . He would prefer not to have "active discrimination" in favour of Polynesians but it could only be said it was not necessary when 8 or 9 percent of Maoris were in good jobs'.[1] In 1983, an official who was experienced in the Department of Maori Affairs and in the Department of Health wrote to his peers in their journal, *Public Sector:* 'The contemporary challenge for bureaucracy is to legitimise discriminatory programmes. Based on the assumption that a minimum aim of social administration is to solve poverty and ethnic disadvantage, the political will to seek more equal and equitable outcomes must underlie effective programmes of differential action'.[2] Nor did the 'challenge for bureaucracy' recede in the later 1980s. In January 1987 the Race Relations Office found it necessary to publish *Towards an Equitable Society: Affirmative Action.* In the booklet, the Office defended 'affirmative action' programmes aimed 'to accelerate the process whereby Maori and Pacific Island employees are encouraged to apply for work in which they have been under-represented and to help them qualify on merit for appointment and promotion'. By 'affirmative action programmes' it meant bursaries and scholarships deriving from the Maori Educational Foundation and from tribal sources, University Polynesian preference schemes, apprenticeship and other Polytechnic training schemes, the Maori Enterprise Development Scheme and Maori Affairs Department housing loans.

Why the 'challenge' to make programmes of differential action seem legitimate, and why the necessity to *defend* affirmative action programmes? If equality of condition was the goal, why the problem?

It was because those programmes encountered a loosely articulated – indeed sometimes contradictory – but powerful and pervasive public ideology of

---

[1] H2:9/2/80.

[2] Harper, 'The Implications for a Bureaucracy of Responding to Special Group Needs', p. 7.

equality that denied their justice. It is because the ideology denied Māori claims to equalizing treatment that it may be called the *Pākehā* ideology of equality, but many Māori in fact embraced it and were often publicized doing so, and reforming Pākehā rejected it with disdain. The ideology was egalitarian in the sense that its proponents believed inequalities in the enjoyment of social goods had to be *justified*. Inequalities were not obviously just and right; where they were, they had to be shown to be so. But the Pākehā ideologists thought in fact that current inequalities in New Zealand were by and large justified. People merited and deserved what they had in fact differentially got. Of course equality of opportunity would have had to exist for that to be true, otherwise the race would not have been fair, and the rewards not distributed according to merit but according to the chances of family wealth, neighbourhood connections, good parenting and so on. The Pākehā ideology held that equality of opportunity did indeed exist, so that those who prospered, prospered deservedly and those who languished deserved what they did not get.

Equality of opportunity and unequal rewards distributed according to past performance: these, in the Pākehā ideology, constituted justice. Anything else was unequal treatment and favouritism: in a word, injustice. More specifically it was the injustice of wrongly distinguishing *some* people solely on grounds of their race and harming *other* people because of the application of the wrong distinction. It was (psychologically speaking) 'racism'; as a political policy it was 'apartheid'; in legal principle, it was 'inequality before the law'. So affirmative action programmes were bitterly opposed. And so were any other arrangements, practices, laws, sayings and activities which distinguished Māori from Pākehā: the four Maori MPs, the Department of Maori Affairs, Maori Land and Maori Land Courts, and so on – even the Maori All Blacks. The Treaty of Waitangi itself, if (and when) applied in modern times, would (and did) issue in racist legislation and judgments. And racism – like apartheid and inequality before the law – was a species of injustice.

In 1979–1980 the Human Rights Commission collected examples of the Pākehā ideology in their preliminary study to *Race Against Time*, which they published in 1980 and called *Racial Harmony in New Zealand*. In their study the Commission asked their respondents to philosophize about the Haka Party incident and He Taua's taking of justice into their own hands by attacking the offending engineering students. The Pākehā ideology emerged with great clarity. One respondent told the Commission: 'I regard any . . . special treatment of whatsoever nature as racist'; another: 'to stretch the law for any section is to distort it. The disadvantaged should obey the law as should the privileged, and to "make allowances" for either a Maori gang member or a Member of Parliament is equally corrupt'; another: 'we are New Zealanders and live by New Zealand law'; another: 'we should not ask for racial privilege; we should not ask for racial exclusiveness'; another: 'I have watched, with growing concern, Maori/Pakeha (instead of white/black) become alternative terms for an us/them ideology which, more and more, bears a striking resemblance to South Africa's Afrikanerdom.' Separation of the races and differential treatment was, the respondents said, both unjust and inimical to social harmony and peace. 'Being Maori is often a state of mind, there being so little Maori blood involved. To be a proud New Zealander is the best and least divisive answer, with race unimportant unless to the private individual. There are already far too many divisions created over land laws [and] voting rolls.' One respondent complained of Māori requiring 'to be treated as if handicapped. Apart from traditional privileges enjoyed by Maoris such as special MPs [and] preferential treatment through the Maori Affairs Department, the most recent developments are . . . hostels . . . and Maori representation on regional authorities. (I know of one successful claimant for a Maori Affairs loan who would be no more than one sixteenth part Maori.)' Others complained of the Maori Trustee's separate existence and funding of Maori Affairs' programmes for Māori.

If the Māori had failed it was their own fault. 'The world does not owe the Maoris a living. They do not look after their children.' 'The Maoris must be made to understand that good things in white man's culture cannot be got without sacrifices. If they want white man's standards of living they must join in the rat race on the white man's terms.' The Māori 'took to beer and bingo'. 'Maoris generally speaking, have not taken advantage of the opportunities that have been and still are offering . . . Maoris have special advantages in welfare and education that are denied to their other New Zealand brethren.' 'Generally a Maori worker is not as ambitious and therefore productive as a Pakeha, which makes him less desirable for employment. By the same token a Chinese person would generally be more industrious than a Pakeha making him most desirable.' 'I think,' said another, 'the last five years have nurtured an arrogance in the Maoris. New Zealanders have *over* favoured the Maoris who now feel superior, without proving it by ethics and character.' Others complained of Māori lawlessness and gang activity, the wearing, for example, of the swastika emblem by the 'Stormtrooper' gang.

Though in substance the precise issues changed during the 1980s, the ideology itself remained constant. As the claims to the restitution of lands, language, culture and fisheries unfolded, and as the Māori demanded institutional reforms appropriate to their separate rights, the same basic conception of social justice was reiterated: equality before the law, equality of opportunity as justifying inequality of condition, and personal and group failure as accounting for the Māori's relative deprivation. The ideology had its radically consistent extremes. Some were expressed in the submissions of interested parties to the Committee to Review the Curriculum for Schools, which was to publish its *Curriculum Review* in 1987. One respondent produced this invocation to the committee: 'one land, one language, one culture, one goal, one people'; another made the suggestion that 'radical feminisim, racism, sexism and other associated radical causes should be banned and people should be accepted

as they are in Christian love without prejudice of any kind'.[3] Dr Paul Spoonley
and others have well recorded and traced the sources and overall shape of
such extreme views.[4] And Spoonley has analysed many more innocent beliefs
as 'racist' in effect, if not in intention.[5] Here my concern is to record the
conceptions of justice which both the extreme and more moderate views
had in common: justice as equality before the law, justice as equality of
opportunity, and justice as (pretty much) the ethnic distributions that currently
existed.

Several separable ideas went under the claim that 'equality before the law'
was required by justice. First, the idea that the Māori ought to be freed
from the disabilities to which they – or more often, it was said, their lands
– were subject and which did not apply to others; second, the idea that
Māori privileges should be removed and that they should qualify for things
on the same grounds as others and not on the sole ground of being Māori;
third, that they should be equally subject to the (single) legal system. In
sum, the idea was that not only should everyone be subject to the same
authorities who should make and administer the law, but that the precise
laws that governed Māori and Pākehā should not differ on grounds of Māori
and Pākehā differences – or on grounds that the Māori had separate rights.

Some argued that the Māori should be freed from subjection to a separate
set of rules, from – as one Māori inheritor of Māori land put it – being
relegated to 'the kindergarten of national life'.[6] She, like many Māori who
made submissions to the McCarthy Commission on the Maori Land Courts
(1980) wanted to be free from the shackles of the Maori Land Courts with
their appalling record-keeping, their insistence that alienation could not be
attained without a large number of consents of people long disconnected
from the land, and their restrictions on the power of bequest. And she spoke
of the Universal Declaration of Human Rights which promised 'equality
before the law', claiming 'New Zealanders are one people . . . all entitled
to recognition and protection under one law and one court system'. For
its part the McCarthy Commission thought there should be as few legal
distinctions on grounds of race and as few special courts as possible, though
the Maori Land Courts would have to remain until their task of registering
all Māori land was done. It quoted the 'kindergarten of our national life'
remark with approval, and noted (as did the media) that many Māori had
told the Commission, as they had told the Pritchard-Waetford Commission
in 1968, that they would prefer to hold their land as 'General' not as 'Māori
Land' and that they were tired of being 'second-class citizens.'[7]

[3] Curriculum Review Committee, *The Curriculum Review*, pp. 83, 97.

[4] Jesson et al., *Revival of the Right*.

[5] Spoonley, *Racism and Ethnicity*, esp. pp. 18–23.

[6] Pamela Te Ruihi Warner, 'Condemned to Live in a Shack Because of Maori Land Laws',
H6:4/2/80.

[7] H3:11/6/80; H6:12/6/80. See also Letter from Kuku Karaitiana, H6:9/5/81.

Others wanted not so much to free the Māori from disabilities as to obliterate their privileges. Hilda Phillips waged a campaign through the 1970s and 1980s against the separate system of land law on grounds that it militated against New Zealanders seeing themselves as equals under the law and sharing a common humanity – and also common blood. The Maori Affairs Department, the Maori Land Courts and the Waitangi Tribunal were institutions devoted to maintaining and extending their own Māori privilege, and were the institutions in fact responsible for the wrongs of which the Māori still complained.[8] Mrs Phillips and others quoted the *Hunn Report*'s count of there being 264 'legal differentiations' between Māori and Pākehā on the Statute books.[9] One, Mr D. McMaster, a retired Auckland farmer, even took a case to the Waitangi Tribunal in 1985 claiming that the 200 'special privileges' the Māori had were 'contrary to the principles of the Treaty of Waitangi'. The Tribunal declined competence to hear him on the ground that he was not a Māori.[10] This, he thought, proved his point.[11] And it was a common argument against the Tribunal that it was not colour blind.

Equally common was the claim that the crucial article in the Treaty which it administered was Article 3 which promised the Māori 'all the *same* rights' as everyone else.[12] The greatest outcry of the 1980's against Māori legal privilege was caused by acquittals of two Māori defendants on charges of illegal shellfish gathering. In August 1986 Mr Tom Te Weehi pleaded in defence of such a charge section 88(2) of the Fisheries Act, which had it that 'nothing in this act [including shellfish regulations] shall affect any Māori fishing rights'. When he was acquitted, even though the nature and extent of Māori fishing rights was not established, locals at Ninety-Mile beach in the Far North began to reap the protected delicacy, the Toheroa. 'I never thought I would live to see the day in New Zealand when different laws applied to different people depending on the colour of their skin', said Dr Lockwood Smith, the local (Opposition) MP. A similar but noisier reaction greeted the acquittal of Jack Hakirau Love in April 1988, who pleaded section 88(2) also. Noisier, for this time his Pākehā gathering companion had been found guilty and the commercial fishing industry was in any case spoiling for a fight over the Māori threat to their fisheries. That this was 'apartheid', 'separatism', 'racist law', and that everyone ought to be under the 'same law' were the shibboleths. Thus when the Government was negotiating its fishing deal with the Māori during 1987–1989, for instance, and when it defended its Fisheries Bill which recorded the settlement it imposed, it continually stated that it

---

[8] Letters from Hilda Phillips at AS6:5/2/79; H12:31/8/79; H6:4/2/80; AS6:28/4/80; AS6:30/5/80; AS6:16/7/80; AS7:13/8/80; H6:2/6/81.

[9] Hunn, *Report*, pp. 77–8, and App. F, pp. 92–3. A good analysis of the tenor of the differentials as mostly to do with Māori lands is in Metge, *The Maoris of New Zealand*, p. 43.

[10] Waitangi Tribunal, *D. McMaster (re "Special Privileges")* (May 1985).

[11] NZT:24/3/85; Hii7:21/7/87. Cf. Waitangi Tribunal. *D. McMaster (re "Special Privileges")* May 1985.

[12] H6:6/2/81, Letter Mrs Pamela Te Ruihi Warner; H6:6/2/81, Letter 'Proud New Zealander'; AS8:17/9/86. Letter Hilda Phillips.

was concerned to get a 'non-discriminatory' law in place. Richard Prebble foreshadowed it, talking of the Government's determination that 'from now every New Zealander will fish subject to the same laws', and that 'the law will apply equally to Maori and non-Maori'.[13] And the preamble to the Bill precisely designed to settle *Māori* claims, to distribute Individual Transferable Quotas to *Māori* and to set up *Māori* committees to oversee coastal recreation fishing, continued the understandable equivocation. It stated its aim to be that 'All New Zealanders involved in fishing should be subject to the same laws'.[14] The Opposition, for its part, played clumsily with the matter, continually talking of the Government favoring 'apartheid on the high seas', 'racism', and 'separate laws' for Māori and Pākehā. In the climate of debate, no one wanted to be accused of favouring *them*.[15]

There was, it will already be evident, a hint of equivocation on 'equality before the law'. It could mean, as well as people being subject to the same particular rules of law, that they should be equally subject to the same legal system. Of course it is entirely possible for people, equally subject to the same legal system, to have different rights and duties under it. Employers, for instance, have different rights and duties from employees, and teachers from pupils. And the Māori claims were often precisely that under the legal system to which Māori and Pākehā were equally subject, they were guaranteed different rights from the Pākehā – for instance, in the fundamental law that was the Treaty of Waitangi, in the common law of aboriginal rights, and in the Fisheries Act which recognized (either or both of) these. But possibly because New Zealanders thought of the legal system as primarily a system of criminal law in which the same rules must apply to all, they were not at all sympathetic to the idea that there might be different rules for different people.

In 1979 and 1980, Judge B. H. Blackwood had occasion to state the line of thought very clearly.[16] In 1979, in the Haka Party Case (*Police* v *Dalton*), Judge Blackwood contemplated the insult offered He Taua – the plastic skirts imitating female Polynesian dress, the obscene paintings on the bodies of the students, the obscene and trivial words substituted for those of the haka, the students' gestures, their drunkenness, the years of refusals to desist when asked. None of the students' activities, he agreed with the defendants, could be justified in a truly 'multicultural' society. But:

However offended these defendants may have felt, that does *not* entitle them to take the law into their own hands, which is exactly what they chose to do. They chose to operate a type of lynch law, a concept unacceptable to our law, and, I believe,

---

[13] NZPD1:42,pp. 6823-4. 21 September 1988.

[14] Maori Fisheries Bill (1988, No.81-1), pp. 3-4.

[15] NZPD1:41, pp. 6844, 6887-90, 6892-4.

[16] And see also Sir Thaddeus McCarthy, AS4:29/8/79, responding to New Zealand Maori Council's suggestion that the powers of the Maori Land Court be extended to cover minor offences, family matters, and adoption. 'He thought the suggestion might provoke criticism along the lines that there would be one rule for European offenders and another for Maori offenders.'

unacceptable in any civilised society. We are one people, of differing religious beliefs, cultural heritages and racial backgrounds. We are governed by one law. Every civilised society has rules by which it lives, and it makes those rules of necessity so that the society may survive; without those rules the law of the jungle would operate. . . . Commonly in these courts we refer to it as the rule of law, and it is the duty of the Court to uphold the rule of law. Expressed simply the rule of law is that every citizen of this country, irrespective of his colour, creed, sex or status, *is equal before the law, but is equally subject to that law*. There cannot be one set of laws, for example, for one ethnic group and another set of law[s] for others. If the rule of law is not upheld, we have anarchy. If we have anarchy then civilised society will perish.[17]

In 1980, Judge Blackwood had another occasion to speak of equality before the law. He insisted that the protest leader Joe Hawke pay a fine of $150 for assaulting a man on a bicycle on Bastion Point. Hawke had claimed in defence that the ground was tapu because of the death of his niece there two weeks before the incident, and that 'our right to mourn was trampled on'. Convicted, he had refused to pay the fine. The newspaper report was: 'Judge Blackwood said as far as the Court was concerned there was one law to govern New Zealand citizens. "It is my duty to see the fine paid . . . otherwise I'm not applying the law as I would to all citizens" '.[18]

The idea-set of equality before the law was this: that judges must apply the laws impartially; that every citizen must be subject to the laws; that citizens may not with unauthorized violence administer the laws for themselves; that every citizen, as in the criminal laws, ought to be subject to exactly the same set of requirements and prohibitions as any other citizen; that only if there were one set of requirements could there be 'one people'; that if laws are broken, anarchy is likely; that if there are different rules governing different groups, anarchy is likely. The propositions that made up the set were all of them very different – the maxim of impartiality, the distinction between being in authority and being subject to it, the empirical claims about anarchy, the definition of a nation, etc. – and so are the arguments for and against them. Yet they were commonly found unselfconsiously yoked in the thought of laymen as well as judges. Jane Kelsey saw Blackwood's yoking of the propositions as nothing other than a demonstration of the 'contempt' with which 'British justice' had always 'treated assertions of Maori cultural and political integrity within Aotearoa'.[19] That is too harsh a judgement if it refers to conscious intentions: no doubt as with others, so with Blackwood, the truth and persuasiveness of some of the propositions led to the adoption – as true and persuasive – of those that were not.

Equality before the law was transmuted, though, in lay thought into the ideal of undifferentiated treatment of people by governments and other authorities and into opposition to Māori separatist tendencies. Unequal

---

[17] *Police* v *Dalton*, pp. 42-3.

[18] AS8:20/5/80.

[19] Kelsey, 'Legal Imperialism', p. 20.

treatment was the enemy of equality of opportunity; separatism was 'apartheid' and destroyed the unity of society. Perhaps it would even destroy the country. Governmental equalizing welfare policies expressed by or built on legal distinction were objected to as 'privilege'; and there were allied objections to the 'favouritism', 'separatism', and 'apartheid' practised both by the Māori themselves and by governments.

The tone of correspondence in newspapers on Māori privilege was not amiable; talk-back radio was even more passionately angry at the insult to justice. In deeply ironic tones, a correspondent of 1981 said 'we should have houses specifically for Maoris and Islanders all over Auckland . . . These could be administered by their own Maori and Island Affairs Department. We should have scholarships specially for Maoris, and perhaps special community centres, special seats in Government, maybe even a Maori-only football team. Then of course, being a democracy we must do the same for the whites. Oops! Apartheid?' Another correspondent, 'Kiwi', said much the same thing on the same newspaper page,[20] and similar sentiments were commonly heard throughout the late 1970s into the late 1980s. The Royal Commission on Social Policy collected a number and recorded them in 1987.[21]

Newspaper correspondents disapproved of the Maori Trustee using Māori money to provide houses to Māori. Even worse, houses were provided to Māori gang members; and when in the 1980s, special make-work schemes were provided for them, there was a huge outcry.[22] In 1984 there was objection to the Hui Taumata as being 'separatist';[23] and in the same year objections to continued Māori claims to Bastion Point were yolked with their trying to segregate themselves in separate institutions: 'I was taught that we are one people.'[24] Others complained of the Māori exclusivity of Maori International and the *Herald* wrote an editorial on its 'explicitly racial name and purpose' raising, it said, 'legitimate challenges' to the very idea.[25] Others complained through the 1980s about the policy of Maori Affairs of developing Maori Lands. Did the Pākehā get the same service?[26] There was a bitter recurring argument from 1979 through 1988 as to whether the Māori people ought by right to have a representative on the planning committee of the Auckland Regional Authority,[27] and the very idea – recurring through the late 1970s and 1980s – that there should be separate Maori Community Courts for dealing with young Māori offenders met with an indignant public reception and a careful one from the politicians. 'In a multiracial society . . . all races

[20] AS6:21/5/81, Letter Peter J. Thompson.

[21] *The April Report*, i, p. 328.

[22] H6:22/2/79.

[23] H6:5/11/84.

[24] AS8:12/9/84, Letter Shane Kemp. See also Hiii5:22/10/84, Letter 'New Zealander'.

[25] H6:28/8/80, Letter 'Discrimination'; H6:18/12/84, Letter 'Perplexed'; H6:30/1/84; Hiii4:3/2/84 Letter Arnold Braden; H6:5/11/84, Letter J. C. Wilson.

[26] Hiii4:3/2/84, Letter Arnold Braden.

[27] For its beginnings, Hii11:24/10/79; Hiii6:7/11/79. It was still going on in 1989.

. . . must enjoy on equal terms all benefits – protection by the law, health, education, welfare. . . . But all races must give the same allegiance accepting that all are one before the law and no one race can have special privileges.'[28] When in November 1988, Mr Moana Jackson suggested in a report to the Department of Justice a 'bicultural restructuring' of the criminal justice system, his recommendations, opposed by the Minister of Justice, were hardly taken seriously by Pākehā public opinion.[29]

But what if, as seemed to be the case, the Māori did *not* enjoy the same benefits in law, health, education, and welfare? The answer tended to be that they *had* every opportunity to attain these, but, out of a tendency to gripe at their misfortunes, out of laziness or out of a cussed desire to be Māori, had not grasped them. So that their inequality of condition, while lamentable, had been earned by them. Only they could do what was best for them and the nation – overcome that condition by application to the real tasks in hand. A common argument was that part of the problem was that the Māori were paralysed by their sense of grievance as to their losses at the hands of the Pākehā. They should take their minds off these, which were simply, according to one correspondent, 'excuses to avoid the disciplined activities that will help their race to achieve satisfaction, not in a "Pakeha society" . . . but in the shrinking world of the silicon chip'.[30] Māori sometimes said the same: 'I believe that all Maoris should forget the land and look towards our youth, for they are the future. We all must become more aware of their needs and help them cope with the pressures of today's life.'[31] Educated 'activists and protesters', said another, should help their people, not incite hatred: 'Teach us to be good parents, to keep our children out of prisons, away from suicides and drug abuse'.[32] When Mr Te Awa Heke, a descendant of the famous Hone Heke (signatory of the Treaty and warrior against the Pākehā state in the 1840s), started to organize a 'March for Harmony' to Waitangi in 1983, he was praised for saying that 'Maori have no reasons to complain about lack of opportunity in education, job finding, and gaining the respect of other members of the community'.[33] The Māori should forget their grievances and improve themselves. They had every chance. This was the Pākehā ideology.[34]

Such sentiments were the stock in trade of populist politicians like Robert Muldoon and Ben Couch. Lives – Pākehā radical as well as Māori – should not be wasted on the futile and dangerous fomenting of grievance and disharmony: young Māori in particular should not fritter away their chances

[28] AS6:3/12/79, Letter 'Oppressed'; AS6:11/2/79.

[29] Jackson, *The Maori and the Criminal Justice System*, ii, esp. pp. 205 and following. And see Chapter 12 of this book.

[30] H10:18/3/81.

[31] AS6:27/11/81.

[32] AS10:23/3/88.

[33] Hiii13:27/1/83, Letter Senior Citizen.

[34] See also letters at Hiii:19/3/79; H3:22/2/80.

to succeed. They should also realize they had a duty to their country and people to do so. 'A certain type of Maori,' said Couch, 'blames other people for his problem.'[35] Mr Norman Jones MP (Opp), the archetypical redneck, professed himself in 1986 'sick and tired, as a fourth generation pakeha, being told I am responsible for Maori offending'. 'If the leaders of Maoridom spent as much time and concern and care and money looking after young Maoris as they did on Taha Maori and ramming Maori culture down our throats, then we'd all be better off. . . . You've got to hold the parents culpable.'[36]

Not all blamed the Māori. They simply recorded that it was hard to get the message of self improvement through to them; and Hon. Aussie Malcolm, Minister of Health in 1982, spoke this way.[37] Others however – both people and politicians – called on the notion that the Māori were just lazy, and did not therefore do well at school or deserve work when they left. 'Fair go, mate, they're not up to it!' said a *Sunday News* headline quoting the unemployment statistics of 1981 and its readers' reactions: 'I think it's half their own fault anyway – and it's all because they didn't make it at school.' 'All these reports in the paper make out as if Maoris are useless and can't get a job, but I think half of them aren't even looking.' One Māori who had got a job did not think that employers gave Māori and Islanders 'a fair go'. They were racist and did not hire them. All the same, she thought that 'parents are partly to blame, and it's sad to see these kids on the streets with nothing to do'.[38] Ben Couch remarked that 'Health has no race; and neither has self-indulgence, and lack of self-discipline. If we have lost our health . . . it is largely because we have lost pride in our own bodies. We cannot blame anyone else but ourselves for that. . . . Our people of earlier days would have felt themselves disgraced to be fat and out of condition.'[39]

In the late 1980s Winston Peters took up Couch's baton and exhorted the Māori to greater effort, especially in view of the 'millions of dollars poured into Maoridom through funding, such as social welfare benefits'.[40] Pākehā gave paternal – and as often, maternal – advice to the Māori as to how to do better as parents;[41] and Māori correspondents to newspapers often lamented the failure of Māori parents to discipline their children for the sake of their health, education, and law-abidingness.[42]

In 1984 Mr John Graham, Headmaster of Auckland Grammar School, said Māori pupils did not do well because they were 'lazy'. 'They're just lazy. If you attack a system because one section can't handle it, for God's sake

[35] AS2:5/6/84; H5:14/6/82.

[36] AS8:17/9/86.

[37] AS6:8/9/82.

[38] DST9:11/1/81.

[39] Quoted in Pat Booth, 'Are Maoris Getting a Fair Deal?', *Metro*, Sept 1985, p. 69.

[40] DST3:1/5/88.

[41] H6:10/3/80, Letter (Mrs) E. M. Wright; AS6:26/8/81, Letter 'Teacher'.

[42] H8:21/3/88.

look at the section rather than the system.'[43] The Race Relations Office received complaints; but he was widely supported in his views. Bob Jones, financier, and leader while it was successful of the libertarian New Zealand Party, thought that those who failed were either inactive out of discontent, lazy, or unlucky. If they wanted to do better they should try harder and stop 'moaning'.[44] And one anonymous parent told the Curriculum Review Committee that 'other cultures manage to get on without a chip on their shoulders – we have all been treated badly at some time'.[45] 'Attempts to "pacify" the lazy members of racial minorities with racially segregated sports teams, Government departments, loan amenities, university quotas, schools, prison visiting rights, and so on have resulted in the current racial backlash from the "non-pacified" population. When will these bludgers stop whinging and work for their benefits?' asked one belligerent letter-writer.[46]

Often the case for Māori non-deserving was linked with praise of other cultures in the vivid, 'multicultural', mosaic which made up New Zealand, in which each culture was free to live out its own ways, in which individuals were free to stick with customary practices or not, and in which each man and woman had an equal chance of fulfilment. As 'New Zealander' said in 1988: 'We are all foremost New Zealanders, all able to practise our homespun traditions without interference from anyone'.[47] Another, objecting to Māori 'radical troublemaking', intoned: 'Let us live together in harmony, as one race, New Zealanders. Practise their own culture, if they wish, others do, Dutch, Chinese, Indians, Vietnamese, all come here speaking little or no English and in a very short time by their own efforts (no Government handouts or mollycoddling) achieve high academic marks, own businesses, land and property, all the while retaining their own culture, in their own groups, in their own time.'[48] But culture was a matter for the home and the ethnic group, not for the schools: 'the present pushing of cultural diversity will lead, inevitably to cultural separatism, not unity,' the Curriculum Review Committee was told.[49]

---

[43] Quoted in Marion McLeod, 'Starting Fair', NZL14:6/2/88.

[44] He summed up his attitude in a letter, NBR:30/9/88.

[45] *The Curriculum Review*, p. 83.

[46] H8:20/9/88. See also AS6:26/4/84, Letter 'New Zealander'; H11:2/7/88, Letter R. Eggers.

[47] AS6:24/4/84.

[48] AS10:23/3/88, Letter G. Kay. On the industry of others, see Hii7:19/3/79, Letter Vernon Yates.

[49] *The Curriculum Review*, p. 83.

II

Amelioration through Differential Treatment and Multicultural Distributivism

The Pākehā ideology was no monolithic system. It was too full of contradictions. It shaded gradually, via a lack of confidence that 'equality of opportunity' really *was* available for the Māori, into an ameliorative liberalism. This ameliorationism shaded in turn into the indigenous[50] egalitarianism of New Zealand/Aotearoa. Despite its variety and contradiction though, the general and inescapable tendency of the Pākehā ideology was not to treat the Māori as something special but simply as cases of deprivation with consequent needs which must be met. And such cases could also be found among the Pākehā, so that Māori people were to be treated like any others in the same condition of need.

To be an ameliorationist was to be willing to contemplate state intervention for the sake of meeting both personal and group needs; and policy-makers and people could construct that position on either (or both) liberal or egalitarian foundations. For their part, liberals could contemplate with equanimity the fact of many and competing forms of life and culture – but (with varying degrees of equanimity) they could also face the fact that the dominant Pākehā form might disadvantage those who practised others. And while a liberal commitment to equal opportunity could easily lead to equalizing policies that would bring about that distribution of things that the figures on relative deprivation showed to be so lacking, there was no obvious reason why that equalization of opportunity should lead to the provision of different opportunities for separate *ethnies* to do different things. In brief, liberalism could suggest (among other things) a homogenizing egalitarianism.

But because it was in *New Zealand* that policies of equalization were being defended and contemplated, they could hardly be spoken of as 'egalitarian' and could never be spoken of as 'socialist'. They were rather presented as being designed to 'give everyone a fair go' and as counters to the 'élitism' of established arrangements. This was the language of that indigenous egalitarianism which did not and could not identify itself with state socialism. It could not (as a matter of rhetoric) because 'socialism' had long been an unpopular word in the country and (as a matter of political theory) because whereas socialism often implied public ownership of productive resources, indigenous egalitarianism was more interested simply in equalizing the consumption of, and enjoyment of, the goods of life. It was not so much interested in the processes of making things – including people and lives – and did not have much to say about what good people and lives were like.

Submissions made in 1985–1986 to the Curriculum Review Committee

---

[50] Creole indigenous, shared by Māori and Pākehā.

provide a good general idea of the ideological milieu. The Committee was told that: 'The schools don't reflect the cultural backgrounds of minority/ ethnic subcultures'; and: 'However Anglos are hurting, people from other cultures are hurting more'; and: 'There should be proportional representation of Maori, Pakeha and other groups represented on school committees and boards, depending on the number of children in schools. If there are 54% Maori children in the schools, then there should be 54% Maori on the school committee or board'; and (more commodiously): 'If the widening gap between rich and poor, have and have-nots and educated and educationally disabled in our society is to be bridged, more genuine recognition of the significance of taha Maori must be given at levels of the education system'; and: 'Because the largest non-European group are the Maori people, it is only right that this be the starting point of multicultural education'; and: 'Schools tend to be run by people who have "made it", and are very much geared to supporting the status quo, and the institutions which train our teachers, i.e. the universities.' Asked how 'fairness' could be achieved, the respondents spoke of the necessity for: 'unequal treatment. Benefits, help, individual tuition to those who need it. (A political death knell, as the nice white families with average/above average children/backgrounds will be outraged). As it is, free boarding schools, uniform etc. to Maori students is looked on with disfavour to vociferous outrage.' 'Fair treatment for all, or equity, may require unequal treatment.' Respondents firmly denied that 'equality of opportunity' actually existed, and said that the belief that it did exist constituted a 'barrier' to bringing it about. The way things were, 'some people cannot grasp the opportunity owing to ethnic, cultural, financial, parental and location influences.'[51]

A battle for those who would argue in these ways for special treatment for the Māori was to contest the ground claimed by those who said that such treatment was 'discriminatory', was 'racism', and was 'apartheid'. Descriptive and normative meanings had to be untangled, and usage rectified. And here the ameliorationalists had to work against the grain of normal public understandings of the words. It was not going to be easy for the reformers to speak of 'unequal treatment', 'reverse discrimination' or 'positive discrimination'. As in the United Kingdom and the United States of America it was better to call such policies 'equity policies', policies of 'equal opportunity' or policies of 'affirmative action', so as to avoid implications of inequality and discrimination.[52]

The Labour Prime Minister in 1974, the Rt. Hon. Norman Kirk, had felt constrained to argue that while the Treaty of Waitangi 'stressed equality', there was still a case for allowing 'discrimination in fields such as Maori education where discrimination existed to favour the Maori'.[53] But it was left rather to out-of-doors reformers than to parliamentary politicians to

[51] *The Curriculum Review*, pp. 70, 83, 27, 71, 72, 88, 92, 94, 95–7.

[52] Interestingly, on the UK, see Reeves, *British Political Discourse about Race*, p. 144.

[53] H1:2/4/74.

attempt the rehabilitation of the idea of discrimination. As the Māori demand took shape in the the late 1970s to 'correct what many see as the crux of the problem – too many Maoris in manual jobs and too few in the professions', measures were taken to combat the problem. They were named 'affirmative action' rather than 'positive discrimination', and they were defended not as equalizing policies but as 'just a matter of recognising ability, promoting and nurturing it'.[54] The word 'discrimination' was generally avoided.

Mary Hume, President of CARE (the Citizens' Association for Racial Equality) undertook the rehabilitative task on 'discrimination' in 1979. She wrote to newspapers: 'I looked up "discriminate" in the *Concise Oxford Dictionary*. The first meaning given is "observe a difference between; distinguish from another". The second meaning is "distinguish unfavourably". What Hilda Phillips . . . fails to acknowledge is that discrimination can enhance; it does not have to injure. Recognising racial difference can be an important part of accepting a person, or people, it can answer a need; it can help to ensure genuine equality of opportunity in all fields. It is the spirit in which it is done that counts'.[55] In the same year, Miss Mary Grey, president of the New Zealand Association of Social Workers, undertook a defence of 'positive discrimination' against a complaint to the Race Relations Office that the Education Department had advertised for a Māori language teacher of 'Maori descent'. 'It is time', she told the Association, to advocate measures to improve the relative position of Māori: 'We are the ones who see the situations of Maoris; who see them falling victim to a culturally different system. It is time we started questioning our own Pakeha systems and institutions . . . started tackling causes.'[56] From about that time on, the idea that there was a Pākehā 'system' which disadvantaged other cultures and which would need to be transformed if minorities were to enjoy equality, took root among anti-racist groups and spread into the bureaucracy. It took time – the complaint about the Education Department's advertisement for a Māori was met with an assurance that 'suitable applicants of any race will be considered' – but ameliorationalist liberalism was to be the bureaucratic ideology by the late 1980s.

The accusation that these policies of amelioration were specifically 'racist' as well as generally 'discriminatory' had to be met. And the first and most obvious thing to say was that the policies were designed rather to counter racism than to entrench it. For that reason, reformers sought for and exposed personal prejudice where they found it. In the nature of things in New Zealand/ Aotearoa personal prejudice of a publicly-demonstrable kind was not easy to find. The last celebrated cases had occurred in the late 1950s.[57] But everyone knew it was there, and it was a notable blow in the fight against injustice when a 1986 study by the Office of the Race Relations Conciliator, *Racism*

[54] AS5:1/9/77. See also AS12:11/11/80.

[55] AS6:29/11/79.

[56] H4:5/11/79.

[57] Metge, *The Maoris of New Zealand*, pp. 295–300.

and Rental Accommodation, exposed it. Landlords and real estate agents were found to be much less willing to rent accommodation to Māori and Pacific Islander applicants than to whites: Polynesian names and (more powerfully) skin colour were the triggers for rejection. Māori and Polynesians were successful in initial phone applications less than half as often as others; in face-to-face encounters, about one-sixth as successful. No one disputed the results. No one denied that the landlords and members of the Real Estate Institute had done grievous wrong. To be 'racist' where this was for someone to discriminate against people simply on ground of their skin colour, or perhaps culture, was not a thing to be defended in public at all.

The reformers sought to go still further and take the battle against racism into the enemy camp. The National Council of Churches and other reformers borrowed an American Black Power analysis for that purpose. There were, they taught in the 1980s, three kinds of racism: personal, cultural, and institutional. Because the teaching depended on opaque distinctions between individual human consciousnesses on the one hand, and on the other systems of belief and activity ambivalently external to individual consciousness, it is not easy to reproduce. And there is some difficulty caused by the collapsing of a 1970s distinction between 'racialism' on the one hand and 'racism' on the other. 'Racialism' used to refer – in the usage of the Race Relations Conciliator in the 1970s – to invidious discrimination 'resulting from stereotyping with the implication of inferiority only in particular areas with the possibility of change' not ruled out. 'Racism' was, however, based on a belief in permanent relations of subordination with no prospect of future equality. It was discrimination on the basis of a belief 'in the biological hereditary superiority of one race over another'.[58] But during the 1980s the distinction went – a victory to those reformers and those of their opponents who did not understand or did not want it, but a defeat for those who would wish to describe doctrines more clearly and therefore needed distinctions that referred to real differences.[59]

Therefore, it is best to show the doctrine on racism simply by describing an instance. *Puao-Te-Ata-Tu/Day Break*, the report of a Ministerial Committee 'on a Maori perspective for the Department of Social Welfare', taught it in 1986, in an attempt to suggest reforms of the Department which might improve its performance for those who were not Pākehā. An Appendix on 'The Faces of Racism' explained that 'personal racism' occurred when an individual saw members of other races as inferior 'because of skin colour or ethnic origin'.[60] This was simple 'race prejudice', easily identifiable in jokes and disparaging comments. 'Cultural racism' was 'less obvious'. Nevertheless it was identifiable in the beliefs and actions of its perpetrators. It was a 'parcel of attitudes' and assumptions: the 'assumption that Pakeha

---

[58] Metge, *The Maoris of New Zealand*, pp. 297–8.

[59] See Lloyd Geering, 'Prejudicial to healing', NZL93:25/4/87, who also argues along the lines suggested by his title.

[60] PTAT, ii, Appendix 3. See also vol i, pp. 19, 25–6 for what follows.

culture, lifestyle and values are superior to those of other New Zealand cultures . . . that Pakeha values, beliefs and systems are "normal". . . [also] the unshakeable belief in the cultural superiority of Europeans'. It manifested itself, for instance, when the 'power culture' arrogated to itself 'the right to select those aspects of Maoritanga it wants to use or include in general New Zealand culture. These selections range from tail motif in our national airline to the inclusion of Maori words in the Dictionary of New Zealand English.'

Personal racism, one might say, could be intended by persons, whereas cultural racism was not so much chosen and pursued of a set purpose by individuals; it was rather the milieu of understandings in which they operated without giving much thought to it. It informed consciousness and damaged its victims without being the object of conscious scrutiny.

But 'institutional racism' was more problematically a question of intention, purpose or consciousness at all. 'Whilst personal and cultural racism may be described in their own right, institutional racism is to be observed from its effects. It is a bias in our social and administrative institutions that automatically benefits the dominant race or culture, while penalising minority or subordinate groups.' The effects were the statistics of inequality. Inequalities were caused, not by the failure of the Māori to adapt, but by 'monocultural bias' – and the culture which shapes and directs that bias is 'Pakehatanga'.

The bias can be observed operating in law, government, the professions, health care, land ownership, welfare practices, education, town planning, the police, finance, business and the spoken language. It permeates the media and our national economic life. If one is outside, one sees it as 'the system'. If one is cocooned within it, one sees it as the normal condition of existence. Institutional racism is the basic weapon that has driven the Maori into the role of outsiders and strangers in their own land.

Puao-Te-Ata-Tu/Day Break concluded by drawing on the complex logic of their analysis by arguing that individuals, while they might 'personally' not be 'racist' could still be called – and actually *be* – 'racist'. 'If those in positions of influence within institutions do not work to reduce and eliminate the monocultural bias that disadvantages Maoris and minorities, they can be accused of collaborating with the system, and therefore of being racist . . .' Further, *Puao-Te-Ata-Tu/Day Break* spoke as if only the dominant or 'power' culture and its members and institutions could be racist. Individuals of other cultures and other cultural groups or institutions could not be.[61] This was orthodox teaching, also emanating from reforming circles. *Broadsheet* magazine, for instance, complained when the Race Relations Conciliator found that Donna Awatere's *Maori Sovereignty* breached section 9a of the Race Relations Act. Right-wing anti-Jewish books might well have been found to 'excite hostility or ill-will . . . on the grounds of colour, race or ethnic or national origins'. For the Jews were a minority attacked by powerful interests. But

---

[61] PTAT, i, p. 26.

when a majority were being attacked, 'how can the same criteria apply?' The purpose of the Act was to protect the weak from the strong; not to give further grounds for persecuting the weak.[62] Mr Walter Hirsch, who became Race Relations Conciliator soon after the *Maori Sovereignty* decision, came to embrace this view in public, as did, on a famous TV occasion in 1987, Canon Hone Kaa; and Paul Spoonley made the same point more systematically in his 1988 monograph, *Racism and Ethnicity*.[63] Individuals of minority cultures could be personally 'prejudiced'. But they could not be 'racist'; for 'racism' was 'prejudice plus power'. It was in any case racism rather than prejudice which ought to be the central concern of the law, for the law ought to be most concerned with the powerlessness and oppression of minority cultures and their members. There was not much it could do about personal attitudes.

Obviously, one point of the tripartite distinction of 'racisms' was to pre-empt meanings and be in a position to include the innocent (in mind) with the guilty (Māori-hating, fearing, despising) Pākehā as 'racist'. The distinctions issued in a wide definition of 'racism' so that every element of the social whole was subject to classification as 'racist' or 'non-racist', as was the social whole itself. This Manichaean dualism took its moral force from the publicly-accepted idea that 'personal' race prejudice was wrong, was a species of injustice, and ought to be eliminated as much as possible.

The other purposes of the Manichaeism – the division of the whole of life into 'racist' and 'non-racist' elements and its depiction as a power struggle between the forces of good and evil – were educative, and they were expressive of a doctrine of what may be called distributive multiculturalism.

Even though it was becoming official policy in the 1970s,[64] 'sustained discussions regarding [the] definition, properties, impact and significance' of multiculturalism was, lamented a visiting academic in 1984, 'virtually non-existent'.[65] That is true; but *Race Against Time* and some other quasi-official sources went a good way towards elaborating the ideal of distributive multiculturalism for the 1980s.[66] Cultural variety was taken to be an axiomatic fact, axiomatically also something not to be criticized. It was even something to be enjoyed. Further, all cultures, all systems of value, were held to be equal. The values embedded in the customs, practices and institutions of no one culture were to be rated more highly than those of any other. This position confronted, to deny, the justice of existing arrangements which had discrimination embedded in them, and it denied the existence of equality

[62] Joyce and Rosier, 'Maori Sovereignty Racist?' *Broadsheet* (March 1986), pp. 12–13.

[63] Hone Kaa speaking on racism on TV1's *Tu Kupenga*, 13/3/88; Spoonley, *Racism and Ethnicity*, pp. 5, 23–5 and following. See also Radio New Zealand, *Beyond Guilt*, pp. 7–11.

[64] See, for example, the 1976 report of the New Zealand Task Force on Economic and Social Planning, *New Zealand at the Turning Point*, p. xviii.

[65] Augie Fleras, 'Monoculturalism, multiculturalism and biculturalism', at p. 53.

[66] See, for example, Human Rights Commission, *Report of a Seminar on Human Rights held in Wellington, New Zealand, on 9-10 December 1978*, p. 20.

of opportunity. The doctrine thus both explained and excused Māori failure under 'monoculturalism'. It also demanded institutional reform to accommodate cultural difference, and it required separate treatment for members of separate cultures: partly as an expression of their right to group autonomy, partly to equalize their condition, partly as reparation for the past and continuing wrongs of the monoculture.

Race Against Time asserted all this directly: 'Right and wrong,' the reader was told, 'differ from society to society, as the moral principles on which a society's customs are determined by the culture of that society'; 'a society of many cultures must respect and accept those cultural differences, if racial harmony is to be maintained'. 'What has developed', said Hiwi Tauroa, when interviewed in 1982, 'is a monocultural society built on a foundation of institutionalised discrimination and inequality. . . . Those who can and choose to accept the majority culture get a good bite of the educational and social cake. Those who cannot or do not choose to, get left with the crumbs.'[67]

He was echoing those who told the Human Rights Commission that to object as He Taua had done to the debasement of a culture was to join in the articulation 'of our search for justice and equality'. He was echoing others too, who spoke to the Commission: 'I for one was brought up by my people to be proud of what I am and there is no way I am going to be anything else but Maori;' 'the new generation is concerned with full social equality and respect for cultural integrity in all its diverse forms. For this they are prepared to fight;' 'I began to see that the Maori in New Zealand had suffered by the white man's domination of the superiority hierarchy. That the Maori had lost all sense of his cultural identity. And that all peoples *need* a cultural identity'; 'white middle-class values' predominate, 'for instance Maori marae are subject to Pakeha ideas on Town and Country Planning'; 'ignorance, ethnocentricity, disrespect for another's culture, are racist behaviours which stem from attitudes which are a product of our colonial history, and now permeate all institutions of our contemporary society. Along with unquestioning stereotyping, these attitudes have a cumulative effect, resulting in entrenched inequalities to minority groups.' It was not equality in monocultural terms that was sought – 'all too often it is assumed that *equality* means *sameness*' – but there must be 'a right to be different,' and a space for Māori liberty: 'The Maori must have full autonomy to make decisions. Ethnically, the Pakeha has no right to intrude. In sociological terms, it demeans the standing and culture of the Maori if the decisions are to lie, in the main, with the Pakeha.'[68]

In 1982 a discussion group of state servants at Waahi Marae in Huntly repeated the same themes as to the origins of inequality and as to a cure lying in respect for cultures. In a publication of their discussions, *Public Service in a Multicultural Society* (1983), they held that 'a multicultural society rests on the understanding and the acknowledgement of equality of values and

---

[67] Reported in Part 3 of Pat Booth's, 'Maori: *Race Against Time*', AS12:7/9/82.

[68] HRC, *Racial Harmony in New Zealand*, pp. 3, 6–8, 10, 16 etc.

the respect for differences'.[69] In these conditions the insistence that there should be one rule of life for all just would not work. Nor, consequently, would New Zealand domestic laws, practices, and institutions. They were 'monocultural', whereas they ought to be 'multicultural'. *Puao-Te-Ata-Tu/Day Break* repeated the same claims as to the origins of inequality lying in monoculturalism: 'The evidence seems overwhelming that the Maori underperformance in social and economic status and law observance is symptomatic of alienation and mono-culturalism leading to the disintegration of traditional sanctions.' Inequalitites were 'the outcome of monocultural institutions which simply ignore or freeze out the cultures of those who do not belong to the majority. National cultures are evolved which are rooted in the values, systems and viewpoints of one culture only. Participation by minorities is conditional on their subjugating their own values and systems to those of "the system" of the power culture.' The aim should be to attain 'socio-economic parity between Maori and non-Maori by the provision of resources to meet Maori needs on Maori terms'.[70]

The distributional consequences of this position were in fact not altogether different from Hunn's: that each culture ought to have resources roughly proportional to the number of individuals who made up its membership in the relevant field of activity. But whereas Hunn seems to have thought such arrangements might well be transitory and a means to what would end it – the merging of Māori and Pākehā – multicultural distributivism seems to have regarded them as a permanent feature of things. They would be permanent not because a Hunn-style equality would not be brought about, but because it was additionally essential that differences between cultures should be maintained.

Hunn had hoped that 'integration' of the races would be brought about as their material lives were brought more closely to resemble one another's: as they lived as neighbours in the towns and experienced similar housing conditions, and as they shared the whole range of educational and work experiences.[71] A mix of increasing similarity in material conditions on the one hand, and familiarity with (diminishing) cultural difference on the other, would eliminate personal prejudice, the complex emotion that led to the Māori not being treated as an equal. And was it Hunn himself who spoke thus to the Human Rights Commission in 1978?

To ameliorate race relations a fundamental social and economic equality needs to be achieved. Negative attitudes and inequality operate on each other. . . . Attitudes need to be altered but this will be meaningless unless the Polynesian is more equally distributed throughout the various social and economic hierarchies that exist throughout New Zealand. As long as they continue to be concentrated in the low status occupations and areas, then they will be seen as a problem group. . . . Until then, low status

[69] Race Relations Counciliator, *Race Against Time*, p. 14; *Public Service in a Multicultural Society*, p. 24.

[70] PTAT, i, pp. 19,36.

[71] Hunn, 'Can Race Relations be Left to Chance?'

jobs simpl[y] reinforce poor educational performance and combine with other factors like low standard housing, poor health, and associated problems to produce a circle which becomes very difficult to break.[72]

Such voices, often those of National MPs, but in general those who wished to minimize reparations for past wrongs and (perhaps) maximize equalization of condition, were, as was recorded earlier in the book, commonly heard. In 1988 and 1989 especially, Winston Peters combined the pleas for more jobs and better education for the Māori with attacks on the idea of reparation; and the National MPs always spoke of equalization policies being better than the unreasonable 'fears' and 'expectations' raised by the prospect of reparation through the Tribunal.[73] Jim Bolger put it in 1988: 'Race Relations will be very much better when all New Zealanders have the satisfaction of achievement in education, a decent job, a decent income and a secure future.'[74] Labour MPs did not disagree, as far as it went. Social peace was in danger. Equalization of condition was the palliative.

Though no New Zealand politician would say so – for fear of the socialist-Marxist slur – Hunn's was basically a class analysis of the causes and cures of inequality. The maxim of action with which it operated was that to obliterate the close alignment of class with race inequality would be to eliminate race problems. The maxim however, expressed only a universally-accepted appreciation of the way the political and social world worked. It did not express a generally agreed *aim*. The generally-accepted aim was rather to bring about peace, co-operation and a decent life for everyone, not to eliminate class differences as a matter of justice.

The doctrine of multiculturalism was however an ethnic one, and it was aimed not simply at peace and reasonable harmony, but at ethnic justice. It did not reject the equalities of condition promised by entry into the magic circle, and thus the figures on inequality could be used both by Hunn-style (integrationist) ameliorationists and by multicultural distributivists as well. But it added to the list of things to be distributed and the series of dimensions on which disproportionate distributions could be located. It demanded respect for cultures, the reconstruction of institutions and practices so that they would reflect and respond to cultural purposes, and the right of all cultures to more self-determination. It was from that perspective that it opposed the Pākehā ideology of equality. And thus the recommendations of *Race Against Time* included not only 'affirmative action' to bring about equality but also actions to strengthen and sustain the many cultures that there were: Māori (and Polynesian Islanders) must be appointed to decision-making positions and to a wider range of employment. They must be encouraged in reformed education and work-training systems, and the Māori must be helped to find a new pride and identity in the reinvigoration of their language. The

[72] *Racial Harmony in New Zealand*, p. 8.

[73] NZPD1:41 (8 Dec 1987), pp. 1727; (15 June 1988), p. 4401 (22 Sept 1988), p. 6894.

[74] H4:2/5/88.

bureaucracy, the legal system, and the churches must transform themselves, adding, firstly a Māori 'dimension', and other dimensions later. Better arrangements must be made for the ownership and control of Māori land. Māori women and youth must be catered for. The media must reflect the facts of multiculturalism and not hide them.[75] 'The aim is to remove all forms of discrimination; to develop policies of equal advancement for all members of the community.'

All this too, was a matter of strict justice. *Race Against Time* insisted that the inequalities be addressed, not only for the sake of avoiding – as its name suggested – a dark future of racial conflict, but as a matter of obvious rightness. *Public Service in a Multicultural Society* spoke the same way. It warned not only of the danger of inequalities' creating permanently alienated groups, but of living in a world 'which gives increasing emphasis to issues of racial justice'.[76] Justice was the issue, as well as peace. For its part the State Services Commission (which had called the hui on administration in a multicultural society) reiterated an objective it had foreshadowed in 1979 and committed itself to in 1981: 'to ensure that the systems and processes of Government administration are consistent with equal opportunity for all social groups and that the attitudes and values of staff at every level reflect and promote that objective.'[77] The hui agreed that 'equality of opportunity' was undermined in its purpose of bringing about equality by the 'operation of discrimination in less obvious ways'. And the conclusion was reached that 'until the achievement levels of minority groups compare with those of the majority, fair treatment is seen to be a myth'. Apprehensive about the reception of the idea of 'affirmative action' within the ranks of the state services, the conference nevertheless adopted a policy of 'equal representation' of all groups especially at the top management levels and added that 'the disadvantaged position of the Māori people needs to be recognised as a first priority'.There were problems: did a Māori or a Samoan or a Chinese without their languages or culture *count* as Māori, Samoan, or Chinese? and could knowledge of precisely those things count as a 'qualification', alongside other educational ones, for recruitment and promotion?[78] But the doctrine of multicultural distributivism was clearly in the ascendant.

And so it also was largely in *Puao-Te-Ata-Tu/Day Break*, where the language of 'equity' was now thoroughly adopted. 'Equity' and 'justice' were directly appealed to as well as peace and co-operation as the reason for adopting a policy of multicultural distributivism. The inequalities, the low socio-economic status, the 'underperformance in status and law observance' of the Māori were noted. So was their 'sense of injustice' in the face of employment, housing and education problems, compounded by the 'monocultural' legal and bureaucratic systems with which they had to deal.

---

[75] HRC, *Race Against Time*, Chapters 4, 5.

[76] *Public Service in a Multicultural Society*, p. 11.

[77] *Public Service in a Multicultural Society*, p. 13.

[78] *Public Service in a Multicultural Society*, pp. 26,32,34.

Puao-Te-Ata-Tu/Day Break quoted approvingly the 1968 USA *Report . . . on Civil Disorders:* 'Ignorance, discrimination, slums, poverty, disease, not enough jobs. We should attack these conditions - not because we are frightened of conflict, but because we are fired by conscience.'[79] And it recommended a raft of reforms to 'attack and eliminate deprivation and alienation' by 'allocating an equitable share of resources' and 'sharing power and authority over the use of resources'. Unfortunately the largest consumers of Social Welfare, the Māori people should for instance largely control, on a representative basis, its delivery by the state.[80]

Later governmental studies – in early 1987 – also used the language of equity to express the multicultural ideal. *The Curriculum Review* included the Māori in its prescription for 'fair treatment for all - equity'. 'There must be fairness for all in both opportunities and outcomes.'[81] The first volume of Moana Jackson's Justice Department study, *The Maori and the Criminal Justice System*, also supported equity measures. It described the legal system, and the studies of it so far carried out, as 'monocultural' and suggested the modification of the system in the name of justice. It quoted with approval a 1981 report of the USA Commission on Civil Rights which argued the necessity of affirmative action: 'many normal, seemingly neutral operations of our society create stereotyped expectations that justify unequal results; unequal results in one area foster inequalities of opportunity and accomplishment in others; the lack of opportunity and accomplishment confirm . . . prejudices or engender new ones that fuel the normal opportunities generating unequal results.'[82]

But the language of equity and talk of multicultural distributions, had, from the Māori point of view, its drawbacks. It could not express all their demands, and it drowned them in the clamour of others.

III

The Cloudy Rhetoric of Equity

Around 1983 the phrase 'social equity' found a voice in public. By 1987 it was the cant of the day.

One of the first signs of the new language was the publication in 1983 of a Planning Council booklet, *Issues in Equity*. It addressed itself to public perceptions of 'injustice' and 'unfairness' in current social, economic, and political arrangements and called them 'issues in equity'. It concerned itself with issues of equality of opportunity and 'barriers' to it, with equality of access to advantage-giving institutions, and with the fairness of current distributions of social goods. Consequently it asked its respondents questions

---

[79] PTAT, i, p. 44.
[80] PTAT, i, pp. 26, 32–4.
[81] *The Curriculum Review*, p. 99.
[82] Jackson, *The Maori and the Criminal Justice System*, i, p. 12.

as to the proper distribution of socially-produced resources and whether 'affirmative action' policies were justifiable.

It recorded considerable discontent with the 'disadvantages' suffered by women, handicapped people, the unemployed, ethnic minorities and others. But it recorded also the opposition to thinking this way: assertions that equality of opportunity actually existed and that the disadvantaged really could blame no one but themselves. And it was by translating these two sets of contradictory plain feelings about injustice – the indigenous egalitarian and the opposing Pākehā ideology of equality – into the language of the science of economics that the Planning Council came to call them 'equity issues'.

Briefed in 1984 by Treasury on 'equity' issues in departmental papers published as *Economic Management*, the incoming Labour Government adopted the new discourse with enthusiasm. It is true that it followed Treasury's lead in distinguishing between matters of 'efficiency' and 'equity', and it also limited the scope of 'equity' considerations to matters of 'social' and not 'economic' policy. But within the sphere of 'social policy' it energetically used the language, though at times in service of the Pākehā ideology, at other times of indigenous egalitariansim. Its new Ministry of Women's Affairs was devoted to obtaining 'equity' for women, including Māori women, for and by whom a separate section was constituted. The Government also established a Cabinet Committee on 'Social Equity' under Geoffrey Palmer, responsible for 'social policy'. The Human Rights Commission and the Race Relations Office were already becoming publicly involved in elaborating and defending policies of 'affirmative action' or 'reverse discrimination' for the disadvantaged. And Government departments developed 'equity' policies. Education, for instance, consulting the public with questionnaires and meetings, carried out curriculum reviews of schools and tertiary education in a process extending from 1984 until the publication of its *Curriculum Review* for secondary schools in 1987 and a 1988 report on post-compulsory education. Mrs Anne Hercus, the Minister for Social Welfare as well as of Women's Affairs, gingered into action by a women's group,[83] instituted in 1985 the enquiries into monoculturalism in Social Welfare that were to issue in *Puao-Te-Ata-Tu/Day Break*. Urged on by the State Services Commission (the control department responsible for personnel and organizational policies) other Government departments undertook internal assessment.[84] Programmes to promote 'equality of opportunity' and 'equality of access' were developed. In January 1987 the Race Relations Office defended them as they related to ethnic and racial groups in *Towards an Equitable Society: Affirmative Action*.

Also in 1987, in its papers designed to brief the Government in its second term, Treasury's *Government Management* undertook a serious study of 'equity' as well as 'efficiency' in social policy. In the same year the Terms of Reference of the Royal Commission on Social Policy asked it to find out from the

---

[83] See 'Racism is Alive and Well in N.Z. Institutions', *Broadsheet* (Oct 1985), pp. 16–20.

[84] See State Services Commission, Equal Employment Opportunities Unit, *Departmental Equal Employment Opportunities Monitoring Report, 1 April 1985–31 March 1986*.

public and make recommendations on social policy, and for its part the Planning Council in *Social Policy Options* proffered suggestions among other things, as to 'equity'. In 1988, the *April Report* of the Commission set out its own and the public's view on equity at great length in five large books.

This list could be extended and the milieu elaborated. But the central facts were that all these were public exercises in the elaboration of conceptual confusion and the discovery of substantive disagreement. What the concept of equity referred to was never clarified, and what ought to be done in the name of equity was not agreed upon. In brief, the adoption of the terminology went no way to defining and resolving issues in social justice. Worse, from a Māori point of view, it was a language which suggested the proliferation of equality groups according to variously-stated criteria of need, desert and social equalization. It did not speak of the Māori unequivocally as a unique nation, defined not by their needs or their deserts or their inequality, but by their *ethnie* – their common consciousness of a common past and a common way of being.

The language of equity could not in fact be used to speak that way. Those who used and developed it in New Zealand thought that social arrangements, including societies themselves, had (when they were justified) a utilitarian and individualist justification: they were for the good of each individual. Individuals were organic wholes, the units of cosmic significance. What did not figure for individuals figured for nothing at all. Individuals made institutions and societies; they could join and leave them; they could modify or destroy them. And thus equity was the virtue of ameliorating individual lives as they were distorted by laws and social practices, so that individual fulfilment could be better attained. Nothing could have been further from the Māori view, which was that Māori was a primordial and cosmic entity. It embraced, formed and sustained individuals indeed; but those were not its purposes, functions or ends. It was instrument to nothing beyond itself (in a way that, in the language of equity, individuals were not the instruments of any purposes beyond their own). Individuals might exist organically. But it was the spirit, the wairua, that had the truer reality; individuals simply bore the wairua through a time sequence that was as insubstantial as the human body itself. Individuals were mortal and circumscribed. Māori was immortal and limitless. In the order of things, it was not – it could not be – that the individual human being preceded the collectivity.

Great conceptual confusion as to the nature of 'social equity' was evident. *Issues in Equity* was at the mercy of its clients, simply reporting what they thought. 'Equity,' the pamphlet said, 'has been defined as social justice or "getting a fair go".' But as to what would characterize *those* states of affairs, it was not clear to the Council's descriptive ethics whether 'equality of opportunity' should be interpreted as the injunction to let people 'sink or swim' in the sea of life, or whether it indicated that 'affirmative action' was a necessary part of the idea. At another point, when commending to their clients the ideal of 'equality of opportunity', the authors nevertheless seemed to worry about whether 'equality of opportunity would of itself' achieve 'equality of outcome'. 'In some areas positive discrimination may be justified to promote equity.' And here 'equality of outcome', which came to be called 'equality of result' in later years, seems to have been the preferred option. The authors stressed continually that 'freedom of choice' was an important constituent of equity, and worried that Government intervention in the economy might limit it. In their analysis, if not in their professed belief, the concept of 'equity' denoted a variety of contradictory and incompatible judgements as to the evaluation of policy.

The Planning Council was no clearer as to its concept of social equity in its *Social Policy Options* of 1987, even though it had a history of disputes between women's movements and the Employers' Federation to guide it.[85] Sometimes it spoke as if 'equity' was – or included – social justice: 'How are we to claim adherence to the principles of equity and still allow social injustices to be perpetrated?' Sometimes 'fairness' was considered to be the same as both. It was also suggested that 'access' to state-provided services was 'equity'. But the distinction between equity and justice was denied as well as asserted, and equity was assimilated to a variety of other virtues of social arrangements as well as justice. 'Equity' it was said, was a 'value' which could be *distinguished* from the 'values' (that is, valued things) of 'access' and 'autonomy'. In other parts of the text, 'equity' was taken to stand in relationships varying between synonymy with, and opposition to, 'autonomy', 'freedom', and 'tolerance'.

The 'value' (the force, weight or importance?) of the 'values' was not made clear. Like the other values, 'social equity' was said to be 'grounded' in 'human needs at different stages of the life-cycle'. The Council said all four (equity, autonomy, freedom and tolerance) had been 'influential' in its thinking while developing a series of thirteen unprioritized 'social objectives' or 'principles' that it wished to put up for public discussion, as indicating a 'general area of need or aspiration'. But the reader was cheerfully told that the thirteen objectives were not *really* separate: 'Overlap is to be expected, as human lives are not compartmentalised.' All in all, the Planning Council's authors seem to have been so impressed with the holistic complexity of social life and the values it expressed that they were unwilling to analyse and specify its moral components – let alone judge the competing claims. Clearly disliking conceptual legislation, they put themselves at the mercy of the substantive ideals of those they were studying when deciding what the concept of equity referred to.

Only one thing was clear in both Planning Council studies. They thought they could see some conceptual and moral truth in one of the 'abstract themes' which they discerned as having been stated by their clients: 'Equity is not the same as equality.' 'Equity' but not 'equality' was a 'justifiable aim'. 'It is necessary to make a distinction between equity and equality; they are

---

[85] For traces of the disputes see HRC, *Women in Banking* and Downey, *Human Rights*, pp. 14–21 and 21n.

associated but different. An over-emphasis on equality would ignore essential differences between people. Equity is therefore a more justifiable, and a more feasible, goal for society.'

In fact *Social Policy Options* was to examine the matter of the relations between equality and equity a little more than that. To treat someone 'fairly' was to treat like cases in a like way. Thus 'anomalies' in the distribution of social benefits and taxes, and differences in people's conditions of work when they did the same work were inequitable. Also 'anomalous' was inequality of opportunity for job training and promotion. But equality in the distribution of other goods of life was not thought to be 'inequitable'. Equality was a ground of the distribution of some things but not of others. Considerations of desert, reward for risk-taking and so on might override equal distributions of things, though at certain unspecified points. The Council argued that something would be wrong until the invidious inequalities under which ethnic groups, the disabled, the aged, one-parent families, homosexuals, and women all laboured were 'addressed'. However, it neither suggested how much equalization of condition was necessary, nor could it bring itself to describe the inequalities as inequitable, unfair, or unjust. What *could* be said was that in those conditions, New Zealand was not 'making the best use of its human resources and potential'.

The language of efficiency and social productivity was at that point more in evidence than the language of justice in distribution. 'Efficiency' and not 'equity', 'economic policy' and not 'social policy' was at issue. In fact, it was a distinction between the two languages that Treasury had taken up in *Economic Management* in 1984, and it was to pursue that distinction in *Government Management* three years later. There were moments when the will to analyse – registering doubtless the weakness of the analysis itself – faltered. In 1987 it ceased seriously to use the distinctions at all. 'Social policies can be characterised as being particularly involved with people and with equity considerations but this is equally true of economic policy in general . . . For the purposes of this discussion it is suggested that social policy should be regarded as that list of activities which are normally deemed to be social policies.'[86] Treasury now saw the distinction between equity and efficiency – like that between economic and social policy – as 'contrived', and was content to note and contribute to what were normally thought of as social policy debates on employment, crime, education, health, cross-cultural relations, and poverty. The department proclaimed itself very aware of the dangers of being 'seduced' by too great an 'intellectualism' in searching for precision where it could not be got, and thought that in the end it was public acceptance of policies by voters that mattered, not the 'intellectual acceptance of philosophical bureaucrats'. In general, in this context as in others, Treasury set out to clarify and organize intuitive and commonsense feelings, arguing on commonsense grounds that: 'Social stress', 'deprivation', and 'significant inequality in opportunities . . . or . . . access to resources'

---

[86] The Treasury, *Government Management*, i, p. 125.

were obvious signs of inequity which called for an analysis as to the 'reasons for such unfairness and explorations as to whether there were grounds (and means) to "redress the balance".'[87]

It determined that such 'bumper sticker thoughts' as 'the achievement of a fair distribution', or 'giving everyone a fair chance', should be translated as far as possible into policy options.[88] Not that it succeeded. For instance, it made a distinction between 'equality of opportunity' and 'equality of result' that could not really work. For what is equality of opportunity except equality in the goods of life animated by the thought that the powers and rights constituting that equality provide a starting point (not a result) in the race or adventure of life? What people have is not abstract 'opportunity' or 'freedom', but concrete things like houses and incomes and capital and cars and school buildings and teachers and computers. What they have, animated by the will to future success, *is* their 'opportunity'. What they have, animated by a will to judge it as the consequence of their past, is their 'result'. So in the distinction between equality of opportunity and equality of result, the things distributed are nothing (they are the same in either case) and temporal perspective is everything. But if equal opportunities are to be provided then the temporal perspective is irrelevent too. Any distribution at any time can be looked at as a beginning or an end, as an opportunity or a result. From a policy perspective the distinction is therefore unreal. Equality of opportunity must mean – whether one likes it or not, and Treasury did not – continuous equalization of condition.

The point of this slight digression is simply to show that Treasury, despite its economistic jargon, would think like everybody else and play on the public prejudice that to distribute equality of opportunity was to distribute freedom and not much else.

Like everybody else too, Treasury would talk of 'equity' rather than of 'justice': because equity, unlike justice, could be modified in the face of other demands. It was distinguished from other virtues of social arrangements, notably 'security', 'social harmony', and 'individual freedom' and – not just a narrowly economic virtue – the 'smooth functioning of markets'.[89] The art of economic and social management was, according to Treasury advice, to reconcile, balance, and trade off considerations of efficiency, equity, security, harmony and liberty.[90]

It was not, in any case, clear to the department exactly what 'just' arrangements would be like at all. The question was addressed specifically in an essay annexed to its *Government Management*: 'Ethics and Social Justice'.[91] The essay 'wove together', without attempting to decide between them, the 'threads' of what the profoundly disagreeing Anglo-American professional

[87] The Treasury, *Government Management*, i, pp. 394–9.

[88] The Treasury, *Government Management*, i, p. 398.

[89] The Treasury, *Economic Management*, p. 252.

[90] The Treasury, *Government Management*, i, pp. 211–12, 251–2.

[91] The Treasury, *Government Management*, i, pp. 406–26.

philosophers and decision-theorists said: that justice was giving people their rights; that justice was what people would contract for; that justice was the maximization of welfare. The essay claimed that it was best to trade off 'some elegance of theory for comprehensiveness of result', and to take elements from each 'approach'. It advised the Royal Commission on Social Policy, recently announced, that trade-offs between individual rights would be necessary to encourage the maximization of welfare. Also, that 'those trade-offs should not be carried so far as to abridge individual rights and the normative judgement that the Commission must strive for is a definition of those rights.'[92] Justice would be what it was decided it would be.

And finally, also like everyone else in government circles, Treasury adopted an individualistic ontology and an ethic which was both individualist and utilitarian. The appearance of 'Ethics and Social Policy' probably represented the first time that the professional study of ethics had been applied by officials to questions of social policy in New Zealand. It was entirely in keeping with the practice of New Zealand thinking (for instance, on compulsory membership of Trade Unions, and on a Bill of Rights) that the starting point should have been that kind of liberal moral philosophy, the point of which has been to begin with the separate individual and then wrestle with the problem of tying that individual to collectivities.[93] In this sense, the essay actually codified a popular (perhaps predominant) liberal democratic ideology that was only seriously challenged in public by Māori ideologists and a few politically ineffective socialists.[94]

The essay asserted that issues in equity were questions of 'political philosopy' which 'obviously stem from prior conclusions of moral philosophy'.[95] And if political philosophy was subordinate to moral philosophy, moral philosophy itself was primarily a philosophy of individual identity and action. The basic reality was individuals: 'Families and tribes are not organic entities with mortality, rationality or senses, they cannot feel pleasure and pain . . . . Families and tribes (and other collective organisations) are fundamentally collections of people.'[96] And thus, the essay argued, codifying popular belief: 'Without a logical starting point of the well-being of individual people then policy is likely to be built on prejudice and simple adherence to existing

---

92 The Treasury, *Government Management*, i, p. 426.

93 Andrew Sharp, 'The "Principle" of Voluntary Unionism in New Zealand Political Debate', and 'An Historical and Philosophical Perspective on the Proposal for a Bill of Rights for New Zealand'.

94 But it is an open question as to how much it is to suffer from illusion to think of the popular ideology in this way. Treasury thought so and the media too. But they obviously ignored the powerful current of co-operative welfarist thought expressed, for example, in *Issues in Equity* and which is one of the bases of creole egalitarianism. And the media largely ignored opposition to the Labour Government from such quarters.

95 The Treasury, *Government Management*, i, p. 408.

96 The Treasury, *Government Management*, i, p. 410.

social structures'.⁹⁷ Social policy and the rules of justice were to be seen as derivative from the good of individual persons.

Treasury was not alone. The Royal Commission on Social Policy's treatment of the same issues by Maxine Barrett in 1988 took the same line.⁹⁸ In her essay 'Standards and Foundations for Social Policy', she held, like Treasury, that collectivities were instruments for the good of individuals. And though she thought collectivities could be rights-bearers, provided they could be clearly enough defined, she also thought that: 'It makes little sense at all to consider the group or the tribe as being of final, or intrinsic value.' Neither paper quoted any collectivist philosophers – even the liberal collectivists who were developing communitarian and feminist critiques of liberal-individualist epistemology and ontology – writing in the 1980s. John Rawls of the *Theory of Justice* (1971) was quoted, for instance, rather than the revisionist, and much more collectivist, Rawls of the 1980s.⁹⁹ There was no examination of the relevant philosophical work of Michael Walzer, Virginia Held, Michael Sandel and others; work which set out to show the limits of the individualist-contractualist model of social relations and altogether denied its applicability over large ranges of human activity. This literature stressed rightly that human beings might be more plausibly regarded as radically encumbered with responsibilities, loves, friendships, and unchosen duties, than as unencumbered by any obligations except those they undertook as 'free' and 'equal' traders. The facts of individual's actual lives certainly pointed that way. What kind of thought is it, for instance, that the relationship between mother and child is a contractual one, undertaken for mutual individual benefit? And how many act out the mother-child relationship in their lives compared with the relationship of equal contractors? Why should the trading model be taken as paradigmatic of reality and as a pattern for behaviour over all relationships?¹⁰⁰ When Treasury quoted part of a Māori proverb, 'he tangata, he tangata, he tangata' ('it is the people, it is the people, it is the people') its point was to show that groups were made up of individual persons, not to stress the importance of the collectivity. Perhaps they would even have translated 'the people of Rome' as the collection of individuals who made up that republic?¹⁰¹ Certainly the department saw the Pākehā nuclear family as a creature of long-term contract between individuals: 'The sacrifices involved in family life reflect the long-term caring understandings (contracts) that people can enter into.' And more: 'No third party can hope to replace these sensitive understandings. Similarly the whanau, the hapu, the iwi, the

---

⁹⁷ The Treasury, *Government Management*, i, p. 405. See also pp. 406, 413.

⁹⁸ *The April Report*, iii (2), pp. 64–7 especially.

⁹⁹ Rawls, 'Kantian Constructivism in Moral Theory' (1980) and 'Political Theory: Political not Metaphysical'.

¹⁰⁰ Walzer, *Spheres of Justice*; Held, *Rights and Goods* and 'Feminism and Moral Theory; Sandel, *Liberalism and the Limits of Justice* and 'The Procedural Republic and the Unencumbered Self'. Closer to home, see the Australian, Robert Ewin's *Liberty, Community and Justice*, which was perhaps published too late for Treasury and for the Commission.

¹⁰¹ The Treasury, *Government Management*, i, p. 410.

church and friendship networks provide institutional contexts within which differences can be worked through and mutual support offered. Clubs and societies provide further opportunities for social exchange and the trading of obligations and favours. All of these social institutions provide a framework within which the individual can lead a richer and more rounded life.'[102]

Society was a contract: among living, breathing, separate, unencumbered, *real* individuals; and central government had best keep out of their lives as much as possible. In arguing this way Treasury was either ignorant of or rejected the European heritage of political thought, as well as the Māori. And not just the socialist tradition, and the various communitarian beliefs that individuals are born into permanent and unchosen commitments to (say) their families or their churches or their localities. When the traditionalist Edmund Burke said society was 'indeed a contract' in 1790, he was being deeply ironic. If it was a contract it was one which encompassed state, society and individuals; it was indissoluble by individuals or corporations, even by the state; and it was not made by individuals, but entered into as an inheritance:

Society is indeed a contract. Subordinate contracts of mere occasional interest may be dissolved at pleasure – but the state ought not to be considered as nothing better than a partnership agreement in a trade of pepper and coffee, calico or tobacco, or some such low concern, to be taken up for a little temporary interest, and to be dissolved by the fancy of the parties. It is to be looked on with other reverence. . . . It is a partnership in all science; a partnership in all art; a partnership in every virtue, and in all perfection. As the ends of such a partnership cannot be obtained in many generations, it becomes a partnership not only between those who are living, those who are dead, and those who are to be born. . . . [States] . . . are not morally at liberty at their pleasure, and on their speculations of contingent improvement, wholly to separate and tear asunder the bands of their subordinate community, and to dissolve it into an unsocial, uncivil, unconnected chaos of elementary principles.[103]

Treasury simply expressed the current New Zealand ideology of liberal individualism and forgot that there were competing views, both Māori and Pākehā. It took as its model of human reality (and of the bonds between individuals) the circumstances which hold between unencumbered equals, bargaining among themselves for what they happen to want – a circumstance comparatively rare in human experience. Organizations, including the state, were analysed as having existences which maintained that rare form of circumstance and which were justified only so far as they did.

On this ontological and ethical basis of radically separate individuals, what particular inequities and equities did the official publications draw attention to? And what equality classes were there thought to exist and why?

A great variety of each, since the Planning Council, Treasury, and others (not having a theory themselves as to what equity actually was) largely reported

---

[102] The Treasury,*Government Management*, i. p. 402.
[103] Burke, *Reflections on the Revolution in France*, pp. 194–5.

simply what they heard. Respondents to *Issues in Equity* ran the gamut. As to desert; they thought that market income was deserved – when it was deserved – as 'the return for labour'. Inequalities generated in 'labour', reported the authors, 'were not generally seen as unfair'. 'Labour' included (probably) risk-taking, because 'the dominant ideology recognises the need to reward effort, expertise and risk-taking'. But when the authors suggested that equity could well imply 'equal pay for equal work' and 'equal pay for work of equal value', it could hardly have been that risks were at that point in their minds. And many of the respondents thought that income from speculation and tax avoidance was *not* deserved. Speculation and tax avoidance were not the right *kind* of applications of skill, work, and risk. They did not generate desert.

Need, too, made its demands on equity in income distribution as well as desert. And so did the ideal of a degree of equalization of wealth. In fact need and equalization were not always clearly distinguished. *Issues in Equity* said that 'unfairness and social injustice' were 'highlighted' by 'shortfalls in various areas of need'. Those unable to suport themselves 'from their own efforts' should be aided. 'What is "fair" in these cases depends on the nature of the inability and the likely duration of this state.' And the overall aim should be 'to achieve an equitable distribution of income and to ensure that everyone has adequate financial support'. It was said to be 'inequitable' that both 'need' and 'disadvantage' were not attended to. Families with only one market-income were thought to suffer especial hardship; also those who for good reason *could* not labour to deserve; and those on welfare benefits were said to suffer 'inequities of income in a broader sense'. They 'were seen to be at a social and economic disadvantage'.

Most often considerations of desert, need, and equalization – often in the guise of equality of opportunity – revolved in uneasy combination. There was disagreement as to the 'fairness' or not of the superannuation benefit which was paid purely on grounds of entitlement by age. Some respondents thought it unfair that all those over sixty should receive it because not all of that group needed it. A smaller equality class should be constructed excluding those still working and the wealthy. Need was the distributive criterion. Other respondents thought the payments rightly went to the larger equality class of all those 60 years old and over: it was a 'just reward' for 'a lifetime of contributions to the community.' Desert was the criterion. Still others just thought it unfair that not all the aged should get it – an application of the formal principle of justice to the larger equality class, specified, without reason, according to age.

Treasury and the Government were soon to begin to pose this and other like issues as ones of 'universal' versus 'targeted' benefits. *Economic Management* was to predict a future conflict between those social welfare benefits based on need (unemployment, domestic purposes, sickness and invalid benefits) and those which were 'universally applied without regard to income' (national superannuation and the family benefit). The real issues were (in the language adopted here) the size, composition, and critieria of entry into, equality groups.

Commitment from 1984 onwards to 'free market' policies further complicated questions of deciding what it was 'equitable' to give to whom and why. Treasury's *Economic Management* remarked that free wage-bargaining in a flexible wage market might lead to 'outcomes for some people which are incompatible with the community's objectives in relation to an equitable distribution of income and social justice'; but, counterwise, it also noted that if, as it also recommended, professions and other monopolies were denied control of their members and services, a 'more equitable distribution of incomes' *was* likely to result. The empirical relation between 'efficiency' and 'equity' was already vastly unclear, as their conceptual relationship was to be by 1987. For its part, *Social Policy Options* recorded well the tensions in equity that subsequently developed during the free-marketeering years of the Labour Government. It contrasted the expressed views of income equity as getting what one was individually worth, getting what the market would provide, and getting the same as others in the same job. The Council said it was 'inequitable' that 'wages and salaries are arrived at not necessarily on the basis of individual worth, but through bargaining systems'; and it thought in regard to wage fixing procedures that 'a balance must be struck between standardisation in the interest of equity, freedom to negotiate by both workers and employers, and the benefits of diversity and choice'. No advice as to principle was given. The politics of trade-off would have to do the job.

Issues in Equity also covered other applications of different conceptions of 'inequity' to different equality classes: in the unfair treatment of families and children, in the non-consultation of communities by central and local government, in housing, legal justice, health, and in regard to women's employment. General claims were heard that the further society went down the materialistic, affluent, white, middle-class male path, the less chance those not white middle-class males 'would have of receiving fair consideration'. It was said to be 'unfair to label people and apply stereotypes' as this caused suffering among old people, young people, men, women, the Māori people, Polynesian islanders, solo parents, the unemployed, ex-offenders, state house tenants, landlords, businessmen, and farmers.

Nor was differential access to knowledge and power fair. Indeed – and to proceed no further with illustrations – educational matters provided the official publications with further instances of the rich variety of the 'inequitable' and of inequitably-treated classes of people. *Issues in Equity* noted the poor success rate of Māori and Polynesian children, and observed that 'many people thought it unfair that educational goals were set by the white middle class'. Also 'questioned' was the unequal distribution of resources by which schools in richer neighbourhoods and the 'higher levels of the educational system – despite the acknowledged importance of early learning' – got more than their share. Treasury's *Economic Management* pretty much agreed: 'middle class capture' of the education system meant that it did not function as well as it might as a 'means of improving income distribution and reducing social inequality'. It argued that 'the distribution of successful education outcomes is inequitable. This calls into question the effectiveness of education as a vehicle for equalising opportunities.' The system did particulary badly for Māori and Polynesian students. *The Curriculum Review* heard (and encouraged) similar doubts about the fairness of the school system. Respondents told the Committee that girls were unfairly restricted by their lack of confidence in mathematics, the physical sciences, and sports, together with their lack of assertiveness. Boys were unfairly treated because they were not encouraged in music and dance. Ethnic groups did not get opportunities to do language work in their own tongues, especially in te reo Māori and the Polynesian languages. Bad children, quiet children, rural children, boarders, and both fast and slow learners were disadvantaged because their special needs were not met; and those who wanted manual skills could not get them as easily as academic ones. The Committee summed it up by saying that no one who was not 'average' was getting a fair go: and this included the 'well-behaved, middle-of-the-road students' because their teachers' time was taken up with other demands![104]

At the end of the day, in the Government's August 1988 statement of policy on schooling, *Tomorrow's Schools*, 'equity issues' were approached with the same lack of rigour and lack of promise from the Māori point of view. The 'equity objectives' of the proposed new system of school administration were to be: 'to ensure that [the] system . . . promotes and progressively achieves greater equity for women, Māori, Pacific Island, other groups with minority status; and for working class, rural and disabled students, teachers and communities.'[105] A similar brevity and vagueness as to equity issues characterized the *Report of the Working Groups on Post Compulsory Education and Training*, the Government's proposals for the reform in areas of higher education.[106]

Much, much more, could be said. But the Māori might have been forgiven if they had judged that this way of thinking was not entirely suited to approaching their problems. It mixed their demands with others'; it defined groups according to multiple criteria – need, desert and equalization etc. – which could cut across ethnic criteria. It uttered multiple prescriptions, many of which had nothing to do with Māori and Pākehā at all, and in all their variety simply reproduced the leading ideals of social justice that happened to exist in New Zealand, and which tended therefore to treat the Māori not as members of an irreducibly real *ethnie*, but as individuals in need who happened to be Māori. So while the claim to 'equity', and the allied claim to multicultural distributions, were arms of Māori strategy, they were never the whole.

They claimed, in addition, to be special.

---

[104] *The Curriculum Review*, pp. 86–8.

[105] Department of Education, *Tomorrow's Schools*, p. 25. On p. 26 the new opportunities and the access that Māori would have under the new system are listed.

[106] Hawke, *Report*, paras. 2.4–2.5.

Chapter 12
The Bicultural Distributive Claim and the Māori Code

I

The Bicultural Distributive Claim

None of the sources of the official doctrine of multicultural distributivism quoted in the last chapter were entirely unequivocal in their support for the idea. *Race Against Time* and *Public Service in a Multicultural Society* did not entirely embrace it, and *Puao-Te-Ata-Tū/Day Break* in fact pretty much ignored it. The equivocation on multiculturalism hinged on the doctrine of distributive biculturalism. This was the doctrine that distributions of things in Aotearoa/ New Zealand should be made primarily between the two main cultures, Māori and Pākehā, and that since Māori and Pākehā were *ethnie* worthy of equal respect, the distributions should be equal between them. It was not numbers of persons within each *ethnie* that weighted the balance; it was the equal value of each culture. So that, for instance, in regard to the distribution of political authority, it was (so to say) representative ethnocracy rather than representative democracy that was sought for.

Māori political argument to this effect became evident in the early 1980s. It was not only Māori leaders and publicists who came to argue this way. Churches, informed by the theological colleges,[1] followed suit. So too, did those governmental institutions which we have already seen speaking the cloudy rhetoric of equity. For as well as speaking of equity, they partly reflected emerging Māori demands for distributive biculturalism. But in speaking the language of biculturalism they also deflected the demand for bicultural distributions. To adopt the way of speaking was not necessarily to adopt the policy. By 1987 the two most significant bureaucratic debaters on social policy – Treasury and the Royal Commission on Social Policy – were speaking a Māori code as well as the language of equity: the Commission's *April Report* sympathetically, Treasury not. The Māori code can best be seen as a muffled, legalized, and bureaucratized version of distributive biculturalism.

While preparing *Race Against Time*, Hiwi Tauroa had heard that the case for the Māori was not exactly the same as the case for other ethnic groups. He agreed; he began to develop the idea of the equality between Māori and Pākehā languages and cultures, and he spoke of 'the active promotion of a bi-cultural then a multi-cultural society'.[2] But multiculturalism was still

---

[1] See Healy, 'Theological Colleges and the Maori'.

[2] Race Relations Conciliator, *Race Against Time*, p. 46.

a powerful theme in the booklet and stood balanced against the special emphasis on the Māori.[3] The Waahi Conference, set up to consider and promote 'multiculturalism', went a little further. Participants, many of them Māori, asked: 'if biculturalism could not be achieved, then what is the call for multiculturalism?'; and they spoke of a 'bicultural imperative'.[4] But the time was not yet ripe for a body of government servants to insist on such a change of policy. In 1983, *Issues in Equity* referred to its socially-conscious respondents' lamenting the lack, not of 'biculturalism' but of 'multiculturalism' in the country. Reporting to the Organisation of Economic and Cultural Development in the same year, the Department of Education spoke of a growing recognition in the country of 'ethical and cultural diversity' and reported this as evidence of a 'resurgence of a sense of Maori identity', which it placed alongside 'a growing awareness of the rights of ethnic minorities'. It did not recognize, that is, the *fundamental* nature of distributive biculturalism. Nor did the OECD, when it congratulated the nation on its attempts to 'create a genuinely multicultural society based on a core of shared values'.[5]

But by 1985 it was clear that an official movement away from the ideal of multiculturalism towards an accommodation with the ideal of biculturalism had occurred. The Law Commission Act clearly recognized some of the force of biculturalism, though not as an exclusive ideal. It embraced a multicultural ideal, but gave special consideration to the Māori. Section 2 (2a) required the Commission both 'to take into account te ao Maori (the Maori dimension)', and 'also give consideration to the multicultural nature of New Zealand society'.[6] And in July 1986 the bicultural ideal emerged as entirely dominant in a document already examined for its doctrines as to the nature of 'racism': *Puao-Te-Ata-Tu/Day Break*. The form of the report's title – put in both languages – expressed biculturalism. So did the composition of the membership of the advisory committee on 'a Maori Perspective for the Department of Social Welfare' which prepared it. It was graced with four distinguished Māori members alongside three Pākehā, and it was chaired by Mr John Rangihau, a man of great knowledge and mana.

The bicultural theme was intrinsic to the report. 'In our view,' the committee said, echoing Māori voices out of doors, 'policies and social objectives rooted in the concept of multiculturalism are commonly used as a means of avoiding the historical and social imperatives of the Maori situation.'[7] And they scarcely spoke from then on of groups other than Māori and Pākehā. They spoke only of Māori problems in criticizing 'personal racism', which attacked 'the fount of personal identity and . . . self worth, as well as denying the indigenous

[3] Race Relations Conciliator, *Race against Time*, pp. 18-19.

[4] *Public Service in a Multicultural Society*, pp. 21-4.

[5] The Treasury, *Government Management*, ii, pp. 220-1. And its source, Benton, 'Te Rito o te Korari: Maori Language and New Zealand's National Identity'.

[6] Law Commission Act's name and address.

[7] PTAT, i, p. 19.

person access to resources and opportunities in the larger society'.[8] The Pākehā needed to understand the Māori perspective and value it; they should understand that the Māori saw a history of Pākehā exploitation by force of arms, fraud, and a monocultural law; they should cease to counter the call for reforms 'with allegations of separatism or privilege'. And the Committee complained of those who 'cannot conceive that indigenous people have particular rights, or [cannot] contemplate that the denial of a way of life to the original inhabitants, is itself divisive and destructive'.[9]

The Māori people had a special place in New Zealand, at least equal with that of the Pākehā and more firmly rooted in the past. Māori culture was one of the two essential cultures in Aotearoa: it was even *the* essential culture.

The Treaty of Waitangi expressed these two claims. 'The importance of the Treaty as a driving force in contemporary Maori protest cannot be overemphasised. As our people have, in this generation, sought to find a philosophical base for relating to Pakeha society, the Treaty has become a symbol and a charter.' It gave the Māori 'all the rights and privileges of British citizens, presumably total equality in social, cultural, economic and political spheres of the community'.[10] Thus the Department should 'interpret biculturalism as the sharing of responsibility and authority for decisions with appropriate Maori people'.[11] On this basis, *Puao-Te-Ata-Tu/Day Break* elaborated a mode of bicultural distributivism alongside its multicultural one, suggesting a devolved system of social welfare provision with very much more Māori involvement in the localities.

So even as the ideology of multiculturalism was in the early 1980s attaining its most sophisticated development, and as it was taken over and developed by others who opposed its original purposes, its drawbacks were becoming apparent to Māori interests and a theory of biculturalism was being developed. The multiculturalist mode of thought made each culture equally important, and so te iwi Māori took its place as only one people among many, with no special claims against other iwi, and no special place in Aotearoa. They for their part wished to restate their special claims against others and to assert their unique place in the land. Against the suggestions of what the bureaucracy came to call 'social equity', they had to assert the strict claims of biculturalism in a way that would overcome the universalism of discourse on equality and of multiculturalism.

After all, the ideal of equalization of condition could be, and was, applied to ameliorate the lot of *all* persons and groups in need; and the ideal of multiculturalism equalized to deny the special claims of any culture. The Māori needed to insist on their special position in the history and destiny of Aotearoa/New Zealand. The issue was not simply and alone one of

8 PTAT, ii, p. 25.
9 PTAT, ii, p. 20. Cf pp. 5-11, 15-24.
10 PTAT, ii, pp. 13-14.
11 PTAT, i, pp. 19-20.

distributing and administering the social product. It was an issue also of mana, of authority, of the right to create and sustain a way of life independent of the Pākehā state. And so in various combinations, Māori said they were the tangata whenua o Aotearoa, intimately and indissolubly connected to the land; that by the right of prior occupation, the land was originally and remained spiritually theirs; that by virtue of the Treaty of Waitangi they had agreed to an equal partnership with the Crown and with subsequent settlers who were thus manuhiri (invited visitors); that te iwi Māori had nowhere else to go, whereas the visitors had other homelands in which their cultures thrived; that while the Crown had sovereignty, they had the rangatiratanga appropriate to an equal partner.

When Dr Erik Schwimmer suggested in the late 1960s that New Zealand should be described as and should become a 'bicultural society',[12] he was trying to avoid the ethnic-relations language of the *Hunn Report* with its implication that to partake in full citizenship – in the politics of the state – Māori would have to assimilate themselves to the dominant *ethnie* of the country, or at least to lay aside their Maoriness while they acted on the public stage. Schwimmer wanted to say that not only should there be 'bicultural' individuals who moved within both Māori and Pākehā cultures; not only should each *ethnie* respect and learn from the other equally; there should also be epistemological and organizational correlatives. All people (or if that were too much, all Governments) should adopt the bicultural value of seeing the two cultural sides to each question; and it should be recognized that, organizationally, there is more than one way of skinning a cat. It was these ideas – presented in a Māori fashion as appropriate to their status as tangata whenua and as Treaty partners – that were to be pressed into service in the 1980s as a defence against the inroads of distributive multiculturalism: a defence against the idea that each culture counted for one and only one, and against the idea that the distribution of resources ought to be proportional to the numbers in each culture.

Multiculturalism suggested distribution of things according to the membership size of the *ethnie* in question. Individuals constituted the equality classes. But bicultural distributivism treated the two cultures as the sole equality classes. The numbers of individuals in them did not matter. It was in accordance with *multicultural* distributivism that it was wrong for instance that Māori, 8–13 per cent of the population, did not get that proportion of broadcast media time, coronary by-pass operations, positions in top management, numbers of Māori parliamentary seats, school and tertiary education successes, and so on. It was (similarly) right that they should get 10 per cent of the fisheries as proposed by the Crown negotiators in the stalled deal of 1988 on fisheries, and right that their numbers in tertiary education should be proportionate to their numbers in the population. But *bicultural* distributivism was different. It demanded that the *ethnie*, not the individuals, be represented

12 Schwimmer (ed), *The Maori People in the Nineteen-Sixties*, pp. 11-64. Also Metge, *The Maoris of New Zealand*, pp. 308-10.

in matters or sharing. And it came to this: that the Māori ought to be half sharers in many things, partners in control of others, and sole guardians of still others. Basic to the distributive claims was the assumption that they had the right to exist and persist as a distinct and unique people. Distributive biculturalism was a doctrine built on the idea of Māori sovereignty, mana motuhake.

Nothing of this was new in the 1980s: for instance Pat Hohepa in 1978 and Hirini Mead in 1979 had argued for the 'two people one nation' idea. But the enthusiastic adoption of the Treaty and the combination of that with the idea of 'partnership' gave the doctrine a particular and changing colour as the decade unfolded. It had appeared in New Zealand Maori Council philosophy by 1980. It was in the kaupapa of Mana Motuhake by 1981. The reader will recall the various propositions variously made and weighed by the Waitangi Tribunal, in the proposed Bill of Rights, at the Hikoi, during the two great Treaty hui, and by the Court of Appeal in the *New Zealand Maori Council* v *the Attorney General*. They were discussed from 1984 to 1986 and adopted by the Anglican Church as the basis for its policy of *Te Kaupapa Tikanga Rua* – the philosophy of two ethics – or 'bicultural development'. They were taught by Project Waitangi and other groups of Pākehā reformers; and they were entirely dominant in Māori submissions to the Royal Commission on Social Policy in 1987.

The teaching was most authoritatively expressed by the Tribunal in *Te Atiawa Report* and in *Te Reo Report*.[13] In *Te Atiawa Report* the Tribunal held that the Treaty was 'an acknowledgement of Maori existence, of their prior occupation of the land and of the intent that the Maori presence would remain and be respected. It made us one country but acknowledged that we were two people. It established the regime not for uni-culturalism but for bi-culturalism.' The special claims due the Māori by right of prior occupation (what came to be called 'tangata whenua status') and by the Treaty were reiterated in *Te Reo Report*:

We do not accept that the Maori is just another one of a number of ethnic minority groups in our community. It must be remembered that of all minority groups the Maori alone is party to a solemn treaty made with the Crown. None of the other migrant groups who have come to live in this country in recent years can claim the rights that were given the Maori people by the Treaty of Waitangi.

Because of the Treaty Maori New Zealanders stand on a special footing reinforcing, if reinforcement be needed, their historical position as the original inhabitants, the tangata whenua of New Zealand, who agreed to allow our European forebears to come and settle here with them.

In their discussion paper of 1980 the New Zealand Maori Council spoke of the necessity for a 'bicultural society' and objected to the 'majority culture' deciding what was best for Māori. It claimed that 'as tangata whenua of this country we have a right to special recognition, to control our own

---

[13] *Te Atiawa Report, Te Reo Report*, Section 5.11, at p. 37.

affairs, and to determine our own future'. The Council looked forward to a 'national partnership', 'of equals'. It objected to the imposition of Pākehā names to places: 'such name changes are a denigration of the past and denial of the future. We are given to understand that the future is no longer ours to announce . . . . Our language is the only one that really belongs here.' It ought to be an official language, equally honoured with English, equally used. Te iwi Māori had the right to exist and sustain itself, equal with that of the Pākehā: 'We are not talking separatism. We seek to lay the foundation for Maori self-determination within the total New Zealand society.'[14] It was a matter of distribution of rights of self-determination within the political society of New Zealand.

Not all biculturalists were, of course, Māori. *Te Kaupapa Tikanga Rua* was put together among others by Professor Kenneth Keith, (friend of Geoffrey Palmer and his co-architect of the proposed Bill of Rights of 1985), as well as by Professor Whatarangi Winiata of the New Zealand Maori Council (and the Department of Accountancy at the Victoria University of Wellington). It spoke of the 'special position of the Maori as reflected in the Treaty'. 'The Treaty laid the foundation for the existence together of two main cultural groups – Maori and Pakeha – within one nation'; 'partnership involves co-operation and independence between distinct cultural or ethnic groups within one nation.' It found it 'legitimate' to talk of a 'multicultural society', but thought that kind of talk 'can be used to mask the primary reality expressed in the Treaty of Waitangi, and the obligation to live by its principles'.[15]

Project Waitangi told the Royal Commission on Social Policy in 1987: 'We see the Treaty as the basis of our nationhood: it was and is an invitation to share this land with Maori and as an equal partnership.' The New Zealand Nurses' Association saw the Treaty as the 'basis for building a fair and just society . . . . From that foundation will come the possibility of bicultural development which will redress the inequalities between Maori and non-Maori.'[16] The National Youth Council said 'The Treaty of Waitangi is a document of equal partnership between Maori and Tauiwi.'[17] And Māori spoke the same way to the Commission: Dr Mason Durie, one of the commmissioners, said Maori submissions had 'consistent themes'. 'The main one was that the Treaty of Waitangi was directly related to social policy. Interpretation varied, but many saw it as a means to redress land grievances which were linked to the social and economic status of Maori people.' Ranginui Walker argued to the Commission that 'as a result of the Treaty . . . nation building in future should be based on a policy of bi-culturalism. This would involve the transformation of previously mono-cultural social and political institutions to include a Maori dimension . . . . If a century of encrusted

---

[14] NZMC, *Discussion Paper on Future Maori Development and Legislation.*

[15] Anglican Church in New Zealand, *Te Kaupapa Tikanga Rua*, pp. 19, 33, 34.

[16] *The April Report*, ii, p. 30.

[17] *The April Report*, iv, p. 733.

institutional racism is to be overcome it can only be done on a co-equal basis of power-sharing.'[18]

Plans for the reform and redistribution of political authority on bicultural lines were prepared accordingly. They were extremely various, and ran the gamut from proposals simply to sensitize existing Pākehā institutions to Māori values by requiring consultation with Māori, to more or less full-blown demands for bicultural distributivism. Three bicultural distributivist claims may serve as examples, for the extremes will throw the less far-reaching proposals into focus. Two were to do with the making of law (one at central, the other at district levels) and one with the exercise of legal jurisdiction as well as legislative capacity.

Through their spokesman, Whatarangi Winiata, the Raukawa Trustees began to present a plan for a new form of Government in 1984. It was presented to the Treaty hui of 1984 and 1985, to The Hui Taumata of October 1984, to a Wellington seminar of jurists on the proposed Bill of Rights and to Government Ministers in 1985, and on other occasions from then on, not least to the Royal Commission on Social Policy. The proposal was for the introduction of a second legislative chamber, a Senate, consisting of 10 Māori and 10 Pākehā – 'a 50/50 Senate', Winiata called it. This chamber would not initiate legislation but would ensure that legislation was consistent with the Treaty of Waitangi, and it would 'reconcile' legislation proposed by a now-divided primary legislature: a chamber of 15 Māori Representatives elected according to tikanga Māori (Māori custom), another of 85 Pākehā elected according to tikanga Pākehā. The details might be varied, but the principle was clear:

> . . . the need to restore the principle of one people, one vote in the major institutions of Aotearoa to give recognition to our bicultural heritage as a nation built upon the Treaty of Waitangi. The Treaty was signed by two peoples, the Maori and the pakeha, these were the two partners in the deal. Subsequently, the concept of democracy, one person, one vote, was introduced and the pakeha population multiplied. They were obedient to God in that respect. We now find that the pakeha has 10 votes to one vote of the Maori partner.[19]

Not surprisingly this version of distributive biculturalism did not appeal to many of the directive élite and no response at all was forthcoming, except from academics.[20] It was starkly contrary to majoritarian principles of distribution within one nation. So (to turn to our second example of bicultural distributism in legislation) was the proposal of a Maori Consultative Group set up in May 1988 to advise Hon. Dr Michael Bassett, Minister of Local Government, on Māori participation in local government. The proposals, made in March 1989, included the proposition that 'in accordance with the principle of rangatiratanga (tribal sovereignty), there should be equal

---

[18] H11:18/6/87.

[19] NZ Section of the International Commission of Jurists, *Bill of Rights Seminar*, pp. 66-9.

[20] Mulgan, *Māori, Pākehā and Democracy*, Chapter 5.

representation of tangata whenua and tauiwi on all units of local government': the 50 per cent to be chosen by the locals – the mana whenua. On the same principles there should also be a Māori Local Government Commission working in parallel with the Pākehā one. There were additional recommendations as to the devolution of authority on Māori matters to local government being carried out 'in a manner consistent with the Treaty of Waitangi'; but it was fairly obviously the principle of bicultural distributivism which led the Minister to repudiate the recommendations as coming from a body 'highjacked' by 'unrepresentative activists'. 'The Government', said Bassett, 'is not prepared to accept the recommendations. To do so would be undemocratic since it would put the Maoris, who constitute 10 per cent of the population into the driving seats . . . irrespective of whether they could succeed through the electoral process.'[21] Thus the fate of bicultural distributivism when it cut across the democratic electoral principle of 'one vote, one value'. The two collectivities, Māori and Pākehā, simply could not be counted as 'equal', for to do so would be to count each individual Māori's vote (or other kind of choice) at a value ten times that of the individual Pākehā's. This could not be countenanced by a democratic state.

The third and final example of a recommendation of bicultural distributivism also met the fate of being rejected by the department (and Minister) which had called it up. This was Mr Moana Jackson's proposal in November 1988 for a 'parallel' criminal justice system. He argued from 'the tangata whenua status of the Maori people, the partnership which the Treaty imposes on them and the Crown, and the idea of biculturalism which grows out of it'. As to their being tangata whenua, it was not so much Māori temporal priority as their uniqueness in Aotearoa that Jackson stressed: 'their culture and language developed their uniqueness here. . . . Such uniqueness does not give them an exclusive understanding or sense of belonging to the land, but it does give them a pre-eminent right to be heard and to participate in what happens to and within it.' As to those who did not sign the Treaty in which the Pākehā recognized their rangatiratanga or authority: 'they have subsequently seen it as the cornerstone of Maori/Pakeha relationships. They have frequently used it as a basis for petitions to the Queen, and for dealings with the government. Thus, rather like the decisions of a higher court binding those not directly party to an action, so the Treaty has come to be accepted by Maori people as a covenanted precedent for defining behaviour and establishing a framework of relations with the Crown.' And the framework was that of an 'equal relationship', a bicultural one.[22]

But what *was* a bicultural relationship? In Jackson's work was to be found for the first time an attempt to distinguish what until than had been confounded in theory though not (obviously) in policy proposal. Jackson argued that a 'bicultural relationship' could imply two separable things: the first, adapting Pākehā institutions 'to meet Maori requirements and to address Maori

[21] AS4:8/3/89; H3:17/3/89.

[22] Jackson, *The Maori and the Criminal Justice System*, ii, pp. 168-71.

concerns'; the second, developing 'different and specifically Maori institutions . . . to more meaningfully share the authority defined by the Treaty'. It was the second sort of relationship that Jackson argued for, quoting with approval a National Council of Churches notion of biculturalism as: 'the philosophy that constitutes the spirit and intent of the Treaty [and which] involves notions of an equal partnership . . . reflected in an equality of power, resources and responsibility'.[23] And it was this second sort of biculturalism – what I have called bicultural distributivism as opposed to what might be called bicultural reformism – on which he founded proposals for a separate but parallel Māori system of criminal justice. The first sort of biculturalism was simply a form of 'cultural appropriation' which did not allow for equal sharing in the 'decision-making process'. Ameliorationism on grounds of equality was not only not enough, it was wrong: 'The first criter[ion] of any affirmative action policy needs to recognise the rights the Maori people have to be employed is not based on a minority status, but on their status as tangata whenua partners under the Treaty.' 'Current thinking on biculturalism has different definitions of affirmative action or equal employment. It assumes first that the Maori are just another minority group with minority group disadvantages.' It was not enough either for Pākehā in the bureauracy to have learned te reo Māori and Māori customs: 'fluency and comfort [in Maori settings] did not alter the fundamental Pakeha perspectives they brought to Maori issues, nor their self-interested belief that the institutions they were part of were superior to those of the Maori.'[24] A system of criminal justice needed to be defined and administered by Māori and according to Māori understandings; indeed in wider areas, Māori needed to influence the legal system. These aims Jackson approached suggesting among other things an autonomous Maori Law Commission (Te Runanga Whakamarama I Nga Ture) to study Māori law, to consult with Māori and respond to proposed legislation, to make proposals as to legislation and to examine and suggest treatments for Māori criminal offending. He also suggested a system of Māori legal services, which would, as well as providing assistance to the Māori, perhaps operate a separate court system and certainly massively reform the existing one.[25]

The details of the proposals cannot further concern us here, nor the fact that they expressed a good weight of Māori sentiment.[26] For the moment it is enough to note that the Minister of Justice repudiated any notion of distributive biculturalism so argued: 'The Minister has made it clear,' said the Secretary for Justice, 'that while he supports the need to make the legal system sensitive to Maori values and needs, he believes it is essential that

---

[23] Jackson, *The Maori and the Criminal Justice System*, ii, p. 205, quoting Murray Short from Church and Society Commission, NCC, *The Pakeha and the Treaty*, p. 46.

[24] Jackson, *The Maori and the Criminal Justice System*, pp. 206-8, and see following.

[25] Jackson, *The Maori and the Criminal Justice System*, i, pp. 218-21.

[26] And organization around the issue: see the earlier call for a Maori Law Commission, H12:5/ 11/88.

New Zealand retains one legal system in which everyone is equal under the law.' And it was not only the Minister, Geoffrey Palmer, who thought this way. The Opposition spokesmen of Justice (Paul East) and Maori Affairs (Winston Peters) agreed. Peters said he was 'implacably opposed' to a 'separatist' system: 'it is essential that New Zealand retains one legal system in which everyone is equal under the law'.[27] This response echoed the fate of all proposals based on the principle of bicultural distributivism. There had to be one law, and the law had to be made by a representative democracy. But bicultural proposals (reformist more often than distributive) did find an echo in a Māori code developed in bureaucratic circles alongside the cloudy rhetoric of equity.

II

The Māori Code in Governing Circles

By 1986, governing circles and members of the directive minority of society were listening carefully to the bicultural claims (both reformist and distributive), not always cheerfully. As a consequence, a special Māori code was developed for speaking of Māori matters, some of the key phrases of which, were: the 'principles of the Treaty of Waitangi', 'partnership', 'biculturalism', 'indigenous' and 'tangata whenua'. The most elaborate official expositions of the code – those in Treasury's *Government Management* and in the Royal Commission on Social Policy's *April Report* – did not come to the same policy conclusions at all. Indeed *The April Report* went out of its way to show where Treasury was wrong. But they shared the language. In April 1988, when the Department of Maori Affairs put out the Green Paper on devolution, Koro Wetere could observe rightly that the Government had 'been involved in lengthy and wide-ranging discussions to see how we can better put the principles of the Treaty of Waitangi into practice'. The Green Paper was called *He Tirohanga Rangapu/Partnership Perspectives*. In naming itself in the two languages, it used the new code to perfection.[28]

Official and quasi-official policy documents mostly mixed the language of equity with the Māori code. *Puao-Te-Ata-Tu/Day Break* has been seen doing this in mid-1986. In December the same mixture of languages (and attitudes) characterized the Royal Commission on the Electoral System's *Towards a better Democracy*. The commissioners consulted and heard submissions in te reo Māori and in English. They held that the Māori differed from other minority groups in being 'indigenous to New Zealand. They are the tangata whenua.' And they noted that 'Maori tribal leaders and the Crown' entered into the Treaty of Waitangi by which 'the Crown formally recognised the existing rights

[27] Jackson, *The Maori and the Criminal Justice System*, Foreword, p. 3. Newspaper reports at SS3:27/11/88; H3:28/11/88; H24:30/11/89.

[28] Department of Maori Affairs, *He Tirohanga Rangapu/Partnership Perspectives*, p. 1.

of the Maori and undertook to protect them. It is in this sense that Maori people have had a special constitutional status, whatever recognition the Government and the legal system may have accorded to the Treaty at various times.' The Commission also noted Māori claims to 'a measure of autonomy or self-determination (mana Maori motuhake)' together with demands for formal recognition of the Treaty and 'the protection of the rights and interests which it guarantees'. But having noted that, it recorded an 'understanding . . . that Maori do not regard the content of these claims as ends in themselves but rather as offering the most effective means of ensuring their cultural survival'.[29]

In the event, the Commission's recommendations denied Māori claims to increased separate representation under the existing first-past-the-post majority system. It recommended instead a multiple member proportional representation system. One major factor influencing their recommendation was that of integrating the Māori into the political system: they thought a proportional representation system would make it more likely that all MPs (and not just, as in the current system, those in Māori electorates) would have to attend to Māori interests. On the other hand another factor was their wish to protect separate Māori interests; they thought their proposed system would yield more Māori MPs who spoke Māori and were capable of operating in the Māori world.[30] All in all, the Commission saw the Māori on the one hand as just one 'important minority' which ought to enjoy 'a just and equitable share of political power'; on the other hand, it saw them as special. Advocating a general overhaul of the constitutional system, it held that 'the Maori people's position would be much more secure if our constitutional and political systems were to reflect the diversity in our society and, more particularly, the special position of the Maori'.[31] The Commission spoke both the language of equity and the Māori code: and it felt the tension they expressed, between treating groups as collections of individuals and treating Māori as an indissoluble unity – treating, that is the *ethnie* itself as a bearer of rights and interests.

The same mixture of languages was evident among the documents on educational reforms put together from 1986 onwards. Two examples may stand for the general trend. Though the Department of Education's discussion paper *Tertiary Education in New Zealand* (April 1987) spoke only the language of equity, the Report of the Universities Review Committee of October, set up by the collected Vice-Chancellors to respond defensively to the discussion paper, spoke the Māori code as well. The report, *New Zealand's Universities. Partners in National Development*, discussed the position of lower socio-economic classes, women, Māori, Pacific Islanders and 'other disadvantaged groups',

---

[29] Royal Commission on the Electoral System, *Towards a Better Democracy*, pp. 81, 86.

[30] Royal Commission, *Towards a Better Democracy*, Chapter 3. See also the remarks of two members of the Commission: Wallace, 'The Case for Electoral Reform', pp. 4-6; Mulgan, *Democracy and Power in New Zealand*, pp. 72-80.

[31] Royal Commission, *Towards a Better Democracy*, pp. 87, 110.

all under the same head: 'accessibility and social equity'. And the Māori case was partly the case for the other disadvantaged groups: one for better 'access' and 'representation' via 'affirmative action policies' and 'equal employment' policies. But the Committee also spoke the Māori code, referring to education and training of the Māori as 'crucial to the solution of their future identity and wellbeing in a bicultural society'. The Committee also referred, in the language of *New Zealand Maori Council* v *the Attorney General*, to a 'partnership' between the institutions of society (at the forefront of which were the universities) and the Māori.[32]

The *Curriculum Review* of April 1987 was even more willing to elaborate a bicultural view, though it *also* spoke the language of equity to such an excess (it will be recalled) that it saw the 'middle of the road' pupil as 'disadvantaged'. It consulted in two languages. It urged the recognition of the 'tangata whenua status' of the Māori, 'the original people of Aotearoa'. It followed the Waitangi Tribunal in interpreting the Treaty as having 'promised Maori people equal status as citizens of Aotearoa, and promised to honour their right to retain their way of life and their language'. Previously cagey in its draft report of July 1986, the committee in its final report 'strongly' supported taha Māori in schools and the Māori expression of aroha, manaakitanga and wairua; it also now supported the introduction of kaupapa Māori schools, which would teach the language and the culture by total immersion.[33]

Even cagier in its use of the Māori code was the Planning Council's *Policy Options*. The Māori were the only group to be actually named in a 'Social Objective' specified in the book; but their interests were to be balanced against those of other individuals. Sub-heading (b) of the 'Objective', called 'Freedom, Participation and Tolerance', was 'To ensure that New Zealand society allows adequate scope for the development of the Maori people':

The objective asks for recognition of the Maori as tangata whenua (people of the land) – the original inhabitants. As such the Maori have special rights to the expression of their culture through culturally appropriate processes and structures. (This is not to ignore the rights and aspirations of other ethnic minorities, and other groups, especially women; these are covered in the previous objectives.) Barriers in society, both institutional and attitudinal, should be removed; not just barriers to cultural expression, but also those which have held back the Maori people from achieving the standard of living and quality of life enjoyed by the non-Maori population. Moves towards this objective must, however, be consistent with the other objectives already stated – respect for individual rights, tolerance and participation.

But if the Planning Council hedged their recognition of special Māori rights, at least they recognized them. They spoke the code.

Treasury was still less whole-hearted about the Māori code, and adopted it partly to counter it. By July 1987 it had no choice. Reparations were an important issue and the claims of the Māori to being a special people

[32] Universities Review Committee, *New Zealand's Universities*, Chapter 4.
[33] *The Curriculum Review*, pp. 26-7, 29, 30.

were insistent. So *Government Management* devoted a whole chapter to the 'Implications of the Treaty of Waitangi', and the question of partnership was further discussed in a separate chapter on Māori education. Over all Treasury was non-committal but decidedly cautious about the use of the Māori code, and it utterly rejected the doctrine of bicultural distributivism and what it sensed to be the underlying claim to Māori sovereignty.

Treasury reported: 'The Maori are the longest established of all the ethnic and cultural communities that exist in New Zealand. They have a unique attachment to the land because of their long history of settlement and the nature of their spiritual beliefs. They are the tangata whenua. In 1840 they were the owners of New Zealand.'[34] Thus the report. It is not easy to say *what* normative weight or imperative force the Department thought any of these propositions might be thought to have. The best gloss is probably to see the questions not far beneath the surface: what has long-establishment and ancient ownership got to do with current claims? And why should a people's beliefs give them claims over others who do not share those beliefs?

This would certainly be suggested by the Department's very un-Māori analysis of the Treaty 'partnership'. It was – conventionally enough – one between the Māori and 'the Crown'. It was one requiring the 'reasonableness' and 'good faith' of which the Court of Appeal had spoken, and one respecting the 'wairua' of 'the Maori approach'; and Māori rights were certainly 'Treaty rights'. But the rights, besides not being legal rights (they were Treaty rights only), were remarkably unspecific and not much adapted to the 'complexities and sophistication of the modern state'. They far from covered every aspect of life: only those specified in the Treaty. Their precise content would have to be decided by the Crown at those points where Māori claims came (as they inevitably would) to conflict with the sovereignty of the state and with private property rights. As to bicultural distributivism, when the Māori claimed special rights to 'tax revenue' and 'power sharing', the state had the legitimate power to decide those claims too, in the light of Bisson J's remarks in the *New Zealand Maori Council* v *the Attorney General* on the state's duty to 'provide laws and make related decisions for the community as a whole having regard to the economic and other needs of the day'. It must decide sensitively, realizing that to adopt a doctrine of multiculturalism 'tends to submerge Maoridom'. But on the other hand – and Treasury quoted Dr Richard Benton here (who would not have appreciated his authority being used in this way) – 'Benton is careful to warn against the danger of other ethnic groups feeling "put down" as a consequence of a restoration of the Maori language.'[35]

Thus Treasury. Many other examples of usages of the Māori code could be identified: in the the 1988 review of laws for managing air, land and water use, and mining, for instance, and in the Education Department proposals of the same year to give the Māori language a 'central place' in the senior

---

[34] The Treasury, *Government Management*, i, 319, and thereafter to p. 355.

[35] The Treasury, *Government Management*, i, Chapter 5; ii, Chapter 8.

school English syllabus.[36] It was, however, in *The April Report* of the Royal Commission on Social Policy that the Māori code found its greatest elaboration and application. The full name of the Commission was reproduced in te reo Māori on the covers of the five books which made up the four large volumes: Te Komihana A Te Karauna Mo Nga Ahuatanga-A-Iwi. It made 35 marae visits attended by 1584 people and analysed their submissions.[37] It produced a bilingual chapter on 'The Treaty of Waitangi: directions for Social Policy/Te Tiriti o Waitangi: He Tohutohu: Te Kaupapa Mo Nga Ahuatanga a Iwi'; and one part of a two-part chapter on women and social policy was devoted to Māori women.[38] Associated papers reported on the 'standards and foundations of Maori society' as well as 'standards and foundations for social policy';[39] and the Commission reported the extensive discussions and advice taken on the Treaty,[40] on the current concerns of the Māori people,[41] and on Māori attitudes to wellbeing and welfare.[42] There were papers too on Māori education,[43] on the teaching of te reo,[44] on hapū and iwi resources,[45] and on the Māori and the mass media.[46] There was more on the Māori, but only two separate pieces on Pacific Islanders and other ethnic groups.[47] While Māori issues, on a very modest count, took up about 650 pages – they were also discussed under functional headings like housing, immigration policy, and so on – other ethnic groups took up about 50 pages. In brief, *The April Report* adopted, as well as it knew how, a bicultural approach to its task.

The elements of the Māori code pervaded the Commission's own quasi-recommendations (it was not given time to finish its job) and attitudes. Of the commissioners, only Mason Durie, brother of Judge Durie, was Māori. But despite accusations by their Māori clients that they were not bicultural enough, the Chairman and five commissioners held that 'a Māori dimension is basic to New Zealand society'. They attempted to provide such a dimension as a twin aim with providing a 'coherent approach to the goals and values and principles which are the foundations of New Zealand society'. The sections on the Māori dimension they called 'The Treaty of Waitangi: Directions for Social Policy'. Fundamentally, they held that the Treaty 'acknowledged

---

[36] Core Group on Resource Management Reform, *Resource Management Law Reform*, paper E. On the syllabus proposals, H8:17/11/88.

[37] *The April Report*, i, pp. 253-98.

[38] *The April Report*, ii, pp. 40-186.

[39] *The April Report*, iii (1), pp. 5-41.

[40] *The April Report*, iii (1), pp. 79-278.

[41] *The April Report*, iii (1), pp. 363-404.

[42] *The April Report*, iii (1), pp. 491-6.

[43] *The April Report*, iii (2), pp. 285-404, iv, pp. 89-114.

[44] *The April Report*, iii (2), pp. 703-43.

[45] *The April Report*, iii (2), pp. 789-803.

[46] *The April Report*, iv, pp. 481-503.

[47] *The April Report*, iv, pp. 561-91.

Maori sovereignty and, in so doing, recognised the status of the indigenous people.' 'In return' (they enigmatically continued) 'the role of the British Crown was acknowledged by the Maori signatories . . . and priority was given to British settlers over those of other nations'. It should thus, the Commissioners emphasized, be understood clearly that the Māori had 'indigenous status', like many 'who have become minorities in their own lands', and that New Zealand was fortunate in having a Treaty 'which sets out the relationships, responsibilities and conditions under which further development can proceed in a harmonious manner'.[48] They spoke of the Treaty 'not only as an historical record upon which grievances from the past can be based, but more importantly we see it as a pro-active agreement with relevance into the twentieth century and beyond'. They quoted the Waitangi Tribunal's *Orakei Report* with approval to the effect that the Treaty was 'not intended to fossilise the status quo but to provide a definition for future growth and development'; but they could not help thinking that the 'proactive provisions' of the Treaty might be 'insufficiently recognised unless other measures are introduced to complement the mechanisms already in place for dealing with past grievances', and they recommended the establishment of a Waitangi Commission to 'give emphasis to the application of the Treaty to New Zealand's current and future development'.[49]

Not only was the Treaty a prospective document, it covered almost all aspects of life. The Commission remonstrated with Treasury for having thought that 'where the Treaty is silent, as in respect of employment, incomes, and economic development, there would be no special claim to partnership or power-sharing other than as provided under Article III'. On the contrary, the Commission held, 'within the Treaty, economic, social, constitutional, cultural and spiritual dimensions are intended'. Because the Treaty 'obviously' referred to 'the ownership and management of such resources as lands, forests, fisheries and villages', and because of the relationships of the Māori with 'that environment', Article 2 'must also be concerned with economic and social issues and with the many factors that contribute to wellbeing'. Their view was that 'few, if any aspects of wellbeing could be seen to stand outside the Treaty'. In this mode, regarding their thinking as to the proper relation between Māori and the state, the Commission almost entirely reduced issues of distributive justice to the one issue of justice as the keeping of contracts. Such a way of thinking was in one obvious respect close to Treasury's – in the emphasis it put on contract. But where Treasury thought that justice consisted in the keeping of contracts between individuals, the Commission thought that the contracts were between two corporate beings.

The Commission did not quite think however that the sum of justice in Treaty contract was the unanalysable sum of all justice. They could summarize and specify their view of what the Treaty entailed mainly; and when speaking

48 *The April Report*, ii, p. 45.

49 *The April Report*, ii, pp. 40-1, 62.

of Māori-Pākehā issues, they also ranged 'equity' considerations alongside those of justice in contract – although the emphasis was on the Māori code.

Sharing the prevailing mania for racy slogans, the Commission produced its own: 'partnership, protection, participation'.[50] What then, would justice between Māori and the state, Māori and Pākehā, be?

As to 'Partnership': The Māori people, individually (by Article 3) and collectively (by Article 2) were one partner, the Crown the other. The Commission held that, despite those who did not sign, 'all Maori people are party to the Treaty of Waitangi both as individuals and members of tribes and tribal confederations'; and it held (rejecting the view of most of the churches that 'the spirit of partnership must operate at an individual level if it is to have any real meaning') that local and central Government were the other partners, not Pākehā individuals. As to the substance of the 'partnership' and its location in society, it is not easy to say precisely what the Commission had in mind as to what 'partnership' was, except that it was neither 'entrenched separatism' on the one hand, nor 'assimilation and homogeneity' on the other. This does not tell us much; but the Commission did go further. The Māori-Crown partnership was not the *only* partnership, but it was the predominating one. 'Multiculturalism' for instance was a function of the Crown's 'addressing the cultural needs of those within its mandate', whereas 'biculturalism' was a fundamental constituent of the partnership and absolutely incumbent on the Crown. Immigration policies ought not to continue to be made with 'minimal consultation between the principal partners' – and similarly in 'all areas of social policy'. The Commission thought it saw a reaction to 'élitist' decision-making structures. It saw instead the welcome growth of partnerships between 'local-central; private-public; employer-employee; [and] voluntary-statutory' agents, and it seems to have thought that the Māori-Crown partnership was to be listed with that (heterogeneous) group. But there was no doubt that the Commission put the Māori-Crown partnership to the fore. The proposed Waitangi Commission, set up to audit future legislation, would be developed on the 'principle of partnership involving tribal authorities, federating Maori organizations and the Crown'. And generally, 'fairness, equality and justice will be best addressed when partnership is vigorously pursued at all levels with recognition of differing values and perspectives and an acknowledgement of the other partners' prerogatives'.[51]

As to 'Protection' and 'Participation':[52] It was the failure of the Crown to protect the lands, fisheries and, in general, tribal bases, that had led to claims to the Waitangi Tribunal for compensation; and the Commission agreed with Treasury that 'solutions to these claims need to be found urgently if disparities in social-wellbeing are to be seriously addressed'. Thus reparations became

---

[50] *The April Report*, ii, pp. 49 and following. M. H. Durie further developed this line of thought in 1988-89, in 'The Treaty of Waitangi — Perspectives on Social Policy'.

[51] *The April Report*, ii, pp. 49-56, 63.

[52] *The April Report*, ii, pp. 56-69.

a form of prospective social policy designed to bring about equity. The protection of taonga – language and 'human and cultural resources' – was also especially required by the Treaty (as well as a crying need of those Māori alienated from their 'tribal identity'). All this was essential if Māori participation in New Zealand society was to be developed from a basis of their 'lower standards of health, education, housing, employment and all other aspects of social and economic wellbeing'. Earlier, Europeanizing, Māori leaders of the Young Maori movement (Sir Apirana Ngata, Te Rangi Hiroa, Sir Peter Buck, and Dr Maui Pomare) had got it wrong if they had thought that 'Maori participation in New Zealand would be more equitable and fruitful if it were on the same basis as for all other citizens'. And here the Commission supported the more separatist Māori leadership of the 1970s and 1980s in criticizing the pre-war Māori politicians. A degree of Māori autonomy was allowed for in the Treaty and must now be provided. 'Social and economic policies for Maori should be determined by Maori people, in accord with their own values, systems and due resources, but within the framework of a unified New Zealand.'[53] More precisely, the Commission urged that election procedures for election to Hospital Boards, University Councils, City Councils, and Parliament be so modified that Māori representatives might be chosen according to the custom of the Māori themselves. Although it cautioned against too great a haste in conditions where few iwi authorities were yet ready to take on powers devolved on them by central government, devolution was also clearly on the Commission's agenda.

Throughout its report the Commission joined considerations of equity with the Māori code. It spoke often of the 'terms of the partnership ideals of the Treaty of Waitangi and the need to reduce inequalities and disparities between the Maori and non-Maori'.[54] But overall the emphasis was on the Treaty and the Māori code; and perhaps its main conclusion was that 'the uniqueness of the Treaty . . . in Maori eyes is not adequately conveyed in debates on its place in the country's statutes, or as an element in the New Zealand Constitution. . . . Simply, the Treaty itself is the authority.' The Commission thus thought 'that the Treaty of Waitangi, in its entirety, should be entrenched as a constitutional document and that deliberations to that end should proceed according to the principles of partnership and with due speed.'[55]

There were of course many differences between the official and quasi-official documents discussed here; and many have not been discussed. But it may well be concluded that in the official point of view, the case for the Māori was the case for social equity in general, plus the case for special Māori rights. The location of the Māori in official thinking was, from 1982 through 1988 (from *Race Against Time* to the *April Report*), in the process of becoming

53 *The April Report*, ii, p. 63.

54 *The April Report*, ii, p. 71.

55 *The April Report*, ii, pp. 3, 17, 21, 39, 41, 42.

like that of the Amerindian in the USA or in Canada. They were seen firstly as ordinary citizens in a society which was committed to equal rights to (disputed) things but secondly they were coming to be seen as having special rights by virtue of their aboriginal position in the land and consequent special relations with the state.[56]

Of course the development of such a complex, uncertain, and inconsistent ideology was one thing, and practice (including the greater clarification of the thinking) was another. Vine De Loria Jr., a Professor of Political Science and a Sioux, has attested to the difficulties all parties in Indian-USA relations have had with distinguishing between Indian 'self-determination' and 'self-government' – and this after more than fifty years' concentrated discussion. He has recorded many and bitter disputes as to the distribution of social welfare over an even longer period.[57] With even less national experience, things might have been expected to proceed slowly in New Zealand. The Pākehā-Māori debate on self determination and self-government for the Māori was just beginning, the debates on distributive justice and reparations were highly confused, and new redistributive policies and practices emerged only slowly.

The Government's reaction to the recommendations of the Waitangi Tribunal was, for example, pretty much what might have been expected in such a fluid situation. It was not in line with Māori expectations, nor Pākehā opinion's rejection of them. The years 1983–1989 saw a promise to return Orakei lands to Ngati Whatua and the return of Ngati Paoa to Waiheke; they saw a decision to dispose of Rotorua sewage on land, and they saw the beginnings of moves to implement environmental and organizational reforms; they saw it accepted that te reo Māori could be the language of citizens appearing in Court. Not all of these actions – especially the return of the Orakei lands – were approved by the Government's Pākehā constituency, yet they hardly satisfied Māori demands. Aila Taylor was, by 1988, tolerably satisfied with the progress Te Atiawa was finally making in Taranaki after five years of frustration, and Ngati Pikiao were satisfied as to the land disposal of the Rotorua sewage. But Mrs Nganeko Minhinnick continued to express the dissatisfaction of the Manukau hapū with the slowness of progress, and the te reo claimants still smarted at the Crown's Maori Language Act (1985) which 'preempted' the Tribunal's findings and did considerably less than what had been recommended in the way of making Māori an official language. They were not happy, either, with the Government choosing to ignore the invitation to take up the question of Māori broadcasting, after the Royal Commission's report.[58]

As to any devolution of power: a liveable outcome would require from the Government that it understand the Māori aspirations to self-determination

---

[56] See for a brief and clear exposition of this: E. Schusky, *The Right to be Indian*, and see the essays in De Loria (ed.), *American Indian Policy in the Twentieth Century*.

[57] De Loria, *The Nations Within*, p. 244, and throughout.

[58] See Hughes, *Environmental Management and the Principles of the Treaty of Waitangi*.

and define the legal powers necessary for that in a way that would (more or less) satisfy all interested parties. It would also require that it provide finance for self-government. The road would be long and difficult because of the Pākehā ideology and also because the Government was committed to retrenchment in conditions where monies devoted to Māori, as Māori, had never been great. (From 1975 through 1985, Maori Affairs received between 0.61 per cent and 0.85 per cent of funding made available to Government departments.)[59] The road might even *disappear* if the Māori should (as was possible) disappear as an *ethnie*. In the meantime, the Māori's internal problems would be like those of the Amerindians: to define what 'behaviour and beliefs constitute acceptable expressions of tribal heritage . . . and invoke the conscience of the community to maintain those standards; to construct tribal identities and stable institutions to express them; and to avoid the invasion of the tribal communities by decultured aliens'.[60]

As between Māori and Pākehā, it would be a matter of scale, of limits, of agreements to live separately in some ways, but to retain a common membership of the civil state. Such agreements were doubtless what the fourth Labour Government was trying to achieve in collaboration and confrontation with its subjects, Māori and Pākehā alike. David Lange, the PM, and one who had been instrumental in encouraging debate on the Treaty at the Waitangi hui in 1985, always sought to encourage this way of thinking. In late 1988, he spoke typically of the process of consultation with Maoridom as not easy, nor likely to be short: 'If that means we have to talk ourselves into a state of exhaustion we are better off than working ourselves up into a state of belligerence.' He made it clear that he recognized that 'Maoris were fundamentally different from Europeans and fairness demanded that the Government deal with Maoridom differently'; and (not for the first time over the years) he expressed a certain dissatisfaction with the developing habit of seeking solution to the problems of differences through legal adjudication. He was reported as saying: 'To ask what the treaty meant in terms of everyday activities of the Government was not to be found in the courts. Complicated legal arguments about the meaning of the words of the Treaty would never solve any differences between European and Māori.'[61]

Time and gentleness were what he asked. But from time to time, certain Māori who were frustrated at the slowness of change and outraged at the continuing injustice, rejected the idea of limiting and negotiating their claims. They demanded absolute Māori sovereignty. Their legalism called up an equally legalistic response: the assertion of state sovereignty. It is to these assertions of sovereignty, inevitable in conditions where justice is thought not to be done, that we now turn in the final section of this book.

---

[59] Spoonley, *Racism and Ethnicity*, pp. 80–1.
[60] The problems defined by De Loria (ed.), *American Indian Policy in the Twentieth Century*, p. 253.
[61] H2:19/11/88.

Part Four
Justice and Sovereignty

Chapter 13
Absolute Māori Sovereignty

I

The Commonplaces of Māori Sovereignty

Ms Ripeka Evans of the Maori Economic Development Commission spoke in 1985 at a seminar on a Bill of Rights for New Zealand. She only slightly startled her audience of lawyers, academics, and social workers by telling them that 'at the crux of the debate about the Treaty of Waitangi is the question of Maori Sovereignty.' [1] She might well have added that the question was at the crux of the debate on reparative justice, or she might with equal justification have said that it lay at the crux of the debate on inequality. For the Māori, all paths in Māori-Pākehā debate led to the assertion of Māori sovereignty: to the assertion of tribal rangatiratanga, of mana Māori and of mana Māori motuhake. This chapter tries to explain and illustrate what this doctrine (or more precisely some of these various doctrines) were; for as the doctrines were crucial to Māori views as to what justice was and how to attain it, so they were crucial in calling up the response of the state in the assertion of its own absolute right to make and judge of law: to be the sole fountain of justice.

In the English language the claim to rangatiratanga might be rendered as the claim of Māori (and more precisely of tribal groups) that they should control their own lives within an ambit defined and limited by the extent of that rangatiratanga or chiefly authority which the Crown swore an oath to protect at Waitangi. In English, mana Māori in its political aspect might be best rendered as an intrinsic, inalienable right-and-duty to be Māori; 'mana Māori motuhake' asserted the same, with the added implication spelled out, that the right-and duty was to be *separately and distinctly* Māori. To assert intrinsic mana Māori motuhake was, among other things, to assert fundamental rights. They were rights, that is to say, not subservient to a higher end – the way a person's rights to life and liberty might be derived, for instance, from a belief that our lives are not our own to do with as we will, but that they are God's and that we are duty-bound to Him. Being Māori was *itself* the fundamental source of all duties. Maoriness laid duties on each inheritor, and it was these fundamental duties that were the source of all right claims against those who would encroach on mana Māori. Being Māori was thus a duty-to-be and a right-against. It was an inalienable right and an inescapable duty.

Such (translated into the language of rights and duties) was the core of the series of doctrines that in the early 1980s came to be known as 'Māori

---

[1] See Sharp *et al.*, *A Bill of Rights for New Zealand*, at p. 197.

Sovereignty'. My English translations might suggest to the reader that, by conflating rangatiratanga with mana Māori motuhake, the protaganists of Māori sovereignty could easily have come up with a doctrine of sovereignty much like that of the modern nation state, and could then have claimed that sovereignty for the Māori over and against the claims of the 'Pākehā' state. In fact, though their language often suggested it, few propagandists took the path clear through the terrain prepared by the modern nation state. Their claims were more limited.

What though, *are* the claims of the modern nation state? We read in Thomas Hobbes's *Leviathan* (1651) that among the essential governmental powers of sovereignty are the right to make laws, the right of judicature, the right to make war and peace, the right to appoint office-holders, the right to reward and punish, the right to honour subjects with titles and dignities, and the right to regulate what opinions are allowed to be propagated in public (allowed to be spoken 'to multitudes of people' says Hobbes). These rights (and there were others), he concluded, constituted 'the essence of sovereignty'. They 'are the marks, whereby a man may discern in what man or assembly of men, the sovereign power is placed, and resideth. For these are incommunicable, and inseparable': they may not be given up.[2] In Hobbes, this is a harsh and absolutist doctrine, and he pictures the sovereign power as Leviathan, the great sea monster of *Job*, Chapter 41. Leviathan had the right and power to coerce its subjects, together with the right to define the content of justice for the territories over which it ruled. The doctrine incorporated all men and women into the state as Leviathan's 'subjects'. Leviathan 'bore their body'; it 'represented' them. The people were 'subjects' and not 'citizens'. They were people under a ruler, not people equal each with each and sharing rule with one another. They were indeed imagined to have consented to subjection – to have 'authorised' it – but this gave them no rights at all against the sovereign. People had given up their rights to act for themselves (to act, that is, on their own 'authority') and Hobbes pictured the state as 'acting for' each individual. The state was thus incapable of 'injustice' to its subjects. 'For he that doth anything by authority from another' cannot 'injure' (that is, breach the rights) of that other. The sovereign *can* hurt or damage subjects, and can act evilly towards them; but cannot treat them 'unjustly'. All rights, the breach of which is injustice, flow from the sovereign. The content of justice is the same as the content of the law of which the sovereign state is the sole author. And the sovereign, Leviathan, will enforce his justice. Thus Hobbes quotes *Job*: 'None is so fierce that dàre stir him up. . . . When he raiseth himself up, the mighty are afraid. . . . Upon the earth there is not his like.'

Harsh the doctrine may be; but this is the doctrine of the sovereignty of the modern state which was to triumph over the three hundred years after Hobbes's death. Hobbes is the foremost political theorist of these states.[3]

---

[2] Hobbes, *Leviathan*, Chapter 18.

[3] See de Jouvenel, *Sovereignty*, for the history of sovereignty and its derivation in Europe.

It is now scarcely at issue that modern states have an indefeasible moral right to control the politics of their territories by means of law and if necessary by means of force. Without sovereignty there would be chaos. And this was the core doctrine of state brought to New Zealand by Captain Hobson.[4]

It was also (as we shall see in the next chapter) the doctrine of state pretty much accepted by the legal and political leaders of New Zealand in the 1980s. It is true they thought that sovereign powers might be devolved so as to be exercised by a wide range of institutions and groups; but in this they may not have differed much from Hobbes. It is hard to say what Hobbes meant by sovereign powers being 'incommunicable and inseparable', and the New Zealanders certainly believed that ultimately all legal power came from the state and could be recalled by it.

But this was not the doctrine typically espoused by the Māori on their own behalf. Mostly they did not claim Māori coercive and legal sovereignty over the territory of Aotearoa. Most argued rather for areas of immunity from Pākehā and Crown control, and for powers to administer in separated parcels, their lands and waters, their education, health and social welfare policies for themselves. They argued for their rangatiratanga. This was the point of arguing biculturalism in the sphere of governing power; it was the point of arguing multiculturalism or biculturalism in distributions; it was the point of their supporting (where they did) devolutionary policies. These would sustain and enhance mana Māori. But generally, Māori propagandists did not assert mana Māori as the prime and absolute authority in the land.

The assertion of Māori sovereignty was usually more a strategy of avoidance of Pākehā totalitarianism and the assertion of separate rights than the claim to rule everything. 'At present,' complained Mrs Betty Williams in an article in 1985, 'we have neither power nor freedom, and the direction we are heading is being manipulated by those who own the capital and technology as well as those who wield political power.' Māori sovereignty was, in her case, immunity from that manipulation.[5] Mr Derek Fox, a broadcaster, argued similarly for less than absolute Māori sovereignty in urging a greatly expanded Māori presence in the broadcasting media: 'Maori people have a right to arrangements which give expression to the "tino rangatiratanga" (authority) guaranteed in the Treaty of Waitangi. That implies "mana whakahaere" (control); Maori are not interested in being advisors or "colour consultants". We are ready to make our own way in the world, but we want to take our equitable share of resources with us to do so.'[6]

Many more examples of limited claims could be given. Professor Kawharu, for instance, contemplating a title for a collection of essays on the Treaty which he edited in 1988, at one time wished to call it 'sovereignty versus

---

[4] See the works of Mark Francis in the Finding List.

[5] Betty Williams, 'The Maori Struggle Against White Racism's Destruction of our Resources'. But she often tended to argue absolute sovereignty as well: and see also her *The Passage of Maori Land into Pakeha Ownership*.

[6] *The April Report*, iv. p. 484

rangatiratanga'. This was not to stress the clash between two sovereign authorities, one of which must extinguish the other. He rather held that the two were separate things, each with their own sphere of action, and that they could live together – that indeed they must. The book would show, he argued with the aid of the contributors, that the Treaty (and thus the sovereignty of the state) could 'have no meaning without the honest acceptance of . . . rangatiratanga'. It would also show that 'there is every reason to recognize rangatiratanga, every reason to reconcile it with the Crown's sovereignty, and no reason to think that that is not possible.'[7]

But because they saw two separate sources of authority in the state, Kawharu, Fox, and Williams can be seen in Hobbesian terms as proposing not only a limitation on state sovereignty, but a division of sovereignty. This was something quite inimical to a Hobbesian view of the matter. No man, Hobbes thought, could follow two masters; and he attacked (for instance) the pretensions of churches to a separate base of authority in society – to a 'divine right' separate from that of the state. Separate authority bases made men 'see double', 'forget their allegiance' and ultimately led to war. It was only by virtue of there being a single sovereign that a political system – a state – was a state at all.[8] And nothing less Hobbesian can be imagined, for instance, than Shane Jone's rehearsal of the idea of divided sovereignty at the same 1985 seminar as Ripeka Evans. He argued that if the Treaty in Māori had specified that the Māori gave up their mana ('the essence of sovereignty, that is, supreme authority') rather than simply kāwanatanga, they would never have signed. They *did* sign, and signing therefore did not give up their mana. They also retained their rangatiratanga ('power and authority', 'jurisdiction') over their 'lands, homes, estates, valued possessions and institutions'.[9] And that rangatiratanga was thought to be more impervious to sovereign legal control than the property rights of the Pākehā or the institutions they had constructed using the provisions of Pākehā law. Rangatiratanga was never given up; it was secured by fundamental contract; it could be alienated only with the consent of those to whom it belonged. It was in the Treaty that 'the two sovereign partners, the Crown and the Maori people, laid down the scope of each partner's law-making power'. The Crown's power over the Māori was thus radically limited by a Māori sovereignty that had been retained. Sovereignty was, in fact, divided.[10]

This notion of divided sovereignty was the one most often heard from Māori quarters; and it was the one that expressed the most authoritative Māori opinion on the matter. But these doctrines of divided sovereignty were not the only ones; and some Māori approached a Hobbesian understanding of what was at issue and adapted the Māori claims to that understanding.

[7] Kawharu (ed.), *Waitangi*, p. xviii.

[8] And see Hobbes's, *Leviathan*, Chapter 41 for 'subordinate' systems existing only by virtue of the sovereign's will.

[9] Jones in Sharp, *A Bill of Rights*, p. 211.

[10] Jones in Sharp, *A Bill of Rights*, p. 216. See also NZL16:19-25/11/88, Letter Moana Jackson.

They so extended the vague limits of mana and rangatiratanga as to entirely extinguish the pretensions of the sovereign state of New Zealand. Ranginui Walker once went so far as to say that he thought that what 'Maori nationalists' like Atareta Poananga were 'demanding' was 'Pakeha adherence to their part of the bargain [in the Treaty of Waitangi], namely recognition of the rangatiratanga (sovereignty) of the Maori over their lands, forests, fisheries and treasured possessions'.[11] Nothing more. But, if I am not mistaken, he was plainly wrong. The remainder of this chapter records the theoretical construction of a Māori state in the image of, and absolutely denying the legitimate existence of, the Pākehā state. Māori should become *Leviathan* and everyone, and all else subject.

The movement in thought towards absolutism could have gained momentum only in conditions where gross and persistent injustice was felt. The doctrine of absolute Māori sovereignty was the response to justice denied. In reclaiming rangatiratanga and mana Māori motuhake and fusing them into a new doctrine of state, the doctrine was built on the idea that reparations were due and had been denied; and it was built on feelings of outrage at current inequalities. It appealed to the commonplace in Māori political thought that the Pākehā had not only done particular wrongs in relation to the authority, lands, fisheries and villages of particular iwi and hapū, but (consequently) had done general wrong to te iwi Māori as a whole. The Pākehā had subverted Māori taonga and mana and rangatiratanga in general: had, purposefully or not, attempted to deprive the Māori of their culture – collectivist, ceremonial, Māori speaking, and at harmony with nature. Reparations by restitution of sovereignty was due. These were teachings, said one activist of the 1970s who had retired by the mid-1980s, that Māori had 'imbibed like porridge' from their youth.[12]

The doctrine of absolute sovereignty was often argued from the Treaty. Some, like the Arahua Maori Komiti of Hokitika, despite the growing Māori respect for the Treaty kept on arguing through the 1970s and 1980s that it was an attempt at fraud, was void for lack of widespread Māori consent, and that the 'indigenous' (that is, aboriginal) people had in fact retained their right to national self-determination.[13] And despite the many and routine assertions that in signing the Treaty the Māori had irrevocably committed themselves to recognizing the absolute sovereignty of the Crown, others denied or doubted this. In particular they asserted the consequences of the Treaty's violation to be the reawakening of the right of absolute Māori sovereignty. Whiti Te Ra Kaihau, speaking for Ngati Te Ata, told the Royal Commission on Social Policy for instance: 'Maoridom can with precision argue that the TRUST [set out in the Treaty] has been truly busted. That no amount of

---

[11] NZL64-6: 2/11/85.

[12] ASiii6:9/3/85.

[13] Arahura Maori Komiti, 'Self-Determination and Territorial Title for the Indigenous Maori People of Aotearoa', (July 1986), pp. 1-5. See also their similar submission to the parliamentary committee on the Treaty of Waitangi Bill, 1975: MA/ 75, 13a-21a.

patching up will ever repair it short of returning our Maori sovereignty.'
Tuaiwa Hautai/Eva Rickard put it: 'If the Treaty is not legal then I am
the ruler of this land. Simple as that.'[14]

But what could be said by appealing to the Treaty could equally be said
without reference to it. Some argued from the wording of the Maori
Declaration of Independence, recognized by the British in 1835, that the
Māori were then, and were recognized to be, a 'sovereign' nation, and that
they had never given up that sovereignty in the Treaty.[15] More fundamentally,
the proposition that sovereignty (mana and rangatiratanga) had not been given
to the Pākehā in 1840 was taken simply to express an eternal truth. Mana
and rangatiratanga never had been ceded, and could never be ceded. Cession
was a moral impossibility. This was the thought which lay behind the
declarations at the Turangawaewae and Waitangi hui that the Treaty did
not stand alone as a basis for Māori claims, that it was rather a symbol
of something pre-existent and continuing through time: the tangata whenua
status of the Māori and te mana Māori motuhake. The Treaty was not the
source of mana. Mana was the power and the glory which came from Māori
communal descent from 'Supreme Spiritual Beings', a descent reaffirmed by
groups of people in their tribal whakapapa, and a descent expressed in the
duty of each generation to guard and protect the land and the world in
which it lived, both for itself and for future generations: mana wairua; mana
tuku iho, mana tangata i mana whenua.[16]

Māori sovereignty then, survived; and the sovereignty of the state could
be forfeited if it failed to protect it. Ripeka Evans began her 1985 remarks
by quoting a speech of the Anglican Māori Bishop, Rev. Manuhuia Bennett,
to the effect that 'Maori Sovereignty became an issue immediately the first
musket shot was fired over the acquisition of land. There have been attempts
to re-establish it in every generation. It challenges the rest of New Zealand
either to put its house in order or vacate.' It could have been Bennett's
view that Aotearoa was Māori land, that the tangata whenua alone had
the right to rule there, and that Māori rights flowed from that condition,
not from the grace of the Pākehā state. Equally he might have believed
that the Pākehā were bound by the Treaty, and denying it, had forfeited
their right to live (and thus rule) in Aotearoa. Either thought would have
been possible, and both were expressed often enough. Whatever: it was
evidently his view that the Māori never gave up but always retained the
(sovereign) right to evict the Pākehā and would be justified in exercising
that right if the Pākehā did not act well. Reparative justice could demand
the restitution of Māori sovereignty, and in modern conditions, this would

---

[14] *The April Report*, ii, p. 44; iii (1), pp. 101, 253.

[15] See the Arahura reference above. On the declaration, see Buick, *The Treaty of Waitangi*, Chapter
1; Orange, *Treaty of Waitangi*, pp. 19-22.

[16] See Blank *et al.* (eds.), *He Korero*, p. 3, and Evans' gloss on it in Sharp, *A Bill of Rights*,
p. 198.

be a sovereignty indistinguishable in kind from the sort of sovereignty exercised by the Pākehā state.

This was the distinct movement in thought which could be clearly observed in the words and writings of Donna Awatere, Ripeka Evans, and Atareta Poananga at certain points of their lives in the 1980s. There were others who said much the same; but these three will serve as my examples of practitioners of a style of thought carried to its logical conclusions. They appealed to the commonplaces of Māori thinking, but the idea of absolute Māori sovereignty was normally tempered by a vivid appreciation, not only of the complex politics of a complex people, but of a complex relation, through a common history expressing itself often in family and blood ties, with the Pākehā. It was an idea tempered by the fact that it was not the *only* idea, and it expressed itself according to the temperament of Māori individuals and gatherings. The Waitangi Tribunal itself, in a remark not at all approved of by the Court of Appeal, spoke of Māori sovereignty thus: 'When European New Zealanders deny the Maori his "treaty rights"' . . . they deny their own right to be here too';[17] but this was not the Tribunal's only thought. In 1988, Koro Wetere found himself saying precisely the same thing as the Tribunal; but this was not his only thought either. When, too, Bruce Gregory told Parliament that he could not understand the unwillingness of Jim Bolger ever to contemplate differential legislation based on race, he came close to arguing absolute Māori sovereignty: 'I had to scratch my head and think that the Chinese governed China and the English tended to govern England. I suppose those different races have a right to govern. But for some unknown reason the Maori does not seem to exist as a race.'[18] Yet he did not always speak that way. Tipene O'Regan was reported by a worried MP as having written in the *National Geographic* September 1987: 'Our aims and wishes are basic. We had these islands, we lost them to the Europeans, and now we want them back.'[19] But O'Regan was not always so global in his ambitions.[20]

The three women had not always, and did not continue always, to think in this way. Perhaps – though I think they did – they did not quite think this way at all.[21] However, the thought is worth examining in its purer forms, if only to see the logic of mana Māori motuhake which could unfold in conditions of social and personal storm and stress, and in the face of the Pākehā state.

[17] Waitangi Tribunal, *Manukau Report*, p. 6.

[18] NZPD1:41, p. 6898, (22 Sept 1988).

[19] NZPD1:42, p. 6616, (15 Sept 1988).

[20] See his 'The Ngai Tahu Claim'.

[21] See, for example, Pat Hohepa's discussion of Awatere's not pursuing her theme fully enough to deliver a theory of the reassertion of sovereignty in *Craccum* 3: 16 April, 1985.

II

Absolute Māori Sovereignty: Awatere, Evans, and Poananga

What was new and what caused great public reaction, was, in Donna Awatere's case, the sheer systematic power of her exposition of absolute Māori sovereignty, seemingly unalloyed by any authorial doubts as to the truth of her vision. Her style and attitudes had been forged in the crucible of the radical politics of Nga Tamatoa in the 1970s, and in the heat and strife of anti-racist, feminist and left-wing politics. The anti-Springbok tour demonstrations of 1981 had radicalized many young Māori and Polynesians, and there were clear strains between them and the always-fractionated Pākehā left. For its part, the feminist movement (ideologically at odds within itself anyway as liberal and radical argued with socialist) was not clear what to make of the claims of Māori women that the source of oppression was not to be found in capitalism, or sexism, or men, but in Pākehā racism. Awatere's mission was to tell them. Embroiled in legal proceedings (and in a police cell) as a consequence of her protest activity in Hamilton, her passionate commitment to her cause led her to write (at very high speed and inspired by anger)[22] what was to become a series of articles entitled 'Maori Sovereignty'. The articles were published in 1982 and 1983 in the feminist periodical *Broadsheet*, addressed especially to an audience of feminists, trade unionists, anti-racist groups, left-wing radicals, and socialists. But in 1984 her articles, expanded slightly and revised as a book, reached a wider public. And her style and attitudes made an immediate impact. She began to feature in the mainstream press, where she was portrayed as good-looking and charming (she was once going to be an opera singer), articulate (she was a psychologist and educator) – and as a scary harbinger of violence.[23] Once a figure known only in left-wing political circles, she had become a national figure.

Awatere began, she later said, with the idea of arguing for biculturalism:

. . . because in those days, the early 80's, multiculturalism was the big issue. But the more I thought and researched and observed and thought again the more I could see clearly biculturalism is not possible. Because of something completely invisible to Pakeha people, the main currents of white culture. Things like individualism, materialism, alienation. Two certainties came through. Firstly that we cannot become a bicultural society because deep-rooted elements in Pakeha culture will prevent it and secondly that even if it were possible it is eminently undesirable, something like trying to mate with a barracouda . . . . I wanted to look at the basic cause of the difficulties that beset our people. To do that I did something that hadn't been

---

[22] See her account of the context in her 'Waiora: Health from a Maaori Point of View', p. 7.

[23] For example, ASii1, 4: 5/2/85.

done before. I looked at Pakeha society and culture. I didn't look at us at all. I looked at them.[24]

Inevitably though, it was not Pākehā alone that she studied: it was Pākehā as faced by Māori. She depicted the confrontation as one of war. 'The war began 140 years ago. New combatants have come and gone. The style of battle, the place of battles has changed. It has entered a new phase.' It was now total war. 'In our response we must break the habit of seeking to rectify grievances one at a time and instead formulate a battle plan based on full knowledge of the battle conditions as the confrontation of two ways of life where one side determines the rules.'

The war was for the 'return' of what had been taken – *never* surrendered', but taken 'by trickery, by numbers, by force, by accepting no opposition, by chauvinism, and by cultural imperialism'. What had been taken was Māori sovereignty, mana Māori Motuhake. 'Maori sovereignty is the Maori ability to determine our own destiny and do so from the basis of our land and fisheries. In essence Maori sovereignty seeks nothing less than the acknowledgement that New Zealand is Maori land, and further seeks the return of that land.'[25] Nor could the Māori *not* fight for the restitution of sovereignty and what it guaranteed. The battle called to all generations who lived in a timeless unity. Those who oppressed one generation, oppressed all. 'To the Maori, the past is the present, is the future. Who I am and my relationship to everyone else depends on my whakapapa, on my lineage. . . . One needs one's ancestors therefore to define one's present . . . . It is easy to feel the humiliation, anger and sense of loss which your tipuna felt. And to take up the kaupapa they had. This means the grievances of the past, of one's tipuna, are the grievances of the Maori person in the present.'[26]

Moreover, Māori sovereignty overrode any other principle of governmental legitimacy or organization. Aotearoa was irreducibly Māori. 'White liberals . . . can accept that Azania [The Republic of South Africa] belongs to black people. This is probably because blacks are in a majority; and whites are so keen on majority rule. In New Zealand this means that all is well. Justice is being seen to be done. *Who says?* Blacks should have control of Azania because it is their country. Maoris should have control of New Zealand because it is our country.' And: 'who the *hell* gave British and European immigrants the right to take over another place, whether is is Zimbabwe, Azania or Aotearoa?'

Awatere could just imagine it possible that Māori and Pākehā might have lived together: 'at the very least one could relate to a richness, fairness, and Aotearoaness that included the Maori'. But this she judged impossible

[24] Debbie Rewhiti, 'Maori Sovereignty', *Broadsheet* (Nov 1984), pp. 13-15 at 13. And see Awatere's 'Address to the Royal College of Psychiatrists, Rotorua, 29 March 1984', printed in *Craccum*, 10 April 1984, pp. 12-13.

[25] Awatere, *Maori Sovereignty*, pp. 9, 10, 13.

[26] Awatere, *Maori Sovereignty*, p. 54.

in fact because of the contempt and hatred that the Pākehā had demonstrated they felt for the Māori: in their disregard of the Treaty, in the infamous injustices of the 'Land Wars, of Parihaka, of Bastion Point, of the Waitangi protests'. It was demonstrated in continuing racial prejudice and the desire of whites to separate themselves from Māori, and it was also demonstrated in current inequalities. Awatere rehearsed the evidence, concluding that Māori women, doubly despised because of their sex as well as race, had the worst of it all. 'The irony of the present situation is that white people see themselves as essentially moral, as essentially just and fair people. But the only justice there is in this country is for white people; *only* for white people.'[27]

In those conditions of past and continuing wrong, with no reparations and no cessation, Māori sovereignty could be the only hope for justice. 'Justice for Maori women doesn't exist without Maori sovereignty.'[28] 'There is no justice while Maori sovereignty is not acknowledged, until Maori land, *all* Maori land is returned to us.'[29] The only right the Pākehā might have had would be, according to Māori custom, as manuhiri, or visitors. If they had respected the customs of the people they might have been welcome. But 'all immigrants to this country are . . . rude visitors who have by force and corruption imposed visitors' rules upon the Maori'.[30] In brief, Pākehā injustice demanded the restitution of the Māori ability to exercise a sovereignty that had never been extinguished.

Mediatorial Māori tended to say there was something 'un-Māori' about Awatere's extreme development of her thesis. And, even laying aside her remarkable aggression which ran counter to Māori customs of politeness, there were indeed marked European elements in it. There was, for instance, a romantic rejection of the modern west of a kind visible in Europe since the German of the *sturm und drang* (storm and stress) of the 1770s. She exhibited a degree of nostalgia of an arcadian past of limited resources and limited appetites. And the whole was mixed with modern Marxist and feminist considerations.

But her protest was not only with *elements* of a European culture. It was more fundamentally with the total milieu of European-inspired existence. In its essence, it was a Māori argument. No other people could quite make it. Certainly no one but a Māori could have made such a non-negotiable demand to a world which could not answer it. Rejecting contemporary feminist concerns, she cried: 'Look, we are *Maori* before anything. What does cancer, sexuality, rape, individual survival, death, or anything mean without the survival of the Maori as a Nation? It is empty. Meaningless.'[31] Awatere's was not a relaxed and confident Māori voice. It was hardly the voice of a person serenely enjoying the benefits of a culture and an ethnicity. It was

[27] Awatere, *Maori Sovereignty*, pp. 20, 24, 27, 32, 39; and see Part One generally.

[28] Awatere, *Maori Sovereignty*, p. 44.

[29] Awatere, *Maori Sovereignty*, p. 20.

[30] Awatere, *Maori Sovereignty*, p. 35.

[31] Awatere, *Maori Sovereignty*, p. 45.

the voice of a modern intellect, devoid of an easy faith in living, transmissable traditions, and entirely lacking the serenity and balance which accompany that easy faith. Her sayings were informed and corrupted by a western world she now largely hated. Hers was without doubt a Māori voice, very much in touch with a widely and deeply shared reality.

Much the same themes were to be heard from Awatere's friend of the early 1980s, Ripeka Evans.

When Evans was appointed to the Broadcasting Corporation in 1987 as a cultural advisor, she was remembered by her adversaries as a Cuban-trained ideologist, if not terrorist, of the late 1970s and early 1980s.[32] In fact she did not practise terrorism though her views had a Cuban edge to them – that is, if to be a Cuban revolutionary is to embrace the idea of the overthrow of the state without either waiting for the appropriate economic conditions or without convincing the populace.[33] She was actually rather more devoted to aggressive public argument and demonstration of her views. A veteran of the Waitangi Action Committee campaigns against the celebration of Waitangi Day and of the Springbok Tour demonstrations, for a time in 1983-1984 at the forefront of the Kotahitanga movement, Evans developed views typical of the 1980s: tribal reparationism, Māori nationalism, New Zealand egalitarianism, and optimistic revolutionism. Taken together, for instance in an article of hers, 'Aftermath of Waitangi', which appeared in 1982, they could add up to an argument for absolute Māori sovereignty. There she stressed rather more than her friend and collaborator the conviction that Māori sovereignty was in line with a world movement of liberation. She saw the Māori rather more in accord with the international doctrines of the rights of 'indigenous peoples' which were being elaborated in the corridors of the United Nations.[34] She stressed rather less (though she was far from denying) the uniqueness of the Māori, rather more their sharing the plight of those aboriginal races who had been the victims of white colonialism. And where Awatere spent much time setting the terms on which Pākehā might collaborate with the Māori in the emerging new state, Evans philosophized rather more on the quisling role of the Māori collaborator who sustained the Pākehā 'system'.

Noting that Māori protest of the 1970s seemed to be about two separate things: (firstly) 'civil rights' to language, to Māori production units in radio and TV, to justice in courts, to equal opportunities, housing and health; and rights (secondly) to land – she held that 'Common to both areas of protest is the element of "Maori dispossession".' The Māori now had 'virtually no land, little language, no justice and no white or Maori education'. As with

---

[32] The latest accusation, I think is in NZL12:7/5/88, Letter G. R. McDonald.

[33] See her account of herself in 'Rebecca Evans'.

[34] On which see Knight, 'Territory and People or People and Territory?'; Barsh, 'Indigenous Peoples: an Emerging Object of International Law'; Kingsbury, 'The Treaty of Waitangi: Some International Law Aspects', pp. 134-49; Mulgan, 'Indigenous Rights and the Legitimacy of Former Governments'.

Awatere, so with Evans – justice in reparation demanded Māori sovereignty. It was not, she argued, a new demand. It lay behind ' "Te Mana Maori Motuhake" – "Kotahitanga" – etc.' But 'what we have lacked is a decisive drive towards that goal and a national involvement based on the demand for Maori sovereignty'.

Now Māori sovereignty *was* essential, for the drive to equality which might otherwise have provided a just solution to dispossession had not worked. 'To all in the struggle and some who have left I mean no disrespect to you personally to say that to a large degree these struggles have failed.' Accommodation had not and could not work. It was:

> . . . a hangover from the white-wash philosophies of the racist Hunn and Maori Affairs Reports of the 1960s and the "well-gone-overboard" belief of brown-skinned Pakehas – that is, the belief that a Maori could still be Maori and succeed in the system – straddle two roads at the same time. Never will it happen. . . . . Academia successfully dressed-down Maori demands so that Maori language was taught from the top down. The hidden intention was to make Maori language a language of the bourgeoisie and a weapon for the middle and ruling class to use against the Maori people.

As to the Polynesian Preference Schemes at law schools, they had produced 'more Maori and Pacific Island lawyers who either don't want to do anything for Maori and Pacific Island causes or want to harm such causes'. 'One of the most horrifying aspects of the PIG [Police Investigation Groups] patrols which Nga Tamatoa, Polynesian Panthers and ACORD conducted was that now ten years later most of the Polynesian Panther members are Pigs [police officers]!!' As in the USA, the 'affirmative action type approach gives you stoolies and house-niggers'.

If the civil rights campaign had failed, so had the campaign for land rights that began with the Great Land March of 1975. There was no common aim that united the protestors. Each group had acted separately pursuing its own grievances: Takaparawha, Awhitu, Horowhenua, Tauranga. But the Cuban voyage of 1978 had taught her the importance of unity and a way of seeing the Māori struggle as part of a world struggle.

> We met and lived with the Palestine Liberation Organisation. After exchanging stories about our respective struggles many long discussions took place about the similarity of both struggles. In many instances there is an identical comparison to be made with the position of the Palestinian people. Maori people are dispossessed people – we live in a country which is ours but we have no recognition of that right . . . One of the best lessons I learnt in Cuba was the necessity to articulate long term revolutionary goals in fundamental language. Living with the PLO gave us the opportunity to articulate the aim of fighting for the complete return of Aotearoa and have that aim taken seriously.

A romantic reparationism, even quest for vengeance, would bind the Māori people in the struggle for the restoration of sovereignty. They must come together as tanagata whenua. They might have to work with 'whites'; but 'there is no revolution of indigenous people in the world that is led by foreign people'. So the Māori must lead, and 'if whites do not accept their role as mutineers of their own system then they clearly place themselves away from our aims and in the camp of the enemy. It is whites who confront the first contradiction which they brought to our country . . . That contradiction was the theft of our land.'

Nor was Evans against utu. 'There are thousands of our ancestors who were killed and died an unjust death. *"It is with vengeance that we seek to stand tall and with pride in our own land and in our own country"*,' she concluded.[35] And it was this threat of retaliation which was to haunt her career from then on as she went on to work for Māori causes within 'the system'.

The third woman, Atareta Poananga, took the opposite route - out of the system, into confrontation with it. After an unhappy career in the Department of Foreign Affairs, still the élite Government department in the early 1980s, she suffered what she called the 'death of an honorary white',[36] was eased out from there and became a union organizer and polemicist for Māori rights. It is hard to be precise about *her personal* thinking, because she continually insisted that she spoke, in Māori style, not for herself but for those with whom she was tied: Te Ahi Kaa. But she developed much further than Awatere or Evans the idea that the Māori shared the same colonial oppression as indigenous peoples throughout the world; and with her husband, Pat Hohepa (who already had them), she made contacts with Amerindians, with the United Nations Committee on Indigenous Peoples, and with other 'fourth world' groups. She shared with Awatere the passionately believed thought that, were the Māori culture to perish, life would be worthless. Like Evans, she philosophized on Māori collaborators. Like both Awatere and Evans, and supported by Te Ahi Kaa, she held that Māori sovereignty should be fostered and restored.

Again, as in the thought of Awatere and Evans, the argument for absolute sovereignty was not the only one Poananga could make; and nor was absolute Māori sovereignty all that she could see. So that, for instance, alongside her support for the Fijian revolution, and her stronger words, must be placed the fact that she and Hohepa travelled in late 1987 to the USA to study the forms and problems of limited self-government among the tribes, hoping to bring some help to Waima on the Hokianga where they lived, witnesses to great unemployment and distress as well as hope for a better life. But at the extreme, she presented the case at issue as that of *Māori* v *Pākehā*, her language was the totalistic and inflamed language of injustice, her arguments were unrelievedly reparationsist, and she demanded the practical restitution of absolute Māori sovereignty.

It was with these ideas in mind that she had travelled to Melbourne in May 1985 to deliver a paper on the rights of indigenous peoples to an academic conference held by ANZAAS (The Australian and New Zealand Association

---

[35] Evans, 'Aftermath of Waitangi – Building a National Movement'.

[36] See Poananga, 'Death of an Honorary White', *Broadsheet* (April 1986), pp. 13–19.

for the Advancement of Science). She believed that the Māori case was the case of all 'first peoples': those who were in their places in the world first. 'Many original peoples of colonised lands were referred to as Fourth World but call themselves First Nations.'[37] She argued against the colonization, both physical and mental, of such people. She spoke of Pākehā taking the land, and of near genocide of the Māori. She argued that the Māori had never ceded sovereignty in the Treaty, and she argued that in any case the Treaty did not bind the Māori because it had never been 'ratified'. Speaking thus, she was baited by rednecks in the audience,[38] and was reported in the New Zealand media as replying that the first European settlers in Aotearoa were the 'riff raff, flotsam and jetsam of British culture'. The general reaction was immediate and hostile. On her return she made it clear to television audiences that she meant what she said: that the Māori people were tangata whenua, the Pākehā unwelcome manuhiri.[39]

The complaints were many and vocal, including over one hundred to the Race Relations Conciliator as to breach of section 9a of the Race Relations Act; and, as in the case of Donna Awatere, a long string of newspaper and magazine articles followed, almost all of them expressing the obvious agitation of their readerships. She remained famous through 1987 and 1988. She was a symbol along with Mr Syd Jackson and Mrs Titewhai Harawira, fellow members of Te Ahi Kaa, of extreme Maori nationalism.[40] The best public expositions of her ideas were to be found not in the popular media however, where she was subjected to unrelievedly hostile questioning and analysis, but in the pages of *Broadsheet* in 1986 and 1987.

In 'The Death of an Honorary White', published in 1986, the burden of her case against the Pākehā was that they had occupied and colonized not only Aotearoa but the Māori people themselves. As Aotearoa was to be decolonized, so were individuals to be decolonized: only with extreme difficulty though. She followed Franz Fanon (the Mozambican psychiatrist and political theorist who worked in Algeria supporting the independence fighters) in stressing the 'psychological emasculation' of the 'indigenous people'. 'You are socialised from birth into believing everything Maori is inferior. You see there is only one destiny – to be white, to succeed in white things.' Many Māori stayed that way, 'auxiliaries' to the Pākehā system, 'uncle Toms', 'house niggers', 'brown Pakeha'. 'Individual ambition, awards, knighthoods, and status in society' were a continual threat to Maoriness.

Like Awatere, Poananga thought of biculturalism both as a public and outward division of rule and (within each person) as a privately-constructed

---

[37] Quoted from Geoff McDonald, *The Kiwis Fight Back*, pp. 28-63.

[38] Her account to me soon after the event.

[39] A record of these matters in *Metro*, vol. 5, no. 57, pp. 44-58 (March 1986).

[40] Jackson (author of regular articles in *Metro*) was a visitor in search of aid to Colonel Gadaffi's Libya in 1988, and Harawira was at the centre of a battle for the control of the Whare Paia (a Maori Mental Health Unit) at Carrington Hospital in Auckland from which she was dismissed in March 1989.

sharing of identity. Like Awatere too, she thought both public and private biculturalism to be impossibilities. 'White supremacy' expressed in the idea of 'one people, one nation', 'will *always* deny biculturalism or real power-sharing'. And no individual could be both Maori and Pakeha. Also in *Broadsheet*, Poananga criticized Witi Ihimaera, her ex-colleague in Foreign Affairs, for portraying it as a not unattractive possibility (or at least unavoidable necessity) in his novel, *The Matriach*. She argued that: 'The inextricable relationship between Maori and Pakeha is a parasitical one, blandly called biculturalism, but in reality [it is] the visitor feeding off the host.' And she attacked Māori 'auxiliaries' for joining the 'white male club', which 'crosses a broad spectrum of Maori male leadership from almost all Maori academics (mistakenly named as "radical") to the "Sirs" and recognised Uncle Toms of the Maori Council, bureaucrats in the public service and other Pakeha-created auxiliary organisations.'[41]

One must choose. She for herself was now (by 1986):

. . . free of the colonised mind – proud to assert and insist on recognition of my culture, values and traditions, of living and feeling totally Maori, to insist I will no longer be a black skin under a white mask. To reject biculturalism and instead insist upon Mana Maori Motuhake or Maori self-determination . . . I am proud to be part of a Maori nationalist movement which has existed in its various forms for the 150 years of Pakeha occupation. This movement questions the very legitimacy of Pakeha rule. We are tangata whenua and our way is the only way. We are growing stronger culturally, economically and politically. Our minds and thought processes have been decolonised. Integrating our needs with the colonisers' institutions (biculturalism) we recognise now as a fatally flawed philosophy – another attempt at cultural subjugation. The Pakeha have been here for over a century and have *never* shared power . . . We must move past political, economic and social assimilation and develop instead Maori nationalism as a positive assertion of a people who were never conquered. Many Pakeha's response will be anger, outrage and an affronted cultural arrogance that we have chosen *our own* separate path. So be it. We will turn over a new page in history. We know time is on our side. Our population is increasing so that by the year 2000 we will be 30%. We know we will reclaim our heritage as tangata whenua. The process is long but our destiny is clear.

Poananga concluded her 'Death of an Honorary White' with a Māori proverb: 'Time will see the return of the mana, the land, the people.'[42]

But what more precisely would be returned in this imagined future, and on what grounds? A long TV interview in April 1988 gave some of the answers to a nervous audience.[43] 'Infinite power' – mana Māori motuhake – would be returned. The 'two worlds' of Māori and Pākehā, in 'fatal conflict' could never coexist. Pākehā brought the cancer of their society with them, a cancer 'related to their white skin'. Without sovereignty, Māori would never achieve 'parity' in all institutions. Devolution was not enough;

[41] Poananga, 'The Matriarch: Takahia Wahine Toa,' *Broadsheet* (Dec 1986), pp. 24-8; (Jan-Feb 1987), pp. 25-9

[42] *Broadsheet* (April 1986), pp. 13-19.

[43] *Encounter*, TV1, 22 April 1988.

'collaborators' and kūpapa ('crouchers': like those who had fought with the Pākehā in the internal wars of the 1860s and 1870s) were repudiated and a warrior ancestry claimed. Each tribe would decide what should be done in its own area, for 'we are not a Maori people. . . . We are Maori tribes.' 'We were the first people of this land,' she insisted. And it came to this: that the first people (historically) now ought to be the first people (morally, politically, and legally).

She was, in all this, repeating the demand she had made at the ANZAAS conference:

What we had in the past we want in the future . . . in the end our goal is Maori control of Aotearoa . . . *All* land is Maori land – not Crown land or private land or Maori incorporation land . . . these titles are a legal fiction. We are saying we want *all* the land back . . . We want the whole of Aotearoa back under Maori control as it had been for 2,000 years – 50 generations. It's only been the last six that we haven't had control.

These then were claims to absolute Māori sovereignty. Extreme in themselves (in the senses: 'not widely held to be persuasive' and also 'unmitigated by countervailing considerations') they were the mirror image of the extreme right-wing Pākehā claim: 'one land, one language, one culture, one goal, one people'. There were important differences: the Māori claim to sovereignty in the state emerged not from a history of triumph but from one of suffering and a feeling of injustice; the Pākehā ideology did not so much argue for the predominance of its views as to assume them; and while the Māori claim to absolute sovereignty was sheer political fantasy, the Pākehā ideology could very easily have been put into practice. But they had this in common: both extreme views denied the possibility of justice except in a homogeneous society. Both denied the possibility of doing justice where there were competing *ethnie* and separate 'cultures'. Both held that in substance there should be one way of doing things and one way of living in Aotearoa/ New Zealand. Both in effect claimed the hegemony of one culture – of one *ethnie* over the other. Though the right-wing Pākehā claim was not put in *terms* of sovereignty, and rather assumed the power of the state to act on its principles, the outcome was the same. In effect there were two claims to two (contradictory) sovereignties. And for *either* sovereign power to act along the lines urged by its supporters would be to deny the substance of what many subjects thought to be just.

That is the logic of the demand for justice in conditions where it was thought (as some did) that there ought to be a common conception of justice shared by the two peoples. For if it were thought (as it was) that the conception ought to be something like the Pākehā ideology of individual equality of opportunity and equality under the law, then injustice would be thought to be done. According to the Pākehā way of thinking there would of course be none at all; but those who did not share that way of thinking would feel and smart under what *they* took to be injustice. It would naturally also be thought that the injustice was enforced by an alien and evil sovereign power, however 'democratic' it might seem to the majority. If, on the other hand, it were a Māori conception of justice that were to be insisted upon – something along the lines of recognizing Māori rights to exercise rangatiratanga separate from the Pākehā – then equally, injustice would be thought to be done. The Māori would not see it that way, but the Pākehā would; and they in turn would deny any sovereign the power to enforce such a kind of justice.

It will by now be clear that the logic of such a discourse on justice and injustice was played out in the real world of argument. But it would be a mistake to think that the issue as to sovereignty was only one between Māori and Pākehā conceptions of justice and the authority to enforce them. A certain number of articulate citizens may have seen things that way, but the state did not at all. Its claims to sovereignty simply did not take ethnicity into account: it was not an ethnic but a nation state. There might be two peoples but there was one nation. Made legitimate in its origins by the British sovereign, and worthy of continued support because it embodied a democracy, the sovereignty of the state transcended (and ought to regulate) the differing conceptions of justice held by all its subjects. So, and to bring the historical part of this book to a conclusion, what kind of sovereignty *did* the state of New Zealand and its defenders in fact claim and assert? Was it absolute or limited? And on what grounds was it argued that the state possessed a sovereignty that stood for the political culture of the territory as a whole – that incorporated all its subjects, Māori and Pākehā, indifferently?

Chapter 14
Putting Bounds to the Wairua, to Mana and Rangatiratanga: The Assertion of State Sovereignty

I

Legal Sovereignty

It will now be evident that governing circles in New Zealand found themselves in the 1980s operating in conditions of extreme uncertainty in Māori-Pākehā and Māori-Crown relations. It must be said immediately that this did not present an unmitigated challenge to them and to the legitimacy of Government. The linguistic, conceptual, and policy-forming uncertainty, besides simply expressing ignorant confusion, was very largely an expression of a calm willingness and co-operative agreement not to push things – a willingness to act out a cool, and not a hot, politics. Confusion, silence, and unclarity were not only modes of tactfulness; they were also the expression of much agreement and a mutual commitment to a joint life. But the uncertainty also expressed concrete, commonly-sensed disagreements between the peoples. It bore a tinge of danger as well as being reassuring. Violence was often mentioned as a possible consequence of continued injustice. Of more immediate concern, it was made obvious to all that the state as it was constituted and as it operated was hardly the object of devotion of many Māori and that it stood to lose the adherence of still more.

In the event, the reaction of governing circles to all the judgements expressed as uncertainty – the confusion and the cordiality and the fear – was the same. Not only did they emphasize the importance of a negotiated, political solution to Māori claims; they also reasserted the sovereignty of the state. This was not surprising. For where there is no unforced and easy agreement in a political society, then decision may have to be taken as to what rules are to be made and followed. They have of necessity to be made when life cannot go on without them, notably where there is danger to the state in not deciding. And it often seemed to law-makers and law-enforcers in New Zealand that that unfortunate condition, if not upon them, was not far off. So they insisted upon the absolute sovereignty of the state.

Absolute sovereignty is a simple enough concept. It is the legally unchallengeable supreme and unlimited power to make, declare, enforce, and administer the law and policy under which a political society lives. And this is precisely what was claimed. But the simplicity of sovereignty in idea is often matched by the difficulty of observing its instances in the concrete conditions of social and political life. Sovereign power is after all a characteristic of an organizational system – of a whole form of life – not (as Hobbes seems to have thought) of a single part of it. Sovereignty permeates political life: hence Rousseau's remark that it was the incorporated people who are to be called 'the state' when they are passive, 'the sovereign' when active (and when dealing with outsiders, a 'power').[1] Its powers do not necessarily lodge in one person, or one institution alone; it may be that one institution has supreme authority in one area of activity, but not in others. Sovereignty informs all official institutions in their mutual relations; and its location is to be discovered in the commonly-followed prescriptions of law and lawful practices in particular societies. Hence there are divisions of power between executive, legislative, and judicial arms of Government; sharings of legislative power between assemblies, federations, and so on. There are 'rules of recognition'[2] by which we may know its location: which court is to judge, which assembly is to legislate on this or that matter, which army is the state's and so on.

Nevertheless it is a characteristic of systems of sovereignty that they are, so to say, 'closed' and 'hierarchical'. They are closed in that one cannot appeal outside the legal rules accepted as valid within them, and one cannot claim that breach of an extrinsic rule invalidates an act of the system. The act may be (extrinsically to the system) wrong, iniquitous, sinful, and unjust. It may breach (say) natural law, old customs which have fallen into disuse, common sense morality, the word of God or whatever; but it is not illegal and it does not contravene legal justice. Hence Hobbes's saying that the word of the sovereign was the sum of justice; that a sovereign could not breach the law of which he or they were the sole authors. Closure further suggests the hierarchical nature of sovereignty: its theorists have typically insisted that no law within the system, and no institution within it, may limit or bridle sovereign power. In the end there must be a final arbiter, or else legal life would be impossible because of conflict between rival adjudicators. And there must be, at the summit, a supreme legislator who can give laws to the arbitrators both to meet new exigencies and to solve problems caused by the conflict of laws.[3]

Because sovereignty can be seen as both diffused within a state and yet hierarchically distributed, there are obviously difficulties in deciding upon its location – difficulties which can be solved only by complex technical arguments in law and philosophy which defy the common sense of ordinary citizens. But at least this may be said, that to claim sovereignty is sometimes to assert the right of a state, over and against the claims of other states, to rule itself or a colony or a dependency. That is a matter of external relations and is, for instance, what was mainly at issue when the British claimed sovereignty over New Zealand. They aimed to exclude the potentially

---

[1] Rousseau, *The Social Contract and the Discourse*, Book 1, Chapter 6. p. 175.

[2] Hart, *The Concept of Law*, Chapter 6.

[3] An account based on Goldsmith, 'Hobbes's "Mortall God" '; and Hart, *The Concept of Law*, Chapter 4.

competing claims of France and the United States. And the issues were those of international (as opposed to domestic) law. The arguments about sovereignty in New Zealand/Aotearoa in the 1980s were, however, hardly to do with external relations at all. They were rather to do with the internal constitution of the state. And they did not only concern domestic *legal* questions as to the location of the powers of legal sovereignty and how it might happen to be diffused among the people acting in capacities authorized by law. They also concerned the foundations and justification of the very existence of sovereignty, and the reasons why the legal system ought to bind the inhabitants of Aotearoa/New Zealand. Was it right that the legal system which actually existed should harbour the Leviathan, the great sea monster who was king over all the children of pride? Was it right that the legislators, judges, and local bodies constituted by law should deliver justice to the Māori? Was it right that the state's schools and prisons and welfare institutions should do so too?

These were the questions the Māori were asking, both directly and in their assertions of Māori sovereignty.

New Zealand governing circles hardly hesitated in their answers. They were very definite in their views and very easy to understand. The idea was that it was for the political process – in Cabinet and Parliament in particular – to decide the fate of Māori claims to both reparative justice and to equity. It had the moral authority as representing the people at large to do so. Democratic right was the foundation of political power. The governing institutions also had legal right. Together with the law courts, which were instituted to interpret and enforce its laws, Parliament as the supreme legislative power had the legal authority, devolved originally from Britain but now as legislator in an autochthonous system, to do so. And in the end – it was hardly said but it was known – the state apparatus had the coercive power of the army, the police and the bulk of its citizens to back up its decisions.

The legal fraternity's views, put forward by scholars as well as in the courts were not much different from those of the bureaucrats and politicians. The legists added a filigree of legal learning to the overall structure and complicated the detail of its design. They concentrated rather less on the political purposes and justifications of sovereignty, rather more on its characteristics of closure and hierarchy. So that to examine the legal doctrines first is to appreciate better the simplicity of what the politicians said. It was in any case the work of the courts, especially the Court of Appeal in the *New Zealand Maori Council v the Attorney General*, which most influenced debate.

The subtlest of the independent legal theorists on the issue were Professor Jock Brookfield in 1985 and Dr Paul McHugh in 1989. Both of them sympathetic to many of the Māori claims (McHugh especially so), in the end they argued the supremacy of the state, and the hierarchy and closure of its system of law.

In a widely-publicized address on the occasion of his inauguration to the

Chair of Constitutional Law at Auckland University in late 1985, Brookfield diagnosed a crisis of 'legitimacy' in the Pākehā state.[4] Quoting Donna Awatere and Jane Kelsey (a Pākehā legal theorist), he spoke of 'a crisis in the right of governments to rule'. It was not this Labour Government, nor was it the National Government before it, whose title to rule was at issue. The moral title of *any* government must be defective, the critics informed him, because all New Zealand governments came to power according to legal rules contained in a legal system, the operation of which denied Māori rights.

Brookfield was not unsympathetic to the idea that mistaken legal adjudication in New Zealand had denied Māori what should have been their legal rights. He followed emphatically current legal scholarship, notably that of Paul McHugh, in thinking the Māori correct in asserting that New Zealand judges *had* systematically and wrongly (as a matter of law) denied them. And he thought that reparations, of a nature and quantum to be decided by common sense, were due. As a lawyer, he differed from the Māori in thinking that the rights denied were not Treaty rights[5] – they were rather the aboriginal rights that had indeed been recognized in the Treaty but were not dependant for their legal validity on it. Still, legal rights had been violated, and observing that many Māori were coming to think that the state had no moral claim on them at all, he clearly sympathized with their conclusions. For how could a state, he might have asked, governing badly, claim a title to rule? How could a tyrant in the exercise of power ever be thought to be other than a tyrant with a defective title?

But Brookfield did not intend to side with those who impugned the legitimacy of the state. He rather thought that the aspersions on its legitimacy made it prudent for the sovereign state to judge and legislate in accord with the temper of the times. He argued that sovereign power depended in fact for its 'legitimacy' – maybe for its very existence – on the continuing consent of people. Perhaps he thought consent was even a morally necessary condition, and that people who did not consent to the state's power over them were not morally bound to obey it at all. He did not say. But he *did* think obviously that consent represented the condition of mind in which people *thought* they should obey the state. It was also the condition of mind in which people agreed to a large extent with the policies of the governments the regime produced from time to time. So the goal of the state must be to attain and maintain the consent of the disaffected. Accordingly Brookfield suggested that the state should ensure that the aboriginal rights of the Māori were made legal tender by the sovereign's willing them – or enough of them to settle the practical issue of consent – as law. Thus the fishing rights and rights of land occupation and use that used to be recognized by colonial

---

[4] Hiil, 3:9/11/85, reporting his inaugural address. The text was revised in 1988 (unimportantly for my purposes) and published in his 'The Constitution: The Search for Legitimacy'.

[5] It was possible, but not usual, for lawyers to think that they were (or should be) Treaty rights: see Hackshaw, 'Nineteenth Century Notions of Aboriginal Title', and David V. Williams, 'Te Tiriti O Waitangi'.

courts in the states that descended from Britain and were recognized in New Zealand, at least in the 1840s, must be re-examined and perhaps reaffirmed.

As to the Treaty of Waitangi, Brookfield argued that it must be put at the centre of their claims to legitimacy by the governing powers. The legitimacy of the state could in fact be revived only in a process of re-examining, reinterpreting and re-enforcing it. 'The legitimacy of the Constitution . . . rests to an essential extent on reconciling the authority of the New Zealand Crown and Parliament developed from the kawanatanga ceded in the first article . . . with the rangatiratanga and mana of the Maori which should have been preserved under the second article.' The problem was that of 'reconciling' these things 'within the legal order'. It might help, as the White paper on a Bill of Rights proposed, to 'recognise' and 'affirm' Treaty rights, 'applied to circumstances as they arise so that effect may be given to [the Treaty's] true spirit and intent'. That much at least would be necessary to win the hearts and minds of the Māori; and together with the recognition of aboriginal rights, it would go some way to recognizing 'the place of the Maori people as the indigenous people of the country'. In a revised version of his address written in 1988, Brookfield, while lamenting that the Constitution Act of 1986 had not provided a substitute for what it had repealed – section 71 of the old Constitution Act (1852) which had provided for Māori self-government in Māori districts – was nevertheless pleased to note the legal revolution which had begun to write the 'principles of the Treaty of Waitangi' into statute.

Brookfield's was a call for legal reform, and a welcome to it. But it is worth stressing that he always insisted that such a process of redefining and re-enforcing both aboriginal and Treaty-derived Māori rights would have to be done by the established courts of law. He expressed no doubts, and gave little reasoning, for what he assumed: the necessity of a sovereign legal system in the state and the existence of that sovereignty in the lawful institutions of the actual state in New Zealand. Where he had argued with learning, sophistication, and practical good sense how the sovereign state should act, he did not so much argue as simply assert these other essential elements in this case.

As to why there must a sovereign, Brookfield's answer would no doubt – because of his interest in the legal normalization of revolutions – have been the classical one drawn from the European political and legal tradition from the sixteenth centuries. It would have been the answer drawn especially from Jean Bodin, Sir Robert Filmer, Thomas Hobbes, Sir William Blackstone, Jeremy Bentham, John Austin, George Cornwall Lewis, and Herman Merivale.[6] In common with all their positions was his assumption that sovereign legal power was a conceptual and practical necessity in a state. He was no more capable than they – no more than most New Zealanders – of imagining

---

[6] See for the transmission of the tradition to the nineteenth century colonies, Mark Francis, 'The Contemplation of Colonial Constitutions as Political Philosophy', pp. 144-5, 150-9 especially.

a modern state without a legal sovereign. Somewhere there must be powers of supreme legislation and final adjudication; and in the end the legislative power, because it could change the law, was sovereign. State sovereignty must be the source and guarantor of all legal right in the land. Were there no sovereignty there could be no legal system, no state; and people would simply not have enforceable rights and duties. There would in principle and in practice be an endless succession of unsettleable disputes as the disputants went from authority to authority making their cases, and rejecting authority after authority as often as their causes were denied.

There are clear signs that Brookfield thought in this classical, European, way. But though he must have contemplated, he did not mention what his mentors had insisted upon – that 'the sword' at the end of the day could be called on to keep the peace. He did not himself see a practical threat to the state. Yet he had, like his teachers who lived through civil wars or the social unrest of modernization in France and England, a vivid appreciation of the fragility of government in general; a student also of modern revolutions in the third world, he seems to have felt, via both these sets of experience, the force in New Zealand of the serious questioning of the regime's legitimacy.

As to why it should have been the particular legal system that New Zealand happened to have that should harbour sovereignty, Brookfield simply gave the conventional legal historical case and pointed to the integrity of the judiciary. He rested content with showing the historical origins and development of the state from 21 May 1840 when, in two proclamations, Captain Hobson had announced to the world British sovereignty over the North and South Islands. Such was the undoubtedly correct legal doctrine. That took care of the authority which created the regime's original title; it was absolutely nothing to do with the Treaty at all, and was a creation of the will of the sovereign of the United Kingdom. He then traced the changing forms of the constitution until (most notably) the New Zealand General Assembly in 1947 claimed and was granted autonomy by Britain in terms laid down in the Statute of Westminster. That took care of the transmission of legal sovereignty through time – of the title to rule in New Zealand. As to the 'professionalism' and 'integrity', of the judges: *that* in 1985 was rather an affirmation of confidence in the possibility that the legal system could deliver the right decisions rather than an assertion of its entitlement to do so. The entitlement was not in question. In 1988 he could comment on *Te Weehi* v *Regional Fisheries Office*, the *New Zealand Maori Council* v *the Attorney General* and other recent cases as vindicating his confidence, and as having 'confounded the objectors' low expectations' of the courts. But the fundamental assumption remained – that the title of the judges to judge was, like the rest of the legal system, inherited, and legally unimpeachable. There was no question of there being a Māori sovereignty at all comparable with the sovereignty of the state.

As to the 'legitimacy' of the constitution, Brookfield was briefer and professedly more unclear. He seems to have thought that the British constitution before 1832, even though its legal title was sound, was not very (morally) legitimate because it did not represent the people well enough. And he seems to have thought that, what with the gradual withdrawal of British legal influence in New Zealand (at first creating, then sustaining, then merely influencing the constitution), the *legal* as well as the moral title of the New Zealand state came increasingly to rest on the consent of its subjects. But overall, Brookfield is probably best thought of as having provided an assertion of the sovereignty of the New Zealand state, married with some advice on how it should best act to conserve the allegiance of its Māori subjects. The legal theory was one of closure and hierarchy, the political theory a common sense and practical one designed to meet a current problem.

Less may be said of McHugh's 'constitutional theory', mainly because of the technicality and complexity of his argument.[7] But it can be noted that his approach was that of a constitutional lawyer, and his aim was to show that there were some limitations on the legal power of the sovereign state. 'Whilst it is obvious,' he argued, 'that the task of the constitutional lawyer must be to square rangatiratanga with the fundamental principle of our constitution, the sovereignty of the Crown [exercised through Parliament], it does not follow that they are antagonistic.' To this purpose he uncovered a tradition in British constitutional commentary in which it was argued that what gave the constitution its moral grip on the people was their original (and, in some versions, continuing) consent to it; he showed that it was also widely held that the function of such a government was to protect the 'property' of its subjects; he showed how, when New Zealand was annexed, it was clearly the legal custom of the British to obtain the consent of the sovereign nations whose sovereignty they intended to replace with their own; he showed how the British certainly intended that this procedure be followed in New Zealand; and he showed how it was. His end position was that while 'legal sovereignty' was lodged in the Parliament of New Zealand, 'political sovereignty' (as the great jurist Lord Dicey had named it) lodged not only in the ordinary people of New Zealand, but also, by virtue of the Treaty of Waitangi and the rangatiratanga guaranteed them in it, the Māori tribes. This 'political sovereignty' generated in the state of New Zealand, when it governed, an obligation to rule so as to protect the 'property' of the people at large, and in particular the 'rangatiratanga' of the Māori. The detail of the historical argument need not detain us,[8] nor the precise meaning he gave to the idea of 'political sovereignty' using legal commentators to do so. What matters is that his procedure was to translate the claim to

[7] In his 'Constitutional Theory and Maori Claims'.

[8] Though it is curious that 'the levellers' of the English civil war period, John Locke (a political exile, who never admitted his authorship of the famous *Second Treatise on Government*, and is notable for the atypicality of his arguments), Algernon Sidney (executed for treason) and Tom Paine (an exile vilified by the ruling classes) are quoted as British constitutional experts. And it is odd that he does not discuss the seventeenth-century notion of an immemorial constitution, the virtue of which was, that because its origins were not known, no sovereign could be located creating it and the rights and properties of the people had the same original footing as the rights of government.

rangatiratanga into the vocabulary of law. 'It is suggested that the traditional vocabulary of British constitutional theory provides the equipment to clarify the relationship of rangatiratanga to our system of government.'[9] The lawyer's response to the Māori claims to sovereignty was to bring them within the ambit of law and legal tradition. McHugh did not do this, it must be stressed, to deny the substance of the claims (he urged the recognition and constitution of many autonomous areas of tribal action). Rather he put the issues into the language of the law so that he could deal with them the only way lawyers (and the state) know how: as legal claims. In the last analysis too, he lodged sovereignty in the legal system — the creation of the state.

The Court of Appeal in the *New Zealand Maori Council v the Attorney General* was no less firm on the doctrine of state sovereignty than the constitutional theorists, and it was scarcely less willing to suggest that the state should act better towards its Māori subjects. Most importantly, the judges did not simply give opinions that had authority only with the learned; faced with legal questions that required an answer, they gave legally authoritative views as to some of the relations between state sovereignty and Māori sovereignty. And their views were to become the common coin of political argument from then on.

In deciding the case, the judges attended as carefully as they could do to the Treaty issues raised by the jurisprudence of the wairua. For they seem to have seen that the Māori jurisprudence of the wairua pointed in two different directions. On the one hand it pointed in the direction of negotiation between two peoples in a co-operative partnership in which mere rights should not be too strictly stood upon. On the other hand – and this was the problem – it also pointed in the direction of the claim that perhaps only the Māori, in Māori institutions, could decide what the wairua was. Only the Māori – it could be argued – could say what constituted the rangatiratanga they retained by Article 2 of the Treaty; to suggest otherwise would derogate from a mana that had never been relinquished. And while a Court of Common Law could, and did, quite willingly accommodate to the idea that wide areas should be created and sustained in which negotiation between the two separate iwi, or an iwi and a state could occur, it could not contemplate any derogation from the rule of law and the sovereign right of the courts to decide what it was. The law in brief had its non-negotiable mana too. The right to decide what the law was, and in particular what rangatiratanga was, would stay with the courts.

The Court, in developing its jurisprudence of 'partnership', made it quite plain that the partnership was one of a sovereign state with the Māori. There was no dissent from Mr Justice Somers' judgment that, notwithstanding the differences in the two language versions of the Treaty/te Tiriti, 'I am of the opinion that the question of sovereignty in New Zealand is not in doubt

---

[9] 'Constitutional Theory and Maori Claims', p. 47.

. . . Sovereignty resides in Parliament.'[10] And it was not just a strict interpretation of Article 1 which would accord sovereignty to the Crown. Sir Robin Cooke, the President of the Court, argued the Government to be as much *empowered* as limited by the fact of the Treaty partnership, because to 'try to shackle the government unreasonably would . . . be inconsistent' with the 'principles of the Treaty'.[11] *Sovereignty once established*, the flexible relationship of a partnership instituted for mutual benefit was the spirit of the Treaty. The 'reasonableness and good faith' which the court insisted upon implied first the subjection to Pākehā law of the Māori and secondly, within the ambit of that subjection, the fullest 'partnership' possible.

Even the decisions which enhanced Māori rights made them a function of state sovereignty. Even the decisions which seemed to bind Government to constitutional principles were in fact reassertions of state sovereignty. All the judges agreed that 'the principles of the Treaty of Waitangi override everything else in the State Owned Enterprises Act'.[12] The Treaty was, within the ambit of the Act, to be treated as a 'basic constitutional document'[13] and its 'spirit' was to override if necessary any particular provision of the Act. It had the 'impact of a constitutional guarantee within the field covered by the State Owned Enterprises Act'.[14] The Court held too that the Treaty could operate as a constitutional guarantee of Māori rights, and suggested that a 'duty of reparation' might well be owed for past violations of its spirit. The President went further, suggesting that it might well be 'inconsistent with the principles of the Treaty for the Crown to act inconsistently with' a recommendation of the Tribunal that lost lands should be returned.[15] But why all this? Because Parliament made it so in legislation: in section 9 of the SOE Act. And who said all this? The Court of Appeal. There was no derogation here at all from the principles of state sovereignty.

There is no doubt that in prescribing these limits on Government activity and in suggesting such legal obligations, the Court of Appeal took from Parliament more than the Parliament had wished to concede. Yet state sovereignty was preserved, even enhanced. The injunction to abide by the 'the principles of the Treaty of Waitangi' was by the time the Appeal Court made its judgment, contained not only in the Treaty of Waitangi Act and the SOE Act, but also in the Long Title of the Environment Act (1986) and in section 4 of the Conservation Act (1987). And the Court held that it must be that wherever the injunction appeared, the Treaty was, as it had never before been, incorporated in municipal law. Perhaps the Treaty was

---

[10] Somers J. in Government Printer, *The Treaty of Waitangi in the Court of Appeal* (Henceforth TWCA) at p. 15.

[11] Cooke P. in TWCA at pp. 37, 40.

[12] Cooke P. in TWCA at p. 44.

[13] Richardson J. in TWCA at p. 9.

[14] Cooke P. in TWCA at p. 21. Compare Casey J. at p. 13.

[15] Cooke P. in TWCA at p. 27. But note his statement as to the latitude of possible settlements, pp. 37-8. See also Richardson J. at p. 17, pp. 41-2.

even, within the ambit of those statutes, a basic 'constitutional' law. But why? By virtue and only by virtue of the force of the statutes which commanded respect for its principles. The statutes passed by Parliament made the Treaty valid law. It was not binding either in and of itself, or as expressing mana Māori motuhake.

The legislature and the judiciary together then had in a sense 'ratified' the Treaty: not in its provisions but in its spirit; and not in a blanket way so that it would be a foundation for all law, but rather piecemeal, in particular statutes and judgments. It is far from clear – and the Court could not find it so[16] – whether the legislature knew that this is what it was doing in passing section 9 of the SOE Act. It probably did not, given the disconcerted surprise the Government expressed at the prospect of the Maori Council's case, and given the vigour with which it fought it. But there is no doubt that a revolution in jurisprudence had occurred. The politicians and the judges had partly stumbled into, partly been forced into, bringing home the Treaty into law. Doubtless also, the Māori had now been given enormous legal opportunities, long to be explored.

But at a price. For while from the judges' point of view the conclusion they reached was inescapable and could not be denied by Parliament, they insisted equally that it was built on the premise of parliamentary sovereignty. Cooke P. put it this way: 'If the judiciary has been able to play a role to some extent creative, that is because the legislature has given the opportunity.' Somers J., this way: 'Neither the provisions of the Treaty of Waitangi nor its principles are as a matter of law, a restraint on the legislative supremacy of Parliament.'[17] And the price was, more generally, the reassertion of the subjection of the Treaty, the Tribunal, and Māori claims to the sovereign legal system. The rulings of the Tribunal as to the meaning of the Treaty, in any case applicable only within the ambit of the Treaty of Waitangi Act, would not bind the *Courts*. Courts would enforce a recommendation of the Tribunal on the Crown only if they were satisfied for themselves that the principles of the Treaty had been breached. On the other hand the Tribunal *would* be bound by the judgments of Courts working within the ambit of all Acts, including the Treaty of Waitangi Act, as to the legal effect of the Treaty. Thus, though the Court of Appeal did indeed take important heed of what the Tribunal said – as had the High Court earlier in the year[18] – it did not consider itself bound by its interpretations. Both the interpretation of the 'principles of the Treaty' and the 'practical measures' to achieve their working out would, in the final arbitration, be for the courts of common law.[19]

The basis of the Court's decisions was something like this: that as Māori mana did not depend for its existence on the Treaty but pre-dated it, state

---

[16] Cooke P. in TWCA at pp. 22-4; Casey J. at pp. 14-15; Bisson J. at p. 13.

[17] Cooke P. in TWCA at p. 47. Somers J. at p. 17.

[18] In *Huakina Development Trust v Waikato Authority and Bowater*, unreported decision of Chilwell J.

[19] I take this to be so on a reading of Cooke P. in TWCA at p. 30, and Somers J. at p. 13.

sovereignty did not depend for its existence on the Treaty either. The principles on which state sovereignty was claimed predated the Treaty 'time out of mind', and what activated the Crown's right to rule was not the Treaty at all.

This was not precisely the matter at issue, and it is therefore noteworthy that while the Court did not pronounce on it at all definitely, it did choose to speak on the origins of legal sovereignty, and the tendency of what it said was clear. It seems likely that in providing such dicta on a matter not at issue, the Justices were responding to the claims to Māori sovereignty implicit in the doctrines of the wairua, of mana, and of rangatiratanga. Richardson J. held that it was the approval by the Crown and the gazetting on 2 October 1840 of Hobson's two proclamations of 21 May 1840 that 'established Crown sovereignty in New Zealand'. Hobson, Richardson recounted, had in one proclamation declared that the Māori signatories had ceded the North Island to the Queen, and in the other that the South Island was the Queen's by right of discovery. Although he reported the preambular rationale of cession in the first proclamation, Richardson also noted that that 'some chiefs refused to sign, others were not reached'; and it was clear he was not about to hold that the Treaty was a Treaty of cession and the basis of British sovereignty in New Zealand. Instead, he remarked, more ambiguously and capaciously, avoiding the issue out of politesse: 'It now seems widely accepted as a matter of colonial law and international law that those proclamations approved by the Crown and the gazetting of the acquisition of New Zealand by the Crown . . . authoritatively established Crown sovereignty over New Zealand.' In another place Richardson characterized the Treaty as a 'compact, . . . through which the peaceful settlement of New Zealand was contemplated', and one 'through which the Crown sought from the indigenous people legitimacy for its acquisition of government'. But 'legitimacy' did not mean 'title to sovereignty' here. It seems to have indicated simply Māori acquiescence in the British assuming sovereignty by an act of royal prerogative. For, concluding his history of the Treaty-making, Richardson said: 'I think it is clear that the Treaty was presented and accepted as providing a path for the orderly colonisation of New Zealand under British Government protection of Maori and British interests alike.' It 'provided a path' and it justified the assumption of sovereignty. But it neither constituted legal sovereignty, nor authorized it in legal form. It is hard to escape the conclusion that the Crown and the Crown alone authorized the sovereignty and acquired the government. It was the proclamations, and crucially, the gazetting that registered the royal will. The Treaty was at best a means of adding 'legitimacy' – that is the agreement of the people – to that acquisition.

Mr Justice Somers also told of the signing of the Treaty and the differences in interpretation of it. But his emphasis was also on the two proclamations and the gazetting. Notwithstanding the 'important differences between the understanding of the signatories . . . I am of the opinion that the question of sovereignty in New Zealand is not in doubt'. Following the Treaty there were the proclamations, and, he concluded: 'These proclamations were approved in London and published in the London Gazette of 2 October 1840. The sovereignty of the Crown was then beyond dispute and the subsequent legislative history of New Zealand evidences that. Sovereignty in New Zealand resides in Parliament.' At most he seems to have been prepared to think of the Treaty as some kind of prerequisite to the Queen's constituting British sovereignty. *If* it was though, it was as a Treaty of cession. On that view, mana Māori would have been given up, would have been extinguished in submitting itself to the sovereignty of the British monarch; utterly extinguished and unrevivable. But the point was not pursued.[20] Nor did Mr Justice Bisson go further. He clearly thought the chiefs had ceded their right to govern themselves. But he had no comment to make as to the relationship of that event with the constitution of British sovereignty.[21]

No judge was going to say outright that the signing of the Treaty was not really the act that created sovereignty in New Zealand, that rather it was an exercise of the Queen's prerogative that did so. Though this was undoubtedly the legal position, to state it would have been an affront to Māori belief. But this is most likely what they meant in including the Treaty in the story of the creation of sovereignty, but in not ruling on its legal status in the story. For how else, given the doctrine of the indestructibility of the mana Māori lodged from 1840 in the Treaty, could there *be* sovereignty in the legal system? How else could Parliament have got and retained the right to make laws, and the Courts to declare what they were? If mana Māori was part of what constituted the sovereignty of law, then the withdrawal of mana Māori would deconstitute it. The doctrine of deconstitution clearly could not subsist with the idea of common law.

The preferred gloss on the Treaty seemed to the judges to be that contained in the recital to the Maori Affairs Bill in Parliament at the time (the bill it may be recalled set in motion by Ben Couch and prepared by the New Zealand Maori Council after five years' consultation with the Māori people). In the recital to the bill there was no question as to the extinction of mana Māori if 'mana' was to be taken to have anything to do with legal sovereignty. That kind of mana was simply extinct. The issue was rather for the sovereign legal system to decide what rangatiratanga was. The recital stated that:

. . . The Treaty of Waitangi symbolises the special relationship between the Maori people and the Crown: And . . . it is desirable that the spirit of the exchange of sovereignty for the protection of rangatiratanga be reconfirmed: And . . . rangatiratanga . . . means the custody and care of matters significant to the cultural identity of the Maori people in New Zealand in trust for future generations . . .[22]

[20] Richardson J. in TWCA at pp. 8-9, 34, 36. Somers J. at p. 15, and pp. 17-19, quoting *Haoani Te Heuheu Tukino* v *Aotea District Maori Land Board* (1941), which notoriously treated the Treaty as a treaty of cession.

[21] Bisson J. in TWCA at p. 23.

[22] Cooke P. in TWCA at p. 29; Bisson J. at p. 24.

The bill then went on to define rangatiratanga for purposes of Māori land ownership and utilization and in regard to the proposed reorganizations revolving around the Department of Maori Affairs. But the judges in quoting the preamble had something more general in mind. In regard to reparations, existing institutions, and the law, their thought was that the Tribunal, the government and the New Zealand Maori Council should explore the avenues of settlement and if possible settle by agreement. If that exploration were not successful and agreement were not reached, then rangatiratanga would be defined by the Courts and repaired according to the common law. Rangatiratanga would become legal right. Legal right violated would require legal remedy. Perhaps reparation defined by law.

In this way the jurisprudence of the wairua, of mana, and rangatiratanga was adapted to meet, on the one hand, the Māori demand for justice in reparations combined with a tendency to argue for Māori sovereignty, and on the other hand the Pākehā (and much Māori) desire for a future-oriented justice and policy together with the Pākehā insistence on the sovereignty of the law and equality under it. The Court suggested that *both* sides must pay a price. The Māori must not claim to be final legal arbiters on what rangatiratanga was; the state must, when all the negotiations were through, make reparations for violation of legal right as defined by the common law courts, and it must recognize the separate rights of the Māori. For the state, state sovereignty, and law were the instruments of neither *ethnie*. Legal justice would not correspond with either's ideology. It might even outrage the sense of justice of both.

II

Political and Moral Sovereignty

This is the way the Government read the decision. Richard Prebble, the Minister of State Enterprises, and thus the man perhaps more discommoded than anyone by the Court's injunction forbidding sales of Crown Land to State Enterprises until the Government and the New Zealand Maori Council should reach agreement, saw this. During the debate on the Treaty of Waitangi (SE) Bill, introduced in December 1987 to give effect to the agreement which was hammered out in the difficult months following the Court's decision, he recognized in two massive understatements that 'it was no secret' the Court's decision faced the Government with 'a fairly major problem'. But equally he saw the other, possibly more important implication of the decision: 'The New Zealand Maori Council brought its case in order to protect land claims by Maori people, but it also recognised that, under the Treaty of Waitangi, not only rights were granted to Maori people but also obligations, and that the Crown has sovereign rights in New Zealand.' Geoffrey Palmer, equally appalled at one time by the New Zealand Maori Council's proceedings and the Court's decision, more suavely noted that President Cooke had said that the Treaty did not authorize 'unreasonable restrictions on the right of a duly elected government to follow its chosen policy'. The deal was: recognition of the sovereign state for reparations negotiated in good faith. Nor did the National Opposition dissent from this view.[23] In fact, because the bill set out to give the Tribunal the power to bind the Crown in cases where SOEs had received Crown land, the Opposition were in a better position than the Government to argue the sovereignty of the parliamentary state during the subsequent debate: 'An important aspect of the Treaty of Waitangi is that the Crown is sovereign,' said Warren Kyd, complaining of the Tribunal's new powers; and Mr Doug Graham asked whether is was 'fair that the Tribunal should have the final say instead of the Government?', adding, 'I do not think that New Zealanders by and large think that it is.'[24]

In brief, the Appeal Court's decision as to the location of sovereignty and its willingness to assert sovereignty was fully in accord with that of the parliamentary politicians. It was in fact a legalistic version of what they had said all along when they had contemplated the nature and powers of the Waitangi Tribunal: in 1974, in 1984 and in 1985. Parliament, in representing the people, was the democratic sovereign. Parliament, by virtue of the Treaty contract, was contractually sovereign. Parliament, by virtue of its political expertise was politically sovereign. Finally – for those were, strictly speaking matters of moral argument – Parliament was also legally sovereign. And the conclusion was that decisions on Māori claims would have to be 'political', made, and enforced by Parliament.

All this was repeated emphatically in the debate over the Tribunal's Muriwhenua findings.[25] Accompanying the themes of the moderating spirit of the Treaty and the need to negotiate a future, there was a definite and clear bottom line: sovereignty. The Opposition was again at an advantage. As in the State Enterprises debate it could be made to seem that the Government was abdicating power and Jim Bolger could firmly assert that there was: 'one country, many people, but there can be only one law'. And the law was to be made by the Crown. 'Article the first of the Treaty of Waitangi is explicit about sovereignty: "The Chiefs of the Confederation of the United Tribes of New Zealand and the separate independent Chiefs . . . cede to Her Majesty the Queen absolutely and without reservation all the rights and powers of Sovereignty which the said Confederation or Individual Chiefs respectively exercise or possess".' Doug Kidd, supporting negotiation on grounds of recognizing Māori rights, nevertheless felt bound to assert legal sovereignty with energy if not precision: 'Some people have said it . . . is contrary to the sovereignty of the Crown. Rubbish . . . No one is denying the sovereignty of the Crown – the tribunal does not do so in its report . . . The House must not confuse the assertion and declaration of the fishing rights of the Muriwhenua people with the question of sovereignty.' Simon

23 NZPD1:42 (8 December 1987), pp. 1716, 1720-1, 1725-6, 1728-9, 1729.

24 NZPD1:42, (21 June 1988), pp. 4576-7, 4585.

25 NZPD1:42 (15 June 1988), pp. 4384-4407.

Upton's insistence that it was a 'political solution' that was required, rested on an idea remarkably like one of Jean Jacques Rousseau, the eighteenth century Genevan: that the right to impose the solution – sovereignty – rested with 'the people' acting in their capacity as 'the Crown'.

Government MPs however were not at all behind in asserting legal, political, and moral sovereignty. Colin Moyle, Minister of Fisheries, reported on the negotiations going on in the working party representing the Crown and the Māori as a result of the court injunctions against allocating more Individual Transferable Quotas. He hoped for a successfully negotiated conclusion, but he nevertheless insisted that: 'It is up to the Government to determine a solution and to make any necessary changes to fisheries administration.' Mike Moore thought it 'not good enough for members of this Parliament to claim that sovereignty has been taken away, because everyone knows that it will be the New Zealand Parliament that makes the decisions at the end of the day'; and Richard Prebble thought likewise: 'It is for the Crown and Parliament to make decisions on the basis of the recommendations made to them . . . I have to act on behalf of [party political opponents] as well as for the people who voted for the Government.' Bruce Gregory, hoping for an extension of his people's rights, nevertheless insisted that: 'There is no denial that this is one country.' He meant that whatever the variety of peoples, and despite the partnership between the two most important of them, all were subject to one legal system.[26] Similar arguments were heard as the reforms of the Waitangi Tribunal made their way through Parliament, from late 1987 through 1988. Richard Prebble insisted, for instance that, 'under the Treaty of Waitangi, not only rights were granted the Maori people, but obligations . . . the Crown has sovereign rights over New Zealand.' Warren Kyd agreed: 'The important aspect of the Treaty of Waitangi is that the Crown is sovereign.'[27]

The Courts and the parliamentarians could scarcely have made less ambiguous cases for the sovereignty of the New Zealand state. State officials were not far behind, though their views were less penetrable, being neither in the language of law nor of the kind of common-sense talked by politicians. Nor in the nature of the case were they so often called upon to speak to the matter. But even officials otherwise disagreeing, agreed on this. In an ambiguous passage in *Government Management*, Treasury glossed the Treaty, showing how 'parental' it was, and insisted with the Court of Appeal that the Māori had recognized there the state's 'right to govern', quoting Richardson's remark that even 'the notion of an absolute and formless duty to consult' with the Māori could not be regarded 'as implict in the Treaty'. *Government Management* did indeed find a Treaty duty on the Crown to sustain and respect whatever rights there were in the document, but it essayed no remarks as to whether these non-legal duties ought *really* to bind the

---

[26] NZPD1:42, pp. 6884–6902.

[27] NZPD1:41 (8 Dec 1987), Prebble at p. 1721 and cf. pp. 1716, 1728-9; (21 June 1988), Kidd at p. 4576, and pp. 4577, 4585; (28 June 1988), pp. 4785, 4789, 4790.

Government, or on what precisely those rights were. In another passage, Treasury made it crystal clear that 'the function of justice and the maintenance of law and order' rested with the Crown.[28]

Thus Treasury. But even the Royal Commission on Social Policy, Treasury's opponent on interpretation of the Treaty, and the body which heard so much of and so respected mana Māori motuhake and the Māori desire for greater autonomy, asserted the sovereignty of the state. 'Maori people . . . have "obligations to protect" under the Treaty. In giving their loyalty to the Crown and accepting the right of the Government to govern, they likewise accepted implicit responsibility to protect the authority of the Crown and uphold its laws.' The Commission reported with obvious satisfaction that 'while criticism of the law and court procedures' was common among the Māori, 'contempt for the judiciary or Parliament was rare . . . such reforms as were suggested were carefully conceived within the framework of the law'; and it had no problem deferring to Somers J.'s dictum that the Treaty was subject to the sovereignty of Parliament.[29] The state was sovereign.

[28] The Treasury, *Government Management*, i, pp. 323-6, 346-7.

[29] *The April Report*, ii, pp. 32, 60-1.

Chapter 15
The Construction of Justice and
Sovereignty

There is nothing . . . on earth to be compared with him. He is made so as not to be afraid.
He seeth every high thing below him; and he is king of all the children of pride . . . But
[Leviathan] is mortal, and subject to decay, as all other creatures are . . .
Nothing can be immortal, which mortals make; yet if men had the use of
reason they pretend to, their commonwealths might be secured, at least from
perishing by internal diseases. For by the nature of their institution, they
are designed to live, as long as mankind, or as the laws of nature, or as
justice itself, which gives them life. Therefore when they come to be dissolved,
not by external violence, but intestine disorder, the fault is not in men as
they are the *matter*; but as they are the *makers* and orderers of them.

Thomas Hobbes, *Leviathan*, Chapters 28-29

From the point of view of anyone committed to mana Māori even if not
to absolute Māori sovereignty, the directive minority of New Zealand thus
asserted Pākehā power. As Jane Kelsey said in critical opposition to the attempt
to incorporate the Treaty/te Tiriti into a Bill of Rights, so might she have
said of the dealings of the state with Māori claims to justice in general:
'the legal structures, values, and ideologies of the courts and the judiciary
are part of the hegemonic apparatus of the post-colonial state, and as such
reflect and entrench Pakeha power'.[1] And Kelsey's historical essay, 'Legal
Imperialism and the Colonization of Aotearoa', set out to show in detail
no less than what Awatere, Evans, and Poananga had asserted in gross –
that law was Pākehā law, that the New Zealand ideology of individualism
and democracy was Pākehā ideology, and that the structure and spirit therefore
of the governing institutions in New Zealand were Pākehā.

Given 'Māori', given 'Pākehā', and given irreducible ethnic difference
between them, this is true. However much the law and politicians may have
renounced the language of race and culture in their proceedings, it is true.
However much they thought the state and its activities to be culturally neutral,
it is true. However many Māori individuals were satisfied with the regime
and worked with it, it is true. It is true as a consequence of discourse about
justice between separate *ethnie*. And given that way of speaking of things
– and seeing things – there never will be justice between the *ethnie*. All
this is true, as it were, as a matter of definition – except that, to take the
equally permissible view, Pākehā consciousness would not think of the system
they imposed as one of brute power and hegemony, but rather of justified

---

[1] Kelsey, 'Te Tiriti o Waitangi', in *Race, Gender, Class* 3, p. 26.

legal authority and the moral authority of a superior civilization; and whatever anyone else might say or believe to the contrary, they would interpret Pākehā acts as having been just, and would repudiate contrary opinions as rooted in a false and alien morality, and see incipient injustice in the Māori attempts to reform things.

How can this be?

Obviously, in some important way, justice and sovereignty are not culturally neutral and their content is culturally specific. For justice, as the Scots philosopher David Hume once argued, is an 'artificial virtue', meaning partly that its content is not dictated by 'nature' but by the judgements of particular societies.[2]

Take reparation. Like justice in general, it may be a practice necessary in most societies if they are to survive. But precisely *what* should be repaired and *how* is arbitrary and unpredictable by the use of reason. It is a matter rather of history, of the conventions of particular societies constructed only semi-consciously over long tracts of time. Real and reasonable reparation – as opposed to socially conventional and historically determined reparation – actually defies the human condition. Human societies construct their different practices of reparation on a substratum of existential fact where it would not grow without cultivation. And the cultivation, the culture, is all. Actions – good, bad and indifferent – just change the way the world is. That is all. Nothing can make the world what it would have been had they not occurred. Nothing can *really* undo past acts. People can and do manipulate stories about the past and they can construct accounts of what might have been but for what actually happened; but they cannot make what happened not have happened and what did not happen, have happened. In fact the individuals who are here now would not be here but for what happened; if what happened could be changed, they would be different persons. And *ethnie* too, would be different, though in a more complicated way.[3] The metaphors of reparation, remedy, restitution, and so on are just that: metaphors. They are no more (or less) than socially-constructed fictions, and what they refer to varies from society to society.

Separate societies make up and manipulate their stories about the past, not only to assert their identity but to claim great acts and disclaim villainy. Separate societies construct rules of right and wrong; they invent methods to encourage the one and discourage the other. Separate societies make their own metaphors, as, for instance, English, United States and Commonwealth common lawyers elaborated a system of rules for recognizing and classifying 'breaches' of 'contract', 'injuries', 'negligence' etc., and a 'system' of 'remedies' to provide 'justice' when they occur. The law, as its practitioners know, is a matter of 'artificial reason', developed over a long tract of time and

---

[2] Hume, *A Treatise on Human Nature*, Book 3, sections 2-6; *An Enquiry Concerning Morals*, Section 3, in *Enquiries Concerning the Human Understanding*.

[3] I am reflecting on e.g. Kavka, 'The Paradox of Future Individuals'; Parfit, 'Later Selves and Moral Principles'; Sher, 'Compensation and Transworld Identity'.

specific to its place, and often so 'unreasonable' (i.e. in defiance of common sense) as to baffle the ordinary man and woman. The Māori for their part had and have their artificial reason. They talked and still talk of utu and muru as means of reciprocation of rights and wrongs, and the rules governing them are complex and specific to that people. Different societies each construct their own systems of reciprocity which work for them and are agreed to.

But obviously where there is *no* agreement as to what would constitute right or wrong, righting or restoring, and thus what would constitute reparative justice or utu, then difficulties will arise. They will arise most notably in societies where there are multiple versions of what it is exactly that justice demands;[4] and such difficulties clearly arose in Aotearoa/New Zealand in so far as it is two cultures which exist in one political society.

That is simply the way it was, and it is the way it must be in the logic of the discourse of reparative justice between the *ethnie*.

It was the same in regard to distributive justice, though in a way more complicated than by only ethnic differences. The demands of need will be met only by those who feel in some way connected – who feel members of a society with – those who need. Strangers and aliens can demand nothing.[5] The deserts of excellent performance will be recognized only by those who know and value and can judge within the appropriate field of activity whether merit has been attained; it will be hard, too, in any territorial and diffused society for most people to appreciate the demands of hard work or dirty work which is nevertheless socially useful; and it is notoriously difficult for people in capitalist societies to appreciate the structural necessity for unemployment and thus the blamelessness – actually the desert – of the unemployed. The merits of equality will not be obvious to those who value excellence or desert, or who think that meeting minimal needs is not the same as and is better than equalization. And so on. Any modern political society continually argues about these matters, and in Aotearoa/New Zealand it was no different. And how to count the Māori in this? As needy? So were others. As disadvantaged? So were others. As deserving? So were others. As subjects of equalizing policies? So were others.

Even the most seemingly solid of rights guaranteed in the practice of justice can be, and are, at issue between *ethnie* (and between nations and persons who have different interests). To take some European and American issues: whether the sea could be made property was a bone of contention between those who claimed it could be 'bounded' and those who denied it, saying that because it was fluid, it could not be 'captured'. When it was agreed that at least territorial waters *could* be the 'property' (or 'dominion') of states, the bounds of the property were disputed: should they lie at a half way mark between two sovereign states? Or at that distance where, from the sea, a mariner could sight the land? Should they lie rather at the limits

---

[4] See especially Wolgast, *The Grammar of Justice*, Chapter 6.

[5] Consider with Ignatief, *The Needs of Strangers*, Chapter 1, what is owed to King Lear by virtue of his needs once he rejects community with his former subjects and family.

defensible from the claimant's shores? A cannon shot's distance? How far was that? Three miles? Twelve miles? And so on.[6] What of the right to landed property? Could no one own it? Or only Christians? Was title to ownership obtainable by the consent of all, or of some (and if some, what of the others)? Or did it follow the 'mixing of labour' in it?[7] Could it be obtained by discovery, first occupation, cession, accession, inheritance (and under what rules) and so on? If one owned the land, did one own the minerals beneath and the skies above?

Law, like common sense and philosophy, has had great difficulty in coming up with universally satisfactory answers to such questions. No wonder, there are none. The answers are conventional, specific to particular places and times. This is not to say they are irrational. (A good answer will relate to the multitude of considerations specific to the times and places, and to the interests people have. Hugo Grotius, protagonist of the open sea theory when working for the Dutch, probably changed his mind when he was Swedish Ambassador to France which had different interests from Holland; the three mile limit began to seem too little with improvement in artillery; title to the sky became more interesting when spaceships got to the moon.) But it *is* to say that peoples with different histories and different interests will come up with separate answers as to the basis and scope of title; and often of course the legal answers will not be exactly those given in the common sense of the people.[8]

So Māori and Pākehā, in so far as they are different peoples with different histories and interests, must disagree on some matters of justice (as many other groups too must disagree). Justice for the Māori in New Zealand/ Aotearoa – the political society conceived as made up of two *ethnie* – can never be done. It never will be done. Nor will the Māori do justice to the Pākehā. To think otherwise would be to indulge in wishful thinking and to seek to escape the logic of justice. Each *ethnie* had to see what the other did as injustice. Each will continue to do so, arguing that rights are being violated and injustice done.

It was no accident either that both Māori and the Crown had recourse to the idea of sovereignty at the points at which they disagreed. They each needed to claim an authority to create and to sustain the distributions of things they saw as just. But again, every culture has its own peculiar ways of showing who should have it and why, according to its history; and its history, which is supposed to show entitlement, will never really bear looking into by others. This is so even within a culture. Obscurity and forgetfulness as to the historical origins of sovereign power is as often a mode of political thought as is (as in ancient Rome) the precisely detailed knowledge of or

---

[6] See Fulton, *Sovereignty of the Sea*, Part 1, Chapter 9, and Part 2.

[7] See an account of the most famous consideration of this series of questions by John Locke in Tully, *A Discourse on Property*.

[8] Ackerman, *Private Property and the Constitution*.

myth of origins.[9] This is because no origin is innocent. An Englishman, Anthony Ascham, may make this point best for me, and draw this book to an end. Writing in the late 1640s of times of 'confusions and revolutions' – after civil wars and clamour as to the rights of sovereigns – he remarked of sovereign's entitlements:

> As for point of right, it is a thing always doubtful and would be for ever disputable in all kingdoms if those governors who are in possession should freely permit all men to examine their titles *ab origine*, and those large pretended rights which they exercise over the people. And though this party's title may be as good or a little better than that party's, yet a man in conscience may still doubt whether he have *limpidum titulum*, a just or clear right, especially in those things which are constituted by so various and equivocal a principle as the will of man is.[10]

If not quite universally the case, that was the way it was in England then, and how it was in New Zealand when the issues of justice and sovereignty raised their heads in the 1970s and 1980s. As the Māori could impugn the state's title to govern, so could the Pākehā speak of the sanguine origins of authority and property in pre-European times.

Further, since there could be no (cross-cultural) agreement on what a regime could do to be accepted as just and therefore *become* legitimate in New Zealand/Aotearoa, there could not be agreement as to the nature, location and scope of sovereignty. If there were two cultures and the cultures had different conceptions of the past and of justice, then they would disagree on sovereignty too. There were no non-conventional answers as to what was just and where sovereignty lay.

In so far then as there was a bicultural discourse on justice and sovereignty in New Zealand, a discourse consciously picking on the differences between the peoples, there was bound to be great difficulty in one culture justifying to the other its notions either of justice or of supreme authority. If both cultures had *equal* reason on their side, whatever they said and thought, then neither could hope to convince the other. Their reasonings were simply contrary on many matters, and there was no way of picking between them. The elements of tragedy, the battle of the 'right against the right', as the philosopher Hegel put it, were fundamental to the situation. They constituted it, and it was all there was.

But that was *not* the situation. The discourse of culture clash was not the only one; it was not impossible to find reasons for agreement; and some ways of seeing things and discussing them are better than others. Justice and sovereignty are fundamental issues in politics. They get raised in times of confusions and revolutions, and they will never be quieted by giving thought to them, so as to work out what they mean. Of course in happy times they

---

[9] See Bruce James Smith, *Politics and Remembrance*, for three sets of tactics as to remembering and forgetting origins.

[10] Anthony Ascham, *A Discourse . . . Confusions and Revolutions* (1648), printed in Sharp, *Political Ideas of the English Civil Wars 1641–49*, p. 220.

can – as is best – be ignored, and other things discussed. But only a politics sensitive to the various claims of justice and injustice could bring those times about; and only peoples supporting those politics. The thing to do is to continue to search out and create agreements as to what the content of justice would best be in this place and this time: on how material goods are to be distributed, for instance, and how tribal authority might be accommodated within the state. There is no reason in New Zealand/Aotearoa why the *ethnie* cannot agree on enough for there to be no question as to the content of justice being based on purely Pākehā ideas of just distributions. They would not be. A political community of the two *ethnie* would have decided; and often communities of interest would in any case have cut across ethnic lines, in which case to talk of culture-specific justice would be to elevate a useful shorthand for characterizing differences into the realms of fantasy.

As to absolute legal sovereignty of the state: whatever cross-cultural disagreements there are, it is *not* a culturally-specific argument to say that sovereignty is justified by reference to its essential role in adjudicating on disputes as to rights and then enforcing them where they must be enforced. There is no alternative for anyone in a territory with a population so mixed and in which members of both (genetic) groups so often sympathize cross-culturally, and where members of the separate ethnic groups share interests in ways quite unconnected with their ethnicity. There is no alternative, in anyone's discourse, where the people will and must live together. The state does not have to be an ethnic state or to be justified in its forms and procedures by arguments that appeal to only one *ethnie*. If, of course, the state cannot provide peace and order, prosperity and security to its subjects, they will give it less (and in extremes, none) of their allegiance, whatever their ethnicity. If, too, that state does not seriously address itself to repairing what wrongs it can, if it abuses its authority by violating the deepest beliefs and the terminal identity of some of its subjects and does not help them to live lives in accord with those beliefs, it cannot be expected that those who feel wronged will think it to be *their* state. Why should they? It will not be theirs. During those times – as it must – *Leviathan* will assert its rule and will be felt to be ruling as an alien and oppressive monster.

The art of politics will be in New Zealand/Aotearoa, to avoid that conjuncture, and there is every reason to expect success. The road has been taken. There is enough political community between the *ethnie* for justice to be negotiated, there are enough cross-ethnic common interests, and the sovereign state is demonstrably not the property of the Pākehā alone.

Part Five
Justice and Agency

Chapter 16
Justice and Agency, 1989–1996

I

Continuities

The previous chapters were completed in late 1989. This one was written in November 1996. Seven years has been a long time in the politics and philosophy of justice and the Māori, and a few additional pages cannot capture much of the colour and detail of that period. But it may be said that the fundamental issues have remained much as they had emerged in the 1980s. Māori are still worse off than the majority Pākehā population. In fact the neo-liberal reforms of the economy, state, and civil society,[1] which had been begun in 1984 by the Fourth Labour Government and were continued by the National Governments of 1990–1996 saw the position of the worst-off Māori become still worse. Things appear to be improving for them in 1996, but over the whole period only Pacific Islanders had a worse record of long-term unemployment as the economic reforms unravelled the traditional forms of employment in state railways, mines, public works, forests, and post offices. Only Pacific Islanders had lower average incomes as a welfare state devoted to providing an income sufficient for the ordinary life of a citizen was replaced by one designed to provide only a safety net against utter poverty.[2] Despite continued official commitment to biculturalism, te reo, the Māori language, has continued to die, although vigorous local Māori efforts in kōhanga reo and kura kaupapa have been made to sustain and spread it.[3] In the new, harsher, climate of life, Māori have continued to demand opportunities for economic development and the resources not only to pursue their own plans of development but also to improve their health, education and housing, to preserve their culture and language, and to engender self-respect among their alienated young.

They have continued, too, to demand reparations for past wrongs, with the logically unavoidable disappointments that this has brought.[4] Remarkably little

---

[1] For an idea of the scope of the reforms see (put here in chronological order) Boston et al., *Reshaping the State*; Kelsey, *Rolling Back the State*; Sharp (ed.) *Leap Into the Dark*; Kelsey, *The New Zealand experiment*; Boston et al., *Public management: the New Zealand model*.

[2] Sharp, 'Civil rights, amelioration and reparation', Section: 'Ameliorative Policies'. On the welfare changes see Scollay and St John, *Macroeconomics and the Contemporary New Zealand Society*, pp. 141-27.

[3] Kohanga reo are language-immersion pre-schools; kura kaupapa are language-immersion primary schools. The facts on the language are usefully laid out in *New Zealand Māori Council* v *Attorney-General* (unreported) High Court, Wellington, 3 May 1991, CP942/88 at 33.

[4] See above pp. 104-24, 283-4. For further reasons as to the logic of the situation see Waldron, 'Historic injustice: Its remembrance and supercession', and Laslett (ed.) *Justice Between Groups and Generations*, throughout.

land was returned as a result of the Waitangi Tribunal's recommendations,[5] though various improvements were made in environmental and planning matters.[6] The Tribunal, starved of funds and rather distracted by a programme of systematic research not directly aimed at hearing claims, was slow to deliver reports.[7] It was also unwilling to use the powers it had acquired in 1988 and 1989[8] to require, and not simply to recommend, that the Crown return lands and forests to claimants whose case it believed justified. Yet, despite as well as because of, its slowness and practical ineffectiveness, claims lodged with it mounted. In March 1989 there were 180 outstanding claims. Under the National Governments, backlogs inexorably grew. In October 1996 it was reported that there was a backlog of 618 claims, seventy of which had been made over the previous year.[9] Throughout all this, media interest in the Tribunal and stories about Māori claims continued to increase.[10]

The mix of Māori appeals to justice as equalization as well as reparation so characteristic of the 1980s has continued into the 1990s, even though equalization has had little appeal to Governments, especially since 1987. Labour abandoned the idea of state-imposed redistributive justice and embraced market justice. National followed in its wake: people would and should get what the market delivered them. In the face of the non-delivery of justice of either kind, claims to tino rangatiratanga have continued. Some have demanded separation from the Pākehā state and absolute Māori sovereignty; others have argued for various degrees of autonomy in particular areas of activity. The politics of negotiation and accommodation have also continued, and continued - according to mainstream political and legal doctrine - under the supreme authority of the sovereign state.

All the Māori claims have continued to be accompanied by a good deal of (though I think less) public disapproval along lines made familiar in the 1980s, especially when they have been accompanied by demonstration, occupation of lands, episodes of arson, and the like. A best-selling book in 1995 was Stuart Scott's *Treaty of Waitangi: The Road to Anarchy*. 'Natural justice and common sense' must, he argued, prevail against Māori claims. The Treaty, intended as 'the Marriage lines of two peoples', would, if the clock were not stopped, become a '*causa belli* within the New Zealand community: a racial time bomb for the

---

5   New Zealand is a land of around 24,500,000 hectares. A modest 96,443.4 hectares were returned to Māori as Treaty settlements without payment from 1978 to 1995, and of that area only 1,064.3 hectares were returned as a result of Tribunal recommendations. See Statistics New Zealand, *Census Education Kit*, p.48.

6   See for detail Te Puni Kōkiri, *Report on Implementation of Waitangi Tribunal Recommendations and Agreements*.

7   Eloquent official testimony to this is in Crown Forestry Trust, *Report to Appointors 1995-96*, pp. 2-3, 6-8. See on its operations: Auditor General, *Report* (1995), and Sharp, 'The Waitangi Tribunal in New Zealand Politics 1984-1996'.

8   By the State-Owned Enterprises (Treaty of Waitangi) Act (1988), and the Crown Forests Act (1989)

9   *Sunday Star-Times*, 6 Oct 1996, p.A3.

10 There was a steady growth in the numbers of news stories on radio and TV from 1984 to 1995 as figures derived from the Robert and Noeline Chapman Audio-Visual Archive show. They rose continuously. The only year defying this generalization was 1992, when the figures reached an isolated peak.

future'.[11] The reader interested in the truth of what the book asserts should read it in conjunction with the Waitangi Tribunal's three reports on Ngai Tahu claims.[12] But however the reader may judge Scott's claims, it is plainly not true that anarchy has ever appeared to be a realistic outcome of the agitations.

II

The Struggles for Effective Authority: The Context of the Problems for Agents

The fundamental issues between Māori and the Crown and Māori and Pākehā may have remained the same, but the passage of political and institutional time from 1989 onwards has rendered some of them both more pressing than others and more interesting to philosophers of justice. These are issues of agency. An agent is a person, either natural (a man or woman) or artificial (the Crown, a Government, an iwi, a Court of Appeal) who has the right to act; and the issues at stake were *precisely* as to who had the right to act, and in acting to wield authority and to dispose of resources. In te reo they were issues of rangatiratanga and mana.

Before the neo-liberal economic and political revolution, there had been as much emphasis on who should by right *receive* resources from constituted authorities as there had been on who had the prior right to *make* (or block) such redistributions. When Māori had felt that their rights of recipience were frustrated, or that the means of delivery were ineffective, they had indeed tended to argue that the issue was not so much who should get what, but who had the authority to deliver what the people needed; and thus Māori sovereignty was argued for. But, accepting that the most important thing was to ameliorate the Māori condition – to acquire the resources necessary to improve the health, welfare, education, and economic development of the people – they had equally been able and willing to work within a Pākehā institutional framework to get what they needed. They did not always think that authority, subjection, and property rights were at issue. The neo-liberal change in ruling ideas, institutional arrangements, and economic policy made it more difficult, however, for Māori to sustain such a balance between being a receiver (a patient or subject) and an actor (an agent or authority). The times were against that balance: there would be individual liberty in the market and individual responsibility for one's own life; human relations would be constructed by contract between individual and individual, worker and employer, Government and its 'agents', grouping and grouping. Men, and women, and team enterprises, would have to look after themselves in a world dominated by the nation's need to survive in the international marketplace; and any agents (natural or artificial) in this world would be

---

[11] Preface. Cf. Archie (ed.) *Māori Sovereignty*, Chapters 3, 9, 14, 16, 17.
[12] Waitangi Tribunal: *Ngai Tahu Report*; *Ngai Tahu Sea Fisheries*; *Ngai Tahu Ancillary Claims*.

advised to act so as to enhance their power in it.[13] They had to act and not be acted upon; they had to be authors of their own destiny and not dependent on others; they had to become *agents* and not *patients*.

New Zealanders living in 1996 may find this ancient distinction between agent and patient difficult to follow.[14] The theories of management to which they have been subjected during the neo-liberal revolution suggest that 'agents' are those who, by delegation (typically via contract), act for those in authority over them.[15] They will think that 'agents' are under the command of the 'manager', who has authority over them. But the very idea that an agent can act for an authority is parasitic on the idea of authority, and authority initially arises from individual agency and not from subjection to a superior. The same Thomas Hobbes who insisted that sovereignty – the highest power of agency there is – must be absolute, also insisted that those who act, unless they have in some way (perhaps by contract) delegated their authority to act, are, and remain, authors of their own actions:

A *person* is he whose words or actions are considered either as his own, or as *representing* the words and actions of another man. ... When they are considered as his own, then he is called a *natural person*; and when they are considered as representing the words and actions of another man, then he is a feigned or *artificial person*. ... The word *person*... has been translated to [mean] any representer, as in Tribunals [and] as [in] theatres,[16] so that a *person* is the same as an *actor* is ... .

Of *persons artificial*, some have their words and actions *owned* by those they represent. And then the person is an *actor* (and he that *owns* his word and actions is the *author*): in which case the *actor* acts by *authority*. For that which in speaking of goods and possessions is called an *owner* (and in Latin *dominus*), ... speaking of actions, is called the *author*. And, as the right of possession is called *dominion*, so the right of doing any action is called *authority*. So that by 'authority' is always understood the right of doing any act, and 'done by authority' [means] 'done by commission or license from him whose right it is'.[17]

There can only be 'agents' in the contemporary New Zealand sense where they are authorised to act. *I* use the term in the old-fashioned way: agents are those who may and can act in their own right; they are those natural or artificial persons who are not commanded or controlled by others unless they delegate that command and control to others to act for them. Only when they have in the first place delegated that authority may they become, in turn, agents of that authority. And if they do not delegate their authority they continue to act for themselves and not for another.

[13] Sharp, 'The case for politics and the state', pp. 4-7.
[14] As indeed Jane Kelsey, an excellent historian of current theories of agency, did when she read an earlier draft of this chapter.
[15] Boston et al., *Reshaping the State*, pp. 2-10.
[16] Hobbes has earlier explained that a 'persona' is a disguise or mask, the outward appearance as presented on a stage. A modern might understand what this means by comparing the idea of an inward self with the idea of an outward person. See Sharp, 'Why be bicultural?', pp. 120-2.
[17] *Leviathan*, Chap 16: 'Of persons, authors, and things personated'. I have modernized Hobbes's text for easier reading.

As the 1990s unfolded, and despite general popular distaste for the direction things were taking,[18] the ideology of distributive justice and amelioration was seldom heard, and its politics became muted, complex, confused, and bureaucratic. In these conditions,[19] the questions for Māori were, inevitably, those concerning their rights to act for themselves, to be authors of their own actions, and not to be subject to authorities whom they did not 'own'. They claimed both their authority and their dominion to be their own, underived from a higher authority.

This, of course, was not the whole of Māori politics. Recognition of the Crown and pleas to it for rights of recipience continued. It was just that the balance had changed. Nevertheless, the politics of Māori agency grew at the expense of the politics of amelioration by way of Government agency. A climax was reached in the early months of 1995, when te tino rangatiratanga was proclaimed as the cause of the occupiers of Moutua Gardens/Pakaitore Marae in the town of Wanganui/Whanganui. The local Council was forced by the protesters to prove in court its legal title to the land in question against the Māori claims; the Government found itself having to refuse to negotiate with any group claiming authority separate from, and not subordinate to, that of the sovereign Crown.[20] Some of the protesters, charged with minor offences arising from the occupation, refused to recognise the right of the courts to try them. In November 1996, Geoffrey Fuimaono, pleading in appeal that he was subject only to tikanga Māori/Māori law, was told by Justice Edward Thomas, the Court of Appeal judge probably more sympathetic to Māori legal claims than any other: 'The courts are subservient to Parliament and must apply an act of Parliament in the terms in which it has been enacted'. It may have been in accord with tikanga that someone, even a policeman, entering slyly by a back entrance to a marae, should have his entrance resisted by force; but the Crimes Act did not recognise this custom and so neither would a court. Only Parliament could authorize courts to recognize tikanga as part of the law.[21]

Such a politics of Māori agency was not confined to the climax of 1995. Both Labour until it was voted out of office in October 1990, and National thereafter, had their problems with it. Nor were the problems simply theoretical and to do with the source and locus of authority and dominion as between Māori and Crown; they were also very practical problems, because certain agents of the Crown (the courts and the Waitangi Tribunal in particular) tended to interpose their findings and directives between the executive Government and its intentions. Governments were to find themselves enmeshed in Treaty litigation.

Governments of neither party could contemplate this. Settlements would have to be 'political' and not 'legal'. In creating the Tribunal in 1975 and in expanding

---

18 Kelsey, *The New Zealand Experiment*, pp. 324–5.
19 As described by Jonathan Boston et al, *Public Management*, Chapter 9.
20 H1:19/5/95.
21 HA4, 5 November 1996. Joe Williams, a Māori lawyer, immediately claimed that an implication of the judgement was that where tikanga was not contradicted by statute it had legal validity. *Morning Report*, National Radio, 7 November 1996. The Law Commission, possibly as a consequence, soon announced that it was undertaking a study of the matter. H A11: 18/11/96.

its powers in 1984 and 1988, the Labour Governments of the time were, besides attempting to provide justice for the Māori, endeavouring to take the reparative issue out of Parliament and party politics and to have it dealt with quasi-legally. This was, and remained, a reasonable move. But the attempt to routinize the problem of Māori affairs and take it out of parliamentary and populist politics was, by 1988, looking distinctly unsuccessful. The Tribunal and the courts were seizing the initiative. As a consequence, Labour reverted to the policy that had preceded the setting up of the Tribunal – direct negotiation with claimant tribes. Cabinet decided that the Government would take the lead role. It set up its own official office for researching and negotiating Treaty claims; and in July 1989 David Lange, the Prime Minister, stated clearly the principles on which it would negotiate. The iwi would certainly have the right 'to organise as iwi, and, *under law*, to control their resources as their own'; 'both the Government and the iwi' were 'obliged to accord each other reasonable co-operation on major issues of common concern'; and the Government was 'responsible for providing effective processes for the resolution of grievances in the expectation that reconciliation can occur'. Granting those principles, however, the Government would have the right to make laws, and all New Zealanders would be treated equally under the law. There would be no special treatment or separate legal system.[22]

Four months later, Geoffrey Palmer, the new Labour Prime Minister, travelled to Port Waikato to reopen direct negotiations with Waikato-Tainui over their raupatu claims – claims to lands confiscated in the Waikato after the Māori/Land/Sovereignty Wars. It was then that he told them (and the country) that settlements would have to be 'political' and not 'legal'.[23] In early 1995 the Waikato leader of the still-unfinished negotiations with the Crown was to comment wryly on what the new direction meant to him: 'As an alternative to the courts, international forums, the Waitangi Tribunal or civil insurrection, [the] process of direct negotiation has both its advantages and disadvantages. What has been learned is that, at the end of the day, outcomes rest solely on the political will of both parties to settle'.[24]

The incoming National Government, in any case beholden to a less Māori-sympathetic constituency, continued and extended the same policy of direct negotiation and assertion of Crown sovereignty.[25] Its leaders, notably the Prime Minister Jim Bolger and the Minister of Justice (and Treaty Negotiations) Doug Graham, proclaimed that they wanted the whole claims issue disposed of rapidly. The Government further strengthened its official research and negotiating

---

22 *Principles for Crown Action on the Treaty of Waitangi.* I have added italics and put the first two principles last for the sake of emphasis.
23 The speech is quoted at some length in Kelsey, *Rolling Back the State,* p. 215. See on the context Sharp, 'The problem of Māori affairs, 1984-89'. The overall state of the case as to Treaty politics near the end of Labour's term is presented in a masterly way by Renwick, *The Treaty Now* (August 1990).
24 Mahuta, 'Tainui: a case study in direct negotiation', p.77.
25 Kelsey, 'From flagstaffs to pinetrees'. And the new government adopted the policy of the Treaty of Waitangi Policy Unit for the Crown Task Force on Treaty of Waitangi Issues, as set out in its *The Direct Negotiation of Māori Claims* (1990).

capacity at the expense of the Tribunal's. It finished the fisheries negotiations that Labour had begun in 1988 under the Māori threat of legal action. In its Treaty of Waitangi (Fisheries Claims) Settlement Act of December 1992 – the 'Sealord Deal' – it instituted a complex pan-Māori deal involving about $170 million's worth of fishing Quota and part-ownership of the Sealord fishing company. In 1995 it also brought the negotiations with Waikato-Tainui to a successful statutory conclusion, also at the cost of about $170 million. By the summer of 1994-1995 these settlements[26] had to be seen as part of what had emerged as a clear plan of overall settlement. For, advised by Treasury, the Government had developed from 1991-1994 a proposed 'settlement envelope' of $1 billion.[27] Such a sum would be used to reach 'full and final' settlements of all 'historical' claims over 'about' the following decade. A land bank of surplus Crown land, which had been set up to meet Treaty claims, would be replenished; conservation estate lands would be used only sparingly in settlements.[28] Claims to natural resources not exploited by the Māori in 1840 would not be met; when claims to natural resources *were* met, only use and not ownership rights would be granted. A procedure for negotiation would be introduced: to get on to a 'work programme', claims would have to be fully researched and proved; claimants would have to produce a 'deed of mandate' from those whom they represented so that settlements could not be disputed by rival claimants. Procedures were set in place for ensuring that the beneficiaries of settlements were defined and that the benefits would be passed in trust to an appropriately constituted legal body. As settlements progressed, so the jurisdiction of the Waitangi Tribunal and the courts would be wound down. In December 1994 the Government published these thoughts as *Crown Proposals for the Settlement of Treaty of Waitangi Claims.*[29]

In doing so, it proved that what I have elsewhere called 'the problem of Māori affairs' had not been solved by National, as it had not been solved by Labour: Māori continued to depict themselves as a separate people – in fact as a series of separate peoples – who insisted on dealing with a sovereign Government as if they were its equals.[30] So it was in the early months of 1995. A series of thirteen consultative hui roundly rejected the *Crown Proposals*, concentrating on their not having been previously negotiated with the Māori 'partner', and on their setting the 'fiscal cap' and a time limit on what must be an open-ended process continuing into the indefinite future. Wira Gardiner, Secretary of Te Puni Kōkiri (the Ministry of Māori Development) during the period, has graphically described the almost universal rage among Māori and the universal rejection of the Government's plan expressed at the hui.[31] A series of land occupations, including that of Moutua Gardens, accompanied and immediately followed the hui. Variously meant and variously interpreted claims to tino rangatiratanga were

---

[26] It was common knowledge that Waikato-Tainui's claim was progressing to a conclusion.
[27] The amount paid to redundant State Servants from 1987-1990: NZPD 2:43 (1992), p.13040.
[28] Crown Lands reserved mainly as National Parks, and devoted to the protection of the natural environment.
[29] 8 December 1994.
[30] Sharp, 'The problem of Māori affairs, 1984-89'.
[31] *Return to Sender. What really happened at the fiscal envelope hui.* See also M.H.Durie, 'Proceedings of a Hui held at Hirangi Marae, Turangi'.

voiced.[32] Nevertheless the Government continued with direct negotiations. By October 1996 it reached agreement with the east coast Whakatōhea for a settlement worth about $40 million and it approached a settlement with Ngai Tahu for $170 million. In November, as a general election loomed, it was enmeshed in negotiations with other east coast tribes and with the large North Island raupatu claims of the Taranaki iwi.

Māori remained calm but firm in a refusal to recognize settlements as 'full and final'. Even Waikato-Tainui, grateful recipients of a settlement they immediately set about translating into development projects, refused to bind future generations to what had been done. The iwi's independent rights of future action would not be expunged. They had in the past refused to work as agents for the Crown,[33] and now their leaders refused to think that the actions of their generation could abridge the rights of future generations. It might be said, that as a current Parliament cannot bind a future Parliament because sovereignty cannot be abridged, nor can present Waikato-Tainui limit the rangatiratanga inherent in the iwi at each moment in time.

But it was not Governments alone that had problems of agency. Māori had theirs too. In the 1980s they had come together to demand Treaty settlements and recognition of their rangatiratanga and mana; they had asserted themselves to be an *ethnie*; they had argued for a bicultural society in which their language and customs would bear equal sway with the Pākehā's. To a remarkable degree they had acted as a unit over and against others. They had acted, as Bertrand de Jouvenel used to put it, as a 'team of action': tolerably united in agreed purposes and intent on evolving authority structures to represent them in their pursuit of them. And they had acted as a team of action, in (to adopt and expand another of de Jouvenel's useful notions) a 'milieu of existence' – a complex reality of belief, custom, habit, law, policies, and institutions (including other teams of action) that constituted the raw material which their policies were designed to change.[34] But, as the milieu changed, so did what was always true become evident: Māori were not just a people or an *ethnie* or a race. They were *also* a complex and volatile set of teams of action. They were as much iwi and hapū (and evolving groupings, divisions and remnants of iwi and hapū) as they were Māori; and among those teams of action – not always personified in the names of their eponymous ancestors – questions were to emerge about just which teams had mana and rangatiratanga over which particular persons and things and how that mana and rangatiratanga might be transmuted into authority to speak and act as representing the contesting teams. This contestation, always endemic in Māori society, was still accompanied by attempts at constructing institutions to represent their kotahitanga (their unity or 'hanging togetherness' as Māori), which also had a long history. But the attempts, though pursued with an urgency

---

[32]   The most convenient place to find a range of views as to what Māori sovereignty and tino rangatiratanga might mean are in twin publications: Melbourne (ed.) *Māori Sovereignty. The Māori perspective*, and Archie (ed.) *Māori Sovereignty. The Pakeha perspective*. See also Sharp, 'Sovereignty: te tino rangatiratanga'.

[33]   Mahuta, 'Tainui: a case study of direct negotiations', p.167.

[34]   de Jouvenel, *Sovereignty*, pp. 59–64.

generated both by Government insistence on dealing only with those with 'mandates' as well as by Māori imperatives, were made more difficult as the Treaty settlement process proceeded. Hui which rejected an interim pan-Māori fisheries settlement of 1989, the Sealord fisheries settlement of 1992, and the fiscal envelope proposal of late 1994, all expressed suspicions that, in settling with undifferentiated 'Māori', and in setting a limit to the sum total of all possible settlements, the Crown planned to divide and rule. Obviously, if one Māori team of action claimed and exploited resources for itself, that team had to demonstrate rights of action over and against other teams who claimed the same rights, often over the same people and things.

The scene was set for a competition among Māori themselves as to who had rights of agency. This was the result of the politics of settlement in conditions of the neo-liberal retreat from social welfare and from state-sponsored economic development. In the event, settlements will be seen to have borne little relation to questions of need or any other conceptions of distributive justice. Reparation has been made and will be made to the best organised teams, not to the most needy.[35]

III

Challenges to the Crown's Agency

In the 1990s a new generation of 'Māori radicals' rose to replace the old, though some remained. The doings and sayings of Hone Harawira, Eva Rickard, and Syd Jackson continued to be reported. Ken Mair, Mike Smith, Tame Iti, and Annette Sykes replaced Atareta Poananga, Donna Awatere, and Ripeka Evans as authors of outrageous acts. But it has not been the radicals whose activities have seriously challenged the Crown. Indeed, that they should openly flout the law and should articulate claims to absolute Māori sovereignty has been a help rather than a hindrance to Governments. Popular indignation was stirred, not least among Māori 'moderates'.[36]

Nor have the continued findings of the Waitangi Tribunal as to the details of past wrongs to Māori – most notably in the *Ngai Tahu Reports* (1991–1993) and the *Taranaki Report* (1996) – seemed likely to transform public perceptions to the extent of causing dangerous friction that might translate into loss of votes. Māori always knew of their wrongs; Pākehā were becoming used to hearing of them. The Tribunal's success in public education, although not complete, has bitten so deep that there was no effective opposition to the remarkable preamble to the National Government's statutory settlement with Waikato-Tainui in December 1995. In the preamble, in both English and te reo, the Crown acknowledged that:

[35] J.D.Gould, 'Socio-economic differences between Māori iwi' (1996). And see on fisheries allocation below.
[36] See Gardiner, *Return to Sender*, Chapter 19.

its representatives and advisers acted unjustly and in breach of the Treaty of Waitangi … in sending its forces across the Mangataawhiri in July 1863 and in unfairly labelling Waikato as rebels … The Crown acknowledges that subsequent confiscations of land and resources under the New Zealand Settlements Act … were wrongful, have caused Waikato to the present time to suffer feelings in relation to their lost lands akin to those of orphans, and have had a crippling impact on the welfare, economy and development of Waikato.

The Crown therefore expressed its 'profound regret and apologize[d] unreservedly for the loss of lives … arising from its invasion, and at the devastation of property and social life which resulted'. It would now seek 'on behalf of all New Zealanders to atone for these acknowledged injustices' by making reparation for past wrongs.[37] When the Tribunal's *Manukau Report* had first brought these wrongs to public attention in 1984, there had been a public outcry of denial and the idea of reparation had been dismissed out of hand. It is evidence of the impact of a new historical consciousness among those who care about such things – and a resigned apathy among those who do not – that in 1996 the wrongs were scarcely denied and that it was accepted that reparation would have to be made.

Governments' difficulties have, rather, been caused by their adherence to the idea that settlements must be made in the light of Treaty 'principles', and by the fact that interpretation of those principles lies not entirely with them but also with the Waitangi Tribunal and the courts.

The Tribunal has been reined in since 1989. Its activity has been hampered by lack of resources in the face of its backlog. The courts have made it clear that while they (and the executive) will give great respect to the Tribunal's interpretation of Treaty principles and to the evidence it collects, it is *their* interpretation of the principles and application of them in defined areas that binds both the Tribunal and Governments, and the courts have firmly insisted that it is up to them to decide what evidence they will find admissible.[38] Although the Tribunal had been given powers to require (and not just recommend) that the Government return lands and forests to Māori, it found it impolitic to use them; further, legislation in 1992 and 1993 meant it could not continue to deal with most fisheries questions and could not suggest that privately owned property might be used in Treaty settlements. The Tribunal has had to accept these practical and legal restraints and tailor its activity accordingly.[39] Nevertheless, in pursuing its duty to pronounce on the principles of the Treaty, it has continued to reflect on issues of agency. Its opinions have fuelled those of Governments' opponents and, to a degree, the courts', and have had to be countered by the Crown.

The issues have remained those of rangatiratanga, mana, kāwanatanga and taonga, over and against sovereignty and dominion, government, and property.[40]

---

37 Waikato Raupatu Claims Settlement Act, pp. 12-14.
38 Sharp, 'The Treaty, the Tribunal and the law', p.140. See also *Taiaroa v Minister of Justice* (unreported) High Court Wellington, 4 October 1994, CP 99/94 at 50.
39 A good introduction to the legal and political position up until 1994 is to be found in the pages of G. McLay (ed.) *Treaty Settlements*, especially Keith, 'The roles of the Treaty, the Tribunal, the courts and the legislature', and Graham, 'Address by the Minister in Charge of Treaty Negotiations'. See also Jane Kelsey, 'Judicialisation of the Treaty of Waitangi: a subtle cultural repositioning'.
40 Sharp, 'Sovereignty: te tino rangatiratanga'; Oliver, *Claims to the Waitangi Tribunal*.

The Tribunal has continually asserted that it is *Māori* interpretations of the Māori concepts that matter. In 1840 Māori had known the connection between mana and rangatiratanga and of both with taonga; they still did, and still claimed them on grounds of inextinguishable right. None of these things had been ceded. None *could* be ceded. The Tribunal's reports recorded and supported what the claimants argued to be the essential elements in any interpretation and application of the principles of the Treaty. And to Māori principles of interpretation of their own words, the Tribunal grafted into Treaty principles a jurisprudence derived from the developing practice of international law – a jurisprudence to do with the inalienable rights of indigenous peoples to autonomy and to the development of their own tribal assets. In the *Taranaki Report* of 1996 the hand of the Chairperson, Chief Judge Edward Durie, may be discerned at work, adding to his other, earlier, pronouncements:

In modern times, overseas countries have seen the indigenous component of a symbiotic relationship with Government under the rubric of 'aboriginal autonomy'. Also called 'aboriginal self-government', it equates with 'tino rangatiratanga' and 'mana motuhake' …

Support for this view may be found in the United States of America and developments in Canada and Australia. These suggest that the recognition of aboriginal autonomy is not in fact a barrier to national unity but an aid. They go further to recognise that conciliation requires a process of empowerment, not suppression.

Precisely what forms the recognition of autonomy would take, Judge Durie argued, was not yet clear. But it certainly entailed the 'right of indigenes to constitutional status as first peoples' and it suggested that Māori had rights to 'manage their own policies, resources, and affairs (within the rules necessary for the operation of the state) and to enjoy co-operation and dialogue with the government'.[41]

Clearly the Tribunal's continued interpretation and application of Treaty principles as seen from these Māori perspectives posed problems for the legal and political system. The problems were not directly *legal* ones, for its interpretations were not binding on the Crown. They certainly, however, posed a rhetorical challenge because the system operated on the basis that the Crown had sovereignty over the people and – as part of that sovereignty – dominion or radical title over all the lands and waters of the country. Sovereignty might be limited in practical exercise by the rights of action of innumerable other persons (both natural and artificial), who held private property or authority, but in the last resort legislation could extinguish those rights. This was constitutional doctrine. Rights of agency derived from the Crown.

Such a view of the constitution and of sovereignty was, and remained, the view of the courts as the Labour Government gave way to National. But the Tribunal, extrapolating from court decisions and developments in international law and practice, could always attempt to persuade the courts that they had decided more expansively for Māori rights than they thought they had. One thing was already clear from the 1987 New Zealand Māori Council Case: that where the courts were required by statute to take the principles of the Treaty

41   *The Taranaki Report*, pp. 19-20. Cf. Waitangi Tribunal, *Appointments to the Treaty of Waitangi Fisheries Commission Report*, pp. 11-12, and E.T. Durie's 'Politics, biculturalism and the law'.

into account, they would see these principles, if not as a bar to legislation which could extinguish their operation, at least as requiring the executive to act according to them within the ambits of the relevant statutes. This legal point could be expanded – in jurisprudential conditions where it was thought that the Treaty and not the British actions of 1840 were the basis of the constitution – to mean that the Crown's sovereignty was inherently limited. And so it was in fact expanded, most fully in the *Ngai Tahu Land Report* (1991). There the Tribunal argued that:

While, as we have seen, legal sovereignty is exclusive and exhaustive, this is not to say it is absolute. It is clear that cession of sovereignty to the Crown by the Māori was conditional. It was qualified by the retention of tino rangatiratanga. As Mr Justice Casey said in the New Zealand Māori Council case, 'the whole thrust of article 2 was the protection of Māori land and the uses and privileges associated with it'. It should, of course, be noted that rangatiratanga embraced protection not only of Māori land but much more. We need to remember that rangatiratanga was confirmed and guaranteed by the Queen in article 2. This necessarily qualifies or limits the authority of the Crown to govern.[42]

If the Treaty were to be seen as the generative basis of the New Zealand constitution – that is, as the source of origin and legitimating myth of the legal system – then it is hard to see how the implication of some kind of equality of status (if not of scope of operation)[43] between sovereignty and rangatiratanga could be resisted. The Tribunal *may* usually have meant its words to apply only within the ambit of Treaty claims, but many Māori and some of the legal profession believed, and have come to believe, that this is too restrictive a view to take of the fundamental law and constitution of the country. Annie Mikaere (who is both a Māori and a lawyer) has argued:

Is not working within the limits prescribed by the Crown the very antithesis of tino rangatiratanga? Is not the term 'qualified autonomy' a contradiction in terms? And why must it be that the reconciliation of tino rangatiratanga with kawanatanga necessarily means first defining kawanatanga in terms of Crown sovereignty and then fitting rangatiratanga into that context? Why not define tino rangatiratanga in terms of Māori self-determination and then fit the *concept* of kawanatanga alongside that *reality*?[44]

The thought that native peoples retain an inextinguishable separate status in constitutions, and that all other authorities are disabled from infringing them, is comparatively new in New Zealand, though not elsewhere.[45] This is not at all what the National Party meant in 1990, when it agreed that the Treaty was the 'foundation document' of the country. Nor is it what the courts have meant to imply when they have spoken of the Treaty in much the same terms. The Tribunal has thus remained an important receptacle and transmitter of a Treaty

---

[42]   *Ngai Tahu Report*, Section 14.7.5. A similar statement is in the *Turangi Township Report*, at p.285.
[43]   In the *Kiwifruit Marketing Report*, Section 4.4 (where it is evident that members of the Tribunal disagree as to the scope, and perhaps, source, of rangatiratanga) the right of government to regulate trade was vindicated against claims to Māori independence of it.
[44]   Quoted and discussed by Brookfield, 'Constitutional law', pp. 383-4.
[45]   See Tully, *Strange Multiplicity. Constitutionalism in an age of diversity*; and for comment, Sharp, 'What is the constitution of "The Spirit of Haida Gwai"?'.

jurisprudence which, while not in itself inimical to the Crown's sovereignty, has placed the Treaty and the immemorial and natural rights it expressed at least alongside the Crown's prerogative as the source from which all constitutional arrangements must flow.

The courts were, however, a more powerful hindrance than the Tribunal to Governments' unfettered agency. The Tribunal had only limited powers to bind Governments and it never used them; but the courts had a duty to hear pleas brought to them, a duty to oversee Treaty settlements, and the power to review Governments' performances in those settlements.

Part of the problem was that, although the courts did not directly challenge the paramountcy of statute and the Treaty's legal inefficacy unless it were incorporated in statute, there were indications that they might move in that direction. After the *New Zealand Māori Council* v *Attorney-General* (1987), Mr Justice Cooke's opinion given there continued to be quoted and echoed:

Counsel for the applicants did not go so far as to contend that, apart altogether from the State-Owned Enterprises Act, the Treaty of Waitangi is a Bill of Rights or fundamental New Zealand constitutional document in the sense that it could override Acts of our legislature. It could hardly have done so in the face of the decision of the Privy Council in *Hoani te Heuheu Tukino* v *Aotea District Māori Land Board* [1941 AC 308] that rights conferred by the treaty cannot be enforced in the Courts except so far as a statutory recognition of the rights can be found.[46]

This was, and remained, the legal fact; and the legal profession's view of the history of law in New Zealand reinforced it: New Zealand had inherited a constitution from Britain, and that constitution brought with it the doctrine of the sovereignty of the Crown, which was now, in effect, exercised by an elected Parliament.[47] But there were indications that the 'broad and unquibbling' application of Treaty principles that Cooke and the other Justices had *also* mentioned in the 1987 case might possibly carry the courts further in the direction of importing Treaty principles into the law and applying them in the interpretation and application of statutes that did not directly mention them.

In the case of *Tainui Māori Board* v *the Attorney-General* (1989), the Court of Appeal found against the Crown's attempt to avoid the provisions of section 9 of the SOE Act[48] by having Coalcorp, an SOE, not the Crown, sell lands under claim by Tainui. This was frustrating enough. But the case led Mr Justice Cooke to raise the 'spectre'[49] of Treaty principles having wider, constitutional, import:

---

46 *NZMC* v *Attorney General* [1990] 1 NZLR 641 at 655. See that and similar dicta invoked the High Court in *Te Runanga o Whare Kauri Rekohu Inc* v *Attorney-General*, [1993] NZCLD C-587-88; *Wikeepa* v *Police* (unreported) High Court, Tauranga, AP62/93; *Tairaroa* v *Minister of Justice* (unreported) High Court, Wellington, 4 October 1994, CP 99/94; and *R* v *Pairama* [1995] 13 CRNZ 496, at 498-99. In the Court of Appeal see in *Mahuta and Tainui Trust Board* v *Attorney-General* [1989] 2 NZLR 513 at 518-09; *R* v *Wikeepa* (unreported) 14 June 1994, CA 479/93; and *Taiaroa* v *The Minister of Justice* [1995] 1 NZLR 411. In the Judicial Committee of the Privy Council see *New Zealand Māori Council* v *Attorney-General* [1994] 1 NZLR 513 at 515 and 524.

47 McHugh, 'The historiography of New Zealand's constitutional history'.

48 'Nothing in this Act shall permit the Crown to act contrary to the principles of Waitangi.'

49 I take the word from Joseph, 'Constitutional law', p.11.

...the main questions turn on statutory interpretation. On these questions counsel for Tainui have not sought to put their case on any basis wider than s 9 of the State Enterprises Act. As in *New Zealand Māori Council* v *Attorney General* ... I think it best not to venture on any wider and unargued issues regarding the Treaty of Waitangi and rights of 'indigenous peoples'. As also in that case, I have no doubt that the subject matter of the statutes, concerned as they are with the Treaty, demands a broad, unquibbling and practical interpretation. With appropriate resignation it must be acknowledged that what was said to that effect in the judgements in that case had no obvious influence on the thorough arguments we heard presented ably for the Crown in the present case.

Perhaps we ought to repeat as well that the Court should be slow to ascribe to Parliament an intention to permit conduct inconsistent with the principles of the Treaty. But it does not seem to me to be necessary to invoke any such constitutional principle of interpretation in order to decide this case.[50]

Cooke retired in 1996, soon after his elevation to the British peerage, but he was to leave in his profession's uneasy mind the underlying idea that some combination of Treaty principles, international law, and administrative reasonableness might suggest that Māori rights were a permanent constraint on Government action. Certainly the principles of the Treaty required more than mere consultation when Māori interests were at stake; possibly some kind of primacy must be given to them when they were not directly inimical to statutory provision – even when the relevant legislation did not mention them. The constitutional position remains unclear, and thus so does the power of the courts to exercise constitutional review over Treaty matters. [51]

These have become issues for theorists of the constitution. A more urgent challenge for Governments was the brute fact of litigation consequent on their reforms of the economy. After the Māori Council Case and the fisheries cases of 1987 there followed a huge amount of Māori-centred litigation, mainly but not entirely hinging on section 9 of the SOE Act. What Jane Kelsey has called the 'judicialisation of the Treaty' intensified, so that from 1987 to 1996 more than 70 cases, many joined in complex combinations, came to the courts.[52] Frustrating as it was to Māori and enriching as it was mainly to lawyers, it was even more frustrating to Governments, and it cost them money. They were intent on privatizing not only profitable Crown lands and the fisheries, but also petrochemical and geothermal resources, the tourist industry, coal mines, forests, telecommunications, hydroelectric generation and transmission, and the radio and television industries. At each attempt by the Crown to divest itself of ownership or control there sprang suits and petitions, claims, counter-claims and revisions of claims – all punctuated by appeals to the Court of Appeal in Wellington and to the judicial committee of the Privy Council in Westminster. There was no respite. The art of Government became much more complex in the Treaty area. While the processes of government were greatly slowed, court

---

50   [1989] 2 NZLR 513 at 518-19. Cf. *New Zealand Māori Council* v *Attorney-General* (unreported) High Court, Wellington, 3 May 1991, CP 942/88 at 17.

51   Joseph, 'Constitutional law', pp. 11-14 refers, with an intention not altogether clear, to *Ngai Tahu Māori Trust Board* v *Director-General of Conservation* [1995] 3 NZLR 553. Cf. Brookfield, 'Constitutional law', pp. 376-85.

52   That count is confined to searching 'Treaty of Waitangi' in BRIEFCASE. Cf. Kelsey, 'The judicialisation of the Treaty'.

decisions were often made in haste; and much debate was generated among the politicians and the public.

The first 'broadcasting case' was brought in December 1988, and what may not be the last ended in June 1996.[53] In 1988 the Crown had proposed transferring the assets of the dissolved Broadcasting Corporation to two SOEs, Radio New Zealand and Television New Zealand. In the face of bitter New Zealand Māori Council opposition to Government proposals to allocate too few radio-spectrum frequencies to Māori (and no FM frequencies in Auckland or Wellington), it was not until May 1991 that the Government was freed by the courts to transfer rights in frequencies to Radio New Zealand. And it was not until 1996 that Radio New Zealand was able to sell its commercial assets. Among other things, it had first to be shown that the Government's actions in removing Radio New Zealand from the schedule of SOEs in the SOE Act – and thus from the prohibition of acting inconsistently with the principles of the Treaty – were not outside the law. And some issues still remain live.[54] The disposal of television assets was quicker, but still slower than the Government would have wished. It took until December 1993 for the Privy Council to hold that they might be sold to private enterprise.[55]

In this field of operation Māori and the courts were a mighty hindrance to Government action. As Lord Woolf noted during the Privy Council case:

Section 9 is not intended to provide a lever which can be used to compel the Crown to take positive action to fulfil its obligations under the Treaty. Nonetheless the existence of s 9 can have the effect of facing the Crown with the option of either taking the steps which will result in it meeting those obligations or being unable to take the action which it wishes of transferring the assets.[56]

Similar stories might be told of the greater and lesser frustration of Government intentions concerning the disposal of coal, forests, geothermal resources, and hydroelectric dams; and it was partly litigation and threats of litigation that brought Governments to the negotiating table with Waikato-Tainui and Ngai Tahu.[57]

The most worrying and intractable problem, however, was that of privatizing commercial fisheries by way of Individual Transferable Quotas (ITQs) in accord with the Quota Management System (QMS) introduced by Labour and continued by National.[58] For here, more than in any other area of law, the coincidence of common law aboriginal title with Treaty rights to taonga made the legal position of Governments highly precarious.[59] The case was bad enough in

---

53 Events to mid-1994 are recorded in Waitangi Tribunal, *Broadcasting Claim*.
54 *New Zealand Māori Council* v *Attorney-General* [1996] 3 NZLR 140. See Justice Thomas's dissenting remarks especially as to the live issues at 168.
55 *New Zealand Māori Council* v *Attorney-General* [1994] 1 NZLR 513.
56 [1994] 1 NZLR 513 at 520.
57 Mahuta, 'Tainui: a case study of direct negotiation', pp. 167–73; Mahuta, 'Tainui, Kingitanga and raupatu', pp. 29–30.
58 A good description of the position in late 1992 is in the Waitangi Tribunal's *Fisheries Settlement Report*, Section 2.
59 See above, pp. 82–85. Add Renwick, *The Treaty Now*, pp. 62–73.

1987-1988 when the joint Māori-Crown working group that had been set up to reach a settlement failed to do so.[60] It was to get worse. In September 1988, following further fruitless Māori-Crown negotiations, Labour introduced a bill designed to enshrine a pan-Māori settlement in statute. Among the clauses were a number designed to repeal section 88(2) of the 1983 Fisheries Act ('Nothing in this Act shall affect any Māori fishing rights'), to nullify interim orders of the High Court that prohibited continued disposal of Quota, to nullify the proceedings currently underway, to prohibit fisheries claims to be taken to the courts on grounds of aboriginal or Treaty title, and to forbid recourse to the Waitangi Tribunal on fisheries claims. The proposals led to almost every tribe in the country bringing claims of trespass, breach of fiduciary duty, and negligence against the Crown.[61] In the face of this pressure, the Government gave up its plan of extinguishing Māori fishing rights in exchange for what it would give. The Māori Fisheries Act of December 1989 simply created a Māori Fisheries Commission which, over a period of three years, would receive from the Crown 10 per cent of the total allowable catch, together with a sum of $10 million. For its part, the Commission was to set up a company, Aotearoa Fisheries, to which it was to commit 50 per cent of the assets it received from the Crown and distribute the proceeds of the company among 'Māori'; the other 50 per cent it might lease to Māori but not otherwise dispose of. But this was not enough. Although in the light of the settlement the outstanding fisheries cases were adjourned *sine die*, the threat of judicial recognition of aboriginal title in further cases should they arise, was to spur the Crown to further action.[62] Māori rights not having been extinguished, court cases continued, as disappointment with the quantum of the settlement and disputes among the beneficiaries intensified. The position was intolerable to any Government. Who knew what proportion of fisheries the courts might award? Who indeed knew the extent of aboriginal title, and whether or not it might be applicable to resources other than fisheries?[63]

In the event, the Government was lucky. It was informed by alert Māori in mid-1992 that Carter Holt Harvey, a joint owner of Sealord, the largest fishing company in the country, wished to sell its share. The Crown negotiated a Deed of Settlement with eight powerful Māori[64] by which it would pay $150 million to establish Māori in a joint venture with Brierley Investments and to

[60]   See above, pp. 120-2.
[61]   *Te Runanga o Muriwhenua* v *Attorney-General* [1990] 2 NZLR 641 at 648-49. An excellent account of the events until July 1994 is Munroe, 'The Treaty of Waitangi and the Sealord deal'.
[62]   P. G. McHugh, 'Sealords and sharks: the Māori Fisheries Agreement (1992)', p.355. See also the remarks of Rt Hon J.B. Bolger and Hon. Mrs T.W.M. Tirikatene-Sullivan: NZPD, 2:43 (1992), pp. 13036, 10356.
[63]   The answer is still not clear in 1996; but some indication of the legal sources for deciding was given by Cooke, P. in *Te Runanganui o Te Ika Whenua Inc Society* v *Attorney-General* [1994] 2 NZLR 20 at 23-27.
[64]   Matiu Rata (Muriwhenua), Tipene O'Regan (Ngai Tahu), Sir Graham Latimer (New Zealand Māori Council), Robert Te Kotahi Mahuta (Tainui) - the groups they represented had all made fisheries claims pending in the courts - together with Whatarangi Winiata, Richard Dargaville, Manu Paul and David Higgins.

buy what amounted to a further 26 per cent of Quota to add to the 10 per cent already held; it would further allocate 20 per cent of any new Quota issued under the QMS;[65] the Māori Fisheries Commission set up in 1989 would become the Treaty of Waitangi Fisheries Commission, and would, appointed by the Government after consultation, provide members to serve on various Government advisory boards. The price? The repeal of section 88(2) of the Fisheries Act and agreement from Māori that the settlement would 'satisfy all claims, current and future, and shall discharge and extinguish, all commercial fishing rights...whether arising from common law (including customary title), the Treaty of Waitangi, or otherwise...'. In section 7, the subsequent act, the Treaty of Waitangi (Fisheries Claims) Settlement Act, which came into force in December, stripped the Waitangi Tribunal of its jurisdiction 'to inquire or inquire further into' commercial fishing or commercial fisheries, the Deed of Settlement, and any further legislation that related to commercial fishing and fisheries.

Few parliamentarians were confident that the settlement would stick.[66] And the story is not yet over. Fisheries claims, even to the Tribunal, have continued – an illustration better than any other of the Crown's problems of agency. Not only has its unencumbered title to rule not been recognised; it has been forced into tedious and expensive negotiations to ends it never quite intended.

IV

Problems of Māori Agency

In December 1990 when Winston Peters, as the National Government's Minister of Māori Affairs, proposed the repeal of the shortlived Iwi Runanga Act, he defended his proposal by pointing to a source of anxiety among Māori at large.

> The Bill I have introduced today will ensure that the number of Māori organisations competing for available resources is not allowed to increase any further. Māoridom, statutory organisations, trust boards, community development committees, Māori incorporations, and the Māori Congress do not need to be inundated with a further 50 incorporated runanga, or possibly 72 quasi-governmental authorities ... If we were to multiply the infrastructure of Māoridom it would serve only to magnify the chaos that already surrounds Māori affairs.[67]

The very Labour Māori MPs who had seen the act through Parliament just four months earlier did not resist its repeal. One of their reasons for non-resistance was that even when they had helped pass the act, they had been and remained uneasy, like Peters, at the proliferation of Māori teams of action, and had

---

[65] This would give Māori perhaps 26 per cent of the total Quota.
[66] NZPD 2:43 (1992), pp. 12932-45 12948-52, 12968, 12972-76, 1305241, 13043, 13059-60.
[67] NZPD 2:43 (1990), p. 603.

sympathy with his idea that effective pan-Māori organisations were also a good idea.[68] Indeed, like most Māori, they found themselves drawn to *both* tribal and to pan-Māori teams of action. And they saw that organizing either was not easy.

For Māori are not a team of action but a family of teams, and often a squabbling family. That they assert their common ethnicity − or more often race − and that they assert that they share a common status over and against Pākehā or the Crown is not sufficient for them to be thought to be a team of action. No artificial group is capable of representing them as a whole. None can, in Hobbes's language, 'bear their person'. None can act for them. Among their teams of action, the right to authorize is so diffused and separated that they tend rather to gather in a series of competing teams than in One Big Team. As they share much culturally and genetically with Pākehā, so they share much, perhaps more, among themselves;[69] but as they differ from Pākehā, so they differ among themselves, though in even more complicated and obdurate ways. Their purposes diverge in all the ways that Pākehā purposes diverge, and they also diverge according to their individual commitments to the mana and rangatiratanga of their own particular iwi − which may number more than one.

Almost to a man and woman, Māori team-leaders have insisted on the unity of Māori and their separate status in life and in the political constitution of New Zealand on grounds of rangatiratanga and mana motuhake. The Māori MPs continued to talk through the 1990s of 'my people', of the 'Māori race' and of their special position in the country; and so did their Pākehā colleagues. A proportion of Māori who recognise their Māori ancestry and yet regard their ethnicity as European/Pākehā − and, with stronger reason, those who do not recognize their ancestry at all − may not agree with those propositions, but most still do.[70] Māori also have a long history of unconcluded attempts at creating kotahitanga among the iwi. And they have a history of pan-Māori organizations which have succeeded in being pan-Māori (in the sense not deriving their legitimacy from the fact of their being representatives of particular iwi) but have failed to extend their authority over all matters and all Māori.[71] The organizations that come closest are the Kōhanga Reo Movement, the Māori Women's Welfare League, the New Zealand Māori Council, the Rātana Church, and (since its establishment in 1990) the Māori Congress.

The Kōhanga Reo Movement, a federation of local kōhanga reo, is extemely effective on matters wider than suggested in its brief to revive the language; but its brief *is* limited and it is dependent on Government funding. The Māori Women's Welfare League, perhaps the most effective on the ground over a wide

---

[68]   NZPD 1:42 (1989), pp. 14235, 14237-8, 14234, 3889, 3895. The Hon. Peter Tapsell perhaps most wanted one Māori representative. 'However, the hardest problem that this country has, if we are to make progress in these areas, is the question of representation ... and I would have thought, in a rather simplistic pākehā way [Tapsell is Māori], that, if there were ever to be some sort of annual hui at Turangawaewae or somewhere, where Māoridom got together in a unified way, then we would make progress faster...'. NZPD Vol 2:42 (1992), p.12952.

[69]   Dr Bruce Gregory, MP for Northern Māori, put it well at NZPD 1:42 (1990), p. 3888.

[70]   Gould, 'Socio-economic differences between Māori iwi', pp. 166-7.

[71]   On this and the theme I am elaborating, see M. H. Durie, 'Mana Māori motuhake. The state of the Māori nation'; M.H. Durie, 'Tino rangatiratanga'; Cox, *Kotahitanga: the search for Māori political unity*; Walker, 'Māori people since 1950', pp. 510, 515-16.

range of issues, continues to suffer because it is composed of women: in the tikanga of most iwi, it remained contentious, in the 1990s, for women to represent men in public fora. The New Zealand Māori Council had no difficulty in being recognized by the courts as representative of all Māori. Even so, it never claimed, and could not claim, to represent all Māori on all issues. Its court actions were occasionally objected to as precluding separate iwi action, and were greatly objected to when, in 1990, a Crown Forestry Rental Trust was set up under Sir Graham Latimer, the Council's President, to administer Crown Forest rentals while coordinating the preparation of iwi claims to the Waitangi Tribunal. It is known by all Māori teams of action that the Council's electoral boundaries are based on those of the old Māori Land Court and do not coincide with the rohe, or territories, of the iwi.[72] It is dominated by its rural membership (the Auckland District Māori Council which can claim to represent urban Māori has been consistently outvoted by the other six, predominantly rural District Councils). Its leaders are depicted by its opponents as 'brown aristocracy'; and its financial viability and its political power depend on its close cooperation with the government. It can never represent Māori interests as a whole. Nor can the Rātana Church. Its claims to represent all Māori were based only on the fact that it is a pan-iwi religion, and that until 1993, all Māori MPs came into Parliament via a Rātana-Labour alliance. Shaken in the 1993 election (Labour lost Northern Māori), in 1996 it lost all its seats to New Zealand First, led by the ex-National Māori politician, Winston Peters.

For its part, the Māori Congress has played a leading role in initially coordinating the activities of some sixty-two iwi, fourteen taura here (urban iwi affiliates) and twenty-five other teams, especially in respect of opposition to the Government's fiscal envelope. It successfully negotiated with the Government on the disposition of railway lands; and in the days before the 1996 election it succeeded in attracting thirty prospective Māori MPs to a pre-election hui. But it is essentially an uneasy confederation of the separate iwi, each claiming its own mana and tino rangatiratanga, where a leading characteristic of both those kinds of authority is that they cannot be devolved. The Congress has been beset by defections, not least by Ngai Tahu, who have claimed their identity and interests to be entirely those of an iwi. By 1996 only about thirty iwi remained members. And because its authority structure is based on tribal principles, it finds it impossible to allow full membership to the Māori Council, the taura here, the Rātana Church, and the Māori Women's Welfare League, which are pan-tribal and based on non-tribal formulae of legitimacy, or else, if tribal, are divorced from their local bases. The fundamental problems in Māori representation are demonstrated in gross in the Council and the Congress: the conflict between traditional and other kinds of authority structures, and the lack of representation of urban Māori, who make up something between 70 and 80 per cent of the Māori population.

The representation of iwi – their personification in Hobbes's language – has been just as difficult for Māori to agree upon in the 1990s. The Iwi Runanga Act had been an attempt to provide a legal mechanism for creating legally recognizable

---

[72] For the events leading up to the creation of the Trust, see Renwick, *Treaty Now*, pp. 73-6.

'artificial persons' called Iwi. These Iwi would represent iwi for the purposes of receiving Government monies to administer various programmes, and they would be held accountable for their stewardship of state resources. The Labour Māori MPs had supported the act in the faith that 'the relationship of the Iwi will be that of a contract partner and not that of an agent of the Crown. That reflects the Māori view of partnership and tino rangatiratanga, and is to be preferred to the subservient status of agent as referred to in existing contracts'.[73] The mana of the tribes would remain intact; it would just be that a better delivery mechanism of services to the Māori would be set up. The statutory Iwi would not be mere arms of Government bureaucracy, but would combine, doubtless with difficulty, the requirements of modern management and accountability with the separate tikanga of the iwi.[74] This was precisely why the Department of Māori Affairs was also to be abolished – replaced with a policy Ministry and an Iwi Transition Agency – and power to be devolved to the people. The Iwi Transition Authority would dissolve as it passed power to the Iwi; the Ministry would devote itself to policy formation and advice to and monitoring of Government departments and ministries. The Iwi/iwi would act for themselves.[75] But the MPs had not succeeded in persuading Māoridom that this was the effect of the legislation.[76] It was the Government and not Māori who had set up the means by which iwi would be recognized and the methods by which each iwi would decide its representation. The act was thus to be seen as an attempt to have iwi define their teams of action in Pākehā legal terms. The law ought not to distort the various tikanga of the iwi in that way, and the tikanga were not susceptible of being overridden by the law. As Tainui had tried to tell the Government in 1988, when negotiating Government contracts on work schemes, they did not like being called 'an agent of the Crown': 'appointed authority' would have been better.[77] In the end, the Māori Labour MPs had to agree with Peters that 'it is up to the tribes and not the Government, to dictate the way in which tribal territory is determined, where tribal boundaries are, and how to deal with members who are no longer living within their tribal boundaries'.[78] And, Peters might have added, it was up to the iwi to decide who the iwi were.

So the statutory Runanga of the Iwi were disestablished in the light of the vexed questions that had characterized all debates on Māori affairs in 1989: who were iwi? How could iwi be represented? How were they to relate to the Crown? How were they to relate each to each and to other teams of Māori action constituted on non-family-based principles?[79] How could Māori operate

[73] NZPD 2:42 (1989) pp. 14228-9. See also Dr. Bruce Gregory at 14234, and others at pp. 3881, 3889, 4044.
[74] 'Iwi' with a capital 'I' = government-recognised iwi; 'iwi with a small 'i' = iwi, or hāpu, or people individually or collectively in accordance with the fluid usage in te reo.
[75] See note above.
[76] NZPD 2:42 (1990), p. 3873 lists some of the objections.
[77] Mahuta, 'Tainui: a case study of direct negotiations', p.167.
[78] NZPD 1:43 (1990), p. 603.
[79] Sir Hugh Kawharu ('Urban iwi: the new tribes of Māoridom?', p. 210) says that basic to the understanding of 'what an iwi is' are 'whanaunatanga' and 'manawhenua' - kinship, and authority within tribal boundaries.

together in pan-Māori organisations? How were the *déiwi-ized*[80] fraction of urban Māori (30 per cent of all Māori) to be cared for? How could Māori (and iwi) development be ensured in this condition of uncertainty and contention?[81]

During the 1990s, these problems were exacerbated as the Government largely withdrew from the ameliorative policies of the 1980s and as there was further reorganization of the remains of the new Ministry of Māori Affairs. It became ever clearer after its establishment in 1990 that Te Puni Kōkiri, the Ministry of Māori Development, would no longer deliver services to the Māori people.[82] Combined with these moves, there was the setting up in 1990 of the Crown Forestry Trust to disburse forest rentals so that claimants could prepare their Tribunal cases, and there was, in 1992, the institution of the Treaty of Waitangi Fisheries Commission, entrusted with the task, among others, of transferring assets to iwi. Both bodies were conceived and born in conditions of inter-iwi competition for resources and control, taonga and mana. Both have lived their lives in the same conditions. Then there was the Waikato–Tainui settlement and the prospect of more to come – all under a fiscal envelope that set bounds to what the iwi might compete for among themselves. Questions of Māori agency became questions as to who had legitimate and often exclusive claims on the spoils of Treaty settlement.

A closer inspection of the history of one pan-Māori organisation – Te Ohu Kai Moana/the Treaty of Waitangi Fisheries Commission – may throw into sharper relief the issues at stake. It was a creature of Government. Its thirteen members were given the statutory duty under the 1992 Fisheries Settlement Act to organize, through a consultative process among Māori, the entry of Māori into the 'business and activity of fishing'.[83] The Commission had to decide, among other things, how to allocate the resources released to it by the Government. Big money was at stake, and important opportunities for Māori to enter the fisheries industry. Five sets of disputes emerged which demonstrated that the Commission did not and could not represent Māori, and that the teams of Māori action could not agree on the rights of agency of the competing teams. The first dispute centred on the Crown's right to nominate the Commissioners, and (if it had the right) on whether it had consulted with proper reference to

---

80   My coinage: from *déraciné*, the French for being uprooted, distanced from one's past commitments.

81   On restructuring of the Department of Māori Affairs, the setting up of Iwi authorities and the Māori Land Court: NZPD 1:42 (1989),10060-1, 10063, 100065-76, 12230-40, 12444-65, 12550-5.

82   Te Puni Kōkiri, *Summary of the Establishment and Achievements of Te Puni Kōkiri (January 1, 1992 to October 13, 1995)* (Wellington: Ministry of Māori Development, 1995).

83   The Commissioners were, as set out in the Statute, appointed by the Governor-General on the advice of the Minister of Māori Affairs after consultation with the Māori fisheries negotiators (fn. 57 above), 'and such other persons who are, in the Minister's opinion, representatives of Māori who are or may be beneficiaries of the Commission's assets'. They were: Sir Tipene O'Regan (Chair), Sir Graham Latimer (Deputy), Hon. Ben Couch, Whaimutu Dewes, Craig Ellison, Shane Jones, Robert (later Sir Robert) Mahuta, Dr John Mitchell, Naida Pou, Phillip Pryke, Anaru Rangiheuea, Archie Taiaroa and Evelyn Tuuta. For a summary of the Commission's role and its membership, see Auditor-General, *Report*, pp. 54-5.

the various tikanga of the iwi. Partly it was a question of rangatiratanga and Māori autonomy over and against kawanatanga and Crown sovereignty and, as such, may be regarded as a further instance of the normal Government problems in dealing with Māori in general. But it was also a question of the correct methods of joint-Māori and inter-Māori team action as conceived among Māori, and so it merged with the four other disputes that arose: the first over the principles of allocation among traditionally recognized iwi; the second over just who were iwi; the third over the relative claims of hapū over and against iwi (whoever they were) to fisheries; the fifth over whether or not Māori who did not affiliate with *any* iwi could constitute a Māori team of action at all.[84] The conflicting claims of the disputants and the consequent problems for Māori teams of action were recorded and soberly discussed in late 1992 by the Waitangi Tribunal in its *Fisheries Settlement* and *Appointments to the Treaty of Waitangi Fisheries Commission* reports. Nothing of substance has changed since then.

At first the Commission assumed that allocation would be among traditionally recognized iwi. Just who were the iwi emerged as a problem, so it set about instituting a mechanism by which iwi might lodge a 'deed of mandate' with it so that there would be no argument as to which iwi existed and who represented them.[85] It proceeded, after some hesitation, to the temporary allocation of fishing rights by way of renting out Quota in accordance with the principle of 'mana moana mana whenua'. Those iwi with coastlines would be allocated the Quota: 'as goes the land, so goes the sea'. Outrage followed. What about the inland tribes who had no coastline? So a new allocative principle was arrived at. Coastal iwi would receive the inshore Quota on the principle of mana moana mana whenua; the offshore fisheries would be divided fifty/fifty: 50 per cent on the mana moana principles, 50 per cent on the mana tangata principle – that allocation should be proportional to population.[86] Thus it might be thought that a traditional allocative principle was married to a modern principle of distributive justice. But things emerged as being not quite so clear. It was widely alleged that the 'traditional' principle was a very recent invention of Sir Tipene O'Regan, Chair of the Commission and leader of Ngai Tahu, and that it was invented in his tribe's interest, since, dominating the South Island, off the shores of which were 70 per cent of the Quota, it would get the lion's share. The allegation was agreed to be true both by the Waitangi Tribunal and the Māori Land Court. The Court went so far as to call mana moana a principle 'rooted in greed and ignorance'.[87] For its part, the Tribunal found the 'modern' principle of mana tangata to be ancient; inland tribes had typically organized access to the sea.[88] It also noted that in any

[84] In addition, Chatham Island Moriori have claimed their Māori standing and rights in the matter of fisheries and Māori rights generally, and have introduced the issue into the courts and the Waitangi Tribunal.

[85] Te Ohu Kai Moana, *Discussion Material on Allocation Models for Consultation with Iwi* (August 1994).

[86] Te Ohu Kai Moana, *Report of Te Ohu Kai Moana/Treaty of Waitangi Fisheries Commission for the year ended September 1993.*

[87] *In Re Ngati Toa Rangatira* (unreported) Māori Land Court, Nelson, 8 December 1994, 21 MB 1; noted MLR December-January 1994-95, p. 2.

[88] Waitangi Tribunal, *Fisheries Settlement Report*, p.21. See Section 9 in general.

case rights to coastal fishing had traditionally been in the hapū not the iwi. And so, in this vein, for the past four years a series of claims to the Waitangi Tribunal and court cases (one brought by six members of the Commission itself; others by iwi and groups of iwi disaffected with the implications)[89] have sought to force the Commission to decide on allocative principles which are tika (fair), and not based on self-interest disguised as traditional tikanga.

Then there was the problem of urban iwi. In April 1996 the Commission was to face a successful legal claim in the Court of Appeal that to deliver Quota and other benefits only through traditional iwi was to ignore the claims of urban Māori. The Commission had been operating on the view that an iwi was a group with 'an existence traditionally acknowledged by other iwi'. This would exclude urban Māori not affiliated with the overwhelmingly rural iwi. The Waitangi Tribunal, in response to complaints about this, had held that 'the application of the word "iwi" to urban Māori groups might well be classical and not a new use of the term'.[90] Iwi had risen and fallen. New ones could emerge. *This* was the traditional Māori view. To think that there always had been and always would be a settled number of iwi showed a misunderstanding of the complexity of Māori life. The Court of Appeal, asked to judge the issue, had to translate it into a legally operative form. It agreed that iwi were fluid, but further insisted that if Treaty principles were to be applied to yield allocations, then it must firmly be said that the word 'iwi' occurs only once in the Treaty, and then with reference to all the individual Māori people then living in New Zealand. The court further agreed with the Tribunal and others that Māori fishing rights, and the rights to rangatiratanga agreed to in the Treaty, were *hapū* rights, but it further insisted that the settlement of 1992 was intended by Parliament to be pan-tribal and the black-letter law required that urban Māori be included in any allocation. This being so, the Commission must not only continue to consult with hapū as well as iwi, but 'natural justice' required that urban Māori also be consulted: and 'the most practicable mode of consultation with them is through the Urban Māori Authorities'. The Court would, it said, retain jurisdiction to require the performance of the Commission's statutory functions.[91] Sir Hugh Kawharu, glossing the case, wryly commented:

A culture may change and adapt to new circumstances ... There comes a point, however, when it suffers violence and loses its distinguishing qualities needed for identity to remain intact. For this reason it would have been preferable for the Court to have undertaken an interpretation more consistent with tradition. It would have been more desirable still for the parties to these proceedings to have resolved the issues without recourse to litigation – either between themselves or at a political level, between the Treaty partners. If any measure of control over the shape of Māori tikanga in law is to be had, litigation of this sort should be the last resort.

89   The latest case, which records many previous ones, is *Te Iwi Moriori Trust Board* v *Treaty of Waitangi Fisheries Commission and The Treaty Tribes Coalition* (unreported) Court of Appeal, Wellington, 14 October 1996. C.A.238/96.
90   MLR May 1995, p. 6.
91   MLR May 1996, pp. 1, 9–7. Cf. *Te Runanga o Muriwhenua* v *Te Runangahui o Te Opoko o Te Ika Assn Inc and Others* [1996] 3 NZLR 10.

The issue of urban iwi is still alive, in November 1996 a matter of appeal to the Privy Council by the 'Treaty Tribes', who rejected the idea of urban iwi.

In this series of events one may see some of the difficulties facing a pan-Māori organization. It will clearly be subject to legal constraint. But, more importantly, as to the scope of operation that it *does* have, there will be difficulties in having it recognized by those it is supposed to represent, especially in cases when it is a state creation and not authorized according to tikanga; its agency will be compromised by the conflicting decision principles as to distribution of taonga used by those for whom it is supposed to act; and it will be hard-pressed to assess the rights of those who claim to represent those for whom it is supposed to act. It will, except for the fact that it is bound by law, be in exactly the same position as the Crown. Consequently, its decisions may bind in law but not in Māori opinion.

Similar difficulties attend the iwi (and hapū) themselves when *they* are considered as teams of action. The Iwi Runanga Act may have been rescinded, but the issue as to what groups were iwi and who could represent them did not die. In its *Fisheries Settlement Report*, the Waitangi Tribunal discussed issues of 'Māori representation', in an uneasily dialectical way, considering now one factor, now another. An idea of the complexity of the issues as between iwi and hapu[92] can be given in a short extract of its reasoning on past and present circumstances as it approached the conclusion that iwi should be the units with rights of action over fisheries:

To reach a conclusion in this matter we have had to have regard to the nature of customary Māori society as we see it. As earlier mentioned, there was not time to meet with all who could have assisted this inquiry although we had some help from submissions from T O'Regan and H M Mead and an affidavit from G S Latimer. Traditionally, it appears to us, Māori society was essentially anti-state and egalitarian. Sections regularly split off to stand alone and form new hapū following leadership or other struggles. They still do, and Tuhuru, which distance themselves from Kati Waewae, well illustrate this. This tendency to fractionate and reform ensured the operational autonomy of small hapū groups and so, though they were forever dividing and reassembling in new shapes, the hapu remained the basic political and resource owning unit. (T O'Regan describes the groups as sub-units, and sub-sub units. They may also divide laterally however to simply create more hapu.)

Nonetheless the fragmentation of hapu was conditioned by the need to band together on occasions, and thus there remained a loyalty to a larger collectivity, to those of the common descent line called the 'iwi', or simply, the 'people'. For the most part 'iwi' effectively describes the parent tribe from whom all hapu have come, or a confederation of tribes, as G S Latimer contended; but the word has been variously applied. Iwi were sometimes a transient collation of hapū members for some expeditionary, military or political purpose, and some iwi crusades involved unrelated hapū. In addition, as H M Mead pointed out, iwi may split to form new iwi, or, as G S Latimer considered with regard to Ngati Wai, larger hapu may claim an iwi status. Most importantly, however, there were times when iwi associations were more regularly dominant, through war or some personal influence, and times when hapu chiefs met in regular conclaves or iwi runanga.

The tension between those two strong desires, for local autonomy on the one hand and unity on the other, has characterised ancient and modern Māori society. Opinions will

---

[92] Individuals were also discussed.

no doubt vary but we venture to suggest that local autonomy was seen as more important for Māori, while yet it was recognised that some things had perforce to be done by the iwi. Major arrangements with outside groups, or tauiwi, were usually at this level.

With Pakeha settlement iwi structures became more necessary, significant and permanent. Pan-iwi structures likewise appeared, with waka or iwi-whanui confederations. Each is a legitimate extension from the customary base in our view, a necessary response to a new circumstance. The present-day position now varies from place to place but the current wisdom appears to be that matters of common policy affecting the people generally, should be determined or ratified at an iwi or iwi-whanui plane. Likewise, though resources are primarily hapu owned, generations of Māori have accepted that some commercial operations should be undertaken on an iwi basis.[93]

But the Tribunal was too optimistic as to the the content of the 'current wisdom'. Emphatically not all Māori agreed on the primacy of iwi rights of action over fisheries.

And similar disagreement occurred in regard to other resources. The leadership of Waikato-Tainui faced opposition to the Tainui Trust Board's negotiation and settlement of its raupatu claims with the Government. The thirteen-member Board, in presenting the iwi with its proposed deed of settlement with the Crown, attempted to gain a 'mandate' from them from December 1994 until May 1995. They held a series of hui; they conducted a postal ballot; they undertook what the judge in a subsequent case called a 'multi-faceted' approach to gaining authorisation from the iwi.[94] Not everyone agreed with the Board's doings, and complaints were made about Waikato-Tainui overriding the independent rights of hapū and iwi sections who maintained they had separate claims and must be represented in negotiating them. The Trust Board could not represent them: a group claiming to represent nineteen hapū complained that 'the hapu do not wish their raupatu land grievances rushed through for the sake of a government, who are determined to disposses them of their lands again, by investing their hapu raupatu lands [in] another hapu (Tainui Māori Trust Board)'.[95] The Ngai Tahu Trust Board, which transformed itself in 1996 into a statutory Iwi, had similar problems thrown in its face as it negotiated with the Crown over the settlement of its own particular Treaty claims and as it attempted to deal with the implications for its peoples of the fisheries settlements. It, too, experienced opposition to its claims to bind all the hapū of the iwi in the settlements they made or might make – and some of the opposition was on grounds that what Ngai Tahu claimed to be a hapū was in fact an anciently separate iwi.[96]

There have, too, been many less spectacular cases in the Māori Land Court of teams of action claiming to be, or to represent, iwi or tangata whenua, over matters not only of fisheries and raupatu, but in the right to be consulted in resource management and development planning issues. It used to be that current iwi existence and the current rights of iwi to certain rohe were legally

[93] *Fisheries Report*, Section 7.2.
[94] *Eva Rickard, Pare Hopa & Ors* v *Tainui Maaori Trust Board* (unreported) High Court, Hamilton, 30 April 1996. M.117/95. A more detailed account of consultations and the Waikato-Tainui 'internal negotiations' is in Mahuta, 'Tainui: a case study of negotiations', pp. 173-4.
[95] See e.g. Forbes, *He Panui*, p. 2.
[96] Waitangi Tribunal, *Fisheries Report*, section 7.2; *Tuhuru Report*.

determined according to 'the 1840 rule': the basis for a successful claim was that the iwi who made the claim existed in 1840 and inhabited the rohe in question. But under section 30(1)(b) of Te Ture Whenua Māori (1993)[97] it became possible to apply to the Chief Justice of the Māori Land Court for a determination not on the 1840 rule, but simply on grounds of what would be 'the most appropriate representation' of 'any groups of Māori for the purposes of any consultations, negotiations or any other matter'. Beginning in February 1994, a series of disputes were taken to the Court. One was between two iwi disputing various rights in the Tararua district, and here the issue was which group had rights of action within a certain rohe. Seven other disputes were between alternate groups, usually of recent creation, each claiming exclusively to represent the same iwi: was the iwi to be represented by a Trust Board, a Land Incorporation, a runanga, a collection of marae? The detail of final results are a matter of detail: but two things may be noted. In the inteiwi dispute, a settlement was made by the Court in the absence, and without the consent, of the contending party; and in the intraiwi disputes the Court has tended to ask the disputants to renegotiate iwi representation under the superintendence of kaumātua, enjoining them to seek unity in new arrangements based on old principles.

So much for the difficulties in the face of Māori teams of action in some particular cases and over all. In conditions where what was to be distributed was scarce and often deeply valued as taonga, questions of justice became in the first place questions of agency, as to who had authority, and dominion, mana and rangatiratanga.

V

Conclusion

My conclusion will have to be brief. It is clear that Māori are not one team of action but many, as Pākehā are. Two kinds of politicians have dreamed of One Big Māori Team: officials and politicians intent on streamlining Crown relations with Māori beyond the bounds of political reality, and Māori leaders, who, seeing the problems and the possibilities of their people, aim for an impossible ideal. I hope that my saying this will not be seen as the old Pākehā ploy of divide and rule. But One Big Māori representative could easily do to groups of Māori just what the Crown has done to Māori in the past. It could violate the rights and ignore the interests of some of those who (it would claim) authorize it to act for them. 'It is not the done thing,' as Koro Wetere rightly observed, 'for one group of Māori to sort out the problems of another group.'[98] No metaphysic and consequent political expression of a single Māori identity will advance settlement processes or distributive justice for Māori. In place of the one systematic

---

[97]   The reformed Māori Land Act.
[98]   NZPD 2:42 (1990) p. 1286.

injustice of Pākehā and Crown to Māori there would be innumerable petty but cosmic injustices done. Politicians and officials do not make such a mistake of assuming unity when they deal with Pākehā. Why should they with Māori? Māori do not often make the mistake when they deal among themselves. In the face of reality they cannot.

On the other hand, the dream of a multitude of Māori teams all organized on traditional grounds and dealing as equals with the state is equally impossible in the swirl of change, cooperation and conflict that marks their relationships. Most, but not all, iwi would sink into oblivion, crushed by the expense and the weariness of battles on every front.

And so the debate will continue among the agents. It is *not* a postmodern debate. Although the identities of the subjects and agents of justice may be fluid and 'constructed', although Māori teams of action are in constant flux as members come and go and the teams adapt and change, the identities at stake are as real as concrete human lives can and do make them.[99] The milieu of their Māori existence provides not only much of the material from which they construct their personal activity, but goes to their deepest selves.[100] Their identities are certainly real enough to suggest that the political nation rethink its constitution so as to regularize the complexities of the politics of Māori and Pākehā and among Māori. If there were a constitution, it would be the creation of *all* the peoples, setting out the rules that would govern them in their relations.

This is certainly the mainstream Māori teamleaders' view – for the obvious reasons that they continue to have problems with the state and among themselves, and that to negotiate a new constitution would mean confronting those problems in conditions where their agency is accepted as a fact and not as the question at issue. Their many and various proposals reflect this.[101] Some want to constitute a single, carefully nuanced Māori body politic that would find its niche in the constitution alongside the Crown and operating under a common constitutional law. Others, not at all opposing a Māori body politic, nevertheless oppose the idea of a constitution that does not emanate entirely from Māori tikanga but is, in some way, still the creature of the Crown.[102] Still others reject elements of both views, claiming that it is only the separate iwi who ought to be in special, constitutional relationships with the Crown.[103] Pākehā teamleaders have less reason to consider a new constitution at all. The state – the embodiment and representative of the peoples – manages to survive reasonably well. It has been subject to loss of agency in a world dominated by global capital.[104]

---

[99] Sharp, 'Representing *Justice and the Māori*'.

[100] Sharp, 'Why be bicultural?'.

[101] Some of the suggestions as to a new constitution are summarised in M. H. Durie, 'Tino rangatiranga', pp. 50-51 and 'Proceedings of a hui held at Hirangi Marae, Turangi', pp. 116-17. See also Melbourne (ed.), *Māori Sovereignty*, pp. 32-3, 39, 50-2, 68-70, 86-7, 116-18, 139-40, 151-2; and two Television New Zealand programmes: *Marae*, 27 August 1995 and *Assignment*, 14 September 1995.

[102] See Hirangi Hui (September 1995) papers, 1-3.

[103] Melbourne (ed.), *Māori Sovereignty*, pp. 141-2, 158-9.

[104] Haworth, 'Neo-liberalism, economic internationalisation and the contemporary state in New Zealand'; Kelsey, *Rolling Back the State*.

Perhaps, too, it has endangered its 'ownership' by the people because it has destroyed many of their institutions and customs[105] – not least Māori ones. But it survives.

Conceptions of justice are inherited by a political society and they change as they are continually argued about and negotiated by persons – artificial as well as natural – who hold them. To fix the persons who now exist in a constitution designed to be a 'full and final settlement' of what the relations between them should be, will, I suspect, be impossible in New Zealand/Aotearoa. It will at least be difficult. It may be said, however, that the polity of the 1960s, with which this book began, has long gone. We no longer have a liberal, individualistic constitution, even though the culture of the liberal individualism permeates much of the law of the state as well as its economic practice. The persons who are now represented in the collectivity of the state and its activities are not just individual men and women. They are also, to mention a few, 'Māori', 'iwi', 'whānau' and 'hapū'. It was the neo-liberal turn in governmental policies which, combined with Māori persistence in their teams of action and milieus of existence, largely brought this about.

[105] Sharp, 'Pride, resentment and change'.

Finding List

A Finding List of references and sources arranged according to the manner of their appearance in the footnotes, including a guide to the abbreviations used.

Ackerman, Bruce. *Private property and the constitution* (Yale University Press, New Haven, Conn., 1977)

Adams, Peter. *Fatal necessity* (Auckland University Press, Auckland, 1977)

Anglican Church in New Zealand, Bicultural Commission. *Te kaupapa tikanga rua. Bi-cultural development* (The Commission, Wellington, 1986)

April Report, The. See Royal Commission on Social Policy.

Archdiocese of Wellington Commission for Evangelisation, Justice and Development. 'Understanding Waitangi', Proceedings of a seminar, Wellington (1982)

'Understanding Waitangi II', Proceedings of a seminar, Wellington (1983)

Archie, Carol (ed.) *Maori sovereignty. The Pakeha perspective* (Hodder Moa Beckett, Auckland, 1995)

Arahura Maori Komiti. 'Self-determination and territorial title for the indigenous Maori people of Aotearoa', *Race, Gender, Class 3* (1986), pp. 1-5

AS: abbreviation for the *Auckland Star*, Auckland city's evening paper. Numbers directly following AS indicate page numbers in the first section, e.g., AS1 is the first page of the first section. Later sections are given a roman numeral interpolation before the page number, e.g. ASii3 is page 3 of the second section. Dates are given in the form: day/month/ year, e.g. 3/1/89 is the third of January 1989.

Asher, George and Naulls, David. *Maori land* (New Zealand Planning Council, Paper Number 29, Wellington, 1987)

Auditor-General [D.J.D. McDonald]. *The settlement of claims under the Treaty of Waitangi* (Report of the Controller and Auditor-General. Second report [to Parliament] for 1995. B29 [95b], Wellington, 12 September 1995)

Avenieri, Schlomo. *The political and social thought of Karl Marx* (Cambridge University Press, Cambridge, 1971)

Awatere, Donna. 'Address to the Royal College of Psychiatrists, Rotorua, 29 March 1984', *Craccum*, 16 April 1985, p. 3. (*Craccum* is published by the Auckland University Students' Association.)

'Maori sovereignty', *Broadsheet*, 'Part 1', (June 1982), pp. 38-42; 'Part 2', (October 1982), pp. 24-9; 'Part 3', (January-February 1983), pp. 12-19

Maori sovereignty (Broadsheet, Auckland, 1984)

'Wahine ma korerotia', *Broadsheet*, (July-August 1982), pp. 23-31

'Waiora: health from a Maaori point of view', in University of Waikato, *Ko taa te Maaori waahanga*, pp. 7-17

Ball, Terence. 'The incoherence of intergenerational justice', *Inquiry*, 28 (1985), pp. 321-37

Ballara, Angela. *Proud to be white? A survey of Pakeha prejudice in New Zealand* (Heinemann, Auckland, 1986)

Barsh, R. L. 'Indigenous peoples: an emerging object of international law', *American Journal of International Law*, 80 (1986), pp. 369-85

Bastion Point Judgment, The. (Department of Lands and Survey, Wellington, 1978)

Becker, Lawrence C. and Kipnis, Kenneth (eds.) *Property: Cases, concepts, critiques* (Prentice Hall, Englewood Cliffs, N.J., 1984)

Beckerman, John S. 'Adding insult to *injuria*: affronts to honor and the origins of trespass', in Arnold Green et al. (eds.), *Studies in legal history*, pp. 159-81

Bedau, Hugo A. 'Compensatory justice and the Black Manifesto', *Monist*, 56 (1972), pp. 20-42

Belich, James. *The New Zealand Wars and the Victorian interpretation of racial confict* (Auckland University Press, Auckland, 1986)

Bennett, Manuhuia. 'Te kupu whaka whakamutanga: the last word', in the New Zealand Planning Council, *He matapuna*, pp. 73-9

Benton, Richard A. 'The Maori language, the Treaty of Waitangi, and race relations in New Zealand', in Archdiocese of Wellington, 'Understanding Waitangi II', (1983)

    Te rito o te korari: Maori language and New Zealand's national identity, reprinted from McDonald, G. and Campbell, A., *Looking forward*.

Berger, Thomas R. *Village journey* (Hill and Wang, New York, 1985)

Bierhoff, Hans Werner, Cohen, Ronald L. and Greenberg, Jerald. *Justice in social relations* (Plenum Press, New York, 1986)

Biggs, Bruce. 'Humpty-Dumpty and the Treaty of Waitangi', in I. H. Kawharu (ed.), *Waitangi*, pp. 300-12

    'Maori Affairs and the Hunn Report', *Journal of the Polynesian Society*, 70, iii (1961), pp. 361-4

Bill of Rights seminar. See New Zealand Section, International Commission of Jurists.

Binney, Judith. 'D. F McKenzie, Oral culture, literacy and print in early New Zealand', *Political Science*, 38 (1986) pp. 185-6

Binney, Judith, Chaplin, Gillian and Wallace, Craig. *Mihaia. The prophet Rua Kenana and his community at Maungapohatu* (Oxford University Press, Wellington, 1979)

Binney, Judith and Chaplin, Gillian. *Ngā Mōrehu. The Survivors* (Oxford University Press, Auckland, 1986)

Bittker, Boris. *The case for black reparations* (Random House, New York, 1973)

Blank, Arapera, Henare, Manuka and Williams, Haare. *He Korero mo Waitangi, 1984* (Te Rununga o Waitangi, Ngaruawahia, 1985)

Booth, Pat. 'Are Maoris getting a fair deal?', *Metro* (September 1985)

Boston, Jonathan, Martin, John, Pallot, June and Walsh, Pat. *Public management: the New Zealand model* (Oxford University Press, Auckland, 1996)

Boston, Jonathan, Martin, John, Pallot, June and Walsh, Pat. *Reshaping the state* (Oxford University Press, Auckland, 1991)

Boxill, Bernard. 'The morality of reparation', *Social Theory and Practice*, 2 (1972), pp. 113-22

Broadsheet: Periodical, Auckland.

BRIEFCASE: electronic index to New Zealand case law (Law Library Management, Ltd., Auckland)

Brookfield, F. M. 'The New Zealand constitution: the search for legitimacy', in I. H. Kawharu (ed.), *Waitangi*, pp. 1-24

'Maori fishing rights and the Fisheries Act 1983: Te Weehi Case', *Recent Law* (1987), pp. 63-8

Brown, M. J. E. 'Equity, justice and Maoridom', in *Ko taa te Maaori waahanga*, (University of Waikato), pp. 47-55

Brown, Michael E. (ed.) *Ethnic relations and public policy in Asia and the Pacific* (MIT Press, Cambridge, Mass., 1997)

Buick, T. L. *The Treaty of Waitangi*, 3rd edn. (Thomas Avery and Sons, New Plymouth, 1936; reprinted by Capper Press, Christchurch, 1976)

Burke, Edmund. *Reflections on the Revolution in France. Edited with an introduction by Connor Cruise O'Brien* (Pelican, Harmondsworth, 1969)

Caldwell, L. J. 'Judicial Sovereignty – a new view', *New Zealand Law Journal* (1984), pp. 357-9

Caselberg, John (ed.) *Maori is my name* (John McIndoe, Dunedin, 1975)

Casey, Des. 'Hanna [sic] Jackson – Maori activist', *New Zealand Monthly Review*, 22, no. 238 (1981), p. 12

Chapman, Robert. 'Voting in the Maori political sub-system, 1935-1984', in Royal Commission on the Electoral System, *Report*, Appendix B, pp. 83-108, plus graphs (20pp.)

Chapman, Robert and Chapman, Noeline. *The Robert and Noeline Chapman Audio-Visual Archive*, Department of Political Studies, University of Auckland, contains records of news and magazine programmes on radio and TV.

Chapple, D. R. 'A timber town' in I. H. Kawharu (ed.), *Conflict and compromise*, pp. 187-211

Checkpoint: Radio magazine programme, National Radio. To find particular programmes, see Chapman, Robert and Chapman, Noeline.

Cleave, Peter. 'Tribal and state-like political formations in New Zealand Maori society 1750-1900', *Journal of the Polynesian Society*, 91 (1983), pp. 51-92

Committee to Review the Curriculum for Schools. *The curriculum review: reports of the Committee*, (Department of Education, Wellington, 1987)

Connolly, W. M. *The terms of political discourse*, 2nd edn. (Martin Robinson, Oxford, 1983)

Core Group on Resource Management Law Reform, Ministry for the Environment. *Resource management law reform: a review of the laws for managing air, land and water use and mining* (Information Kit, Core Group, Wellington, 1988)

Courier: South Auckland suburban weekly.

Cox, Lindsay. *Kotahitanga: the search for Maori political unity* (Auckland, Oxford University Press, 1993)

CRNZ. *Criminal reports of New Zealand* (Brooker and Friend, Wellington, c.1983-)

Crown Forestry Trust. *Report to appointers 1995-96* (Wellington, The Trust, 1996)

Crown Proposals for the Settlement of Treaty of Waitangi Claims (Wellington, Office of Treaty Settlements, Department of Justice, 8 December 1994)

Curriculum Review, The. See Committee to Review.

D: abbreviation for the *Dominion*, a Wellington daily newspaper. See AS for section and page abbreviations.

Davey, Judith. *Social policy options* (New Zealand Planning Council, Wellington, 1987)

Davey, Judith and Koopman-Boyden, Peggy. *Issues in equity* (New Zealand Planning Council, Wellington, 1983)

Day, J. P. 'Compensatory discrimination', *Philosophy*, 56 (1981), pp. 55-72

de Bres, Pieter H. 'Maori religious affiliation in a city suburb', in I. H. Kawharu (ed.), *Conflict and compromise*, pp. 144-66

de Jouvenel, Bertrand. *Sovereignty* (Cambridge University Press, Cambridge, 1957)

De Loria, Vine. *The nations within: the past and future of Indian sovereignty* (Pantheon Books, New York, 1984)

De Loria, Vine (ed.) *American Indian policy in the twentieth century* (University of Oklahoma Press, Norman, 1985)

Department of Education. *Tomorrow's schools. The reform of education administration in New Zealand* (The Department of Education, Wellington, August 1988)

Department of Maori Affairs. *A brief summary of the activities of the Department and of the Maori Trustee* (The Department and the Maori Trustee, Wellington, July 1984)

Department of Maori Affairs. *Integration of Maori and Pakeha* (Government Printer, Wellington, 1962)

   Maatua Whangai policy (Wellington, n.d. [1988], unpaged [15pp])

   Report on the economic and social development of the Maori people 1945-1980 (The Department for the Hui Whakatauira Conference, Wellington, 1981)

   He tirohanga rangapu/Partnership perspectives (The Department of Maori Affairs, Wellington, 1988)

   Te urupare rangapu/Partnership response (The Department of Maori Affairs, Wellington, November 1988)

Department of Maori Affairs (ed.) *Nga korero me nga wawata mo te Tiriti o Waitangi* (The Department, Whangarei, 1985)

de Tocqueville, Alexis. *Democracy in America* (Trans. G. Lawrence, J. P Mayer and M. Lerner (eds.) 2 vols. (Harper, New York, 1966)

Dewes, Koro. 'The Pakeha Veto', *Te Maori*, 1, vi (1970), pp. 5ff

Douglas, E. M. K. *Fading expectations: the crisis in Maori housing* (Board of Maori Affairs, Wellington, 1986)

   'Land and Maori identity in contemporary New Zealand', *Plural Societies*, 15 (1984), pp. 33-51

   'Marine resources and the future, a Maaori alternative strategy', Centre for Maaori Studies and Research, Waikato University. Submission to the Treaty of Waitangi Hearing, Ihumatao, 19 July 1984. Quoted from the

Tainui submissions to the Maori Affairs Amendment Bill 1987, No. 26a, Schedule 9.

Downey, P. *Human Rights and New Zealand* (Human Rights Commission, Wellington, 1983)

DST: abbreviation for *The Dominion Sunday Times*, a Wellington weekly newspaper. *See* AS for section and page abbreviations.

Durie, E. T. J. 'Part II and clause 26 of the draft New Zealand Bill of Rights', in Sharp et al., *A Bill of Rights*, pp. 171-93

'The Waitangi Tribunal: its relationship with the judicial system', *New Zealand Law Journal*, (July 1986), pp. 235-8

'Politics, biculturalism and the law', in Wilson and Yeatman (eds.) *Justice and identity*, pp. 33-44

Durie, M. H. 'The Treaty of Waitangi – perspectives on Social Policy', in I. H. Kawharu (ed.), *Waitangi*, pp. 280-99

'Mana Maori motuhake: the state of the Maori nation', in Ray Miller (ed.) *New Zealand politics in transition*, forthcoming.

'Proceedings of a Hui held at Hirangi Marae, Turangi' (1995), in McLay (ed.) *Treaty Settlements*, pp. 109-17

'Tino rangatiratanga: Maori self-determination', *He Pukenga Korero: A Journal of Maori Studies*, 1, i (1995), pp. 44-53

Dworkin, Ronald. *Taking rights seriously* (Harvard University Press, Cambridge, Mass., 1978)

'What is equality?', *Philosophy and Public Affairs*, 10 (1981), pp. 185-246

Dyall, John R. *Maori resource development: a handbook of Maori organisations* (J. R. Dyall, Christchurch, 1984)

Easton, David. *The political system: an inquiry into the nature of political science* (Alfred A. Knopf, New York, 1968. [First published 1953])

Eckhoff, Torstein. *Justice: its determination and social significance* (Rotterdam University Press, Rotterdam, 1974)

Encounter: A TV1 television magazine programme. For particular items, see Chapman, Robert and Chapman, Noeline.

EP: abbreviation for the *Evening Post*, a Wellington daily. *See* AS for section and page abbreviations.

Epstein, Arnold L. *Ethos and identity* (Tavistock, London, 1978)

Evans, Ripeka. 'Aftermath of Waitangi – Building a National Movement', in Waitangi Action Committee, *Newsletter*, Otara [August 1981]

'Is the Treaty of Waitangi a Bill of Rights?', in Sharp et al., *A Bill of Rights*, pp. 197-205

'Maori economic development, *Race, Gender, Class*, 4 (1986), pp. 18-20

'Rebecca Evans', *Broadsheet*, (October 1982), pp. 12-17

Evison, Harry C. *Ngai Tahu land rights and the Crown Pastoral Leases in the South Island of New Zealand* (Ngai Tahu Maori Trust Board, Christchurch, 1986)

The Treaty of Waitangi and the Ngai Tahu Claim: a summary (Ngai Tahu Maori Trust Board, Christchurch, 1988)

Ewin, R. E. *Liberty, community and justice* (Rowman and Littlefield, Totowa, N.J., 1987)

Eyewitness News: TV2 current affairs programme. To find particular programmes, *see* Chapman, Robert and Chapman, Noeline.

Flathman, Richard. 'Equality and generalisation', in Flathman, R. (ed.), *Concepts in social philosophy* (Macmillan, New York, 1973), pp. 366-81

The practice of rights (Cambridge University Press, Cambridge, 1976)

Fleras, Augie. 'Monoculturalism, multiculturalism and biculturalism', *Plural Societies*, 15 (1984), pp. 52-75

'The politics of Maori lobbying. The case of the Maori Council', *Political Science*, 37, i, (July 1985), pp. 18-39

'Towards "Tu tangata": historical developments and current trends in Maori policy and administration', *Political Science*, 37, ii (1985), pp. 18-39

Forbes, Mary. *He panui* (unpublished), attached to *In a submission to te Whare Ahupiri o Nga Ko Here in the matter of the Crown's fiscal settlement* (Auckland, prepared by Mary Forbes, 30 September 1995)

Frame, Alex. 'Colonising attitudes towards Maori custom', *New Zealand Law Journal*, 1981, pp. 105-10

Francis, Mark. 'The contemplation of colonial constitutions as political philosophy', *Political Studies* 40, i (1988), pp. 142-59

'The nineteenth century theory of sovereignty and Thomas Hobbes', *History of political thought*, 1 (1980), pp. 517-40

Francis, Mark with Morrow, John. 'After the ancient constitution: political theory in English constitutional writings, 1765-1832', *History of political thought*, 9 (1988), pp. 283-302

Frey, K.G. (ed.) *Utility and rights* (Basil Blackwell, Oxford, 1984)

Fried, Charles. 'Rights and the common law', in Frey, R.G., *Utility and rights*, pp. 215-34

Frontline: TV1 current affairs programme. For particular programmes, *see* Chapman, Robert and Chapman, Noeline.

Fulton, T.W. *The sovereignty of the sea* (William Blackwood, Edinburgh and London, 1911)

GAL: abbreviation for the library of the General Assembly [Parliament], Wellington. The signs following (e.g., MA/75/10) are the shelf marks of manuscripts held there and the folio numbers (e.g., Maori Affairs, 1975, folio 10). *See* SCMA and MA.

Gilmore, Myron P. *Argument from Roman law in political thought* (Harvard University Press, Cambridge, Mass., 1941)

Humanists and jurists: six studies in the renaissance (Harvard University Press, Cambridge, Mass., 1963)

Glanville, William (ed.) *Salmond on jurisprudence*, 11th edn. (Sweet and Maxwell, London, 1957)

Glazer, Nathan. *Ethnic dilemmas, 1964-1982* (Harvard University Press, Cambridge, Mass., 1983)

Glover, Denis. 'Prayers in prejudice', in D. Glover, *Sharp edge up* (Blackwood and Janet Paul, Auckland, 1968)

GMNZ, *see Good Morning New Zealand.*

Gold, Hyam (ed.) *New Zealand politics in perspective* (Longman Paul, Auckland, 3rd edn. 1992)

Goldsmith, M. M. 'Hobbes's "Mortal God": is there a fallacy in Hobbes's 'theory of sovereignty?', *History of Political Thought*, 1 (1980), pp. 33-50

Good Morning New Zealand: A news and magazine radio programme on National Radio. To find particular programmes, *see* Chapman, Robert and Chapman, Noeline.

Gough, John W. *Fundamental law in English constitutional history* (Clarendon Press, Oxford, 1955)

Gould, J.D. 'Socio-Economic Differences between Maori Iwi', *Journal of the Polynesian Society*, 105, ii (1996), pp. 165-83

Government Printer. *The Treaty of Waitangi in the Court of Appeal* (Government Printer, Wellington, 1987)

Green, Arnold et al. (eds.) *Studies in legal history on the law and custom of England. Essays in honour of Samuel E. Thorne* (University of California Press, Chapel Hill, 1981)

Green, Mark. 'Reparation for blacks? The question of effective equality through preferential treatment', *The Commonwealth*, 14 June 1969, pp. 359-62

Greenland, Hauraki. 'Ethnicity as ideology: the critique of Pakeha society', in Spoonley, McPherson et al., *Tauiwi*, pp. 86-102

    'The politics of Maori cultural revival', M.A. thesis, Department of Sociology, University of Auckland, (1984)

Gross, Barry R. (ed.) *Reverse discrimination* (Prometheus Books, Buffalo, N.Y., 1977)

Guest, Anthony (ed.) *Oxford essays in jurisprudence* (Clarendon Press, Oxford, 1961)

Gustafson, Barry. *The first fifty years: a history of the New Zealand National Party* (Reed Methuen, Auckland, 1986)

Guy, Camille. 'Getting away from racist guilt', *Broadsheet*, (September 1986), pp. 30-2

H: abbreviation for *The New Zealand Herald*, the morning daily newspaper published in Auckland. *See* AS for the method of abbreviating references.

Hackshaw, Fredericka. 'Nineteenth century notions of aboriginal title and their influence on the interpretation of the Treaty of Waitangi', in I. H. Kawharu (ed.), *Waitangi*, pp. 92-120

    'The recognition of native customary rights at common law', unpublished LLB dissertation, University of Auckland, (1984)

Harper, Jim. 'The implications for a bureaucracy of responding to special group needs', *Public Sector*, 8, iii (1983), pp. 3-14

Harré, John. *Maori and Pakeha. A study of mixed marriages in New Zealand* (Pall Mall Press, London, 1966)

Harrington, Michael and Kaufman, Arnold. 'Black reparations - two views', *Dissent* (1969), pp. 317-20

Hart, H. L. A. *The concept of law* (Oxford University Press, Oxford, 1961)

Hawke, Garry R. *Report of the working group on post compulsory education and training 1988* (Cabinet Social Equity Committee, Wellington, 1988)

Haworth, Nigel. 'Neo-liberalism, economic internationalisation and the contemporary state in New Zealand', in Sharp (ed.) *Leap into the dark*, pp. 19-40

Hazard, Paul. *The European Mind 1680-1751* (Penguin, Harmondsworth, 1964)

Healy, Susan. 'Theological colleges and the Maori', unpublished M.A. thesis, Department of Maori Studies, University of Auckland, (1988)

Held, Virginia. 'Feminism and epistemology: recent work on the connection between gender and knowledge', *Philosophy and Public Affairs*, 14 (1985), pp. 296-307

    'Justification, legal and moral', *Ethics*, 86 (1975-76), pp. 1-16

    Rights and goods. Justifying social action (Free Press/Macmillan, New York, 1984)

    'Feminism and moral theory', unpubl. MS (Hunter College, New York, 1988)

Heller, Agnes. *Beyond justice* (Basil Blackwood, Oxford, 1987)

Heller, Eric, *The disinherited mind: essays in modern German literature anl thought* (Penguin, Harmondsworth, 1961)

Hobbes, Thomas. *Leviathan or the matter, forme and power of a commonwealth ecclesiastical and civil* (1651). A good, available edition is that by C. B. McPherson (Pelican, Harmondsworth, 1968)

Hohepa, Pat. 'Maori and Pakeha: the one-people myth', in M. King (ed.), *Tihe mauri ora*, pp. 98-111

Hohfeld, Wesley N. *Fundamental legal conceptions* (Yale University Press, New Haven, Conn., 1923)

Holland, Martin and Boston, Jonathan (eds.) *The Fourth Labour Government. Policy and politics in New Zealand* (Oxford University Press, Auckland, 2nd edn., 1990)

Honore, A. M. 'Ownership', in Guest (ed.), *Oxford essays*, pp. 107-47

Howe, K. R. *Race relations, Australia and New Zealand. A comparative survey 1770s-1970s* (Methuen, Wellington, 1977)

HRC: abbreviation for the Human Rights Commission.

Huakina Development Trust v *Waikato Valley Authority and Bowater*. Unreported decision at the High Court, Wellington Registry, 2 June 1987, MA430/86.

Hughes, Helen R. (Parliamentary Commissioner for the Environment) *Environmental management and the principles of the Treaty of Waitangi. Report on Crown response to the recommendations of the Waitangi Tribunal 1983-1988* (The Commissioner, Wellington, November 1988)

Human Rights Commission. Inciting racial disharmony. *Discussion paper on Section 9a of the Race Relations Act* (The Commission, Wellington, [1984])

    The proposed Bill of Rights. See Tollemache.

    Report of a seminar on human rights held in Wellington, New Zealand on 9-10 December 1978 (The Commission, Wellington, 1979)

    Race against time. (Produced and developed by the Race Relations Conciliator) (The Commission, Wellington, 1982)

Racial harmony in New Zealand: a statement of issues (The Commission, Wellington, [1980])

Women in Banking (The Commission, Wellington, [1984])

Hume, David. *Enquiries concerning human understanding and concerning the principles of morals.* (1777) (Ed. L. A. Selby-Bigge, Clarendon Press, Oxford, 1955)

A treatise of human nature (1739) (Ed. L. A. Selby-Bigge, Clarendon Press, Oxford, 1951)

Hunn, J. K. 'Can race relations be left to chance?' Paper presented to the annual congress of the New Zealand University Students' Association, 28 January 1963.

Report on the Department of Maori Affairs with statistical supplement (24 August 1960) (Government Printer, Wellington, 1961)

Ignatieff, Michael. *The needs of strangers* (Chatto and Windus, London, 1984)

Ihimaera, Witi. *The Matriarch* (Heinemann, Auckland, 1986)

Inner City News. An Auckland weekly newspaper.

Issues in equity. See Davey, Judith and Koopman-Boyden, Peggy.

Jackson, Moana. *The Maori and the criminal justice system. A new perspective* (2 vols., Department of Justice, Wellington. Vol 1, 1987; vol 2, 1988)

Jagose, Pheroze. 'Section 9a of the Race Relations Act 1971 – the "Tigger" of New Zealand's race relations legislation', *Auckland University Law Review*, 4 (1987), pp. 494-509

Jaques, Elliot. 'Psychotic anxieties and the sense of justice', in J. Elliot, *Work, creativity and social justice* (Heinemann, London, 1970)

Jesson, Bruce, Ryan, Allanah and Spoonley, Paul. *Revival of the right* (Heinemann Reed, Auckland, 1988)

Joseph, Philip. 'Literal Compulsion and Fundamental Rights', *New Zealand Law Journal* (1987), pp. 102-4

Joseph, Philip A. (ed.) *Essays on the constitution* (Brooker's, Wellington, 1995)

Joyce, Peta and Rosier, Pat. 'Maori sovereignty racist?', *Broadsheet*, March 1986, pp. 12-13

Kaituna Report. See Waitangi Tribunal, no. 4.

Karetu, Sam. 'Kawa in crisis' in M. King (ed.), *Tihe mauri ora*, pp. 67-79

Kavka, Gregory S. 'The paradox of future individuals', *Philosophy and Public Affairs*, 11 (1982), pp. 93-112

Kawharu, I. H. *Maori land tenure* (Oxford University Press, Oxford, 1977)

Kawharu, I. H. (ed.) *Conflict and compromise. Essays on the Maori since colonisation* (A. H. and A. W. Reed, Wellington, Sydney, London, 1975)

Waitangi: Māori and Pākehā perspectives of the Treaty of Waitangi (Oxford University Press, Auckland, 1989)

Keith, K. J. 'The Treaty and the Race Relations Act', in Victoria University, Department of University Extension, *The Treaty of Waitangi*, pp. 71-80

Kelsey, Jane. 'Legal imperialism and the colonisation of Aotearoa', in Spoonley, MacPherson et al., *Tauiwi*, pp. 20-43

'Te Tiriti o Waitangi and the Bill of Rights', *Race, Gender, Class*, 3, (1986), pp. 23-30

'The Treaty of Waitangi and Pakeha responsibility - directions for the future' (Typescript paper for the Waitangi Forum, Christchurch, February 1987)

'From flagstaffs to pinetrees. Tino rangatiratanga and Treaty policy today', in Spoonley (ed.) *Nga Patai*, pp. 177-201

'Judicialisation of the Treaty of Waitangi: a subtle cultural repositioning', *Australian Journal of Law and Society*, 10 (1994), pp. 131-63

The New Zealand experiment. A world model for structural adjustment? (Bridget Williams Books, Wellington, 1995)

Rolling back the state (Bridget Williams Books, Wellington, 1993)

Kenworthy, L. M., Martindale, T.B. and Sadarka, S. M.. 'The Hunn Report. A measure of progress on aspects of Maori life', *New Zealand Journal of Public Administration*, 33, i (1970), pp. 31-54

Kia Mohio Kia Marama Trust. *Jaws unmasked . . . The consequences of the agreement between the New Zealand Maori Council and the government* (Xeroxed typescript. Auckland, n.d. [1987])

King, Michael. *Being Pakeha. An encounter with New Zealand and the Maori renaissance* (Hodder and Stoughton, Auckland, 1985)

'Between two worlds', Chapter 11 in Oliver with Williams, *The Oxford History of New Zealand*

Whina: a biography of Whina Cooper (Hodder and Stoughton, Auckland, 1983)

King, Michael (ed.) *Te Ao hurihuri. The world moves on: aspects of Maoritanga*, new edition (Longman Paul, Auckland 1981. First published 1975)

Tihe mauri ora: aspects of Maoritanga (Methuen, Wellington, 1978)

King-Farlow, J. and Shea, W. (eds.). *Contemporary issues in political philosophy* (Science History Publications, New York, 1976)

Kingsbury, Benedict. 'The Treaty of Waitangi: some international law aspects', in I. H. Kawharu (ed.), *Waitangi*, pp. 212-57

Knight, D. B. 'Territory and people or people and territory?', *International Political Science Review*, 6 (1985), pp. 248-72

Landfall: Literary periodical.

Lane, Robert E. 'Market justice, political justice', *American Political Science Review*, 80 (1986), pp. 383-402

Laslett, Peter (ed.) *John Locke: Two treatises of government* (Cambridge University Press, Cambridge, 1964 and later editions)

Politics, philosophy and society (lst series, Basil Blackwell, Oxford, 1956)

Laslett, Peter and Runciman, W. G. (eds.) *Politics, philosophy and society*, (2nd series, Basil Blackwell, Oxford, 1962)

Laslett, Peter and Fishkin, James S. (eds.) *Justice between groups and generations* (Yale University Press, New Haven, 1992)

Laswell, Harold. *Politics: who gets what, when, how* (Meridian Books, New York, 1958)

L'Estrange, Maryanne. 'Learning anti-racism', *Broadsheet* (April 1987), pp. 235

Levine, H. B. 'The cultural politics of Maori fishing: an anthropological perspective on the first three Waitangi Tribunal hearings', *Journal of Polynesian Studies*, 96 (December 1987), pp. 421-43

Levine, Stephen and Vasil, Raj. *Maori political perspectives* (Hutchinson, Auckland, 1985)

Litchfield, Michael. Confiscation of Maori Land, *Victoria University of Wellington Law Review*, 15 (1985), pp. 335-60

Locke, John. *Two treatises of government* (See Laslett)

Luban, David. 'Bargaining and compromise: recent work on negotiation and informal justice', *Philosophy and Public Affairs*, 14 (1985), pp. 397-416

Lucas, J. R. *The principles of politics* (Clarendon Press, Oxford, 1966)

Lyons, David. 'The new Indian claims and original rights to land', *Social Theory and Practice*, 4 (1977), pp. 249-72

MA: abbreviation for 'Maori Affairs', and indicates documents of the Select Committee of the House of Representatives on Maori Affairs. After use they go to the General Assembly Library. See SCMA and GAL.

McDonald, Geraldine, and Campbell, Alistair. *Looking forward - essays on the future of New Zealand education* (Te Aro Press, Wellington, 1984)

McDonald, Geoff. *The Kiwis fight back* (Chaston Publishers, Christchurch, 1986)
  Shadows over New Zealand (Chaston Publishers, Christchurch, 1985)

McDonald, Michael. 'Aboriginal rights, in King-Farlow, *Contemporary Issues*, pp. 27-48

McDowell, Te Aroha. 'Tokenism in the Ministry', *Broadsheet*, (April 1985), pp. 28-30

McHugh, Paul G. 'Aboriginal rights and sovereignty: Commonwealth developments', *New Zealand Law Journal*, (February 1986), pp. 57-63
  'Aboriginal servitudes and the Land Transfer Act 1952', *Victoria University Law Review*, 16 (1986), pp. 313-35
  'Aboriginal title in New Zealand courts', (part 1), *Canterbury Law Review*, (1985), pp. 235-65
  'Aboriginal title returns to New Zealand courts', *New Zealand Law Journal*, (1987), pp. 39-41
  'The Constitutional Role of the Waitangi Tribunal', *New Zealand Law Journal*, (July 1985), pp. 224-33
  'Constitutional theory and Maori claims', in 1. H. Kawharu (ed.), *Waitangi*, pp. 25-63
  'The legal status of Maori fishing rights in tidal waters', *Victoria University Law Review*, 14 (1984), pp. 247-73
  'Maori Fishing Rights and the North American Indian', *Otago Law Review*, 6 (1985), pp. 62-94
  The Māori Magna Carta: New Zealand law and the Treaty of Waitangi (Oxford University Press, Auckland, 1991)
  'The historiography of New Zealand's constitutional history', in Joseph (ed.) *Essays on the constitution*, pp. 344-67

McKenzie, Donald F. *Oral culture, literacy and print in early New Zealand. The Treaty of Waitangi* (Victoria University Press: Alexander Turnbull Literary Endowment, Wellington, 1985)

McLay, G (ed.) 'Treaty settlements: the unfinished business', *Victoria University Law Review*, 25, ii (1995)

Magnusson, Magnus and Palsson, Hermann. *Njal's saga* [c. 1280]. (Penguin, Harmondsworth, 1983. First published 1960.)

Mahuta, Robert T. 'The King Movement today', in M. King (ed.), *Tihe mauri ora*, pp. 33-41

'Race relations in New Zealand', in Stokes (ed.), *Nga tumanako*, pp. 17-27

'Tainui: A Case Study of Direct Negotiation', in McLay (ed.) *Treaty settlements*, pp. 167-73

'Tainui, Kingitanga and Raupatu', in Wilson and Yeatman (eds.) *Justice and identity*, pp. 29-30

Maier, Charles. *Changing boundaries of the political* (Cambridge University Press, Cambridge, 1987)

Mair, Lucy. *Primitive government* (Pelican, Harmondsworth, 1962)

Mana Motuhake. *Nga kaupapa Mana Motuhake*. See Walker, Ranginui J. I., collector.

Mangonui Sewerage Report. See Waitangi Tribunal, no. 13.

Manukau Report. See Waitangi Tribunal, no. 6.

Maori Land Court. *Tai whati. Judicial decisions affecting Maoris and Maori land* (The Court, Wellington, 1983)

Te Maori: Periodical published by the Department of Maori Affairs, 1969-1981.

Mead, S. M. *He ara ki te aromarama (Finding a pathway to the future)* (NZ Planning Council, Wellington, 1979). Printed in summary in the Planning Council's *He Matapuna. Some Maori perspectives.*

'The Treaty of Waitangi and "Waitangi",' included in the kitset *New Hope*.

Melbourne, Hineani (ed.) *Maori sovereignty. The Maori perspective* (Hodder Moa Beckett, Auckland, 1995)

Metge, Joan. *The Maoris of New Zealand, rautahi*. Revised edn. (Routledge and Kegan Paul, London, 1976)

Metro: An Auckland monthly magazine.

Mikula, Gerold. 'The experience of injustice', in Hans W. Bierhoff, Ronald L. Cohen, and Jerald Greenberg (eds.), *Justice in social relations*

Mill, John Stuart. *Utilitarianism: liberty: representative government* (Ed. A. D. Lindsay, J. M. Dent, London, 1960)

Miller, David L. *Social justice* (Clarendon Press, Oxford, 1976)

Ministerial Advisory Committee on a Maori Perspective for the Department of Social Welfare. *Puao-Te-Ata-Tu/Day Break*, 2 vols. (The Department, Wellington, 1986)

MLR. Tom Bennion (ed.) *Maori Law Review* (Esoteric Publications, Wellington)

Montague, Phillip. 'Rights and duties of compensation', *Philosophy and Public Affairs*, 13, i (1984), pp. 79-88

MOOHR is the Maori Organisation of Human Rights. They published a *Newsletter.*

More: A glossy monthly published in Auckland.

MR: *Monthly Review*. A left-wing monthly published in Christchurch.

Mulgan, Richard. 'Aotearoa-New Zealand? Problems of a bi-cultural democracy', in University of Otago, *Government*, pp. 26-42

'Indigenous rights and the legitimacy of former governments', address to the Dunedin branch of the New Zealand Institute of International Affairs, 9 June 1988.

Democracy and Power in New Zealand: a study of New Zealand politics. 2nd edn. (Oxford University Press, Auckland, 1989)

Māori, Pākehā and Democracy (Oxford University Press, Auckland, 1989)

Muriwhenua Fishing Report. See Waitangi Tribunal, no. 12.

Munroe, Justine. 'The Treaty of Waitangi and the Sealord deal', in *Victoria University of Wellington Law Review*, 24 (1994), pp. 389–430

Nairn, Mitzi. 'Some questions and a response, in (and *see*) *New Hope*, and National Council of Churches, *Programme on racism.*

National Council of Churches in New Zealand. NCC *Programme on Racism* No. 1. (August 1985) – No 15 (January 1989) (The Council, Christchurch and Auckland)

   The totara and the rose: a resource kit on cultural interaction (Cabbage Tree Press, Christchurch, 1983)

National Council of Churches in New Zealand, Church and Society Commission. *What happened at Waitangi in 1983?: a report to the New Zealand churches concerning the Treaty of Waitangi* (The Commission, Auckland, 1983)

   The Pakeha and the Treaty: signposts (The Commission, Auckland, 1986)

   Waitangi 1984: a turning point?: a report to the churches concerning the Treaty of Waitangi (The Commission, Christchurch, 1984)

NBR: abbreviation for the *National Business Review*. Originally a Wellington weekly, it became an Auckland daily in 1988. *See* AS for the method of abbreviating references.

NCC: abbreviation for the National Council of Churches in New Zealand.

Nedd, A. N. and Marsh, N. R. *Attitudes and behaviour of the multi-cultural workforce in New Zealand* (Department of Management Studies, University of Auckland, Auckland, [1978])

Neville, R. J. Warwick and O'Neill, C. James. *The population of New Zealand: interdisciplinary perspectives* (Longman Paul, Auckland, 1979)

New Hope: see New Zealand Catholic Commission.

New Outlook: Periodical.

New Zealand Catholic Commission for Evangelisation, Justice and Development. *New hope for our society. Discussion kitset on the Treaty of Waitangi* (Published by the editors, Wellington, 1985)

New Zealand Maori Council. *A discussion paper on future development and legislation* (The Council, Wellington, December 1980)

   Kaupapa: te whanga tuatahi. Discussion paper on Maori Affairs legislation (The Council, Wellington, 1983)

   Maori land. See Asher and Naulls.

   New Zealand Maori Council v the Attorney General and others, reprinted in Government Printer, *Treaty of Waitangi in the Court of Appeal.*

New Zealand Planning Council. *Issues in equity*. Davey, Judith and Koopman-Boyden, Peggy.

New Zealand Planning Council (ed.) *He Matapuna: a source. Some Maori perspectives* (The Council, Wellington, 1979)

   Social policy options. See Davey, Judith.

New Zealand Section of the International Commission of Jurists. *Bill of Rights seminar. Held 10 May, Parliament Buildings* (International Commission of Jurists, Wellington, 1985)

New Zealand Task Force on Economic and Social Planning. *New Zealand at the turning point* (Report, Wellington, 1976)

Nga korero: See Department of Maori Affairs.

Nga take Maori: A TV1 magazine programme. For particular items, see Chapman, Robert and Chapman, Noeline.

Ngata, H. K. 'The Treaty of Waitangi and land: parts of the current law in contravention of the Treaty', in Victoria University, Department of University Extension, *Treaty of Waitangi*, pp. 49-70

Ngati Paoa Whaanui, 'Submissions, to the Treaty of Waitangi Tribunal', Kaiaua Marae, Kaiaua. n.d. [1985], Appendix 6. Copy David Williams (ed.), University of Auckland Law School Library.

Nietzsche, Friedrich. *The birth of tragedy and the genealogy of morals* (Doubleday, Garden City, N.Y., 1956)

Novitz, David and Bill Willmot (eds.) *New Zealand in Crisis. A debate about today's critical issues* (GP Books, Wellington, 1992)

Nozick, Robert. *Anarchy, state and utopia* (Basic Books, New York, 1974)

N.Z.A.R.: *New Zealand Administrative Reports.*

NZCLD. *New Zealand Case Law Digest* (Brooker and Friend, Wellington, 1990–)

NZL: abbreviation for *The New Zealand Listener*, a weekly magazine.

NZLR. *New Zealand Law Reports* (Butterworth and Co., Australia, 1883-)

NZMC: abbreviation for the New Zealand Maori Council.

NZPD: abbreviation for the *New Zealand Parliamentary Debates* (Government Printer, Wellington). The abbreviations 1:42 etc. mean first session of the forty-second Parliament etc.

NZT: abbreviation for the *New Zealand Times*. Weekly newspaper, Wellington.

Oakeshott, Michael. *Rationalism in politics and other essays* (Methuen, London, 1977)

Oddie, Graham and Roy W. Perret (eds.) *Justice, ethics and New Zealand society* (Oxford University Press, Auckland, 1992)

Oliver, W. H. *Claims to the Waitangi Tribunal* (Waitangi Tribunal Division, Department of Justice, Wellington, 1991)

Oliver, W. H. with B.R. Williams (eds.). *The Oxford History of New Zealand* (Oxford University Press, Wellington; Clarendon Press, Oxford, 1981)

Orakei Report. *See* Waitangi Tribunal, no. 11.

Orange, Claudia. 'The Treaty of Waitangi', in the kitset *New Hope*, and in Blank *et al.* (eds.), *He korero*

   The Treaty of Waitangi (Allen and Unwin, Wellington, 1987. Reprinted 1987)

O'Regan, Tipene. 'The Ngai Tahu Claim', in 1. H. Kawharu (ed.), *Waitangi*, pp. 234-62

P: abbreviation for the *Press*, a Christchurch daily newspaper. *See* AS for the method of abbreviating references.

Palmer, Geoffrey. *A Bill of Rights for New Zealand: a white paper. Presented to the House of Representatives by the Hon. Geoffrey Palmer, Minister of Justice* (Government Printer, Wellington, 1985)

   Unbridled power: an interpretation of New Zealand's constitution and government. 2nd edn. (Oxford University Press, Auckland, 1987)

Parfit, Derek. 'Later selves and moral principles,' in A. Montefiore (ed.), *Philosophy and personal relations*, (London, 1973), pp. 137-69.

Parsonson, Ann. 'The pursuit of mana', Chapter 6 of Oliver with Williams, *The Oxford History of New Zealand*, pp. 140-67

Patterson, Orlando. *Ethnic chauvinism: the reactionary impulse* (Stein and Day, New York, 1977)

Pearson, Bill. *Fretful sleepers and other essays* (Heinemann, Auckland, 1974)
'Under pressure to integrate', in his *Fretful sleepers*, and in *Landfall*, (June 1962)

Perry, Thomas D. 'A paradigm of philosophy: Hohfeld on legal rights', *American Philosophical Quarterly*, 14 (1977), pp. 41-50

Pettit, Philip. 'Rights, constraints and trumps', *Analysis*, 47 (1987), pp. 814

Phillips, Derek L. *Equality, justice and rectification* (Academic Press, London, New York, San Francisco, 1979)

Phillips, Hilda. *Let the truth be known* (Hilda Phillips, [Auckland], 2 May 1988)

Piddington, Ralph. *An introduction to social anthropology*, vol 1. (Oliver and Boyd, Edinburgh and London, 1963. First published 1950)

Poananga, Atareta. 'Death of an honorary white', *Broadsheet*, (April 1986), pp. 13-19
'The matriarch: takahia wahine toa', *Broadsheet*, (December 1986), pp. 248 (January-February 1987), pp. 25-9

Pocock, J. G. A (ed.) *The Maori and New Zealand politics* (Blackwood and Janet Paul, Auckland and Hamilton, 1965)

Police v Dalton. Unpubl. Magistrates Court, Auckland. Decision 16 July 1979. B. H. Blackwood Esq. S. M.

Pool, Ian and Pole, Nicholas. *The Maori population to 2011: demographic change and its implications* (New Zealand Demographic Society, Wellington, 1987)

Presbyterian Church, Maori Synod. *A Maori view of the 'Hunn Report'* (The Synod, Christchurch, 1961)

Principles for crown action on the Treaty of Waitangi (Government Printer, Wellington, July 1989)

Project Waitangi: Pakeha debate the Treaty. *Resource Kit*, 3 parts, Wellington, 1987-1988

PTAT: *see* Ministerial Advisory Committee, *Puao-Te-Ata-Tu/Day Break*.

Public service in a multiracial society. See State Services Commission.

Puketapu, Kara. *Reform from within* (Department of Maori Affairs, Wellington, 1982)

Race Relations Conciliator, Office of the. *Let's work together: kia mahi tahi tatou: 'Maori Pakeha Kiwi or New Zealander'* [Auckland], n.d. [1986]
Race against time (Human Rights Commission, Wellington, 1982)

Radio New Zealand, Continuing Education Service. *Beyond guilt. A handbook on racism* (RNZ, Wellington, 1987)

Raureti, Moana. 'The origins of the Ratana movement', in M. King (ed.), *Tihe mauri ora*, pp. 42-59

Rawls, John. 'Kantian constructivism in moral theory', *The Journal of Philosophy*, 77 (1980), pp. 515-72
A theory of justice (Harvard University Press, Cambridge, Mass., 1971)
'Political theory: political not metaphysical', *Philosophy and Public Affairs*, 14 (1985), pp. 223-51

Reddy, William M. *Money and liberty in modern Europe. A critique of historical understanding* (Cambridge University Press, Cambridge, 1987)

Rees, W.J. 'The theory of sovereignty restated' in Laslett (ed.), *Politics, philosophy and society*, 1 series, pp. 56-82

Reeves, Frank. *British political discourse about race and race-related matters* (Cambridge University Press, Cambridge 1983)

Renwick, William, *The Treaty now* (GP Publications, Wellington, 1990)

Republican, The. Periodical. Auckland. Edited by Bruce Jesson.

Resource Management Law Reform: Kitset, Wellington, 1988.

Rewhiti, Debbie. 'Maori sovereignty', *Broadsheet*, (November 1984), pp. 13-15

Rice, Geoffrey (ed.) *The Oxford history of New Zealand* (Oxford University Press, Auckland, 2nd edn., 1992)

Richards, Judith R. *The sceptical feminist* (Pelican, Harmondsworth, 1980)

Riley, Patrick (ed.) *The political writings of Leibniz* (Cambridge University Press, Cambridge, 1972)

Robinson, Nehemiah. *Indemnification and Reparations: Jewish Aspects* (Institute of Jewish Affairs, N.Y., 1944)

    Ten Years of German Indemnification (Conference on Jewish Material Claims, N.Y., 1964)

Rockill, Dennis. 'Understanding racism. Response to ACORD', *The Republican*, (September 1983), p. 10

Ross, Ruth M. 'Te Tiriti o Waitangi. Texts and translations', *New Zealand Journal of History*, 6 (1972), pp. 129-54

    'The Treaty on the ground', in Victoria University, *The Treaty of Waitangi*, pp. 16-34

Rousseau, Jean Jacques. *The social contract and the discourses*, G. D. H. Cole (ed.). Revised and augmented by J. H. Brumfitt and J. C. Hall. Dent, London and Melbourne, 1983)

Royal Commission on the Electoral System. *Report: Towards a better democracy* (Government Printer, Wellington, 1986)

Royal Commission on Broadcasting and Related Telecommunications in New Zealand. *Report. Broadcasting and related telecommunications in New Zealand* (Published by the Commission, Auckland, September 1986)

Royal Commission on Social Policy. *The April Report*, 4 vols. (Vol 3 in two parts), (Royal Commission on Social Policy, Wellington, 1988)

Royal Forest and Bird Society v *W. A. Habgood Ltd and others*. Unreported decision at the High Court, Wellington Registry. (31 March 1987)

Royce, Anya Peterson. *Ethnic identity: strategies of diversity* (Indiana University Press, Bloomington, Ind., 1982)

Sahlins, Marshall. *Islands of history* (Tavistock Publications, London and New York, 1987. First published 1985 by the University of Chicago Press.)

Salmond, Anne. 'On sovereignty and "kawanatanga"', unpublished paper, Auckland University. (October 1988)

    Hui: a study of Maori ceremonial gatherings. 2nd edn., reprinted. (Reeds, Wellington, 1983. First published 1975.)

Sandel, Michael. *Liberalism and the limits of justice* (Cambridge University Press, Cambridge, 1982)

'The procedural republic and the unencumbered self', *Political Theory*, 12 (1984), pp. 81-96

Schwerin, Kurt. 'German Compensation for Victims of Nazi Persecution', *Northwestern University Law Review*, 4 (1972), pp. 479-527

Schusky, Ernest L. *The right to be Indian* (American Indian Educational Publishers, San Francisco, 1975. First printed 1970.)

Schwimmer, Erik (ed.) *The Maori people in the nineteen-sixties* (Longman Paul, Auckland, 1975 (Reprint). [First published 1968.]

SCMA: abbreviation for the Select Committee of the House of Representatives [Parliament] on Maori Affairs. The Committee catalogues its documents (always, in this book, submissions made to the Committee on legislation before the House), under the prefix MA. In due course the documents go to the General Assembly Library where they retain the prefix MA, but where the numeric suffix may change. *See* MA and GAL.

Scollay, Robert and St John, Susan. *Macroeconomics and the contemporary New Zealand society* (Longman, Auckland, 1996)

Scott, Dick. *Ask that mountain. The story of Parihaka* (Heinemann/Southern Cross, Auckland, 1975)

Scott, Stuart C. *The travesty of Waitangi: towards anarchy* (Campbell Press, Dunedin, 1995)

Sharp, Andrew. 'An historical and philosophical perspective on the proposal for a Bill of Rights in New Zealand', in Sharp et al., *A Bill of Rights*, pp. 1-46

Political ideas of the English civil wars 1641-49 (Longmans, London, 1983. Reprinted 1988)

'The "principle" of voluntary unionism in New Zealand political debate', *Political Science*, 31 (1986), pp. 1-26

'Tangata whenua at Snaps Gallery', *Photo Forum*, Auckland (October-November 1977), p. 38

et al. *A Bill of Rights for New Zealand* (Legal Research Foundation, Auckland, 1985)

'Civil rights, amelioration, and reparation in New Zealand' in Brown (ed.) *Ethnic relations and public policy in Asia and the Pacific*, Chap. 11.

(ed.) *Leap into the dark. The changing role of the state in New Zealand since 1984* (Auckland University Press, Auckland, 1994)

'The problem of Maori affairs, 1984-89', in Holland and Boston (eds.) *The Fourth Labour Government*, pp. 251-69

'Representing *Justice and the Maori*: on why it ought not to be construed as a post-modernist text', *Political Theory Newsletter*, 6, i (1992), pp. 27-38

'Sovereignty: te tino rangatiratanga', in Novitz and Willmot (eds.) *New Zealand in crisis*, pp. 26-31

'The Treaty, the Tribunal and the law: recognising Maori rights in New Zealand', in Gold (ed.) *New Zealand politics in perspective*, pp. 123-42

'The Waitangi Tribunal in New Zealand politics 1984-1996', in Ray Miller (ed.) *New Zealand politics in transition*, forthcoming.

'What is the constitution of the "Spirit of Haida Gwai"?', *History and Anthropology*, 10, ii (1997), pp. 1-16

'Why be bicultural?', in Wilson and Yeatman (eds.) *Justice and identity*, pp. 116-33

Sher, George. 'Ancient wrongs and modern rights', *Philosophy and Public Affairs*, 19 (1981), pp. 3-17

'Compensation and transworld identity', *Monist*, 62 (1979), pp. 378-91

Shera, Rick. 'Section 3 of the Town and Country Planning Act 1977: adjudicating the nonjusticiable', *Auckland University Law Review*, 4 (1987), pp. 440-58

Simon, Richard. See Part Two, Chapter 3 in Paul Hazard, *The European Mind 1680-1751*.

Simpson, Tony. *Te riri Pakeha: the white man's anger* (Alistair Taylor, Martinborough, 1979. Repub. Hodder and Stoughton. Auckland, 1986)

Sinclair, I. M. 'Treaty interpretation in the English courts', *International and Comparative Law Quarterly*, 12 (1963), pp. 508-51

Sinclair, Keith. *A destiny apart: the search for New Zealand's national identity* (Unwin paperbacks in association with the Port Nicholson Press, Wellington 1988).

A history of New Zealand (New Zealand University Press, Wellington, 1957. Reprinted 1980.)

The origins of the Maori Wars (Reprinted by Auckland University Press, Oxford University Press, Auckland, 1984. First published 1957, 2nd edn., 1961)

Smith, Anthony D. *The ethnic origins of nations* (Basil Blackwell, Oxford, 1986, New York, 1987)

Smith, Bruce James. *Politics and remembrance. Republican themes in Machiavelli Burke and Tocqueville* (Princeton University Press, Princeton, N.J., 1985)

Social Policy Options. See Davey, Judith.

Sorrenson, M. P. K. 'A history of Maori representation in Parliament', in the Royal Commission on the Electoral System, *Report*, Appendix B, pp. 1-82

'Land purchase methods and their effect on the Maori population 1865–1901', *Journal of the Polynesian Society*, lxv, 3 (September 1956), pp. 183-99

'The politics of land', in Pocock, *The Maori and New Zealand politics*, pp. 21-45

'Maori and Pakeha', Chapter 7 of Oliver with Williams, *The Oxford History of New Zealand*, pp. 168-93

'Towards a radical reinterpretation of New Zealand history: the role of the Waitangi Tribunal, *New Zealand Journal of History*, 21 (April 1987), pp. 173-88. Updated and reprinted in I. H. Kawharu (ed.), *Waitangi*, pp. 158-78

Spoonley, Paul. *Racism and ethnicity* (Oxford University Press, Auckland, 1988)

(ed.) *Nga Patai. Racism and ethnic relations in Aotearoa/New Zealand* (Dunmore Press, Palmerston North, 1996)

Spoonley, Paul, MacPherson, C., Pearson, D. and Sedgwick, C. (eds.) *Tauiwi. Racism and ethnicity in New Zealand* (Palmerston North, Dunmore Press, 1984)

SS: *Sunday Star*. An Auckland Sunday newspaper.

State Services Commission. *Public service in a multicultural society. Waahi conference 1982* (State Services Commission, Wellington, 1983)

State Services Commission, Equal Employment Opportunities Unit. 'Departmental equal opportunities monitoring report', Unpublished typescript. (Wellington, 31 March 1986)

Statistics New Zealand. *Census Education Kit* (The Department, Wellington, 1995)

Sterba, James P: 'Recent work on alternative conceptions of justice', *American Philosophical Quarterly*, 23, 1 (1986), pp. 1-22

Stokes, Evelyn (ed.) *Nga tumanako. Proceedings of the national conference of Maori Committees. [November]* (Centre of Maori Studies and Research, University of Waikato, 1978)

T: abbreviation for *The Truth*, a weekly paper.

Tarei, Wi. 'A church called Ringatu' in M. King (ed.), *Tihe mauri ora*, pp. 60-6

Tauroa, E. Te R. 'Report of advisory committee on youth and law in our multicultural society', Typescript. (Wellington, February 1983)

Tauroa, Hiwi [E. Te R.,]. See Human Rights Commission, *Race against time*.

Taylor, Theodore W. *American Indian policy* (Lomond Publications, Mt Airy, Md., 1983)

    The Bureau of Indian Affairs (Westview Press, Boulder, Colo., 1984)

Te Atiawa Report. See Waitangi Tribunal, no. 3.

Te Hikoi: See Waitangi Action Committee.

Te Maori: Periodical.

Te Ohu Kai Moana. *Discussion material on allocation models for consultation with iwi* (Wellington, The Commission, August 1994)

Te Ohu Kai Moana. *Report of Te Ohu Kai Moana/Treaty of Waitangi Fisheries Commission for the year ended September 1993.* Tabled in Parliament, 29 March 1994

Te Puni Kōkiri. *Report on implementation of Waitangi Tribunal recommendations and agreements 1994* (The Ministry, Wellington, 1995)

Te Reo Report. See Waitangi Tribunal, no. 7.

Te Weehi v *Regional Fisheries Office* (1986), 6 N.Z.A.R. 114-28.

Thalberg, Irving. 'Reverse discrimination and the future', *Philosophical Forum*, 5, i-ii (1973-74), pp. 294-307

Thomson, Judith Jarvis. *Rights, restitution and risk* (Harvard University Press, Cambridge, Mass., 1986)

Thucydides. *History of the Peleponnesian War* (Trans. Rex Warner, Penguin, London, 1954)

Tollemache, Nadia. *The proposed Bill of Rights: a discussion and resource paper prepared for the Human Rights Commission by Nadia Tollemache with assistance from Pam Ringwood* (Human Rights Commission, Wellington, 1986)

Treasury, The. *Economic management* (Government Printer, Wellington, 1984)

    Government management (Government Printer, 2 vols., Wellington, 1987)

Treaty of Waitangi Policy Unit for the Crown Task Force on Treaty of Waitangi Issues. *The Direct Negotiation of Maori Claims* (TOPU, Wellington, 1990)

The Treaty of Waitangi in the Court of Appeal (Government Printer, Wellington, 1987)

Trlin, Andrew D. 'Race, ethnicity and society', in Neville and O'Neill, *The population of New Zealand*, pp. 185-212

Trotter, Chris. 'A reply to Donna Awatere', *New Outlook*, 2, i (Winter 1983), pp. 8-9

Tu Kupenga. NZTV2 Sunday night magazine show.

Tu Tangata: Periodical published by Department of Maori Affairs, 1981-1987.

Tully, James. *A discourse on property – John Locke and his adversaries* (Cambridge University Press, Cambridge, 1980)

    Strange multiplicity. Constitutionalism in an age of diversity (Cambridge University Press, Cambridge, 1995)

Turangi Hui. *Unpublished papers* (November 1995)

    Paper 1: 'Constitutional change or constitutional reform'. Discussion for the Working Group

    Paper 2: 'Political options and the issue of constitutional reform or change'

    Paper 3: 'Constitutional change. We govern ourselves'

Turner, A.R. 'The changing basis of decision-making. Is reason sufficient?', *New Zealand Law Journal*, (June 1985), pp. 181-6

TWCA: abbreviation for, Government Printer, *Treaty of Waitangi in the Court of Appeal*.

Universities Review Committee to the . . . Vice-Chancellors' Committee. *New Zealand's universities: partners in national development* (NZ Vice Chancellors' Committee, Wellington, 1987)

University of Otago, Faculty of Arts and Music. *Government in the 1990s* (University of Otago, Dunedin, 1987)

University of Waikato, Centre for Maori Studies and Research. *Ko taa te Maaori Waahanga: Equity, social justice and Maoridom* (The Centre, Hamilton, 1986)

Vasil, Raj. *Biculturalism – reconciling Aotearoa with New Zealand* (Victoria University Press for the Institute of Policy Studies, Wellington, 1988)

Victoria University, Department of University Extension (ed.) *The Treaty of Waitangi. Its origins and significance* (Department of University Extension, Wellington, 1972)

WAC: abbreviation for Waitangi Action Committee.

Waiheke Report. See Waitangi Tribunal, no. 10.

Waitangi Action Committee (ed.) *Te Hikoi ki Waitangi 1984* (The Committee, Otara, 1984)

Waitangi Tribunal. *Reports.* These are listed in chronological order of reporting according to the current (1996) style of naming. A name of an appellant in square brackets at the end will help the reader to find pre-1988 reports referred to in the bulk of this book. Reports are published by GP Publications, Wellington. When not published, they are available from the Waitangi Tribunal, P.O. Box 5022, Wellington.

1. *Waiau Power Station* (February 1978) Wai 2. [Kirkwood]

2. *Fishing Rights* (March 1978) Wai 1. [Hawke]

3. *Motunui-Waitara* (March 1983) Wai 6. [Taylor]

4. *Kaituna River* (November 1984) Wai 4 [Bennett]

5. *Maori 'Privilege'* (May 1985) Wai 19. [McMaster]

6. *Manukau* (July 1985) Wai 8. [Minhinnick].

7. *Te Reo Maori* (April 1986) Wai 11. [Waikerepuru]

8. *Interim Report (re State-Owned Enterprises Bill)* (8 December 1986), printed in *Muriwhenua Fishing,* pp. 289-91

9. *Memorandum (re Maori Fisheries)* (10 December 1986), printed in *Muriwhenua Fishing,* p. 292

10. *Waiheke Island* (June 1987) Wai 10. [Gordon]

11. *Orakei* (November 1987) Wai 9. [Hawke]

12. *Muriwhenua Fishing* (May 1988) Wai 22. [Rata]

13. *Mangonui Sewerage* (August 1988) Wai 17. [Ngati Kahu]

14. *Ngai Tahu* (3 vols, February 1991) Wai 27

15. *Ngai Tahu Fisheries Report* (August 1992) Wai 27

16. *Fisheries Settlement Report* (November 1992) Wai 307

17. *Appointments to the Treaty of Waitangi Fisheries Commission* (December 1992) Wai 321

18. *Tuhuru* (February 1993) Wai 322

19. *The Broadcasting Claim* (July 1994). Wai 176

20. *Ngai Tahu Ancillary Claims* (April 1995) Wai 27

21. *Turangi Township* (October 1995) Wai 84

22. *Kiwifruit Marketing* (November 1995) Wai 449

23. *The Taranaki Report: Kupapa Tuatahi* (June 1996) Wai 153

Walker, Ranginui. 'Maori people since 1950', in Rice (ed.) *Oxford History of New Zealand*, pp. 498-519

Walker, Ranginui J. I. 'The Maori people: their political development', in Hyam Gold (ed.), *New Zealand politics in perspective*, pp. 252-65

'The meaning of biculturalism', Unpublished paper. Maori Studies section of the Department of Anthropology, University of Auckland, n.d. [1985?]

Ngā tau tohetohe: the years of anger (Penguin, Auckland, 1987)

'The politics of voluntary association', in I. H. Kawharu (ed.), *Conflict and compromise*, pp. 167-86

'The urban Maori', in New Zealand Planning Council, *He matapuna*, pp. 33-41

Walker, Ranginui J. I., collector. *Bastion Point tent town*, unpublished collection of ephemera, n.d., Auckland University Library.

Nga kaupapa: Mana Motuhake: manifesto edited by Ranginui Walker from policy documents. Unpublished collection in Auckland University Library, 1981.

Waitangi Action Committee. Unpublished collection of ephemera, n.d., Auckland University Library.

Waitangi Tribunal, unpublished collection of ephemera, n.d., Auckland University Library.

Wallace, John H. 'The case for legislative reform', *Legislative Studies*, 3, i (1988), pp. 3-8

Wallace, John H. (convener). *Reports of the joint working groups on Maori fisheries* (The Joint Groups, Wellington, July 1988)

Walzer, Michael. *Spheres of justice* (Oxford University Press, Oxford, 1983)

Ward, Alan. *A show of justice* (Auckland University Press and Oxford University Press, Auckland, 1973. Reprinted 1983.)

Wards, Ian McL. *The shadow of the land. A study of British policy and racial conflict in New Zealand 1832-1852* (Historical Publications Branch, Department of Internal Affairs, Wellington, 1968)

Wasserstrom, Richard. 'Preferential treatment', in his *Philosophy and social issues* (University of Notre Dame, Notre Dame, Ill., 1980)

White paper: See Palmer, *A Bill of Rights.*

Williams, Bernard. 'The idea of equality', in Laslett and Runciman, *Politics, philosophy and society*, pp. 110-31

Williams, Betty. 'The Maori struggle against white racism's destruction of our resources', *Race, Gender, Class*, 1, i (1985), pp. 98-105

    The passage of Maori land into Pakeha ownership (Cabbage Tree, Christchurch, 1983)

Williams, David V. Memorandum to the Minister of Maori Affairs Concerning the Waitangi Tribunal, 3pp. [7 June 1977]. Printed in Waitangi Action Committee Newsletter, September 1981 in Walker (ed.), *Waitangi Action Committee*, and in Walker (ed.), *Waitangi Tribunal.*

    'Te Tiriti o Waitangi', in the *New Hope* kitset.

    'Te Tiriti o Waitangi - unique relationship between Crown and Tangata Whenua', in I. H. Kawharu (ed.), *Waitangi*, pp. 64-91

Williams, Haare. *Karanga* (Coromandel Press, Coromandel, [1981])

Williams, Herbert W. *A dictionary of the Maori language*, 7th edn. (Government Printer, Wellington, 1985)

Williams, Robert A. 'The algebra of Federal Indian law: the hard trail of decolonizing and Americanizing the White Man's Indian jurisprudence', *Wisconsin Law Review*, (1986), pp. 219-99

Wilson, Margaret and Yeatman, Anna (eds.) *Justice and identity: antipodean practices* (Bridget Williams Books, Wellington, 1995)

WL: abbreviation for the *Western Leader*, an Auckland suburban newspaper. For abbreviated references, *see* AS.

Wolgast, Elizabeth H. *The grammar of justice* (Cornell University Press, Ithaca and London, 1987)

Wyatt-Brown, Bertram. *Southern honor: ethics and behaviour in the Old South* (Oxford University Press, New York, 1982)

Index